Handbook of Social Cognition
Volume 2

HANDBOOK OF SOCIAL COGNITION

Volume 2

Edited by

ROBERT S. WYER, JR.
THOMAS K. SRULL
University of Illinois

LEA

LAWRENCE ERLBAUM ASSOCIATES, PUBLISHERS
1984   Hillsdale, New Jersey   London

Lawrence Erlbaum Associates, Inc., Publishers
365 Broadway
Hillsdale, New Jersey 07642

Library of Congress Cataloging in Publication Data

Main entry under title:

Handbook of social cognition.

Includes bibliographical references and indexes.
1. Social perception—Addresses, essays, lectures.
2. Cognition. I. Wyer, Robert S. II. Srull, Thomas K.
[DNLM: 1. Cognition—Handbooks. 2. Social perception—
Handbooks. BF 311 H2367]
HM132.H333   1984   302'.12   84-6021
ISBN 0-89859-338-7 (v. 1)
ISBN 0-89859-339-5 (v. 2)
ISBN 0-89859-340-9 (v. 3)
ISBN 0-89859-337-9 (set)

V.2

47,792

Printed in the United States of America
10 9 8 7 6 5 4 3 2

Contents

Preface

Social cognition is currently the most active and dynamic area in psychology. New and important theoretical developments are occurring on a regular basis. Moreover, the flurry of research activity in this area has reached proportions one could never have anticipated as little as 10 years ago. It was a rare event in the mid-1970s to meet someone who was specifically interested in social cognition. In contrast, it is now difficult to meet anyone at all who does not profess to be working on some problem related to this general domain of inquiry.

The emergence of social cognition as a major area of psychology reflects, at its core, a convergence of two hitherto distinct disciplines in pursuit of a common set of problems. This convergence was not instigated by any single individual, nor was it stimulated by any specific set of empirical findings. Rather, it occurred spontaneously as a result of the independent recognition by researchers in each discipline that continued advancement in their own area required at least a partial understanding of phenomena being investigated in the other. For example, social psychologists had long been concerned with the effects of situational and individual difference variables on judgments and behavioral decisions. However, they began to realize that their past efforts had largely been restricted to a description of simple input-output relations. That is, experimental investigations were examining the relations among certain classes of stimulus variables and certain classes of overt responses. Evidence bearing on these relations often provided very little insight into the fundamental psychological processes that underlie their existence. Thus, many social psychologists began turning to cognitive theory and methodology for guidance in conceptualizing the underlying processes that mediate such judgments and decisions.

Simultaneously, researchers in cognitive psychology began to realize that continued advancement in their work would require a far more serious consideration of the role of real-world knowledge in the interpretation and cognitive organization of new information. Accordingly, they literally began to move from the ''word'' to the ''sentence,'' and then to the type of complex stimulus materials that are very similar to those of traditional interest to social psychologists. At the conceptual level, researchers interested in the processing of prose material began talking about things like empathy, the role of attributions in comprehension, and the subjective identification of the reader (an inherently social being) with one or more characters in a story. Moreover, a concern with the role of prior knowledge in interpreting and organizing new information led mainstream cognitive psychologists to consider the effects of self-referential knowledge, and of transitory cognitive and emotional states, on the processing of information. Consequently, questions related to the role of the ''self-concept'' in responses to information, and the influence of emotional and affective states on information processing, which had long been of interest to social psychologists, suddenly became the focus of attention of many cognitive psychologists as well.

Even these brief historical descriptions convey the fact that investigators with quite different perspectives and backgrounds appeared to spontaneously converge on a common set of problems to which both sets of knowledge and skills were necessary. Consequently, the institutional boundaries that have historically existed between many areas of cognitive and social psychology have become more and more artificial, and the ''cognitive'' and ''social'' labels attached to researchers in these areas are often more a reflection of their past history than of their current theoretical and empirical interests.

The present set of volumes reflects this convergence. In combination, the volumes provide a comprehensive treatment by both cognitive and social psychologists, often in collaboration, of issues that are central to social information processing. The volumes are intended to be a resource for researchers trained in both traditional disciplines, permitting them to review the most important conceptual and empirical advances in each area. In doing so, the volumes are intended to increase further the cross-disciplinary communication and cross-fertilization of ideas that we believe is required for continued progress, and that anticipates what we believe will ultimately be an even more formal integration of these two historically distinct disciplines.

The handbook is divided into three volumes. Volume 1 provides an overview of central issues in the field. Two chapters (Ostrom; Holyoak & Gordon) focus on how traditional concerns in social and cognitive psychology have blended into the new discipline of social cognition. Other chapters provide a review and analysis of three basic phenomena that cut across theory and research in the area: social categorization (Lingle, Altom, & Medin), the nature and functions of schemata (Brewer & Nakamura; Rumelhart[1]), and cognitive heuristics (Sherman & Corty).

The focus of Volume 2 is on various aspects of memory, including methodological issues associated with the study of social memory (Srull), theoretical and empirical issues surrounding the cognitive representation of social information (Wyer & Gordon), and reviews of recent theory and research in the areas of social memory (Hastie, Park, & Weber), semantic and episodic memory (Shoben), and visual memory (Klatzky).

Volume 3 addresses a variety of topics of interest to both cognitive and social psychologists concerned with various aspects of social information processing, including the role of automatic and controlled processing of social information (Bargh), implications of theory and research on story comprehension for the interpretation of social events (Black, Galambos, & Read), the dynamics of social communication (Kraut & Higgins), the role of the self in information processing (Greenwald & Pratkanis), and output processes in social judgment (Upshaw).

A project such as this simply could not be completed without the help of many people. Most important, we want to thank the large number of investigators who, as a result of their day-to-day research activities, have made this one of the most enjoyable and exciting areas in which to work. We also owe a large debt to each of the authors. Their enthusiasm and commitment to the project is reflected in the universally outstanding chapters of the handbook. We have found our interactions with them during the course of the project to be professionally stimulating and personally rewarding.

The contributions of others are less obvious. We owe a special note of thanks to Professor Jon Hartwick of McGill University. He has been an important source of intellectual stimulation to us for many years, and our early discussions with him were instrumental in the decision to embark on the project.

Finally, we want to express our gratitude to Larry Erlbaum for his confidence and encouragement throughout the project, as well as for giving us an absolutely free hand in trying to accomplish our objectives. Without his advice, encouragement, and gentle prodding, the project would not have been nearly as successful or rewarding.

Robert S. Wyer

Thomas K. Srull

---

[1]The chapter by Rumelhart, unlike the others in this handbook, is an adaptation of an earlier theoretical analysis of cognitive schemata. It is included in the present handbook because the conceptualization is extremely important and the earlier version was targeted to a very small audience. The original version appeared in *Theoretical issues in reading comprehension: Perspectives from cognitive psychology, linguistics, artificial intelligence, and education,* a volume edited by R. J. Spiro, B. C. Bruce, and W. F. Brewer (Lawrence Erlbaum Associates, 1980).

Contents

Handbook of Social Cognition
Volume 2

1 Methodological Techniques for the Study of Person Memory and Social Cognition

Thomas K. Srull
University of Illinois at Urbana-Champaign

Contents

INTRODUCTION

The present chapter is devoted to a discussion and analysis of the major methodological tools available to one conducting research in the general area of social cognition. Emphasis is given to how the methodological approaches discussed generalize across a wide array of experimental paradigms and can be used in the investigation of a variety of theoretical perspectives. Nevertheless, it is important to keep in mind that the choice of a particular dependent variable, or a more general methodological procedure, will often carry with it an implicit theoretical or "metatheoretical" commitment. A number of examples of the important role played by these commitments is provided throughout the chapter.

Most research in social cognition is concerned with memory processes, higher-order judgment processes, or their interaction. Upshaw (1969, 1978, this volume) has provided a number of cogent discussions of methodological issues in the study of social judgment. This chapter therefore concentrates on the investigation of social memory. Although several shortcomings associated with the "stage analysis" that has guided empirical and theoretical work over the past 15 years have recently been identified (Shiffrin, 1975, 1976), this general information processing paradigm continues to be dominant in virtually all work in contemporary cognitive psychology (Lachman, Lachman, & Butterfield, 1979), as well as most approaches to the study of social cognition (see e.g., Wyer & Carlston, 1979; Wyer & Srull, 1980). Because both empirical and theoretical work within this tradition has emphasized the investigation of organizational and retrieval processes, the present chapter will concentrate on those methodological procedures that are most consistent with this orientation.

A chapter of this type is necessarily fragmented in nature and an initial word on organization is appropriate. The major methodological approaches to the study of memory and cognition are initially described and the advantages and disadvantages of each are briefly noted. Several methods that have not yet appeared in the social cognition literature, but nevertheless appear to be potentially useful, are included for completeness. Those already familiar with cognitive methodology may want to skim over the initial part of each section, or refer to several excellent papers for a more technical analysis of some of the issues discussed (e.g., Murdock, 1976, 1982; Murphy & Puff, 1982; Pellegrino & Hubert, 1982; Postman, 1976b; Tulving & Bower, 1974; Watkins & Gardiner, 1982). The latter part of each section then turns to a detailed analysis of how these methods can be applied to some of the issues that have thus far generated the most research and theoretical debate in the field of social cognition.

Since social cognition is a relatively new field, few formal theoretical models are currently available to guide our empirical research. This is, of course, somewhat hazardous because each new construct or hypothesis that is introduced into the literature carries with it a great deal of "surplus meaning." Moreover, that surplus meaning is often supplied as much by the reader as it is by the original investigator (cf. Srull & Wyer, in press). Because of this, it is particularly important for those currently working in the area of social cognition to adopt a method of converging operations in which distinctly different methodologies are used to investigate theoretically similar (or even identical) problems. From this perspective, constructs are first postulated and then "triangulated" by more and more precisely specifying their place within a more abstract nomological network of theoretical relationships (cf. Garner, Hake, & Eriksen, 1956; Pryor & Ostrom, 1981; Runkel & McGrath, 1972). This is most effectively done by thoroughly investigating theoretical constructs with a wide array of methodological approaches. It is firmly believed that the cultivation of more methodologically eclectic attitudes in researchers will speed progress in the field considerably.

Since there are only a limited number of dependent measures available to those interested in cognitive processes, the discussion is organized around such measures. Although there will often be definite advantages associated with assessing one dependent variable as opposed to another, particularly significant progress is likely to come in two additional ways. First, well-articulated theoretical frameworks are more likely to be developed and refined as investigators begin to examine more than a single dependent variable (cf. Cattell, 1966a, 1966b). Although this can often be done within a single experiment, it doesn't necessarily have to be. Nevertheless, well-developed theories will often have implications for a variety of dependent measures. While it may often be a good strategy to measure a single dependent variable in an exploratory or initial investigation, subsequent studies should examine the implications of a theoretical hypothesis for as many different measures as possible. In this way, the underlying theoretical construct(s) will be more efficiently triangulated and our theoretical understanding will be enhanced much further than if we continued to be satisfied with the examination of a single dependent variable. As several philosophers of science have recently pointed out (see e.g., Lakatos, 1978; Laudan, 1977; Weimer, 1979), it is useful in this regard to begin thinking in terms of systematic research *programs* rather than isolated experiments. Such research programs are only now beginning to appear in the social cognition literature (see e.g., Bower, 1981; Bower, Black, & Turner, 1979; Ebbesen, 1980; Hamilton, 1979, 1981; Hastie, 1980; Higgins & King, 1981; Krauss, 1981; Lichtenstein & Brewer, 1980; Ostrom, Lingle, Pryor, & Geva, 1980; Ostrom, Pryor, & Simpson, 1981; Rogers, 1981; L. Ross, 1977; M. Ross, 1981; Snyder, 1981; Taylor & Fiske, 1978; Wyer & Srull, 1981; Zajonc, 1980) and, we believe, they mark the beginning of true progress in the field. The second factor that is likely to produce substantial gain in our understanding is the development of *new* dependent measures. The introduction of new measures such as those by Bousfield (1953), Bransford & Franks (1971), Egan (1958), Newtson (1973, 1976), Sperling (1960), and Sternberg (1966, 1969) have almost invariably led to new insights into the processes of cognitive functioning. There is every reason to believe that the development of additional measures will prove to be equally important in the future.

RECALL PROCEDURES

Various types of recall procedures have been popular in the experimental literature ever since the time of Ebbinghaus (1885), and they continue to be widely used in the study of social cognition. Recall procedures can be broken down into several different types and there are often subtle theoretical assumptions underlying the use of a particular measure that need to be considered.

Serial Recall

Any task that requires one to perform a series of "responses" in a particular order involves serial learning. Experiments using serial recall have almost always used a list-learning paradigm in which words are presented one at a time (usually on a memory drum). The subject is then required to recall the words in the same order in which they were presented.

Most of the original studies using serial recall procedures were conducted within an associationistic framework in which each word in the list was assumed to serve as a (stimulus) cue for recall of the next (response) word. Since classical associationism has largely been disbanded in favor of more active "cognitive" approaches, serial recall is much less frequently studied today. Nevertheless, although specific examinations of serial recall have more or less disappeared since the demise of associationistic approaches to verbal learning, several things are worth noting about this. First, there is a considerable literature documenting the fact that serial order information is often retained in memory. This literature is carefully reviewed by Crowder (1976) and Murdock (1974), and as they point out, these empirical findings ultimately need to be accounted for by our theories. The role that this type of information plays in the larger realm of social cognition also needs to be ultimately addressed. Second, Ellis (1978) has noted that a significant portion of everyday learning (including that of many motor responses) can be thought of as involving serial recall. In this regard, it is also interesting to note that many of the rote memory tasks that most of us learn in the typical course of growing up (such as learning of The Star Spangled Banner) show virtually no evidence of reconstructive memory (Rubin, 1977), and such tasks probably involve strict serial recall. Since the "reproductive" and "reconstructive" nature of recall is a primary concern of those working in social cognition, this aspect of serial recall may well become a topic of increased research attention in the future. Of course, simply determining how much of social learning involves a strong serial order component would be a major accomplishment at present.

Free Recall

Measures of free recall are widely used in both cognitive psychology and social cognition. In studies of free recall, a subject is given material (with any number of orienting tasks or "goals") and asked at some later time to recall the material in any order. Although this technique is primarily used with verbal (i.e., spoken or written) materials, it can also be used with pictures or line drawings, in which case the subject is asked to reproduce the picture as accurately as possible.

The major advantage of the free recall method is that it is completely unstructured by the experimenter, and the type, as well as order, of items recalled can often be used to infer organizational properties of the information. This can be done either by holding the information constant and varying the orienting task or goal of the subject, or by holding the orienting task constant and varying the nature of the material to be learned. Several investigators have used both of these procedures simultaneously to uncover very interesting properties of cognitive organization (see e.g., Bransford, McCarrell, Franks, & Nitsch, 1977; Hamilton, Katz, & Leirer, 1980a, 1980b; Hartwick, 1979; Srull, 1981; Wyer & Gordon, 1982).

There are two potential problems with free recall that make it inappropriate in a variety of contexts. First, as Ellis (1978) notes, it is one of the least sensitive measures of memory available. It is not, therefore, an optimal measure when one is investigating small but theoretically important differences. Often, but not always, this will be most problematic when one is studying long delay intervals or other factors that are likely to result in the absolute levels of recall being very small. Measures such as savings or various types of recognition procedures will often be sensitive in detecting differences that do not "show up" in free recall (see Ellis, 1978; Griggs & Keen, 1977). Various types of reaction time procedures can also be used to detect differences that are too subtle to be observed in free recall paradigms.

The second potential problem in using free recall is that in many situations it is not clear what should be considered the appropriate unit of analysis. This is a problem that was once solved by fiat by assuming that each nonsense syllable or word in a list-learning experiment represented a single unit. However, the problem is attracting much more attention in both cognitive psychology and social cognition, both of which typically use stimulus materials (e.g., prose paragraphs) that are far more complex than those used in traditional verbal learning research. The specific assumptions one is willing to make obviously become critical, but several general points are worth mentioning. First, it is well known that people are very poor at remembering "surface" information (Bransford & Franks, 1971; Franks & Bransford, 1972; Johnson, Bransford, & Solomon,

1973; Sachs, 1967), and it will often be extremely difficult to interpret free recall protocols that are scored on a word-by-word basis. Second, many of the most well articulated theories of the way in which information is represented in memory assume a propositional code (e.g., Anderson, 1976; Anderson & Bower, 1973; Frederickson, 1975; Kintsch, 1974; Norman & Rumelhart, 1975) in which it is clearly *inappropriate* to consider single words as the appropriate unit of analysis. As Anderson states, "In a propositional analysis, only the *meaning* of an event is represented. The unimportant details—details that humans tend not to remember—*are not represented*" (1980, p. 101; italics added). This problem can be somewhat alleviated by using a "general meaning" rather than "verbatim" scoring technique, and alternative representational theories are certainly available. Nevertheless, important theoretical assumptions will necessarily be made when one chooses the word, proposition, "idea unit," sentence, paragraph, or some other unit as the one appropriate for analysis. As our theories become more refined, this problem is sure to take on even greater importance.

Intrusions in Free Recall.   It should be noted that situations will sometimes arise in which subjects produce a considerable number of "intrusions" in free recall protocols (i.e., produce items that were not present in the original stimulus material). This raises several additional issues. First, the intrusions themselves can be analyzed in an attempt to determine whether they manifest any systematic characteristic. For example, Conrad (1964) and Wickelgren (1965a, 1965b) used visually presented letter strings in studies of short-term memory and discovered that intrusions were often acoustically, rather than visually, similar to the presented items. This suggested that subjects were acoustically coding visually presented information. Spiro (1977, 1980) has conducted a similar analysis within the social domain.

A more problematic situation exists when the number of intrusions varies over conditions of the experiment. Such intrusions can be thought of as reflecting a guessing bias. Under conditions of varying intrusion rates, comparisons of "percent correct" can be quite misleading and are obviously inappropriate. Perhaps the most common (partial) solution to this problem is to ignore the nature of the intrusions and attempt to correct for guessing by using Hilgard's (1951) "memory improvement" (MI) score. This correction is represented as:

$$MI = \frac{p \text{ (recall)} - p \text{ (intrusions)}}{1 - p \text{ (intrusions)}}$$

where p (recall) represents the proportion of items on the protocol that are correct and p (intrusions) represents the proportion of items on the protocol that are intrusions. According to this scheme, p (intrusions) serves as an estimate of the amount of guessing during the free recall period. Hilgard's memory improvement index continues to be utilized as one way of dealing with the problem of guessing in free recall (see e.g., Graesser, Woll, Kowalski, & Smith, 1980).

Although the issue is far from settled, there is evidence to suggest that the types of materials used in a great deal of social cognition research (e.g., sentences involving behavioral acts, all of which pertain to the same individual or group) typically produce few intrusions, even under conditions of relatively long delays. For example, Hastie and Kumar (1979), Reyes, Thompson, and Bower (1980), Snyder and Cantor (1979), and Srull (1981) all presented relatively large amounts of behavioral information and found very few intrusions in free recall. The one consistent exception to this seems to involve memory for events that fit a well-defined script. Bower, Black, and Turner (1979), Black, Turner, and Bower (1979), and Graesser et al. (1980) all report substantial intrusion rates using these types of materials. In addition, however, there are a surprising number of studies that do not even report intrusion rates. Researchers should be cautioned to report these findings and explicitly examine whether they vary considerably across conditions of the experiment. Wyer and Gordon (this volume) discuss theoretical reasons why large numbers of intrusions may occur in some contexts and not in others. Obviously, constructing specific theories of person memory that can account for this will represent substantial progress in the field.

Order Information in Free Recall. Bousfield published a classic study in 1953 that was to be extremely influential in a number of different ways. Briefly, Bousfield presented subjects with a 60-word list that was composed of 15 instances from four different conceptual categories (animals, names, professions, and vegetables). These items were presented in random order at the rate of 3 seconds per item. Using a free recall task, Bousfield discovered that the output order for a given subject typically did not reflect the input order. Moreover, there was much more "category clustering" than would be expected by chance. That is, once an item from a particular category (e.g., a vegetable) was recalled, the next item recalled was more likely to be from that same category than from some other. These results demonstrated that contiguous presentation was far less important than category membership and suggested that people use very active organizational strategies in processing new information. Although observations such as these are taken for granted today, they were dramatically inconsistent with the associationistic framework that was dominant in the early 1950s. They also stimulated researchers to closely examine the order in which items were produced in free recall. The overall goal was to develop an objective index that would reflect internal cognitive organization.

Bousfield and his brother, a mathematician, later collaborated in developing what has probably become the most widely used measure of category clustering in free recall. This measure is essentially a ratio of observed category repetitions to the number of such repetitions expected on the basis of chance (Bousfield & Bousfield, 1966). Researchers have remained interested in clustering in free recall ever since, but through the years a number of important problems with interpreting the Bousfield and Bousfield index have been discovered. Perhaps the most important is that higher levels of organization will presumably lead to greater overall recall, yet this is not necessarily reflected in the index. For example, a subject who recalls items from two conceptual categories in the order AABB will receive the same clustering score as a subject who recalls twice as many items in the order AAAABBBB. It is reasonable to assume, however, that greater *overall* levels of recall reflect greater organization on the part of the subject. Another problem is that the measure will not detect higher-order (e.g., hierarchical) forms or organization. For example, a subject who recalls items from three conceptual categories in the order ABCABCABC. . . will receive a score indicating no clustering at all.

These problems are mentioned primarily because the Bousfield and Bousfield index continues to be heavily relied upon, apparently because of its important historical status. There are, however, a large number of alternative clustering measures currently available (Bower, Lesgold, & Tieman, 1969; Colle, 1972; Dalrymple-Alford, 1970; Frankel & Cole, 1971; Frender & Doubilet, 1974; Hubert & Levin, 1976; Lambert, Ignatow, & Krauthamer, 1968; Roenker, Thompson, & Brown, 1971; Robinson, 1966; Wallace & Underwood, 1964). Although there is no perfect or even "best" measure for all purposes, and many of the indices will often be highly intercorrelated (Hamilton et al., 1980b; Murphy, 1979), it is encouraging to see more recent researchers and theorists becoming concerned with specifying the unique advantages of each. It is also noteworthy that several writers have independently come to the conclusion that the adjusted-ratio-of-clustering (ARC) index developed by Roenker et al. (1971) may be the best overall measure currently available. The computational formula for this is

$$\text{ARC} = \frac{R - E(R)}{N - K - E(R)}$$

where R is the observed number of repetitions, $E(R)$ is the expected number of repetitions, N is the total number of all items recalled, and K is the number of conceptual categories represented in the presentation list. Also, $E(R) = (\Sigma\ m(i)^2 / N) - 1$, where m is the number of items from category i that are recalled.

Ostrom, Pryor, and Simpson (1981) point out that ARC is more easily interpreted than the Bousfield and Bousfield index because 0 always represents chance clustering and 1 represents perfect clustering. In addition Ostrom et al., as well as Wyer and Gordon (1982), recommend ARC because it corrects for different numbers of categories that are presented as well as the number of categories recalled. Thus, ARC seems to have a number of desirable descriptive properties. Interestingly, Murphy (1979) has recently conducted a series of computer simulations with various clustering measures to determine how they are influenced by factors that are not specifically organizational in nature (e.g., list length, number of categories, number of items per category, etc.). Murphy states, "ARC is again the least confounded with extraneous factors, with less than 2% of its variance due to effects other than organization" (pp. 74–75). He concludes that, although it is not without fault, ARC may be the single most desirable index of order information in free recall currently available.

It is probably clear that the literature on category clustering is not only large, but also growing rapidly. Without going into detail, several additional observations need to be made. First, particular clustering techniques are often based on a subtle but nevertheless important set of assumptions. Many of these are discussed by Shuell (1975) who points out the confusion that may arise when researchers are not completely aware of the nature of these assumptions. Similarly, Colle (1972) has discussed in detail how "clustering only becomes well defined by reference to a theory" (p. 624). Fortunately, Colle and more recently Murphy (1979) and Pellegrino and Hubert (1982) have provided excellent discussions of the theoretical purposes and implications that can be associated with investigations of category clustering. Researchers considering using measures of category clustering are strongly encouraged to consult these papers.

The second point that needs to be made concerns what we have been referring to as "conceptual categories." These categories need to be specified a priori by the experimenter. While this is typically quite easy in list-learning experiments, the category boundaries may be much less clear with the type of materials generally used in social cognition experiments (cf. Rosch, 1975a, 1975b, 1977, 1978). This is particularly true when one is interested in investigating behaviors that are considered to be indicative of certain personality trait categories (Cantor & Mischel, 1977; Cantor, Mischel, & Schwartz, 1982). Thus, it may be necessary to collect extensive normative data before using such materials in social cognition or person memory experiments that examine category clustering. The reason for this is that all of the procedures discussed above assume that subjects will form (and use as a basis for organizing the information) the same equivalence classes as those identified a priori by the experimenter. To the extent that the equivalence classes differ, clustering scores will necessarily be deflated (i.e., underestimates of "true" underlying organization).

Tulving and Bower (1974) point to a related but slightly different concern. "Since clustering of items with respect to one attribute usually precludes clustering on the basis of other attributes that nevertheless might be represented in memory traces of retrieved items, the method is not well suited for describing traces in all their presumed richness and variety" (p. 282). Thus, it is important to remember that only a single, nonoverlapping set of categories can be examined at any one time.[1]

---

[1]It should be noted that Buschke (1977; Buschke & Schaier, 1979) has recently introduced a technique for assessing "two dimensional recall" that potentially can alleviate some, but not all, of these problems. Unfortunately, very little work using this technique has thus far been reported in the literature. It is therefore quite difficult to evaluate its full potential.

Finally, although objective clustering measures are the most popular measures of examining the order in which items are recalled in free recall experiments, they are not the only techniques available. In fact, at least five separate alternatives have recently been introduced. First, the general concern of all clustering measures—determining the number of observed category repetitions minus the number of such repetitions expected on the basis of chance—can be thought of in terms of conditional probabilities. Specifically, a high degree of category clustering indicates that the probability of recalling an item from category A *given* that an item from category A was recalled on the previous trial ($P_{A/A}$) will be greater than the probability of recalling an item from category B or category C given that an item from category A was recalled on the previous trial ($P_{B/A}$ and $P_{C/A}$, respectively). In other words, high degrees of category clustering are indicated by *within*-category repetitions rather than *between*-category transitions. Srull (1981) has used this approach to examine a very well articulated theory of person memory (Hastie, 1980) that makes specific predictions about when and how the process of recall should alternate from one category to another. The data were approached in the following way. Given that an item from a particular category was recalled on the previous trial, what are the probabilities that an item from each of the possible categories would be recalled on the next trial? It was demonstrated with this technique that, although levels of category clustering were near chance levels, there was a highly systematic nature to the order (pattern) of items recalled. The important point here is that it is possible to construct theories that make predictions about *between*-category transitions as well as *within*-category repetitions, and it is possible to use transitional probabilities of recall to diagnose the underlying (hypothetical) memory representation. It is important, however, to realize that this technique also requires the experimenter to determine the conceptual categories on an a priori basis.

A slightly different method from that noted above was introduced by Bower (1970, 1972a) who examined transitional error probabilities in serial recall. In several different experiments, Bower demonstrated that the probability of making an error (i.e., missing a particular item in the serial recall task) was greater when it was preceded by an item from another category than when it was preceded by an item from the same category (cf. Srull, in press; Tulving & Pearlstone, 1966). By systematically varying the pattern of within-category and between-category transitions in the presentation list, one can obtain very sensitive measures of the probability of making the two types of errors. Unfortunately, this procedure does not seem to immediately generalize beyond the serial recall task.

The last three alternative methods for examining order information in free recall are noteworthy because they do *not* require the experimenter to define nonoverlapping conceptual categories. Friendly (1977, 1979) has developed a technique in which he begins by constructing an item-by-item proximity matrix.

Such a matrix represents each item recalled in terms of how "close" it is to every other item recalled (i.e., the relationship of every item recalled to every other item recalled, rather than to only adjacent items, is considered). Friendly is able to derive from this a hierarchical structure that presumably reflects how clusters of items are organized in memory. The final result is a hierarchical tree structure similar to that produced in multidimensional scaling studies. While Friendly has actually developed several methods that are continuing to be refined (see Friendly, 1979), the general technique is noteworthy because: (a) it can be used in single trial recall studies or in multitrial free recall, (b) it provides a convenient method of examining individual differences, and (c) it can easily be adapted to the study of interitem response times as well as recall. All of these are major advances over the traditional clustering measures.

The fourth major alternative to category clustering measures for examining order information in free recall has recently been proposed by Reitman and Rueter (1980). Their technique is similar to Friendly's but it represents organization in terms of an "ordered tree." The specific model, however, can be applied to the order of items in multitrial recall from different starting points. This model would seem to provide a very flexible tool for examining a number of questions that are important in the area of social cognition. Unfortunately, with the exception of a recent study by McKeithen, Reitman, Reuter, and Hirtle (1981), no empirical work using the method has thus far appeared in the experimental literature.

Finally, there are also a variety of measures of *subjective* organization in free recall. With these measures, the experimenter does not predetermine equivalence classes but attempts to determine the way in which a person subjectively organizes the information to be recalled. Each of these measures requires that a subject be presented with the same set of items on a series of trials (always in a different random order) and attempt to recall as many items as possible after each trial. Thus, these measures are only appropriate for *multitrial* free recall. In a typical experiment, a subject will recall more items on successive trials and the order in which items are recalled will become increasingly systematic. This increasingly systematic nature in which items are recalled is assumed to reflect an increasing degree of subjective organization on the part of the subject. As Sternberg and Tulving (1977) state, "Since the order of words presented for study varies unsystematically from trial to trial, the increasing sequential organization of words over trials must be imposed upon the material by the learner" (p. 539).

Sternberg and Tulving (1977) have recently reviewed some of the psychometric properties of the various measures that have been proposed. Their overall recommendation is the bidirectional "pair frequency" measure. This can be represented as

$$PF = 0 \ (ITR2) - E \ (ITR2) = 0 \ (ITR2) - \frac{2c \ (c-1)}{hk}$$

where $0 \ (ITR2)$ is the number of pairs of items recalled on Trials t and $t + 1$ in either of the two possible orders, $E \ (ITR2)$ is the expected number of such pairs,

c is the total number of common items recalled on Trials t and $t + 1$, h is the total number of items recalled on Trial t, and k is the total number of items recalled on Trial $t + 1$.

Since measures of subjective organization require a multitrial free recall paradigm, they would seem to be more suited to list-learning experiments that employ a random selection of single words as items than to the types of experiments typically conducted in the area of social cognition. Hamilton et al. (1980b), however, have recently conducted a very interesting examination of subjective organization in memory for behavior statements, all of which pertain to the same target person. Their study is particularly noteworthy because they compared organization according to a set of predetermined categories with assessments of subjective organization according to dimensions that were not immediately apparent to the experimenter. While there are likely to be scaling problems in trying to compare the results of two different types of numerical indices, it is likely that measures of subjective organization will be used increasingly often as researchers in social cognition begin to ask more and more detailed theoretical questions.

Once again, the most appropriate general suggestion is to remain eclectic in terms of adopting methodological approaches to examine memory organization. All of the methods discussed above are useful, and the "best" method to choose is really dependent upon the theoretical issue in question and the assumptions one is willing to make. As noted above, it is hoped that more investigators will begin to collect multiple dependent variables from the same experimental paradigm, and as this occurs, we are sure to learn much more about the interrelations among the various measures, as well as the specific psychological structures and processes they tap.

Savings Technique

The savings or "relearning" technique is a method that was introduced by Ebbinghaus and later used extensively in his own memory investigations. In fact, his classic retention curve (Ebbinghaus, 1885) is based on a savings score as the dependent variable. With this procedure, a subject learns the material to a specified criterion and, at some later point, relearns the material to the same criterion. The extent to which a subject is able to learn the material faster the second time is considered a measure of the degree to which the original material was retained. Specifically, a "savings" score can be represented as

$$\% \text{ saved} = \frac{\# \text{ of trials to learn} - \# \text{ of trials to relearn}}{\# \text{ of trials to learn}} \times 100$$

Although Ebbinghaus used a "complete exposure" procedure in which all of the items were constantly available, a serial exposure procedure in which items are presented one at a time can also be used.

The savings technique is only rarely used today but it is a very general procedure that need not be confined to list-learning experiments. We would agree with Bransford (1979), Bugelski (1979), Ellis (1978), and others who have argued that such techniques are potentially quite valuable. The major advantage is that the savings technique is extremely sensitive to small differences that will not be detected by recall or even various types of recognition measures. Accordingly, it should often be a very good method for assessing the retention of material over long periods of time. For this reason, its popularity seems to have increased substantially in recent years (see e.g., Bahrick, 1967; Bahrick & Bahrick, 1964; Conover & Brown, 1977; Kolers, 1976; MacLeod, 1976; Nelson, 1971, 1978; Nelson, Fehling, & Moore-Glascock, 1979; Nelson & Rothbart, 1972; Nelson & Smith, 1972; Nelson & Vining, 1978).

Nelson and his colleagues (Nelson, 1971, 1978; Nelson, Fehling, & Moore-Glascock, 1979; Nelson & Rothbart, 1972; Nelson & Smith, 1972; Nelson & Vining, 1978) have recently used the savings technique to investigate profitably a number of issues where only very small degrees of retention would be expected on an a priori basis. Nelson et al. (1979) have also discussed some of the practical issues that are involved in designing an optimal strategy for the retention of information over long periods of time (see also Chant & Atkinson, 1978; Groen & Atkinson, 1966). At any rate, since many issues in social cognition are concerned with the retention of large amounts of information over very long periods of time, it is to be expected that the savings technique will be used increasingly often in these types of investigations as well. In fact, Burtt (1932, 1941) and Titchner (1923) have each provided classic demonstrations of how the retention of information over several decades can be identified by using the savings procedure.

Cued Recall

One of the most significant influences on the development of cognitive psychology and the adoption of an information-processing framework for the study of memory and cognition was the primary consideration given to retrieval and computational processes, as well as to instances of retrieval failure (see e.g., Eysenck, 1977; Friendly, 1979; Pellegrino & Ingram, 1979; Smith, 1978; Sternberg, 1969; Tulving, 1974; Watkins, 1979). The use of cued recall tasks has become increasingly common as more and more theoretical issues concerning retrieval have been raised.

It is important to distinguish between cued recall as a process and as an experimental procedure. Several theorists (e.g., Battig & Bellezza, 1979; Voss, 1979) have argued that much of one's recall involves the use of self-generated cues. Thus, a free recall task might involve "cued recall" in terms of the underlying processes being activated. As an experimental procedure, however, a cued recall task involves a situation in which the experimenter provides cues (at the acquisition stage, retrieval stage, or both) that may aid the subject in recalling other material.

There are two major advantages to using cued recall as an experimental procedure. First, it can often be used to detect information available in memory that less sensitive methods (e.g., free recall) are unable to detect. The second advantage of cued recall is more subtle but even more important. Many contemporary theorists (e.g., Anderson, 1976; Anderson & Bower, 1973; Eysenck, 1977; Kintsch, 1977; Raaijmakers & Shiffrin, 1980, 1981; Tulving & Watkins, 1975; Wyer & Srull, 1980) postulate that all information encoded into long-term memory is potentially available from that point on, and "forgetting" is due to the inability to retrieve a given piece of information in a particular context. By experimentally varying the nature of the cues available to the subject (i.e., experimenter-generated cues), one can examine under what conditions people will and will not be able to retrieve given information.

Consider one simple example of how cued recall has been used to address a very important (and historically lingering) theoretical question. Twenty years of verbal learning research served to document the importance of interference. Much, if not all, of forgetting was said to be due to interference (e.g., McGeouch & Irion, 1952; Underwood, 1957). It is important to note, however, that such a statement is descriptive rather than explanatory in nature. It tells us that prior learning will inhibit the recall of subsequent information (proactive interference) or that later learning will inhibit the recall of previously acquired information (retroactive interference). It does *not* tell us anything about what cognitive processes might be responsible for such effects, and specifying the nature of such processes has been a major concern of those adopting the information-processing framework. For example, Tulving and Psotka (1971) recognized the ambiguity noted above and reasoned that learning later material could "interfere" with previously acquired information through at least two mechanisms. First, subsequent learning could result in a general decay or weakening of the traces associated with earlier items. Alternatively, subsequent learning may have no effect on earlier traces, but it may make it more difficult for a subject to independently access or retrieve previously learned information (perhaps by making it more difficult for the subject to produce relevant cues). To test these hypotheses, Tulving and Psotka presented subjects with various numbers of word lists. Each list contained 24 words, consisting of 4 words from each of six semantic categories. The words were always blocked by category in the presentation lists but the category names themselves were not provided. Some subjects learned the target list and then recalled as many words as possible. Other subjects learned the target list and then learned from one to five other (interpolated) lists before attempting to recall words from the original target list. The results of the study were quite clear-cut. First, the number of words recalled from the target list consistently declined as the number of interpolated lists increased. These results are consistent with those of many other studies showing the effects of retroactive interference. However, it was still not clear whether such results were due to a weakening of the original traces or to some retrieval failure. Tulving and Psotka addressed this question by administering a second (cued) recall test in which category cues for the six semantic categories were also presented. When the cued recall procedure was used, the number or words recalled from the target list was virtually unaffected by the number of interpolated lists. These results suggest that traces for the original items were still available and the "forgetting" associated with the number of interpolated lists was really due to an inability to retrieve the original items. Thus, Tulving and Psotka were able to take a descriptive statement and at least begin to explain it in terms of specifying the underlying mechanisms involved. Studies such as this one (see also Buschke, 1977; Tulving & Pearlstone, 1966) have led many theorists to postulate that most, if not all, forgetting is due to retrieval failure (cf. Loftus & Loftus, 1980).[2] Correspondingly, cued recall procedures are being used increasingly often in an attempt to discover under what conditions particular types of information will be recalled. While several studies using cued recall have appeared in the social cognition literature, we would expect their number to increase dramatically in the coming years.

Applications and Implications for Social Cognition

Serial Recall. There have been very few serial recall tasks used in the study of social cognition thus far. As noted above, these tasks particularly lend themselves to the investigation of simple associationistic models. However, Bower (1970, 1972a) has nicely demonstrated that they can be used to address the type of organizational questions that researchers in social cognition are interested in as well. For example, Bower and Winenz (1969) presented digit strings using various perceptual groupings (e.g., audio presentations with pauses such as 12–548–36–723–49 and subjects were asked to reproduce the same sequence of digits). The data were then analyzed by examining "transition error probabilities." These represent the conditional probability that item in serial position i is *not* recalled given that the item in serial position i-1 is correctly recalled (cf. Johnson, 1968). Representative data from one of Bower's studies are displayed in Figure 1.1. Notice that there is a relatively small transition error probability

---

[2]Loftus and Loftus (1980) report an informal survey of 75 psychologists who responded to various questions about their own view on memory. They found that 84% agreed with the position that "Everything we learn is permanently stored in the mind, although sometimes particular details are not accessible. With hypnosis, or other special techniques, these inaccessible details could eventually be recovered." In contrast, only 14% of the psychologists agreed with the position that, "Some details that we learn may be permanently lost from memory. Such details would never be able to be recovered by hypnosis, or any other special technique, because these details are simply no longer there."

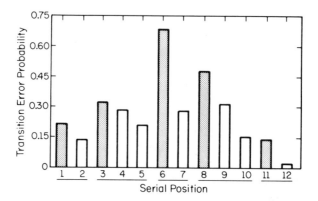

FIG. 1.1.   Characteristic transition error probabilities for a digit series presented verbally with pauses creating a 2-3-2-3-2 group structure. Over Serial Position 1 is the error probability associated with item 1. For any later position n, the bar indicates the conditional probability of an error for Element n, given correct recall of Element $n-1$. The initial transition into each group is cross-hatched. (After Bower, 1970.)

when the transition is *within* a perceptual grouping but consistently a dramatic increase in making an error when the transition is *between* perceptual groupings.

It is important to realize that *subjective* organization or "groupings" should also be reflected in transition error probabilities, and this type of procedure can therefore be used to address a variety of organizational questions. For example, Pryor and Ostrom (1981) have recently pointed out that although it is usually assumed that social information is organized around persons, apparently this does not always occur (see also Ostrom, Pryor, & Simpson, 1981; Srull & Brand, in press). If one were interested in whether subjects spontaneously organize (e.g., behavioral) information pertaining to various members of a group around individual target persons, one could use a similar serial recall procedure. Specifically, such an organization would suggest that, in a blocked presentation format, higher transition error probabilities will result when the transition is between targets rather than within a single target. By systematically varying the number of stimulus persons and the number of behaviors per person, very dramatic differences in the pattern of transition error probabilities should occur. For example, Figure 1.2 shows the predictions for a case in which subjects receive a varying number of behaviors about nine separate stimulus persons.

It should be noted that researchers such as Rothbart, Fulero, Jensen, Howard, and Birrell (1978) have reported several elegant investigations of some of the variables that might affect this type of organization by relying on more indirect judgment measures. However, the resulting inference about memory organization is one more step removed when judgment measures are used. Consequently, any conclusions that are drawn are that much more tenuous. At the very least, techniques such as the analysis of transition error probabilities should prove to be very useful as one of several converging operations that can be applied to problems such as this.

It should also be noted that the same type of procedure as that described above can be used to investigate whether subjects spontaneously encode behaviors in terms of the more abstract personality traits they imply or any other of a number of organizational issues that have been raised in the social cognition literature (for a discussion of some of these issues, see Wyer & Carlston, 1979; Wyer & Gordon, 1982).

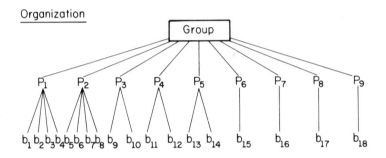

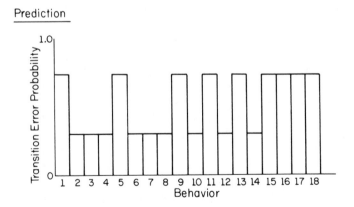

FIG. 1.2. Hypothetical structure that might result when a subject organizes behavioral information around individual members of a group, and the pattern of transitional error probabilities that should result from such an organizational structure.

Free Recall. It is not surprising that a large number of studies in social cognition have examined free recall. Many of these are reviewed in Hastie (1981), Taylor and Crocker (1981), Wyer and Srull (1980), and several of the chapters in this volume. Such a review is beyond the scope of the present chapter but it should be pointed out that an ever-increasing number of "social" variables are being found to have a strong impact on the retention and subsequent recall of information. For example, Hamilton and his colleagues (see Hamilton, 1981; Hamilton, Katz, & Leirer, 1980a, 1980b), Srull (1981), and Wyer and Gordon (1982) have all found that actively trying to form an impression of a person leads to greater recall of (personality trait and specific behavioral) information than simply trying to learn or memorize the information in the first place. Hastie (1980; Hastie & Kumar, 1979), Rothbart, Evans, and Fulero (1979), and Srull (1981) have also found that information incongruent with a prior impression is better recalled than information congruent with a prior impression. Similarly Reyes, Thompson, and Bower (1980) found that courtroom trial evidence that was inconsistent with prior perceptions of a defendant's "favorableness" was better recalled than information consistent with the prior impression. Reyes et al. also found that this differential recall of various types of evidence was paralleled by judgments of apparent guilt.

Other socially relevant variables have also consistently been found to affect the type and amount of information recalled. Bower (1981; Bower, Gilligan, & Monteiro, 1981; Bower, Monteiro, & Gilligan, 1978) and Isen (this volume, Clark & Isen, 1982) have described at least some of the influences that affect can have on recall. Rogers and his colleagues (Kuiper & Rogers, 1979; Rogers, 1981; Rogers, Kuiper, & Kirker, 1977) have consistently found greater recall of information that is related to the self than similar information that is not, and Bower and Gilligan (1979) found enhanced recall of information that is related to a well-known other (e.g., one's mother) as opposed to a person that is not so well known (e.g., Walter Cronkite).

Several researchers (e.g., Bower, Black, & Turner, 1979; Graesser et al., 1980) have found that recall of specific information is affected by its relationship to a more general social script, and Black and Bern (1981) have found that causally related events are better recalled than those that do not share a causal dependency (cf. Schank, 1975). Similarly, Lichtenstein and Brewer (1980) found that goal-directed actions are better recalled than events that are not perceived to be goal directed. Finally, Bower (1978) and Fiske, Taylor, Etcoff, and Laufer (1979) have both found that empathizing with a particular character in a story influences the type of information that is subsequently recalled.

Perhaps the most surprising aspect of the work that has thus far been done in the area of social cognition is that a considerable amount of attention has been given to order information in free recall. In general, this has paid off quite handsomely. For example, Hamilton et al. (1980a, 1980b) presented subjects with a list of sentences in random order that reflected four separate conceptual

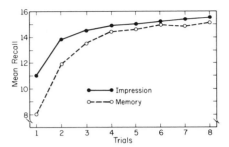

FIG. 1.3.   Mean levels of recall as a function of instructional set and trials. (After Hamilton, Katz, & Leirer, 1980b.)

categories; behaviors related to interpersonal activities, behaviors related to intellectual activities, behaviors related to interests in sports, and behaviors related to religious activities. Hamilton et al. found that subjects given an initial impression set not only recalled more items than those given a memory set, but they manifested a much higher degree of category clustering as well. These data suggest that impression set subjects were much more active in organizing the individual behavior items into what the authors call "personality-relevant schematic categories" than the memory set subjects. This increased organizational activity on the part of the subjects was presumably responsible for their greater ability to retrieve the individual items at a later time. Note, however, that this type of category clustering analysis requires that the experimenter define the relevant categories on an a priori basis. In a subsequent study, Hamilton and Lim (1979) used a multitrial free recall paradigm and analyzed the order of items recalled with the bidirectional pair frequency measure of *subjective* organization (see Sternberg & Tulving, 1977). Two of their findings are particularly relevant. First, one can see from the mean levels of recall (displayed in Fig. 1.3) that the impression set subjects were noticeably better than the memory set subjects on Trials 1–3. Beginning on the fourth trial, however, the difference between impression set and memory set subjects in the total number of items recalled becomes negligible.

The mean levels of subjective organization found by Hamilton and Lim are presented in Figure 1.4. Here again one can see that the impression set subjects show higher degrees of subjective organization, but only on Trials 1–3. After the third trial, the difference between impression set and memory set subjects begins to converge for *both* the levels of subjective organization and the mean number of items recalled.[3] This type of analysis offers much greater insight into the dynamics of person memory than could possibly be gained by simply examining overall levels of recall.

Ostrom, Pryor, and Simpson (1981) have also used measures of category clustering in free recall to investigate the way in which social information is

---

[3]It should be pointed out that Hamilton et al. (1980b) offer a slightly different interpretation of these data than that provided here.

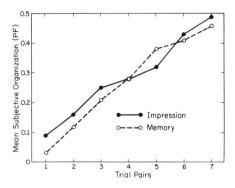

FIG. 1.4.   Mean levels of subjective organization as a function of instructional set and trials. (After Hamilton, Katz, & Leirer, 1980b.)

organized. In an elaborate series of studies they have found that levels of clustering (around individual target persons) is much greater when the target individuals are already familiar persons than when they are previously unfamiliar. However, in a subsequent study, subjects received information that could be organized around individual persons or temporally (e.g., what each of the targets did on Monday, Tuesday, etc.). In this case, subjects showed greater temporal clustering for unfamiliar targets but greater person clustering for familiar targets. These studies, along with several others reviewed by Ostrom et al. (1981), are important because one of the most fundamental issues facing researchers and theorists in social cognition is developing a way to trace the development of person impressions over time. Although this is an extremely complicated problem, the studies reported by Ostrom et al. suggest that the use of measures such as category clustering may provide at least one way to begin addressing it (see also Srull, in press).

It should be remembered that order information in free recall can be investigated in a number of ways in addition to measures of category clustering or subjective organization. Moreover, there will be times when order information is important but these measures are inadequate or strictly inappropriate. For example, Hastie (1980) has developed one of the few formal models of person memory that currently exists. In a typical experiment used to test the model, a subject is presented with a short ensemble of personality trait adjectives describing a target person to create an initial expectancy of the types of behaviors that would normally be expected from this person. The subject is then presented with a sequence of behaviors, of which some are congruent, some are incongruent, and some are irrelevant to the initial expectancy. Hastie has found a number of interesting results with this paradigm (for a summary, see Hastie, 1980; Hastie & Kumar, 1979). Most important, free recall of items incongruent with the expectancy is consistently superior to recall of items congruent with the expectancy, and these in turn are better recalled than irrelevant items. These basic results have been obtained with a variety of trait expectancies, written and visual materials, under short and long delay conditions, and correspond to a wide array of results previously reported in the experimental literature (for an excellent review, see Hastie, 1981).

Hastie (1980) accounts for such results with an associative storage and retrieval network model that permits the formation of interitem associative links. Briefly, he suggests that behavioral items incongruent with a prior expectancy are difficult to comprehend and are therefore held in working memory for a relatively long period of time. This gives any incongruent item an opportunity to be considered in relation to other items in working memory and, whenever this occurs, an interitem associative linkage between the two is established. On the other hand, congruent items are relatively easy to comprehend and simply mapped into the network. The final representational structure that results is similar to that presented in Figure 1.5. Since the retrieval process is assumed to traverse these associative pathways, and a greater number of links are attached to incongruent than congruent episodes, the model predicts that a greater number of incongruent than congruent items should be recalled.

Using this general paradigm, Hastie (1981; Hastie & Kumar, 1979) and Srull (1981) have consistently found only chance levels of category (type of item) clustering in free recall. However, a careful examination of the model indicates that there should be a systematic nature to the order in which items are recalled. For example, note that the associative paths emanating from incongruent items can be attached to other incongruent items or congruent items. However, the overwhelming number of paths attached to congruent items should be emanating from one of the incongruent items. Assuming that the retrieval process underlying free recall follows these paths, this implies several things (see Srull, 1981, for a complete discussion). For example, the probability of recalling an incongruent item given that one has just recalled a congruent item ($P_{I/C}$) should be greater than the probability of recalling a congruent item given that one has just

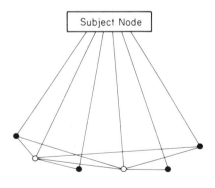

FIG. 1.5. Hypothetical associative network representing information about a single individual. (After Hastie, 1980.)

● Congruent Episodes
○ Incongruent Episodes

recalled an incongruent item ($P_{C/I}$). Srull (1981) has found a considerable difference between these two conditional probabilities. He has also reported a number of additional findings that support this basic type of model. The important point, however, is that this type of analysis is an extremely powerful method for discriminating between competing theoretical frameworks that may not be distinguished on the basis of mean levels of recall alone (see also Belmore, 1981; Johnson, 1968; Tulving, 1967).

In sum, order information in free recall has already provided a number of insights into the organization of social information in memory and the retrieval strategies subjects use in a variety of settings. Although there are a number of techniques for examining order information that may or may not be appropriate for any given situation, they generally appear to be quite sensitive ways to examine various theoretical frameworks.

Cued Recall.   There are many reasons to believe that the organization of social information is a very elaborate process involving a number of both encoding and retrieval factors. Many of these have been discussed by Wyer (Wyer & Carlston, 1979; Wyer & Gordon, 1982, this volume; Wyer & Srull, 1980). As a result of this organization, trait information can cue the recall of various behaviors, specific behaviors can cue the recall of one another, information about one person can cue the recall of information about another person, and so on. Although theoretical progress in this area has been slow, cued recall tasks will undoubtedly be relied upon increasingly often to investigate these effects and the conditions in which they occur (for examples, see Wyer & Gordon, this volume).

In this section we would like to present one technique that may be particularly useful to those interested in social cognition. One of the most enduring issues in the field concerns whether mental representations of persons are configural in nature with "emergent" properties or simply additive in nature (see e.g., Asch, 1946; Bruner, Shapiro, & Tagiuri, 1958; Hamilton & Zanna, 1974; Higgins & Rholes, 1976; Schneider, Hastorf, & Ellsworth, 1979; Zanna & Hamilton, 1977). Although most of the empirical research related to this issue has been conducted within some type of judgment paradigm (for partial reviews of this literature, see N. Anderson, 1971, 1974; Ostrom, 1977; Schneider et al., 1979; Wyer, 1974; Wyer & Carlston, 1979), cued recall tasks can also be used profitably. For example, consider one retrieval cue (X) and another retrieval cue (Y) that convey distinct types of information. These cues could involve information related to a target's physical appearance, past behavior, personality traits, or nearly anything else depending upon the particular setting. Now consider a "double probe" (X + Y) that contains all of the information conveyed by each of the two cues noted above. The empirical question is whether the retrieval of information in response to cue X + Y can be predicted from the independent contributions of cue X and cue Y presented separately. Evidence for a configural representation would result when the cuing effectiveness of the double probe is greater than that of the two single probes in isolation.

It should be noted that this is also a very general technique. Obviously it can be extended to situations that combine three or more probes, and it can be used in a wide array of experimental settings.

Although this procedure has apparently not been used in social cognition research, it has recently appeared in a number of memory investigations (e.g., Jones, 1976, 1978, 1979), and Bruce (1980) has generated predictions for a number of general models. Although some investigators have found results using this procedure that are consistent with a general additive model (Anderson & Bower, 1972a; Bruce, 1980), Foss and Harwood (1975) have investigated recall of sentences and interpreted their findings in terms of a model that has both additive and configural components to it. In addition, R. Anderson (1974), Goetz, Anderson, and Schallert (1981), Horowitz and Prytulak (1969), and Marschark and Paivio (1977) have reported findings that appear to support some type of configural model. In general, a comparison of the relative effectiveness of single and double probes would appear to be a procedure that is ideal for investigating a number of theoretical issues that have long been debated in the social cognition literature.

RECOGNITION PROCEDURES

Hintzman (1978) makes the interesting observation that recognition measures were first reported early in the century but used very infrequently from 1930 to 1960 "apparently because the task does not lend itself easily to an analysis in terms of S-R bonds" (p. 231). However, the introduction of the information-processing approach brought with it a great concern with exactly what is represented in the "memory trace." Since recognition measures are ideally suited to addressing such questions, they have increased dramatically in popularity during the past 20 years. Recognition procedures are also becoming quite common in the study of social cognition.

Several different types of recognition procedures can be distinguished, each of which offers particular advantages and disadvantages. Many of these are reviewed in great detail by Murdock (1982) in a chapter devoted especially to that topic. Once again, the choice of a particular method really depends upon the questions being asked and the assumptions that need to be made.

The common element in all recognition procedures is that the subject is not required to reproduce any of the information. Rather, a subject is given information and, at some later time, given a new set of items and asked to indicate which were previously presented and which were not. Thus, they are really tests of discrimination (Hintzman, 1978). The major advantage of recognition procedures is that they are generally more sensitive to the retention of virtually any type of information than recall tests (see e.g., Crowder, 1976; Murdock, 1974; Nickerson, 1968; Shepard, 1967; Standing, 1973). Another advantage to the testing of recognition memory is that the procedures are easy to use in any modality. For example, the testing of recall for pictorial materials requires that the subjects have the ability to draw an identifiable picture (even in simplified form), and they are often quite difficult to score. Moreover, while it is not at all clear how one could examine recall for material acquired via the tactal, olfactory, or taste sense organs, recognition procedures can easily be adapted for all of these purposes (see Baddeley, 1976, for a review of representative studies in these areas).

Yes–No Recognition

The most simple type of recognition procedure involves a test in which single items are presented, and the subject must indicate which were previously presented and which were not. As is the case with all recognition procedures, it is critically important to make sure that there is no basis, outside of the experimental context per se, for discriminating between old and new (sometimes called "distractor" or "lure") items. That is, care must be taken so that the old and new items do not differ along any dimension whatsoever.

Two potential problems need to be considered when using such a procedure. First, overall performance on such a test will be strongly affected by the degree of similarity between the distractors and the actual items (see e.g., Bahrick & Bahrick, 1964; Bruce & Cofer, 1965; Klein & Arbuckle, 1970). In general, the best procedure is to draw the distractors and old items from a common pool. A more subtle problem involves the number of distractors that are used. Most experimenters typically construct a test in which 50% of the items are "old" and 50% of the items are "new." More importantly, subjects seem to expect a test in which old items and new items are equally represented. A procedure in which more than half of the items are "new" may therefore produce an unusually high number of false alarms, and a procedure in which fewer than half of the items are new may produce an unusually low number of false alarms. More generally, there is always the possibility that factors other than memory per se will affect a subject's criterion for responding "yes" or "no" to items on the recognition test. These factors are often discussed under the rubric of "guessing bias" or "guessing strategy" and procedures based on the Theory of Signal Detectability have been specifically designed to control for this (see below).[4]

---

[4]A few brief comments should also be made about what Kintsch (1977) and others have referred to as the "traditional correction for guessing" in a yes-no recognition task discussed by Woodworth (1938). Woodworth recognized that there was an important guessing or decision process that operates in responding to recognition test items and he suggested that this could be controlled by using the value for P("old"/old item) − P("old"/new item). It should be noted that this correction assumes a high-threshold model (see e.g., Egan, 1958; Thurstone, 1927) in which the individual values for P("old"/old item) and P("old"/new item) are linearly related. In the terminology of signal detection theory, high-threshold models assume that there are straight-line operating characteristics. Kintsch (1977) provides an excellent discussion of alternatives to high-threshold models and he points out that the available evidence (Egan, 1958; Murdock, 1965; Parks, 1966) is clearly inconsis-

Several general guidelines for the use of yes–no recognition tasks can be offered. First, it is ideal if the recognition test can contain all of the old items and an equal number of new items. If the test does not contain an equal number of old and new items, the experimenter can inform the subject of this beforehand. In fact, Murdock (1982) suggests that it is probably a good experimental strategy to inform the subject of the proportion of old and new items in all cases. Murdock (1982) also recommends that the material presented to subjects (i.e., old items) should be a random sample from some clearly defined population *and* that each subject receive a different random sample. While Murdock presents several cogent arguments in support of these recommendations, there are many areas of social cognition where (at present) it is not even possible to clearly define a general population of items. Nevertheless, these procedures are worth striving for. It should also be noted that Murdock (1974; 1982) suggests collecting latency as well as accuracy data. The reasoning behind this concerns an attempt to separate the "memory" and "decision" components of the task. Much more will be said about this in the section on signal detection theory below.

Confidence Ratings

The yes–no recognition procedure can easily be extended to obtain some confidence rating of how certain the subject is that a given item was or was not previously presented. Generally, the subject is presented with a single item and then indicates on a scale his/her confidence that the item was or was not previously presented. Note that the subject is not given the opportunity to make a "neutral" or "undecided" response. Each item must be designated as old or new, and then a confidence rating attached to that judgment. The scales used can be either "marked" or "unmarked," and to the extent that subjects can make such confidence judgments reliably, more precise information is obtained. For this reason, confidence ratings are being used increasingly often. As is the case with the more simple yes–no procedure, however, performance will be affected by the similarity of the distractors and any factor that results in the subject adopting a more or less stringent response criterion. Fortunately, signal detection theory is ideally suited to the analysis of confidence ratings.

Forced-Choice Recognition Procedures

Ellis (1978) notes that the easiest way to control for guessing is to use a forced-choice recognition procedure. With this procedure, each item consists of a set of alternatives (usually, but not always, two alternatives are used), and the subject

tent with the assumption of straight-line operating characteristics in recognition memory experiments. Moreover, this is true with both yes–no procedures and confidence-rating procedures (see below). Thus, Woodworth's correction for guessing is clearly not recommended. However, there are alternative models derived from the theory of signal detectability that do not assume straight-line operating characteristics and appear far more viable.

must identify which of the alternatives was previously presented. This procedure controls for both guessing biases that are due to individual differences *and* factors in the experiment that make one more or less concerned about producing false alarms. It must be emphasized, however, that this procedure does *not* eliminate the need for one to carefully consider the nature of the distractors. In fact, performance will be affected by similarity of the distractors in exactly the same way as that noted above.

Three different phenomena, each from a different domain and none of which is atypical, can be used to illustrate how important it is to carefully consider the nature of the distractors before drawing conclusions from recognition memory experiments. For example, a series of studies once seemed to lead to the conclusion that memory for pictorial materials is virtually unlimited. Shepard (1967) presented subjects with 600 random photographs and then administered a forced-choice recognition test in which each picture was paired with a single distractor. Subjects were able to recognize the correct alternative 98% of the time. Similar findings were reported by Nickerson (1965), Standing, Conezio, and Haber (1970), and Standing (1973) who presented 10,000 separate slides with a procedure that took 5 days to complete! However, a study by Goldstein and Chance (1971) suggests that such results are at least partly due to the fact that the distractors were not at all similar to the actual items. In one of several related studies, Goldstein and Chance used various snowflakes both as presentation items and as lures on a forced-choice recognition test. Under these conditions, subjects were able to recognize only 33% of the items despite the fact that the total acquisition set contained only 14 (as opposed to 10,000) items. A conceptually similar result has recently been reported in a series of studies by Jenkins, Wald, and Pittenger (1978). They used as stimulus items a series of slides, all of which were related to the same sequence of behaviors (e.g., making a cup of tea, answering the telephone). Subjects were then given a yes–no recognition test in which items were either original slides, lures that could have been taken from the portrayed sequence, or lures that did not fit the portrayed sequence. In the "making a cup of tea" study, 80% of the original slides were recognized, 50% of the lures that could have been taken from the sequence were falsely identified as old items, but only 10% of the unrelated lures were falsely identified as old items.

Several studies from the verbal learning literature demonstrate that these effects are not confined to investigations that use pictorial materials. Anisfeld and Knapp (1968) used a yes–no recognition procedure in which the lures were close synonyms of the presented items, high associates of the presented items, or a random selection of "control" words. Many more synonyms and high associates than control words were falsely recognized. Similarly, Underwood and Freund (1968) used a forced-choice recognition procedure in which lures were either high associates, "formally similar" words, or neutral words. The high associates again elicited many more false recognition responses than either of the other two types of distractors. All of these studies indicate that performance on a recognition test (of any type) will be strongly influenced by the items that are used as lures. In many cases, an experimenter may want to "match" the old items and distractor items on variables that are known to affect recognition performance. In list-learning experiments, for example, variables such as word frequency (Gregg, 1976) or imagery value (Paivio, 1976) may need to be controlled. However, this requires that the experimenter know a priori those variables that are likely to be important. Unfortunately, with the exception of studies reported by Jenkins et al. (1978; see also Kraft & Jenkins, 1977), very little is known about the types of factors that are likely to affect recognition memory for the types of materials typically used in social cognition experiments. This is one area in which very important work still needs to be done.

Theory of Signal Detectability

It has become increasingly clear over the past 20 years that almost any cognitive process involves some decision component (see e.g., Lachman, Lachman, & Butterfield, 1979). The theory of signal detectability is an abstract conception of how these decision processes operate and influence performance on a variety of cognitive tasks. To appreciate its flexibility and generality, one need only consider that it has been used in studies of auditory perception (Egan, Schulman, & Greenberg, 1959; Swets, 1959), visual perception (Fitzhugh, 1957), learning (Catania, 1970), personality (LeFave & Neufeld, 1980), and abnormal psychology (Clark, 1966), as well as to the study of memory (e.g., Banks, 1970; Bernbach, 1967; Kintsch, 1967; Krantz, 1969; Lockhart & Murdock, 1970; Parks 1966; Wickelgren & Norman, 1966).

Fortunately, a number of good introductions to signal detection theory exist. Excellent discussions of the underlying logic are provided by Anderson and Borkowski (1978), Coombs, Dawes, and Tversky (1970), and Klatzky (1980), and a very good presentation of the actual mechanics of designing and analyzing various types of experiments using signal detection theory is provided by McNicol (1972). Researchers who are not intimately familiar with signal detection theory but do have a need for it are particularly encouraged to consult this latter source. More advanced treatments of the theory and its derivatives are provided by Swets (1964; Green & Swets, 1966) and Egan and Clark (1966).

Signal detection theory was first developed in the field of perception and engineering psychology to help separate the theoretical process of perception from the decision aspects of one's performance. Conceptually, the theory distinguishes between the observer as a "sensor" and the observer as a "decision maker." Consider a very simple perceptual task in which a person must watch a radar screen and indicate whether a signal appears during a certain period. The radar screen will always contain a certain amount of "noise" (e.g., random atmospheric and electronic disturbances) and only occasionally will a true signal (e.g., a plane) appear. Such a task can generate four different possible responses. A subject can indicate a signal is present when there actually is a signal (a *hit*), indicate a signal is present when there actually is none (a *false alarm*), indicate that no signal is present when there actually is none (a *correct rejection*), or indicate that there is no signal when one is actually present (a *miss*). In perceptual experiments such as this, a subject's overall performance can be summarized by plotting the probability of making a hit as a function of the probability of making a false alarm. Such a plot is referred to as a receiver operating characteristic (ROC) curve and it represents how well a subject is able to discriminate between "noise" and "signal-plus-noise."

Yes–No Recognition.   An exactly analogous situation to that above exists in performance on various types of recognition memory tests. We will use the simple yes–no recognition format as an example in developing the underlying logic of the theory of signal detectability as it applies to memory. With this type of test, a subject is presented with two types of items: *old* items that have been previously presented, and *new* items that have not been previously presented. For each type of item, a subject indicates "old" or "new." A decision matrix outlining the four types of possible responses is presented in Table 1.1. Two different types of correct responses are possible. A hit occurs when a subject responds "old" to an old item, and a correct rejection occurs when a subject responds "new" to a new item. Similarly, there are two types of incorrect responses. A false alarm occurs when a subject responds "old" to a new item, and a miss occurs when a subject responds "new" to an old item.

Note that two values are sufficient to summarize the entire data matrix. Since an old item can generate only a hit or a miss, $P(\text{miss}) = 1 - P(\text{hit})$. Similarly, a new item can only generate a false alarm or a correct rejection. Thus, $P(\text{correct rejection}) = 1 - P(\text{false alarm})$. It is for this reason that researchers typically only report the proportion of hits and false alarms. In addition, since the entire data matrix can be represented by these two values, the information is often presented by plotting the proportion of hits as a function of the proportion of false

TABLE 1.1
A Decision Matrix Outlining the
Four Types of Possible Responses
in a Yes–No Recognition Task

	Recognition Test Item	
Subject's Response	*Old*	*New*
"Old"	Hit	False Alarm
"New"	Miss	Correct Rejection

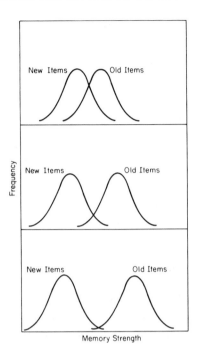

FIG. 1.6.   Several possible theoretical distributions of strengths for old
(previously presented) and new (distractor) items in memory. (After
Klatzky, 1980.)

alarms. Such a graph is analogous to the ROC curve described above and has
been termed a memory operating characteristic (MOC) curve by Norman and
Wickelgren (1965).

Memory researchers using signal detection theory generally assume that there
is a "strength" associated with each item in long-term memory. Thus, there is a
strength associated with each item on a recognition test. However, having an
item presented in the acquisition list serves to increase its initial strength value
for some period of time. The strength for old items will therefore generally be
greater than the strength for new items (cf. Anderson & Bower, 1972b). Moreover, the strength for each of the old items is assumed to be distributed normally,
as is that for each of the new items. The two distributions are also assumed to
have equal variances.

Several possible theoretical distributions are presented in Figure 1.6. In the
top panel, strength for the old items has been increased only slightly. Thus, there
is substantial overlap between the distributions for old and new items. In the
middle panel, there is slightly less overlap. The lower panel represents a case in
which the strength of old items has been increased substantially. Consequently,
there is relatively little overlap between the two resulting distributions.

Signal detection theory uses a value known as d' to represent the difference
between the means of the two distributions measured in standard deviation units.
A larger d' indicates that the two distributions are more discriminable. In Figure

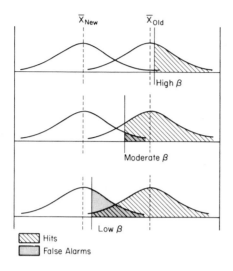

FIG. 1.7. Effects of variations in β when d' remains constant. As β decreases, both the hit and false alarm rates will increase and, as a consequence, estimates of d' will remain constant. (After Klatzky, 1980.)

1.6, top panel would have the smallest d' value, and the bottom panel would have the largest.

The critical assumption of signal detection theory is that the subject implicitly chooses a particular strength as a criterion in deciding whether to respond ''old'' or ''new'' in response to the various recognition test items. The strength value that a subject uses as a criterion will affect the subject's overall performance in a number of ways. Specifically, a ''liberal'' criterion in which a relatively low strength value is used to respond ''old'' will result in a large number of hits but also a large number of false alarms. Conversely, a ''stringent'' criterion in which a high strength value is used to respond ''old'' will result in a small number of false alarms but also a reduced number of hits. Figure 1.7 represents this graphically. The normalized distance between the two distributions (d') is the same in all three panels. The top panel represents a hypothetical subject who used an extremely stringent criterion. Such a subject commits very few false alarms but also gets a relatively small number of hits. The lower panel represents a hypothetical subject who uses a very liberal criterion. Such a subject would have a very high proportion of hits but also commit a large number of false alarms. The middle panel represents the use of an intermediate criterion.[5]

The two values d' and β are assessments of the ''memory'' and ''decision'' components, respectively, and each will be affected by a variety of factors. For example, d' may be influenced by such factors as meaningfulness of the items, interest value in the new information, processing strategies and goals of the subject, and length of the delay between the time in which the new information is

---

[5]The organization of this section is adapted from the excellent presentation by Klatzky (1980).

acquired and the time at which it is tested. Similarly, β may be affected by prior expectancies or any factor that serves to make the subject want to maximize the number of hits or minimize the number of false alarms.

It should be clear that from the perspective of signal detection theory, recognition memory performance is only meaningful when one considers the proportion of hits *in conjunction with* the proportion of false alarms. This information is best represented in terms of the type of MOC curve presented in Figure 1.8. Each point on such a curve represents a different criterion that a subject might use to respond to various items. All points along the diagonal correspond to the case in which $d' = 0$. This line represents chance performance in which the subject is completely unable to discriminate between old and new items. All curves above the diagonal represent situations in which the subject is able to make such discriminations. As d' increases, the ratio of hits to false alarms also increases.

In practice, the experimental data are the probabilities of each subject producing a hit and false alarm. Elliott (1964) has provided tables for determining the associated d' values from the hit and false alarm rates (see also Hacker & Ratcliff, 1979). As Klatzky (1980) notes, "From the table, the experimenter can tell if an experimental manipulation that might have changed both the hit and false alarm rates has actually changed d'. If what has changed is merely the subject's guessing strategy, then the hits and false alarms will have changed together, and d' will be the same for the new values as for the old. In this way, the use of d' rather than a simple percentage of correct responses enables the experimenter to correct for guessing in a theoretically meaningful way" (p. 252). It is for this reason that d' is to be generally preferred over Woodworth's (1938) more simple correction for guessing (see Footnote 4).

In cases where there is reason to believe that one or more of the required assumptions is violated, a variety of nonparametric measures of memory discrimination are also available. Perhaps the most noteworthy is A_g (Banks, 1970;

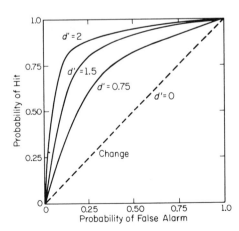

FIG. 1.8.   Theoretical memory operating characteristic (MOC) curves for various values of d'. (After Solso, 1979.)

Green & Moses, 1966; Pollack & Decker, 1958: Pollack & Norman, 1964), which is basically an assessment of the entire area under the MOC curve. Values of A_g range from .5 (random responding) to 1.0 (perfect discrimination) and can be used in place of d'. This nonparametric measure requires no distributional assumptions to be made concerning underlying strength values. Other nonparametric measures and a detailed discussion of the situations in which they are most appropriate are provided by McNicol (1972).

Recognition Confidence Ratings.   In the yes–no recognition task, a subject can only make one of two responses. It is possible, however, that a subject is capable of providing more sensitive information. This can often be obtained through a confidence-rating task. With this type of task, a subject not only indicates if an item was old or new but also rates his/her confidence in the judgment. Between four and ten steps are generally provided on a scale, and subjects appear to be able to make such discriminations quite reliable. For example, the following type of rating scale has proven to be very effective: (1) positive the item was not presented, (2) fairly certain the item was not presented, (3) undecided, but think the item was not presented, (4) undecided, but think the item was presented, (5) fairly certain the item was presented, and (6) positive the item was presented. Note that, similar to the yes–no format, the subject must indirectly respond "old" or "new" to each item (i.e., there is no opportunity to make a neutral or "undecided" response).

Most actual studies using signal detection theory use a confidence rating procedure. The reason for this is that each point on the rating scale can be thought of as corresponding to a different criterion. The fact that high confidence ratings (which correspond to a very stringent criterion) produce relatively few hits or false alarms, whereas lower confidence ratings (a more liberal criterion) produce greater numbers of both hits and false alarms supports this (see Murdock, 1974). Assuming that a sufficient number of items are provided and the subject used all of the confidence-rating categories, an entire MOC curve for each subject can be generated from these data. This makes the confidence-rating procedure ideally suited to the use of signal detection theory.[6, 7]

Latency Data.   As noted above, Murdock (1982) has suggested that latency as well as accuracy data be collected from recognition memory experiments

---

[6]Explicit instructions for how to construct the MOC curve from recognition confidence ratings are provided by McNicol (1972).

[7]There have also been cases in which signal detection theory has been applied to forced-choice recognition procedures, as well as free recall. However, the theory is not particularly well suited to these types of tasks and there is a great deal of controversy over how these type data can be analyzed and interpreted. The many technical issues involved are really beyond the scope of the present chapter. However, the interested reader will find quite thorough discussions in Banks (1970), Green and Swets (1966), and Lockhart and Murdock (1970).

whenever possible. Norman and Wickelgren (1969) reported perhaps the first study in which latency data were collected in a recognition task and related to signal detection theory. The basic tenet of a signal detection analysis is that the strength of an item in memory *and* the strength value that a subject uses as a criterion will determine the response that is made. It is assumed that when the strength of an item is close to the criterion, the decision will be relatively difficult to make and therefore be associated with a longer latency to respond (for discussions of how this general model has been applied to a broad range of phenomena, see Allen & Ebbesen, 1981; Atkinson & Juola, 1974; Ebbesen & Allen, 1979; Shoben, 1980; Smith, 1978; Smith, Shoben, & Rips, 1974). The more general relationships among item strength, recognition judgments, and latency to respond are summarized in Figure 1.9.

Although relatively little work has been done in this area, a number of interesting hypotheses have been tested. For example, since response latencies and confidence ratings are related to the underlying strength of an item in exactly opposite ways, these variables should be negatively correlated. Norman and Wickelgren (1969) and more recently Murdock and Dufty (1972) have both found support for this hypothesis. Second, incorrect responses (either misses or false alarms) will generally be made to items that have strengths relatively close to the criterion. This suggests that latencies for correct responses will generally be shorter than those for incorrect responses. Data reported by Murdock and Dufty (1972) also support this prediction. Finally, one can also consider the relationship between the two theoretical distributions of item strength as depicted in Fig. 1.9. Higher d' values indicate that the two distributions are further separated along the strength continuum. This would suggest that a greater number of items would be associated with shorter latencies. In other words, there should be an inverse relationship between d' and response latency. This prediction has also been supported (Murdock & Dufty, 1972).

Although only a small number of studies have been conducted examining the relationship between response latency and recognition memory, it is hoped that

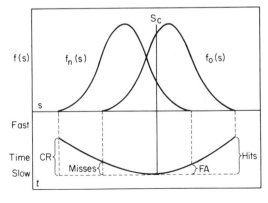

FIG. 1.9.   A strength theory model showing old and new item distributions on a strength continuum (s) and latencies (t) relative to strength. CR represent correct rejections, and FA represent false alarms. (After Norman & Wickelgren, 1969.)

many more will be reported in the future. This would be consistent with our more general suggestion that investigators attempt to collect multiple dependent measures from the same experimental paradigm. Murdock (1982) has discussed in detail many of the advantages of doing just this in experiments utilizing various recognition procedures.

Applications and Implications for Social Cognition

Recognition procedures have been used to address a variety of issues in social cognition. While some studies have used procedures that suffer from severe interpretive difficulties, others have used surprisingly sophisticated methodologies. Since a complete review of how recognition procedures have been used in the study of social cognition is neither necessary nor possible given space limitations, we concentrate in this section on the use of signal detection theory and the "false recognition" paradigm. Each of these general procedures holds great promise for the investigation of person memory and social cognition, but they have appeared in the literature only very sporadically. We hope that by presenting some of the advantages of these approaches, they will become much more fully utilized in the future.

Signal Detection Theory. Perhaps the first area in social cognition where recognition memory procedures were heavily relied upon was concerned with the role of cognitive processes in stereotyping. For example, Cohen (1977, 1981) showed subjects a videotape of a woman returning home from work and interacting with her husband. Some subjects were led to believe that the woman was a waitress, while others were led to believe she was a librarian. The videotape included a number of behaviors, half of which (based on normative ratings) were consistent with prior stereotypes of a waitress and half of which were consistent with prior stereotypes of a librarian. After viewing the videotape, subjects were given a forced-choice recognition test in which each item consisted of one stereotype-consistent behavior and one stereotype-inconsistent behavior. Cohen has found, across a variety of delay intervals, that subjects tend to "recognize" a greater number of stereotype-consistent than stereotype-inconsistent behaviors. As Wyer and Srull (1980) point out, however, it is difficult to know exactly what such results mean because there was no attempt to control for guessing strategies on the part of subjects. For example, it is possible that subjects forgot consistent and inconsistent behaviors at exactly the same rate. However, anytime the subject encounters an item on the recognition test that is not familiar, he/she could use the stereotype label to *guess* which alternative is most likely to be true. This type of guessing strategy would artifactually produce a greater number of stereotype-consistent than stereotype-inconsistent behaviors being "recognized." Cantor and Mischel (1977) and Tsujimoto (1978) have used a confidence-rating, rather than forced-choice, procedure in similar investigations, and they have also failed to take into account the role of any guessing strategies on the part of subjects.

As noted above, the nature of the distractors is critical in any recognition memory experiment, and some consideration must also be given to the potential role of guessing strategies. Hartwick (1979, 1982) has recently reported a series of studies that very nicely deals with both of these concerns.

In an initial study, Hartwick (1979) gave subjects a list of personality trait adjectives that were evaluatively consistent (i.e., either all favorable or all unfavorable) but varied in their descriptive implications (see Peabody, 1967, 1970). Some subjects were given a general impression formation set, while others were given a memory set. All subjects were later given a recognition confidence-rating task. The recognition test consisted of the original 10 trait adjectives, 10 distractors that were evaluatively and descriptively consistent with the original traits, 10 distractors that were evaluatively consistent but descriptively inconsistent with the original traits, 10 distractors that were evaluatively inconsistent but descriptively consistent with the original traits, and 10 distractors that were both evaluatively and descriptively inconsistent with the original traits. Thus, the nature of the distractors was systematically varied (for other examples of this general procedure in very different domains, see Fillenbaum, 1966; Nickerson & Adams, 1979; Sachs, 1967).

Hartwick performed a signal detection analysis of these data that permitted him to separate the ''memory'' from ''decision'' or guessing components of the subjects' performance. In particular, the dependent variable was the total area under the various MOC curves (this is, as noted above, a function of the d' scores). Hartwick found that there was poorer memory discrimination between the old items and either evaluatively consistent distractors or descriptively consistent distractors than there was between the old itmes and evaluatively or descriptively inconsistent distractors. More important, however, the effect of evaluative consistency was much greater under the impression set than under the memory set. On the other hand, the effect of descriptive consistency did not vary across the two orienting task conditions. This suggests that subjects in the impression set condition formed a mental representation of the target person that had a very strong evaluative component to it.

In a subsequent experiment using the same basic procedure, Hartwick (1982) turned to a more fine-grained analysis. Although the results of this experiment are somewhat complex, Hartwick basically found that both evaluative and ''activity'' features (see Osgood, 1969; Osgood, Suci, & Tannenbaum, 1957) are represented in the memory trace. Again, the evaluative dimension appears to be much more important for impression set than memory set subjects. In addition, however, while the representation of activity information largely depends upon evaluative factors, the reverse does not appear to be the case.

While Hartwick has not followed Murdock's (1982) suggestion of including an equal number of old and new items on the recognition test *or* informing subjects beforehand that the test contains a disproportionate number of old and new items, he has introduced an important and creative methodological technique. It should be noted that this is an extremely general procedure that can be used to diagnose which features (attributes) are and are not represented in the memory trace *and* how the nature of the representation is affected by various instructional sets. Thus, the technique is ideally suited to investigating various theories of memory that conceptualize the memory trace as composed of a collection of attributes or attribute vectors (for specific variations of this general approach, see Bower, 1967, 1972a, 1972b; Bregman & Chambers, 1966; Brown & McNeil, 1966; Estes, 1972; Norman & Rumelhart, 1970; Underwood, 1969; Wickelgren, 1965; Wickens, 1970, 1972). The importance of telling subjects how many old and new items are contained on the recognition test is, of course, an empirical question.[8]

It should be remembered that signal detection analyses are based on a general strength theory of item recognition. While we have seen that this procedure has proven to be extremely useful in a number of domains, there are many reasons for wanting to test whether the general strength notion applies to various issues of concern in the study of person memory and social cognition. The most powerful way to do this is to experimentally separate the two strength theory parameters of d' and β. That is, one would like to find an experimental variable that affects d' but not β and another variable that affects β but not d' within the same experiment. Researchers in memory and cognition have found this extremely difficult to do. Nevertheless, an unpublished study by Wells (reported in Murdock, 1974) demonstrates that such an experimental separation of the two parameters is possible. Wells presented lists of individual stimulus items that were either CVCs (consonant-vowel-consonant trigrams) or CCCs (consonant-consonant-consonant trigrams). After receiving a study list of 12 items, the subject was tested on only a single test item and the a priori probability of the test item being old or new was varied systematically across conditions of the experiment. The results clearly show that type of item had a strong affect on d' but not β (with CVCs showing much better memory discrimination than CCCs). However, the a priori probability of any given test item being old or new had a strong affect on the response criterion β but not on d'.

There have apparently been no experimental separations of these two parameters using the types of materials typically employed in person memory experiments. However, such demonstrations will be important for any researcher who

---

[8]It is highly unlikely that this played an important role in any of Hartwick's studies because he has never presented more than 10 trait adjectives to any given subject. Under these conditions it is likely that subjects realized that the vast majority of items on the recognition test were distractors. Nevertheless, researchers who use a greater number of stimulus items should keep this problem in mind and consider Murdock's (1982) arguments very seriously. When a series of related studies are conducted, it is probably wise to inform subjects of the composition of the recognition test in at least several of the studies to determine empirically whether strikingly different results obtain.

wishes to base his/her analysis on a general strength theory of recognition memory.

False Recognition Procedures. It was noted in our discussion of recall procedures that "intrusions" sometimes become the major variable of interest. That is, concern is directed toward the nature of the "false alarms" rather than to the hits. An analogous situation occasionally occurs with recognition procedures. The studies described above by Cohen (1977, 1981), Cantor and Mischel (1977), and Tsujimoto (1978) are of this general class (see also Woll & Graesser, in press).

One of the classic studies examining "false recognition" was performed by Bransford and Franks (1971). They presented subjects with sentences that were individually part of a more complex idea. For example, a subject might be presented with, "The rock rolled down the mountain," "The rock crushed the hut at the edge of the forest," "The hut was tiny," "The rock that rolled down the mountain crushed the tiny hut," "The tiny hut was at the edge of the forest," and so on. Subjects were then presented with test sentences that varied in the number of propositions they contained that were consistent with the general idea. Bransford and Franks found that recognition confidence ratings were a linear function of sentence complexity. That is, the recognition confidence ratings were ordered: FOUR propositions > THREE > TWO > ONE. This occurred despite the fact that subjects never heard *any* sentences that contained four separate propositions. This basic effect has been replicated several times (e.g., Schwartz & Witherspoon, 1974; Singer, 1973) and an analogous finding occurs when a recall test is used as well (Cofer, 1973; Griggs, 1974).

Tsujimoto, Wilde, and Robertson (1978) have recently demonstrated that such results are not confined to the linguistic integration of ideas. They showed subjects slides of athletes finishing an athletic event. Subjects saw TWOS (i.e., two athletes finishing in a particular order), THREES, FOURS, AND FIVES, all of which were consistent with a single linear ordering. The recognition test consisted of old items, new items that were nevertheless consistent with the linear ordering, and "noncases" that were not only new but violated the linear ordering as well. The recognition test consisted of TWOS, THREES, FOURS, and FIVES. While noncases tended to be rejected, old and new items were recognized with equal confidence. In addition, as in the Bransford and Franks (1971) study, recognition confidence ratings were ordered: FIVES > FOURS > THREES > TWOS.

As Hastie (1981) notes, results such as these are often cited in support of some "schema" theory but they are more inconsistent with a simple associationistic account than clearly supportive of a general schema theory. At any rate, the point we wish to make here is that the exact nature of the recognition test also needs to be considered in this type of false recognition paradigm. In particular, although relatively little empirical work has been done related to this, it appears that some types of recognition test formats are more sensitive than others, For example,

Griggs and Keen (1977) attempted to replicate the Bransford and Franks study using two different types of recognition test procedures. In one condition, subjects were given the same type of yes–no confidence-rating task that was used by Bransford and Franks. In the other condition, subjects were presented with all of the test items at once and they had to pick out which ones were old and which ones were new (Murdock [1982] calls this type of forced-choice procedure "batch testing"). Griggs and Keen found that although subjects *apparently* could not distinguish between old and new items with the yes–no /one-item-at-a-time procedure (replicating the Bransford and Franks finding), they could reliably make such discriminations between old and new items when responding to all of the items at once. Thus, the "batch" or forced-choice procedure appears to be more sensitive in picking up differences that are not observed with the yes–no procedure. Griggs and Keen (1977) argue, "The major effect of the forced-choice procedure is the alleviation of memory load and decision difficulties in the recognition task. Decisions can then be based upon the relative strength of individual sentences rather than upon an absolute yes-no criterion (p. 689)."

Any researcher working with this type of false recognition procedure obviously needs to be concerned not only with the type of distractors used but *also* with the sensitivity of the particular recognition test employed. It should be noted, however, that there is one major disadvantage associated with the batch-testing procedure. Specifically, the very nature of the procedure precludes the experimenter from collecting latency data as well as a general accuracy measure. For this reason, some researchers (e.g., Murdock, 1982) have cautioned against drawing inferences based exclusively on this type of procedure. Once again, the ideal situation would appear to be one where various experimental operations are used to carefully converge upon a single interpretation or conclusion.

RECALL-RECOGNITION DIFFERENCES

As we have seen, various types of recall and recognition tests can be used to address a wide array of theoretical issues. It has also been argued, however, that a comparison of free recall and recognition performance can sometimes be used to illuminate those mental processes that are responsible for a given effect. An analysis of the differences between recall and recognition is a much more complicated issue than it initially appears to be and an entire chapter could easily be devoted to the topic. In this section, we try to introduce the major substantive issues and offer one useful way for analyzing the differences between performance on free recall and recognition tests.

The mutually dependent relationship between methodological strategies and theoretical assumptions is seldom more clear than in the study of recall-recognition differences. In short, one simply cannot interpret such differences outside of some (implicit or explicit) theoretical context.

Simple Strength Theory

One of the classic approaches to memory is now known as "simple strength theory." According to this theory, there is a strength associated with each item (e.g., word) in long-term memory. It is referred to as a "simple" strength theory because the strength of any item is assumed to be ahistorical in nature. That is, no mechanism is provided for representing contextual information or "context cues," and the strength of any item is considered to be a function of only the recency and frequency of presentation.

One of the reasons that simple strength theory was proposed is that it can easily account for the most obvious difference between recall and recognition: People are able to recognize many items that they are unable to recall. According to the theory, recall and recognition are processes (as opposed to tasks) that require different amounts of strength for retrieval and activation. As illustrated in Figure 1.10, there are different strength thresholds for recall and recognition. The strength associated with item X is below each threshold and therefore could not be recalled or recognized. Item Y has an intermediate strength and could be recognized but not recalled. On the other hand, the strength associated with Z is very high, and this would allow it to be either recognized or recalled.

Although simple strength theory seems intuitively plausible and it continued to have its proponents through the 1950s, it eventually ran into two separate classes of problems. The first is the very robust "spacing effect" (see e.g., Crowder, 1976; Kintsch, 1977). Since strength is thought to be a function of recency and frequency, massed presentations rather than spaced presentations should lead to superior memory. However, with the possible exception of an immediate memory test, memory typically increases as the lag between presentations increases (for reviews of this literature, see Crowder, 1976; Kintsch, 1977). This is directly opposite to what simple strength theory would predict.

The second general class of problems that posed serious difficulties for simple strength theory is much more important for a consideration of recall-recognition differences. This concerns the many "study-test interactions" that have been

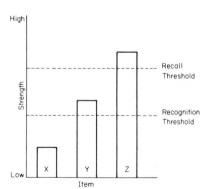

FIG. 1.10.   A simple strength theory model of recall and recognition.

discovered (for a discussion of many of these, see Brown, 1976b). In brief, since simple strength theory postulates that only one theoretical variable (strength) is involved in memory, experimental manipulations should affect recall and recognition in exactly the same way. There is now abundant evidence, however, that this simply is not the case. There are a large number of variables whose effects *depend upon* whether a recall or recognition test is used (for reviews, see Brown, 1976a; Eysenck, 1977; Kintsch, 1970, Tulving, 1976; Watkins & Gardiner, 1979).

Two-Stage Models

The various empirical contradictions to simple strength theory eventually became more and more obvious, and as the information processing paradigm gained in popularity, theorists became increasingly concerned with specifying the theoretical mechanisms involved in the process of recalling or recognizing certain information. In particular, the "generation-recognition" theory was developed as an alternative to simple strength theory. This continues to be one of the most highly regarded conceptual frameworks in cognitive psychology (see e.g., recent reviews by Brown, 1976a; Eysenck, 1977; Glass, Holyoak, & Santa, 1979; Watkins & Gardiner, 1979). While the generation-recognition approach had several early proponents (James, 1890; Muller, 1913), variations of the theory have continued to be developed by Anderson and Bower (1972b, 1974), Bahrick (1969, 1970), Estes and DaPolito (1967), Kintsch (1968, 1970), and Peterson (1967), among others. One of the reasons for its popularity is its ability to parsimoniously account for a large number of reliable differences between recall and recognition.

The generation-recognition theory essentially proposes that recall is a two-stage process in which a person must independently retrieve a particular item and then perform some recognition check on whether, in fact, the item was present in a particular context. Although there is not universal agreement on this point (see e.g., Atkinson, Herrmann, & Wescourt, 1974; Mandler, 1980; Murdock & Anderson, 1975; Tulving, 1976), recognition tasks are generally thought to bypass the retrieval stage and thus only involve the single stage of a discrimination (recognition) check. Thus, recall and recognition are thought to involve qualitatively different theoretical mechanisms.

This has proven to be a very parsimonious conceptual approach, and it can account for a large number of differences that are reliably found between recall and recognition performance. For example, recognition is almost always better than recall. The reason for this is that a breakdown can occur at either stage when a subject must recall an item, but only at one stage when recognition is called for. Another very robust finding in the verbal learning literature is that high frequency words (as determined by their use in the language) are easier to recall than low frequency words (Gregg, 1976). Theoretically, this is because high frequency words are easier to retrieve. In contrast, low frequency words are easier to recognize than high frequency words (Gregg, 1976). The reason for this is that it is harder to distinguish whether high frequency words were present in a particular (experimental) context. In addition, although retroactive interference effects are sometimes quite large for recall, they are negligible when recognition tasks are used (for a review of this literature, see Postman, 1976a). Theoretically, successive presentation lists produce more interference in the retrieval stage than in the discrimination stage (cf. Tulving & Psotka, 1971).

There are also several robust findings that are more closely related to concerns in person memory and social cognition. For example, organization is extremely important for recall but not for recognition, presumably because it is important to have some organizational scheme available if one is going to be able to retrieve various items (for reviews of the pertinent literature, see Kintsch, 1970; McCormack, 1972). Similarly, explicit instructions to learn a list typically produce greater levels of recall than incidental learning conditions (e.g., Estes & Da-Polito, 1967). This is what would be expected if one assumes that intentional learning conditions lead to greater levels of organization than do incidental learning conditions (at least when random lists of words are used as stimuli). Finally, the presence of associative cues is very helpful in facilitating recall, but not at all in recognition (Watkins & Gardiner, 1979). Theoretically, such cues aid in the retrieval stage but not in the recognition stage.

In general, any variable that affects a subject's ability to independently retrieve (i.e., freely generate) a given piece of information should, according to the generation-recognition theory, have a pronounced effect on recall but none on recognition accuracy. Thus, any experimental manipulation that affects recall but *not* recognition is assumed to tap a process that is localized in the retrieval stage of information processing. This makes a comparison of recall-recognition differences ideal for examining retrieval effects.[9]

---

[9]It should be noted that the generation-recognition theory has not been without its critics (see e.g., Tulving, 1976; Wiseman & Tulving, 1975). The major objection is that the theory is unable to account for the fact that words that cannot be recognized are sometimes recalled (Thompson & Tulving, 1970; Tulving & Thompson, 1971, 1973; Watkins & Tulving, 1975). However, these studies are extremely controversial from both a methodological and a theoretical point of view (see e.g., Eysenck, 1977; Reder, Anderson, & Bjork, 1974; Salzberg, 1976; Santa & Lamwers, 1974, 1976). For example, although it is typical in using a within-subject design to administer the recall test first and the recognition test second, the paradigm developed by Tulving and his associates used exactly the opposite sequence. Thus, performance on the recall task may be influenced by the fact that subjects encountered the words a second time in the process of completing the recognition test. It is also important to realize that the generation-recognition theory is inconsistent with these results *only* if it is assumed that the decision (recognition) phase remains invariant across the two tasks. However, there is no guarantee in any of Tulving's studies that this was the case. At any rate, it is important that even those who accept Tulving's apparently anomalous findings defend the generation-recognition theory as the most comprehensive and parsimonious account of recall-recognition differences that currently exists (see Watkins & Gardiner, 1979).

Applications and Implications for Social Cognition

There have been extremely few explicit attempts to compare recall and recognition performance in social cognition. This is probably due to the fact that very few models in social cognition have been developed to the point where specific effects due to retrieval failure can be identified.

One theory in which such effects can be predicted is the associative storage and retrieval model of person memory developed by Hastie (1980) and summarized earlier in the chapter (see Fig 1.5). Since the search and retrieval process underlying free recall is assumed to traverse the associative paths laid down in the network during encoding, Srull (1981, Experiment 1) hypothesized that any variable that affects the nature of these associations should have an effect on recall. Specifically, it was predicted that the encoding of behavioral items incongruent with prior expectancy would form more inter-episode associative paths than the encoding of congruent behavioral items, and the establishment of such paths would occur more often when subjects were attempting to form a coherent impression of the target (as opposed to trying to memorize the information) and when the information pertained to a psychologically meaningful target (as opposed to a group of unrelated individuals). Srull found that all three of these variables had a significant effect on recall. However, when the retrieval stage was bypassed with a recognition task and the number of associative paths that were established during encoding was no longer crucial, none of the variables noted above had a significant influence.

All of the variables investigated by Srull (1981) theoretically affect a subject's tendency to organize and integrate various pieces of information. Although this is a prime topic of concern to those working in the area of person memory, very similar effects have been reported in the experimental literature. For example, Schwartz and Humphreys (1974) used a procedure in which a list of items (words) were presented sequentially. Subjects were either given standard memory set instructions or required to rehearse aloud only the item then being presented, thus reducing the opportunity to organize the material by forming associative linkages between items. This latter condition had no effect on recognition performance but led to substantially reduced levels of recall.

It is clear from results such as these that researchers in social cognition will need to consider much more carefully the relationship between recall and recognition test performance. One of the perennial questions that arises in conducting these types of studies is whether to use a within-subject design in which subjects are first given a free recall test and then administered the recognition test or a between-subject design in which different subjects are given the recall and recognition tests. Unfortunately, there is no simple answer to this, and it is difficult to offer even general guidelines for when each type of design is most appropriate. Clearly differences between recall and recognition are observed in both types of settings. For example, while Srull (1981) used a within-subject design, Schwartz and Humphreys (1974) used a between-subject design.

Moreover, an informal survey of our colleagues who conduct this type of research indicates that they are evenly divided in their recommendations. Some feel that it is always best to use a between-subject design to avoid the possibility of one test contaminating the other. However, others have indicated that they have often compared the results from the two types of designs and have found no differences. Since very few of these comparisons have been conducted on the types of materials used in person memory and social cognition experiments, it really is too early to offer any suggestions. The best overall strategy is for researchers to use both types of designs, compare the results obtained with each, and attempt to delineate those factors that seem to be responsible for any differences observed.

There is one additional way in which a comparison of recall and recognition test performance can be very informative. This is at the individual item level. Perhaps the best way to illustrate this technique is with a specific example.

In one of the most comprehensive and impressive examinations of schema theory, Brewer and Treyens (1981) investigated incidental memory for places. In brief, individual subjects were met by a graduate student experimenter who explained that he needed several more minutes to get ready for the experiment and he then invited the subject to wait in his office for several minutes. After a brief delay, subjects were taken to another room and told that the experiment involved their memory for various objects in the office. Most subjects later reported that they casually glanced around the office in order to gain some general impression of what the experimenter was like or to obtain some clues as to what the experiment would be about.

The graduate student's office actually contained a large number of objects that Brewer and Treyens had independently scaled along several dimensions. For example, "saliency" ratings were obtained by having independent judges rate how noticeable each object would be in that type of room. Objects such as a spare tire and a Playboy centerfold were given high saliency ratings, while objects such as an eraser and paper clips were given low saliency ratings. Brewer and Treyens also obtained "schema expectancy" ratings by having independent judges rate how likely the various objects would appear in that type of room. Objects such as a desk and a calendar obtained high schema expectancy ratings, while objects like a sewing machine and a 45-caliber pistol obtained low schema expectancy ratings.

In one of several conditions of the experiment, subjects first provided a written recall protocol by listing all of the objects they could remember as being in the room. Following this, the same subjects were given a recognition confidence rating task in which they rated each of 131 objects on a scale ranging from 1 ("absolutely certain that you did *not* see the object") to 6 ("absolutely certain that you *did* see the object").

Brewer and Treyens then compared the recall and recognition performance in a number of interesting ways. First, when subjects produced an item on the written recall protocol, 96% of the time they gave a recognition confidence rating of 6 to the same object. However, many of the items that were given recognition confidence ratings of 6 were not recalled. The authors then computed a "retrieval ratio" for each individual object in the room. This ratio was defined as the number of times the object was produced in the written recall task divided by the number of times that the same object was given a recognition confidence rating of 6. A high retrieval ratio (approximating 1.0) reflects the fact that most subjects who rated an object 6 in the recognition task were also able to recall it. A low retrieval ratio (approximating .00) reflects the fact that most subjects who rated an object 6 on the recognition task were not able to independently recall it. Brewer and Treyens then computed correlations between these retrieval ratios and the "saliency" and "schema expectancy" ratings obtained earlier. The correlation between saliency and retrieval ratio was − .04, while the correlation between schema expectancy and retrieval ratio was .56. Moreover, since the saliency and schema expectancy ratings were only slightly negatively correlated themselves, the partial correlations did not change substantially. These results suggest that the schema expectancy was very important in providing (subject-generated) retrieval cues that aided in the recall of various objects. This was not, however, true of object saliency.

Although the computation of retrieval ratios requires that a within-subject comparison be made, this is a very powerful technique for examining retrieval differences at the item-by-item level. It is also a very general procedure. There is no a priori reason to confine the ratio to items that elicit the most extreme recognition confidence rating and it can be used to examine any property of the items that can be independently scaled. It is likely that examining this type of retrieval ratio will become very useful to those working in the area of person memory, as well as social cognition more generally. We would therefore expect to see many more studies reporting this type of analysis in the future.

REACTION TIME PROCEDURES

Even a cursory glance at the literature in cognitive psychology will indicate that reaction time has become a ubiquitous dependent variable. There are several reasons for this, all of which suggest that one can reasonably expect to see reaction time procedures used increasingly often in future social cognition research.

One of the most fundamental distinctions that can be made in social cognition is between *content* and *process*. The content of a mental representation can take many forms (propositional, visual, affective, etc.), but it exists independent of time. In contrast, the processes that operate on such content (the retrieval of information, the transformation of information from one form to another, computational procedures that permit inferences of various types, etc.) are assumed to operate in real time. For this reason, tracing the flow of various cognitive processes over time has become a prime concern of cognitive theorists (see e.g., Blumenthal, 1977; Posner, 1978).

Related to this is the more general issue of how unobservable cognitive processes can be investigated with any degree of precision. Taylor (1976) has noted the problems associated with trying to draw inferences about such processes from simple input-output relationships. Since many of these processes are extremely rapid, and often not open to conscious awareness, retrospective verbal reports are also problematic in many instances (Ericsson & Simon, 1980). As Pachella (1974) has noted, "The only property of mental events that can be studied directly, in the intact organism, *while* the events are taking place, is their duration" (p. 43). This has also contributed to an interest in reaction time.

Finally, reaction time procedures are extremely useful for the general type of stage analysis that is so prevalent in most of cognitive psychology. In particular, a great deal of effort has gone into developing general techniques that allow one to uniquely identify various subsystems (or stages) of a more general process. These procedures have proved to be extremely useful in cognitive psychology and they are being used increasingly often in social cognition as well. It is to these procedures that we now turn.

Subtraction Method

The general logic on which most reaction time procedures continue to be based was originally developed by Donders (1868). He devised three general types of reaction time tasks. These are illustrated in Figure 1.11. The first task, which Donders referred to as the A task, involves a single stimulus and a single

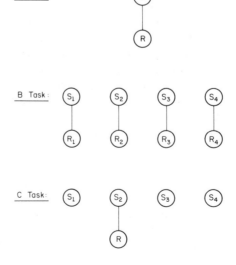

FIG. 1.11. A schematic representation of the three types of tasks used by Donder's. The A Task is thought to measure simple reaction time. The B Task is thought to measure stimulus categorization, response selection, and simple reaction time. The C Task is thought to measure stimulus categorization and simple reaction time.

response. For example, a subject might be asked to press a key whenever a light goes on. Such a task is thought to measure "simple reaction time." In the B task, there are multiple stimuli and multiple responses. For example, a subject might be asked to press a left-hand key whenever the left light goes on, and a right-hand key whenever the right light goes on. Such a task is thought to include three separate processes. First, the subject must categorize the stimulus (stimulus categorization). Second, he/she must choose a response (response selection). Finally, the subject must actually emit the response (again, "simple reaction time"). Figure 1.11 also illustrates Donder's C task. In this case there are multiple stimuli but only a single response. For example, a subject may see four separate lights and be asked to press a key only when the second light goes on. This task measures stimulus categorization and simple reaction time, but the response selection stage is eliminated.

Donders' subtraction method is based on the relationships between these three tasks. For example, task A measures simple reaction time, whereas task C measures stimulus categorization *plus* simple reaction time. Therefore, in order to obtain an estimate of the amount of time required for stimulus categorization, one can simply subtract the amount of time required for task A from that required for task C.

Consider also the relationship between task B and task C. While task C involves stimulus categorization and simple reaction time, task B requires both of these processes *plus* the stage of response selection. Thus, in order to obtain an estimate of the time required for the response selection stage, one can subtract the time required for task C from that required for task B.

It should be noted that this is an extremely general method in terms of its underlying logic and it has been used in a variety of contexts. For example, Sternberg's (1966) well-known research on high-speed memory scanning is based on a variant of the subtraction method. Sternberg's basic task was to present subjects with a list of items such as digits to commit to memory. Subjects then received a probe and had to indicate as quickly as possible whether the probe was in the original memory set. Sternberg found that the time needed to identify a positive match was a linear function of the number of items in the original set, with a slope of 38 msc. Sternberg's (1966) conclusion that memory scanning takes place at the rate of 38 msc. per item is based on a variant of the subtraction method. For example, since it takes 510 msc. to identify an item from a three-digit set, but only 472 msc. to identify one from a two-digit set, the time needed to scan a single digit must be 38 msc.

The subtraction method appears to provide a convenient method for determining the time associated with many cognitive processes. However, as Sternberg (1969a, 1969b) later pointed out, there is a major problem with using such a method. This is known as the assumption of "pure insertion." In the Sternberg task, for example, it must be assumed that increasing the size of the memory set affects scanning but does *not* affect any other component of the process (e.g., the encoding time for a new digit or executing the response). In general, it must be assumed that a single independent variable affects only a single component of the underlying process. However, it has been convincingly demonstrated that this is often not the case (see Pachella, 1974; Teichner & Krebs, 1974). Although there are cases in which the subtraction method will be useful, the method of additive factors, which uses a less constraining set of assumptions, was developed to avoid this major shortcoming of the subtraction method. It is to this method that we now turn.

Method of Additive Factors

While the subtraction method is used to obtain a precise numerical estimate of the duration of a particular mental process, the method of additive factors is used to determine more generally whether distinct stages of information processing can be identified. That is, the issue is whether a mental process can be broken up into *qualitatively* distinct subsystems. The general technique used is really one of converging operations. First, a hypothetical stage model is formulated. Then each stage is linked to a separate independent and dependent variable. By examining the pattern of effects produced by any experimental manipulation, one can determine whether a unique subsystem is being affected.

A concrete example is useful to illustrate. Sternberg (1967) postulated four distinct stages related to the task described above: (1) encoding of the stimulus probe, (2) a serial, exhaustive comparison of the probe to each item in the set, (3) a yes–no decision related to whether the probe was actually a member of the memory set, and (4) a transformation of the decision into an overt response. It is the second stage of the process that relates to memory scanning. The relevant independent variable is memory set size and the relevant dependent variable is the increase in reaction time for each item added to the memory set. The time associated with the other three stages *combined* is reflected in the intercept value (approximately 400 msc. in a typical Sternberg task).

Consider one specific experiment reported by Sternberg (1967) in which the probes used were either normal or visually degraded. Probe items that are visually degraded should be more difficult to encode but they should not affect the rate of memory scanning. Thus, visually degraded probes should be associated with larger intercept values but no difference in the slope relating reaction time to the size of the memory set. This is exactly what Sternberg found. Because stimulus degradation and memory set size produce additive effects (i.e., they do not interact with one another), it can be concluded that they tap into different stages of the underlying process. In other experiments (see e.g., Sternberg, 1975), it has been shown that chronic alcoholics and schizophrenics have much higher intercept values in the Sternberg task, but absolutely no difference in slope, indicating that the rate of memory scanning is not impaired but at least one of the other stages is.

The method of additive factors is an extremely general technique that has been used in a wide variety of contexts. Many of these are reviewed by Massaro (1975), Pachella (1974), and Sternberg (1975). Pachella (1974) also discusses many technical aspects of the procedure that need to be considered in planning a particular study. Like all such reaction time procedures, it should be remembered that there is nothing inherent in the methodology to indicate *what* the particular stages are or the *order* in which they are executed. These must be inferred on the basis of theoretical considerations, along with specific empirical observations.

Speed-Accuracy Trade-Off Methodology

Experimenters who use reaction time as a dependent variable almost universally assume that their subjects can perform perfectly in terms of providing correct responses. Because perfect performance is expected, the time it takes to produce perfect performance is the major issue of concern. Of course, the specific nature of the task can vary enormously. Subjects might be asked to remember three or four digits (Sternberg, 1966, 1967, 1969a, 1969b, 1975), identify when one or two sentences are presented for a second exposure (Anderson, 1976; Anderson & Bower, 1973, Smith, Adams, & Schorr, 1978; Thorndyke & Bower, 1974), indicate when letter-strings do and do not form a complete word (Meyer & Schvaneveldt, 1971, 1976), or be asked simple questions such as "Is a robin a bird?" (Smith, Shoben, & Rips, 1974) or "Which is greater, 13 or 9?" (Holyoak, 1977, 1978). In theory, subjects should be able to perform such tasks perfectly. In practice, they do not. The (major) reason subjects do not produce errorless performance is that performance at a reaction time task is heavily influenced by strategies adopted by the subject. A subject paid for accuracy will become more accurate, and a subject paid for speed will become quicker. Unfortunately, the first subject will also begin to produce much longer reaction times, while the second will begin to produce more errors.

In theory, "reaction time" is generally considered to be the shortest amount of time that is required to produce errorless performance. In practice, there are two important considerations: (1) subjects will almost invariably produce some errors, and (2) in general, there is a "speed-accuracy trade-off" or an inverse relationship between reaction time and the percentage of errors that are made. The issue is what procedures should be used to address this problem.

The most common solution to the problem *by far* is simply to ignore the errors. That is, those trials that produce an incorrect response are not included in the analysis but other than that, the data are analyzed as they would be ordinarily. The justification for such a procedure is the following. Many experiments produce error rates in the area of 2%–3%. It is assumed that "irrelevant factors" entered into the experiment on such trials. Perhaps the subject sneezed, or blinked, or was momentarily distracted, and therefore produced an incorrect response. However, since these factors are not under investigation, they not only *can be* but *should be* ignored.[10]

Ignoring errors is defensible as long as the percentage of trials on which they occur is small, and even more importantly, the percentage of errors is constant across conditions of the experiment. When error rates vary across conditions of the experiment, eliminating those trials that produced an error is *not* sufficient because it is likely that subjects are adopting strategies that also affect performance on correct trials. In other words, the mean reaction time for *correct* trials is also likely to be inversely related to overall error rates.

Occasionally, researchers will attempt to use statistical "corrections" such as treating reaction times and errors as separate variables in a multivariate analysis of variance or by performing an analysis of covariance. However, there is a great deal of evidence (see e.g., Evans & Anastasio, 1968; Pachella, 1974) that none of these are truly satisfactory solutions. The only safe conclusion under such conditions is that irrelevant strategical factors are confounded with the experimental manipulation(s).

The most fundamental problem in using reaction time as a dependent variable concerns the discrepancy between the conceptual definition (the shortest period of time in which one can produce errorless performance) and what actually occurs in practice (relatively short time durations with a small number of errors). It is never clear how close the performance of subjects is approximating the conceptual definition. One way to make this problem more tractable is to build the speed-accuracy trade-off right into the experimental design. Technical details associated with using such speed-accuracy trade-off (SAT) methodology have been described by Dosher (1976, 1979) and Wickelgren (1977), and interesting applications have been reported by Dosher (1982), Reed (1973, 1976), Schouten and Bekker (1967), and Wickelgren, Corbett, and Dosher (1980).

As Dosher (1982) has pointed out, "An RT experiment produces a single point per condition in the processing time-accuracy plane. SAT methods can be used to observe more than one point per condition, so that the relation between time and accuracy can be systematically observed" (p. 175).

In other words, an entire speed-accuracy curve is produced in each condition of the experiment. The most common way of obtaining such a curve is to provide subjects with a signal (e.g., a tone) following the stimulus to indicate when they should respond. Over trials, the delay between the stimulus and the signal is systematically varied. Thus, the amount of time for memory retrieval is manipulated by the experimenter.

---

[10]For this same reason, it is common practice in studies using reaction time as a dependent variable to ignore trials on which an extreme response is made (e.g., all trials on which the reaction time is more than two standard deviations from the mean for that subject). Once again, it is assumed that performance on such a trial must be a function of irrelevant factors.

Figure 1.12 illustrates an idealized speed-accuracy memory retrieval function. It is divided into three general phases. Phase I simply indicates that above chance performance will require some finite amount of time. In Phase II, relatively small increases in time produce significant increases in accuracy. In Phase III, however, additional increases in time are associated with only modest increases in accuracy. Thus, as Dosher (1982, p. 175) points out, "the retrieval functions may be described by a three-parameter function including an *intercept* (minimum retrieval time), an *asymptote* (maximum accuracy), and a parameter that reflects the speed of rise, or a *rate* parameter (where the shape is determined by the function)." The important point is that theoretical predictions can be tested along the entire SAT curve.

It should be emphasized that the basic speed-accuracy trade-off methodology is extremely general. It can be used to test incremental or all-or-none theories, elementaristic or configural theories, models that assume serial or parallel search processes, and continuous or discrete activation models. Dosher (1982) has recently provided an excellent demonstration of how many of these theoretical approaches can be investigated in a single study with SAT methodology.

Signal Detection Approaches

The type of speed-accuracy trade-offs discussed above make it clear that there is an important decision component in many memory tasks. This suggests that the principles of signal detection theory might be used to understand various reaction time procedures as well. One of the most successful attempts to do this is the item recognition model of Atkinson and Juola (1974). Using a general signal detection theory framework, Atkinson and Juola were able to create a model of item recognition that incorporates as a special case the Sternberg model discussed previously. That is, Atkinson and Juola were able to account for all of the Sternberg results *plus* what appeared to be several anomalous findings.

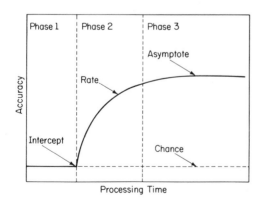

FIG. 1.12. An idealized speed-accuracy trade-off memory retrieval function. (After Dosher, 1979.)

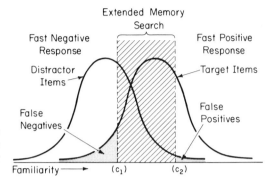

FIG. 1.13. Theoretical distributions of familiarity values for distractor items and target items. (After Atkinson & Juola, 1974.)

Atkinson and Juola (1974) suggest that there is a "familiarity" value associated with each test item (word, digit, nonsense syllable, etc.) in a recognition memory experiment. Essentially, familiarity values are determined by recency and frequency of past exposure. Imagine an experimenter who begins with a pool of 20 words. Ten are presented as to-be-remembered items and 10 are presented as lures on a recognition test. Since the to-be-remembered words are presented during the acquisition phase of the experiment, the familiarity values associated with these words will generally be greater than those associated with the lures. Of course, there will also be differences among the items themselves. This will result in two separate distributions of items (one for the new items and one for the old items) such that the mean familiarity value for the to-be-remembered items is greater than that for the lure items.

The theoretical distribution of old and new items is illustrated in Figure 1.13. In a typical experiment, a subject would then be given each of the 20 words and be asked to indicate as quickly as possible whether the item was previously presented. Atkinson and Juola suggest that a subject will implicitly adopt two separate criteria (C_1 and C_2). An item with a familiarity value below C_1 will elicit a fast negative response. Similarly, an item with a familiarity value greater than C_2 will elicit a fast positive response. Moreover, these responses will be made *without* an extended memory search. When an item has a familiarity value between C_1 and C_2, however, a second stage of processing is required. This is the relatively slow, serial memory search process described by Sternberg. As can be seen from Figure 1.13, although this stage is relatively slow, it will also lead to very few errors. A flowchart of this entire process is presented in Figure 1.14.

The Atkinson and Juola (1974) model has led to a number of ingenious tests and it has generated a great deal of empirical support (see e.g., Atkinson, Herrmann, & Wescourt, 1974; Atkinson & Juloa, 1973, 1974; Fischler & Juola, 1971; Juola & Atkinson, 1971). As we will see, the general approach has also been extended into a number of other domains and it appears to provide a very useful means for conceptualizing several distinct lines of research in contempo-

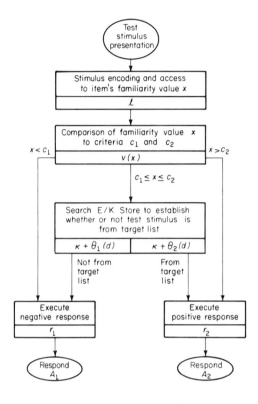

FIG. 1.14. A flowchart representing the memory search and decision stages of item recognition. The bottom entry in each box represents the time required to complete that stage. (After Atkinson & Juola, 1974.)

rary social cognition. One can expect to see much more use of such an approach in the years ahead because of this.

Applications and Implications for Social Cognition

Reaction time procedures are being used increasingly often in social cognition, and Taylor and Fiske (1981) provide a good overview of the various contexts in which they have already been employed. Most of the published investigations have used very simple procedures in which retrieval times for various types of information are contrasted. For example, Pryor and Kriss (1977) examined the relative "availability" of consensus, consistency, and distinctiveness information in making attributions. This work has recently been extended by Sherman and Titus (1982). Markus (1977; Markus, Crane, Bernstein, & Siladi, 1982) has used a similar procedure in investigating how different classes of information are more or less available for different types of subjects. This work is particularly interesting because it examines the "match" between preexisting cognitive structures and the processing of new information.

Perhaps the most sophisticated application of reaction time methodology to examine the availability of information in memory is that reported by Ostrom and his colleagues (Lingle & Ostrom, 1979; Ostrom, Lingle, Pryor, & Geva, 1980). These researchers have been primarily concerned with the effects of making an initial judgment of a person on subsequent (either related or unrelated) judgments of the same person. Their work is noteworthy because they have carefully constructed a number of competing theoretical models that can be used to make divergent predictions in a reaction time task. Within limits, they have found that subjects appear to review nearly all relevant information when making an initial judgment. However, subsequent judgments that are thematically related appear to be based on implications of the first judgment rather than on implications of the original information. Thus, the time required for a second judgment is unrelated to the number of original pieces of information provided. Wyer, Srull, and Gordon (1982) have come to a similar conclusion on the basis of a quite different paradigm, providing the type of converging evidence that is not seen often enough in social cognition.

Several very sophisticated variations of additive factors methodology have also been reported. Anderson and Hastie (1974), for example, have used such procedures to investigate the representation of social information in memory. Imagine that a subject learns that Bob Dylan performed behaviors A, B, and C and that Robert Zimmerman performed behaviors X, Y, and Z. Also imagine that the subject is told either before or after receiving the information that Bob Dylan actually is Robert Zimmerman. The pattern of reaction times needed to verify various statements provides strong clues concerning how such information is represented in memory. It appears, for example, that when subjects are told before receiving the information that Bob Dylan and Robert Zimmerman are the same person, a single node is established in memory and all relevant information is associated to that node. Thus, there is very little difference in the reaction times needed to verify statements such as "Bob Dylan performed behavior A" and "Bob Dylan performed behavior X." However, when subjects are not told of the identity until after receiving the information, two separate nodes are created during encoding and the information associated with one is not necessarily recoded onto the other. Rather, a link is subsequently developed between the two established nodes to indicate the identity. This produces longer reaction times for statements such as "Bob Dylan performed behavior X" than "Bob Dylan performed behavior A." The important point to note is that such reaction time procedures can be used to examine very subtle theoretical issues.

Lynch (1981; Lynch & Shoben, 1982) has developed a paradigm based on similar logic to investigate the conditions under which various types of inferences are made. Imagine that a subject is asked to predict the likelihood of a target performing behavior X in situation Y based on the target's past history of behavior in that situation (i.e., "consistency" information). One possibility is that the subject will consider the implications of each previous behavior for the judgment and then form some composite judgment (i.e., only the consistency information presented will be used). Another possibility, however, is that subjects will attempt to use "consensus" or base-rate information. In this case, the subject would have to infer the likelihood of people *in general* performing behavior X in situation Y before making his/her judgment.

The paradigm developed by Lynch requires that reaction time data be collected for both types of judgments, where the order in which the judgments are made is varied across subjects. One group of subjects would make the likelihood judgment and then the consensus judgment. Other subjects, however, would first make the consensus judgment and then the likelihood judgment. In both cases, the major dependent variable is the time required to make the likelihood judgment. If subjects infer consensus information in the process of making the likelihood judgment, reaction times to make the likelihood judgment should be shorter when consensus information has already been inferred than when it has not. This would also appear to be a very general technique that can be used to investigate the conditions under which any number of social inferences are spontaneously generated. As with many of the other techniques discussed, however, very little empirical work using the procedure currently exists within the domain of social cognition.

The procedure developed by Lynch is related to a fundamental distinction that can be made between storage and computational models. This is a distinction that has proven to be extremely useful in conceptualizing semantic memory (Shoben, 1980), episodic memory (Atkinson & Juola, 1974), and concept formation (Smith & Medin, 1981), and there is evidence to suggest that substantial conceptual advancement can be made in social cognition by taking the distinction into account as well.

In their most basic form, storage models suggest that most, if not all, knowledge is explicitly stored in memory. As a consequence, such models emphasize various types of retrieval processes and inference routines tend to be extremely simple. In contrast, computational models suggest that knowledge is often "computed" on the spot. For example, a subject may be asked, "Is a robin a bird?" A storage model would suggest that subjects directly retrieve the relevant information in order to answer such a question. Computational models, however, emphasize comparison rather than retrieval processes. Thus, a subject would ordinarily have to compute an answer to such a question, perhaps by assessing the degree to which the features of "robin" and "bird" overlap (see e.g., Shoben, 1980; Smith, 1978; Smith, Shoben, & Rips, 1974).

Hybrid models that postulate both retrieval and computational procedures can also be constructed, and Ebbesen and his colleagues (Allen & Ebbesen, 1981; Cohen & Ebbesen, 1979; Ebbesen, 1981; Ebbesen & Allen, 1979) have used such an approach to address a number of important issues in social cognition. Within the domain of "conceptual" or "semantic" memory, for example, Ebbesen and Allen (1979) have investigated the processes that are used to infer one personality trait from another. In particular, they have tested both a retrieval (what they term an "exemplar scanning") and a computational (what they term a "feature comparison") model. The patterns of reaction time data provide a great deal of support for a model that is remarkably similar to the Smith et al. (1974) feature comparison model of semantic memory. If the two traits in question have strong semantic similarity, a fast positive response is generated; if they have very low semantic similarity, a fast negative response is generated; and if they have a moderate degree of similarity, a second stage of feature-based comparison processes is induced. Such a dual cutpoint model establishes two separate threshold criteria.

Ebbesen and his colleagues (see e.g., Allen & Ebbesen, 1981) have also found support for a dual cutpoint model in investigating how trait inferences are made on the basis of behavioral evidence. This model suggests that subjects form both a generalized impression of an actor and a more detailed representation of his/her behavior. The model also suggests that a distinction can be made between "concrete" traits that can be inferred on the basis of a single behavior and "abstract" traits that can only be inferred from multiple instances of behavior.

A flowchart of the hypothesized process is provided in Figure 1.15. As Ebbesen (1981) states:

> In the first stage, the representation of the trait is compared to a generalized impression of the actor. If the similarity of the two representations are above or below a true or a false cutpoint, the rater responds yes or no (respectively). If, however, the similarity estimate falls between these two cutpoints (making it unclear whether a yes or no response is correct), a second stage is entered in which additional evidence is examined before a response is made. Allen and Ebbesen assumed that this additional evidence is a more detailed representation of the behavioral segment—one in which the number of unique elements depends on the length of the behavioral segment. Thus, only traits that are moderately similar to the generalized impression should produce reaction times that increase with the length of the behavioral segment. To complete the argument, they also suggested that (in their experimental task, at least) "concrete" traits would tend to be either very similar or very dissimilar to a generalized impression whereas more "abstract" traits would tend to be *moderately* similar to the generalized impression because the latter have multiple implications and only some of their implications might be represented in the generalized impression (p. 261).

As one test of such a model, Allen and Ebbesen (1981) used a variation of the general Sternberg paradigm. Subjects saw videotapes of an actor, and the length of the videotape was systematically varied across subjects. One particularly impressive finding was that the time needed to answer questions concerning abstract traits of the target was a linear function of the length of the videotape. This suggests that subjects were reviewing some representation of the behavioral

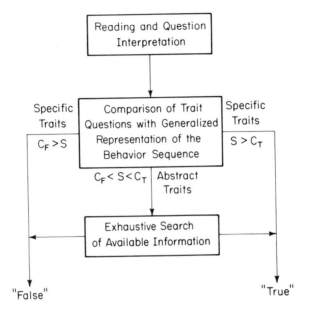

FIG. 1.15.   A flowchart illustration of the Abstract Trait Search model. According to the model, the similarity, S, between the trait question and a representation of the behavioral sequence is evaluated. If the similarity is greater than some standard cutpoint for true responses, C_T, then the response true can be made directly. Alternatively, if the similarity falls below the cutpoint for false responses, C_F, then the response false can be made directly. If the similarity falls between the two cutpoints, $C_F < S < C_T$, then additional information retrieval and comparisons are undertaken. Reading the question and the similarity comparison comprise the first stage of the model, while the exhaustive search process is the second stage. (After Allen & Ebbesen, 1981.)

evidence before making a response. However, the length of the videotape had no effect on the time needed to respond to concrete trait questions.

The dual cutpoint model developed by Ebbesen and his colleagues is very similar to the Atkinson and Juola (1974) model discussed earlier (a comparison of Figures 1.14 and 1.15 points this out clearly), as well as the feature comparison model of semantic memory developed by Smith et al. (1974). In each case, there are two separate threshold criteria, and a corresponding opportunity for the subject to make a quick initial response if either of these thresholds is surpassed. Also in each case, however, a mechanism is provided for a slower, more deliberate second stage of processing. The fact that the same general type of model has received such strong support in three very different content domains suggests that it pertains to a very central part of the information-processing system.

Finally, it is worth reflecting on the fact that important computational procedures are embedded in all three of the models discussed. Not enough attention has been given to such procedures in the social cognition literature, or to the distinction between retrieval and computational procedures more generally. As Shoben (1980) has pointed out, however, one important feature of computational models is that they easily allow for the expansion of concepts such as the mental representation of individuals. This is an issue that poses much more difficulty for simple storage models. Since diagnosing the components of person impressions, and tracing their development over time, are such central issues to many social cognition researchers, one can expect that much greater conceptual weight will be put on various computational procedures in the future. The early work reported by Ebbesen and his colleagues appears to be very promising in this regard.

SUMMARY

It should be clear that there are a large number of methodological techniques available to investigators of person memory. There are distinct advantages associated with virtually all of the procedures discussed in the present chapter. There are also distinct disadvantages. The purpose of the present chapter was to identify these as clearly as possible and thereby offer *general* guidelines for researchers working in the field.

Two more general, but certainly no less important, ways of accelerating progress in the field were also noted. First, most of the theory-testing research that has been conducted in the field of social cognition has relied upon only a single methodological procedure. It should be clear from the discussion presented here, however, that seemingly subtle differences in procedure often turn out to be extremely important, in terms of both the results obtained and the interpretation that can be made. Once again, a research program that relies on converging operations as a general operating framework is more likely to result in meaningful conceptual advance and less likely to be based on premature conclusions.

The second way of accelerating progress is closely related. Specifically, it is important for investigators to develop theories that have implications for more than a single dependent variable. The literature is replete with multi-experiment research reports, but only a small percentage of these examine more than one dependent measure. However, by specifying the implications of a theory for a variety of cognitive measures, basic assumptions of the theory often must be more clearly articulated than they would be otherwise. This will doubtlessly lead to more refined theoretical frameworks, as well as make it easier to discriminate among competing theories in any given domain.

Although much of the early work in social cognition was based on a very limited set of methodological procedures, many of the more recent examples of research cited in this chapter are truly impressive in terms of their methodological sophistication and elegance. Notable progress has been made in a relatively short period of time. This is as it should be, and it is hoped that the discussion provided in the present chapter will contribute to the progressive trend that is already being seen in the field.

ACKNOWLEDGMENTS

Preparation of this chapter was supported by National Science Foundation grant BNS 79–24154. The author would like to thank Ray Burke and Bob Wyer for helpful comments on an earlier draft of the manuscript.

REFERENCES

Allen, R. B., & Ebbesen, E. B. Cognitive processes in person perception: Retrieval of personality trait and behavioral information. *Journal of Experimental Social Psychology*, 1981, *17*, 119–141.
Anderson, D. C., & Borkowski, J. G. *Experimental psychology: Research tactics and their applications*. Glenview, Ill.: Scott, Foresman, & Company, 1978.
Anderson, J. R. *Language, memory, and thought*. Hillsdale, N.J.: Lawrence Erlbaum Associates, 1976.
Anderson, J. R. *Cognitive psychology and its implications*. San Francisco: Freeman, 1980.
Anderson, J. R., & Bower, G. H. Configural properties in sentence memory. *Journal of Verbal Learning and Verbal Behavior*, 1972, *11*, 594–605. (a)
Anderson, J. R., & Bower, G. H. Recognition and retrieval processes in free recall. *Psychological Review*, 1972, *79*, 97–123. (b).
Anderson, J. R., & Bower, G. H. *Human associative memory*. Washington, D.C.: V. H. Winston, 1973.
Anderson, J. R., & Bower, G. H. A propositional theory of recognition memory *Memory & Cognition*, 1974, *2*, 406–412.
Anderson, J. R., & Hastie, R. Individuation and reference in memory: Proper names and definite descriptions. *Cognitive Psychology*, 1974, *6*, 495–515.
Anderson, N. H. Two more tests against change of meaning in adjective combinations. *Journal of Verbal Learning and Verbal Behavior*, 1971, *10*, 75–85.
Anderson, N. H. Information integration theory: A brief survey. In D. H. Krantz, R. C. Atkinson, R. D. Luce, & P. Suppes (Eds.), *Contemporary developments in mathematical psychology* (Vol. 2) New York: Academic Press, 1974.
Anderson, R. C. Substance recall of sentences. *Quarterly Journal of Experimental Psychology*, 1974, *26*, 530–541.
Anisfeld, M., & Knapp, M. Association, synonymity, and directionality in false recognition. *Journal of Experimental Psychology*, 1968, *77*, 171–179.
Asch, S. E. Forming impressions of personality. *Journal of Abnormal and Social Psychology*, 1946, *41*, 258–290.
Atkinson, R. C., Herrmann, D. J., & Wescourt, K. T. Search processes in recognition memory. In R. L. Solso (Ed.), *Theories in cognitive psychology: The Loyola symposium*. Potomac, Md.: Lawrence Erlbaum Associates, 1974.
Atkinson, R. C., & Juola, J. F. Factors influencing speed and accuracy of word recognition. In S. Kornblum (Ed.), *Fourth international symposium on attention and performance*. New York: Academic Press, 1973.
Atkinson, R. C., & Juola, J. F. Search and decision processes in recognition memory. In D. H.

Krantz, R. C. Atkinson, R. D. Luce, & P. Suppes (Eds.), *Contemporary developments in mathematical psychology* (Vol. 1). San Francisco: Freeman, 1974.

Baddeley, A. D. *The psychology of memory.* New York: Basic Books, 1976.

Bahrick, H. P. Relearning and the measurement of retention. *Journal of Verbal Learning and Verbal Behavior,* 1967, *6,* 89–94.

Bahrick, H. P. Measurement of memory by prompted recall. *Journal of Experimental Psychology,* 1969, *97,* 213–219.

Bahrick, H. P. Two-phase model for prompted recall. *Psychological Review,* 1970, *77,* 215–222.

Bahrick, H. P., & Bahrick, P. O. A re-examination of the interrelations among measures of retention. *Quarterly Journal of Experimental Psychology,* 1964, *16,* 318–324.

Banks, W. P. Signal detection theory and human memory. *Psychological Bulletin,* 1970, *74,* 81–99.

Battig, W. F., & Bellezza, F. S. Organization and levels of processing. In C. R. Puff (Ed.), *Memory organization and structure.* New York: Academic Press, 1979.

Belmore, S. M. Imagery and semantic elaboration in hypermnesia for words. *Journal of Experimental Psychology: Human Learning and Memory,* 1981, *7,* 191–203.

Bernbach, H. A. Decision processes in memory. *Psychological Review* 1967, *74,* 462–480.

Black, J. B., & Bern, H. Causal cohesence and memory for events in narratives. *Journal of Verbal Learning and Verbal Behavior.* 1981, *20,* 267–275.

Black, J. B., Turner, J. T., & Bower, G. H. Point of view in narrative comprehension, memory, and production. *Journal of Verbal Learning and Verbal Behavior* 1979, *18,* 187–198.

Blumenthal, A. L. *The process of cognition.* Englewood Cliffs, N.J.: Prentice-Hall, 1977.

Bousfield, A. K., & Bousfield, W. A. Measurement of clustering and of sequential constancies in repeated free recall. *Psychological Reports,* 1966, *19,* 935–942.

Bousfield, W. A. The occurrence of clustering in the recall of randomly arranged associates. *Journal of General Psychology,* 1953, *49,* 229–240.

Bower, G. H. A multicomponent theory of the memory trace. In K. W. Spence & J. T. Spenc (Eds.), *The psychology of learning and motivation* (Vol. 1). New York: Academic Press, 1967.

Bower, G. H. Organizational factors in human memory *Cognitive Psychology,* 1970, *1,* 18–46.

Bower, G. H. Organizational factors in memory. In E. Tulving & W. Donaldson, (Eds.), *Organization of memory.* New York: Academic Press, 1972. (a)

Bower, G. H. Stimulus - sampling theory of encoding variability. In A. W. Melton & E. Martin (Eds.), *Coding processes in human memory.* Washington, D.C.: V. H. Winston, 1972. (b)

Bower, G. H. Experiments on story comprehension and recall. *Discourse Processes,* 1978, *1,* 211–232.

Bower, G. H. Mood and memory. *American Psychologist,* 1981, *36* 129–148.

Bower, G. H., Black, J. B., & Turner, T. J. Scripts in memory for text. *Cognitive Psychology,* 1979, *11,* 177–220.

Bower, G. H., & Gilligan, S. G. Remembering information related to one's self. *Journal of Research in Personality,* 1979, *13,* 420–432.

Bower, G. H., Gilligan, S. G., & Monteiro, K. P. Selectivity learning caused by affective states. *Journal of Experimental Psychology: General,* 1981, *110,* 451–473.

Bower, G. H., Lesgold, A. M., & Tieman, D. Grouping operations in free recall. *Journal of Verbal Learning and Verbal Behavior,* 1969, *8,* 481–493.

Bower, G. H., Monteiro, K. P., & Gilligan, S. G. Emotional mood as a context of learning and recall. *Journal of Verbal Learning and Verbal Behavior,* 1978, *17,* 573–585.

Bower, G. H., & Winzenz, D. Group structure, coding, and memory for digest series. *Journal of Experimental Psychology Monographs,* 1969, *80,* No. 2, Part 2, 1–17.

Bransford, J. D. *Human cognition: Learning understanding, and remembering.* Belmont: Wadsworth, 1979.

Bransford, J. D., & Franks, J. J. The abstraction of linguistic ideas. *Cognitive Psychology,* 1971, *2,* 331–350.

Bransford, J. D., McCarrell, N. S., Franks, J. J., & Nitsch, K. E. Toward unexplaining memory. In R. E. Shaw & J. D. Bransford (Eds.), *Perceiving, acting, and knowing: Toward an ecological psychology*. Hillsdale, N.J.: Lawrence Erlbaum Associates, 1977.

Bregman, A. S., & Chambers, D. W. All-or-none learning of attributes. *Journal of Experimental Psychology* 1966, *71*, 785–793.

Brewer, W. F., & Treyens, J. C. Role of schemata in memory for places. *Cognitive Psychology*, 1981, *13*, 207–230.

Brown, J. An analysis of recognition and recall and problems in their comparison. In J. Brown (Ed.), *Recall and recognition*. London: Wiley, 1976. (a).

Brown, J. (Ed.). *Recall and recognition*. London: Wiley, 1976 (b)

Brown, R., & McNeil, D. The "tip of the tongue" phenomenon. *Journal of Verbal Learning and Verbal Behavior*, 1966, *5*, 325–337.

Bruce, D. Single probes, double probes, and the structure of memory traces. *Journal of Experimental Pychology: Human Learning and Memory*, 1980, *6*, 276–292.

Bruce, D., & Cofer, C. N. A comparison of recognition and recall in short-term memory. *Proceedings, 73rd Annual Convention of the American Psychological Association*, 1965, pp. 81–82.

Bruner, J. S., Shapiro, D., & Tagiuri R. The meaning of traits in isolation and in combination. In R. Tagiuri & L. Petrullo (Eds.), *Person perception and interpersonal behavior*. Stanford: Stanford University, Press, 1958.

Bugelski, B. R. *Principles of learning and memory*. New York: Praeger, 1979.

Burtt, H. E. An experimental study of early childhood memory. *Journal of Genetic Psychology*, 1932, *40*, 287–294.

Burtt, H. E. An experimental study of early childhood memory: Final report. *Journal of Genetic Psychology*, 1941, *58*, 435–439.

Buschke, H. Two dimensional recall: Immediate identification of clusters in episodic and semantic memory. *Journal of Verbal Learning and Verbal Behavior*, 1977, *16*, 201–215.

Buschke, H., & Schaier, A. H. Memory units, ideas, and propositions in semantic remembering. *Journal of Verbal Learning and Verbal Behavior*, 1979, *18*, 549–563.

Cantor, N., & Mischel, W. Traits as prototypes: Effects on recognition memory. *Journal of Personality and Social Psychology*, 1977, *35*, 38–48.

Cantor, N., Mischel, W., & Schwartz, J. Categorical knowledge about the social world: Structure, content, use and abuse. In A. Hastorf & A. Isen (Eds.), *Cognitive social psychology*. New York: Elsevier North-Holland, 1982.

Catania, A. C. Reinforcement schedules and psychophysical judgments: A study of some temporal properties of behavior. In W. N. Shoenfeld (Ed.), *The theory of reinforcement schedules*. New York: Appleton-Century-Crofts, 1970.

Cattell, R. B. Psychological theory and scientific method. In R. B. Cattell (Ed.), *Handbook of multivariate experimental psychology*. Chicago: Rand McNally, 1966.

Cattell, R. B. The principles of experimental design and analysis in relation to theory building. In R. B. Cattell (Ed.), *Handbook of multivariate experimental psychology*. Chicago: Rand McNally, 1966.

Chant, V. G., & Atkinson, R. C. Application of learning models and optimization theory to problems of instruction. In W. K. Estes (Ed.), *Handbook of learning and cognitive processes* (Vol. 5). Hillsdale, N.J.: Lawrence Erlbaum Associates, 1978.

Clark, M. S., & Isen, A. M. Toward understanding the relationship between feeling states and social behavior. In A. Hastorf & A. Isen (Eds.), *Cognitive social psychology*. New York: Elsevier, North-Holland, 1982.

Clark, W. C. The psyche in psychophysics: A sensory-decision theory analysis of the effect of instruction on flicker sensitivity and response bias. *Psychological Bulletin*, 1966, *65*, 358–366.

Cofer, C. N. Constructive processes in memory. *American Scientist*, 1973, *61*, 537–543.

Cohen, C. E. *Cognitive basis of stereotyping*. Paper presented at the American Psychological Association Meeting, San Francisco, September 1977.

Cohen, C. E. Person categories and social perception: Testing some boundaries of the processing effects of prior knowledge. *Journal of Personality and Social Psychology*, 1981, *40*, 441–452.

Cohen, C. E., & Ebbesen, E. B. Observational goals and schema activation: A theoretical framework for behavior perception. *Journal of Experimental Social Psychology*, 1979, *15*, 305–329.

Colle, H. A. The reification of clustering. *Journal of Verbal Learning and Verbal Behavior*, 1972, *11*, 624–633.

Conover, J. N., & Brown, S. C. Item strength and input location in free recall learning. *Journal of Experimental Psychology: Human Learning and Memory*, 1977, *3*, 109–118.

Conrad, R. Acoustic confusions in immediate memory. *British Journal of Psychology*, 1964, *55*, 75–84.

Coombs, C. H., Dawes, R. M., & Tversky, A. *Mathematical psychology*. Englewood Cliffs, N.J.: Prentice-Hall, 1970.

Crowder, R. B. *Principles of learning and memory*. Hillsdale, N.J.: Lawrence Erlbaum Associates, 1976.

Dalrymple-Alford, E. C. Measurement of clustering in free recall. *Psychological Bulletin*, 1970, *74*, 32–34.

Donders, F. C. Die Schnelligkeit psychischer Processe. *Archiv fur Anatomie und wissenschaftliche Medizin*, 1868, 657–681.

Dosher, B. A. The retrieval of sentences from memory: A speed-accuracy study. *Cognitive Psychology*, 1976, *8*, 291–310.

Dosher, B. A. Empirical approaches to information processing: Speed-accuracy tradeoff or reaction time. *Acta Psychologica*, 1979, *43*, 347–359.

Dosher, B. A. Effect of sentence size and network distance on retrieval speed. *Journal of Experimental Psychology: Learning, Memory, and Cognition*, 1982, *8*, 173–207.

Ebbesen, E. B. Cognitive processes in understanding ongoing behavior. In R. Hastie, T. M. Ostrom, E. B. Ebbesen, R. S. Wyer D. L. Hamilton, & D. E. Carlston (Eds.), *Person memory: The cognitive basis of social perception*. Hillsdale, N.J.: Lawrence Erlbaum Associates, 1980.

Ebbesen, E. B. Cognitive processes in inferences about a person's personality. In E. T. Higgins, C. P. Herman, & M. P. Zanna (Eds.), *Social cognition: The Ontario symposium of personality and social psychology*. Hillsdale, N.J.: Lawrence Erlbaum Associates, 1981.

Ebbesen, E. B., & Allen, R. B. Cognitive processes in implicit personality trait inferences. *Journal of Personality and Social Psychology*, 1979, *37*, 471–488.

Ebbinghaus, H. *Uber das Gedachtnis*. Leipzig: Dunker & Humbolt, 1885. (Reprinted as *Memory*. Trans. H. A. Ruger & C. E. Bussenius. New York: Teachers College, 1913; Dover, 1964.)

Egan, J. P. *Recognition memory and the operating characteristic*. Technical Note AFCRC-TN-58-51, Indiana University Hearing and Communication Laboratory, 1958.

Egan, J. P., & Clark, F. R. Psychophysics and signal detection. In J. B. Sidowski (Ed.), *Experimental methods and instrumentation in psychology*. New York: McGraw-Hill, 1966.

Egan, J. P., Schulman, A. L., & Greenberg, G. Z. Operating characteristics determined by binary decisions and by ratings. *Journal of the Acoustical Society of America*, 1959, *31*, 768–773.

Elliott, P. B. Tables of d'. In J. A. Swets (Ed.), *Signal detection and recognition by human observers*. New York: Wiley, 1964.

Ellis, H. C. *Fundamentals of human learning, memory, and cognition* (2nd ed.) Dubuque: Wm. C. Brown Company, 1978.

Ericsson, K. A., & Simon, H. A. Verbal reports as data. *Psychological Review*, 1980, *87*, 215–251.

Estes, W. K. An associative basis for coding and organization in memory. In A. W. Melton & E. Martin (Ed.), *Coding processes in human memory*. Washington, D.C.: V. H. Winston, 1972.

Estes, W. K., & DaPolito, F. Independent variation of information storage and retrieval processes in paired-associate learning. *Journal of Experimental Psychology*, 1967, *75*, 18–26.

Evans, S. H., & Anastasio, E. J. Misuse of analysis of covariance when treatment effect and covariate are confounded. *Psychological Bulletin*, 1968, *69*, 225–234.

Eysenck, M. W. *Human memory: Theory, research and individual differences.* Oxford: Pergamon Press, 1977.

Fillenbaum, S. Memory for gist: Some relevant variables. *Language & Speech,* 1966, *9,* 217–227.

Fischler, I., & Juola, J. F. Effects of repeated tests on recognition time for information in long-term memory. *Journal of Experimental Psychology,* 1971, *91,* 54–58.

Fiske, S. T., Taylor, S. E., Etcoff, N. L., & Laufer, J. K. Imaging, empathy, and causal attribution. *Journal of Experimental Social Psychology,* 1979, *15,* 356–377.

Fitzhugh, R. The statistical detection of threshold signals in the retina. *Journal of General Physiology,* 1957, *40,* 925–948.

Foss, D. J., & Harwood, D. A. Memory for sentences: Implications for human associative memory. *Journal of Verbal Learning and Verbal Behavior,* 1975, *14,* 1–16.

Frankel, F., & Cole, M. Measures of category clustering in free recall. *Psychological Bulletin,* 1971, *76,* 39–44.

Franks, J. J., & Bransford, J. D. The acquisition of abstract ideas. *Journal of Verbal Learning and Verbal Behavior,* 1972, *11,* 311–315.

Frederickson, C. H. Representing logical and semantic structure of knowledge acquired from discourse. *Cognitive Psychology,* 1975, *7,* 371–458.

Frender, R., & Doubilet, P. More on measures of category clustering in free recall-although probably not the last word. *Psychological Bulletin,* 1974, *81,* 64–66.

Friendly, M. L. In search of the M-Gram: The structure of organization in free recall. *Cognitive Psychology,* 1977 *9,* 188–249.

Friendly, M. Methods for finding graphic representations of associative memory structures. In C. R. Puff (Ed.), *Memory organization and structure.* New York: Academic Press, 1979.

Garner, W. R., Hake, H. W., & Eriksen, C. W. Operationism and the concept of perception. *Psychological Review,* 1956, *63,* 149–159.

Glass, A. L., Holyoak, K. J., & Santa, J. L. *Cognition.* Reading, Mass.: Addison-Wesley, 1979.

Goetz, E. T., Anderson, R. C., & Schallert, D. L. The representation of sentences in memory. *Journal of Verbal Learning and Verbal Behavior,* 1981, *20,* 369–385.

Goldstein, A. G., & Chance, J. E. Visual recognition memory for complex configurations. *Perception and Psychophysics,* 1971, *9,* 237–240.

Graesser, A. C., Woll, S. B., Kowalski, D. J. & Smith, D. A. Memory for typical and atypical actions in scripted activities. *Journal of Experimental Psychology: Human Learning and Memory,* 1980, *6,* 503–515.

Green, D. M., & Moses, F. L. On the equivalence of two recognition measures of short-term memory. *Psychological Bulletin,* 1966, *66,* 228–234.

Green, D. M., & Swets, J. A. *Signal detection theory and psychophysics* New York: Wiley, 1966.

Gregg, V. Word frequency, recognition and recall. In J. Brown (Ed.), *Recall and recognition.* London: Wiley, 1976.

Griggs, R. A. The recall of linguistic ideas. *Journal of Experimental Psychology,* 1974, *103,* 807–809.

Griggs, R. A., & Keen, D. M. The role of test procedure in linguistic intergration studies. *Memory & Cognition,* 1977, *5* 685–689.

Groen, G. J., & Atkinson, R. C. Models for optimizing the learning process. *Psychological Bulletin,* 1966, *66,* 309–320.

Hacker, M. J., & Ratcliff, R. A revised table of *d'* for M-alternative forced choice. *Perception & Psychophysics,* 1979, *26,* 168–170.

Hamilton, D. L. A cognitive-attributional analysis of stereotyping. In L.Berkowitz (Ed.), *Advances in experimental social psychology* (Vol. 12). New York: Academic Press, 1979.

Hamilton, D. L. Cognitive representations of persons. In E. T. Higgins, C. P. Herman, & M. P. Zanna (Eds.), *Social cognition: The Ontario symposium on personality and social psychology.* Hillsdale, N.J.: Lawrence Erlbaum Associates, 1981.

Hamilton, D. L., Katz, L. B., & Leirer V. O. Cognitive representation of personality impressions: Organizational processes in first impression formation. *Journal of Personality and Social Psychology.* 1980, *39,* 1050–1063. (a)

Hamilton, D. L., Katz, L. B., & Leirer V. O. Organizational processes in impression formation. In R. Hastie, T. M. Ostrom, E. B. Ebbesen, R. S. Wyer, D. L. Hamilton, & D. E. Carlston (Eds.), *Person memory: The cognitive basis of social perception.* Hillsdale, N.J.: Lawrence Erlbaum Associates, 1980. (b)

Hamilton, D. L., & Lim, C. *Organizational processes in person impressions and memory: Differences in the amount or the nature of organization.* Unpublished manuscript, University of California at Santa Barbara 1979.

Hamilton, D. L., & Zanna, M. P. Context effects in impression formation: Changes in connotative meaning. *Journal of Personality and Social Psychology,* 1974, *29,* 649–654.

Hartwick, J. Memory for trait information A signal detection analysis. *Journal of Experimental Social Psychology,* 1979, *15,* 533–552.

Hartwick, J. *The representation of traits in memory: A study of impression formation.* Unpublished manuscript, McGill University, 1982.

Hastie, R. Memory for information which confirms or contradicts a general impression. In R. Hastie, T. M. Ostrom, E. B. Ebbesen, R. S. Wyer, D. L. Hamilton, & D. E. Carlston (Eds.), *Person memory: The cognitive basis of social perception.* Hillsdale, N.J.: Lawrence Erlbaum Associates, 1980.

Hastie, R. Schematic principles in human memory. In E. T. Higgins, C. P. Herman, & M. P. Zanna (Eds.), *Social cognition: The Ontario symposium on personality and social psychology.* Hillsdale, N.J.: Lawrence Erlbaum Associates, 1981.

Hastie, R., & Kumar, P. A. Person memory: Personality traits as organizing principles in memory for behaviors. *Journal of Personality and Social Psychology,* 1979, *37,* 25–38.

Higgins, E. T., & King, G. Accessibility of social constructs: Information processing consequences of individual and contextual variability. In N. Cantor & J. F. Kihlstrom (Eds.), *Personality cognition, and social interaction.* Hillsdale, N.J.: Lawrence Erlbaum Associates, 1981.

Higgins, E. T., & Rholes, W. S. Impression formation and role fulfillment: A ''holistic reference'' hypothesis. *Journal of Experimental Social Psychology,* 1976, *12,* 422–435.

Hilgard, E. R. Methods and procedure in the study of learning. In S. S. Stevens (Ed.), *Handbook of experimental psychology* New York: Wiley, 1951.

Hintzman, D. L. *The psychology of learning and memory.* San Francisco: Freeman, 1978.

Holyoak, K. J. The form of analog size information in memory. *Cognitive Psychology,* 1977, *9,* 31–53.

Holyoak, K. J. Comparative judgments with numerical reference points. *Cognitive Psychology,* 1978, *10,* 203–243.

Horowitz, L. M., & Prytulak, L. S. Redintegrative memory. *Psychological Review,* 1969, *76,* 519–531.

Hubert, L. J., & Levin, J. R. A general statistical framework for assessing categorical clustering in free recall. *Psychological Bulletin,* 1976, *83,* 1072–1080.

James, W. *The principles of psychology.* New York: Holt, 1890.

Jenkins, J. J., Wald, J., & Pittenger, J. B. Apprehending pictorial events: An instance of psychological cohesion. In C. W. Savage (Ed.), *Minnesota studies in the philosophy of science. Volume IX: Perception and cognition issues in the foundations of psychology.* Minneapolis: University of Minnesota Press, 1978.

Johnson, M. K., Bransford, J. D., & Solomon, S. K. Memory for tacit implications of sentences. *Journal of Experimental Psychology,* 1973, *98,* 203–205.

Johnson, N. Sequential verbal behavior. In T. Dixon & D. Horton (Eds.) *Verbal behavior and general behavior theory.* Englewood Cliffs, N.J.: Prentice-Hall, 1968.

Jones, G. V. A fragmentation hypothesis of memory: Cued recall of pictures and of sequential position. *Journal of Experimental Psychology: General, 1976, 105,* 277–293.

Jones, G. V. Tests of a structural theory of the memory trace. *British Journal of Psychology, 1978, 69,* 351–367.

Jones, G. V. Analyzing memory by cuing: Intrinsic and extrinsic knowledge. In N. S. Sutherland (Ed.), *Tutorial essays in psychology: A guide to recent advances* (Vol. 2). Hillsdale, N.J.: Lawrence Erlbaum Associates, 1979.

Juola, J. F., & Atkinson, R. C. Memory scanning for words vs. categories. *Journal of Verbal Learning and Verbal Behavior, 1971, 10,* 522–527.

Kintsch, W. Memory and decision aspects of recognition learning. *Psychological Review, 1967, 74,* 496–504.

Kitsch, W. Recognition and free recall of organized lists. *Journal of Experimental Psychology, 1968, 78,* 481–487.

Kintsch, W. Models for free recall and recognition. In D. A. Norman (Ed.), *Models of human memory.* New York: Academic Press, 1970.

Kintsch, W. *The representation of meaning in memory.* Hillsdale, N.J.: Lawrence Erlbaum Associates, 1974.

Kintsch, W. *Memory and cognition* (2nd ed.). New York: Wiley, 1977.

Klatzky, R. L. *Human memory: Structures and processes* (2nd ed.). San Francisco: Freeman, 1980.

Klein, L. S., & Arbuckle, T. Y. Response latency and task difficulty in recognition memory. *Journal of Verbal Learning and Verbal Behavior, 1970, 9,* 467–472.

Kolers, P. A. Reading a year later. *Journal of Experimental Psychology: Human Learning and Memory, 1976, 2,* 554–565.

Kraft, R. N., & Jenkins, J. J. Memory for lateral orientation of slides in picture stories. *Memory & Cognition, 1977, 5,* 397–403.

Krantz, D. H. Threshold theories of signal detection. *Psychological Review, 1969, 76,* 308–324.

Krauss, R. M. Impression formation, impression management, and nonverbal behaviors. In E. T. Higgins, C. P. Herman, & M. P. Zanna (Eds.), *Social cognition: The Ontario symposium on personality and social psychology.* Hillsdale, N.J.: Lawrence Erlbaum Associates, 1981.

Kuiper, N. A., & Rogers, T. B. The encoding of personal information: Self-other differences. *Journal of Personality and Social Psychology, 1979, 37,* 449–514.

Lachman, R., Lachman, J. L., & Butterfield, E. C. *Cognitive psychology and information processing: An introduction.* Hillsdale, N.J.: Lawrence Erlbaum Associates, 1979.

Lakatos, I. *The methodology of scientific research programs.* Cambridge: Cambridge University Press, 1978.

Lambert, W. E., Ignatow, M., & Krauthamer, M. Bilingual organization in free recall. *Journal of Verbal Learning and Verbal Behavior, 1968, 7,* 207–214.

Laudan, L. *Progress and its problems: Towards a theory of scientific growth.* Berkeley: University of California Press, 1977.

LeFave, M. K., & Neufeld, R. W. J. Anticipatory threat and physical danger trait anxiety: A signal-detection analysis of effects on autonomic responding. *Journal of Research in Personality, 1980, 14,* 283–306.

Lichtenstein, E. H., & Brewer, W. F. Memory for goal-directed events. *Cognitive Psychology, 1980, 12,* 412–445.

Lingle, J. H., & Ostrom, T. M. Retrieval selectivity in memory-based impression judgments. *Journal of Personality and Social Psychology, 1979, 37,* 180–194.

Lockhart, R. S., Murdock, B. B. Memory and the theory of signal detection. *Psychological Bulletin, 1970, 74,* 100–109.

Loftus, E. F., & Loftus, G. R. On the permanence of stored information in the human brain. *American Psychologist, 1980, 35,* 409–420.

Lynch, J. G. A method for determining the sequencing of cognitive processes in judgment: Order effects on reaction times. In K. B. Monroe (Ed.), *Advances in consumer research* (Vol. 8.). Ann Arbor: Association for Consumer Research, 1981.

Lynch, J. G., & Shoben, E. J. *A causal analysis of the false consensus effect using order effects on reaction times.* Unpublished manuscript, University of Florida, 1982.

MacLeod, C. M. Bilingual episodic memory: Acquisition and forgetting. *Journal of Verbal Learning and Verbal Behavior,* 1976, *15,* 347–364.

Mandler, G. Recognizing: The judgment of previous occurrence. *Psychological Review,* 1980, *87,* 252–271.

Markus, H. Self-schemata and processing information about the self. *Journal of Personality and Social Psychology,* 1977, *35,* 63–78.

Markus, H., Crane, M., Bernstein, S., & Siladi, M. Self-schemas and gender. *Journal of Personality and Social Psychology,* 1982, *42,* 38–50.

Marschark, M., & Paivio, A. Integrative processing of concrete and abstract sentences. *Journal of Verbal Learning and Verbal Behavior,* 1977, *16,* 217–231.

Massaro, D. W. *Experimental psychology and information processing.* Chicago: Rand McNally, 1975.

McCormack, P. D. Recognition memory: How complex a retrieval system? *Canadian Journal of Psychology,* 1972, *26,* 19–41.

McGeoch, J. A., & Irion, A. L. *The psychology of human learning,* New York: Longmans, Green, and Company, 1952.

McKeithen, K. B., Reitman, J. S., Reuter, H. H., & Hirtle, S. C. Knowledge organization and skill differences in computer programmers. *Cognitive Psychology,* 1981, *13,* 307–325.

McNicol, D. *A primer of signal detection theory.* London: George, Allen, & Urwin, 1972.

Meyer, D. E., & Schvaneveldt, R. W. Facilitation in recognizing pairs of words: Evidence of a dependence between retrieval operations. *Journal of Experimental Psychology,* 1971, *90,* 227–234.

Meyer, D. E., & Shvaneveldt, R. W. Meaning, memory structure, and mental processes. In C. N. Cofer (Ed.), *The structure of human memory.* San Francisco: W. H. Freeman, 1976.

Müller, G. E. Zur analyse der gedächtnistatigkeit und des vorstellungsuerlaufe. Ill. Teil. *Zeitschriftfuer Psychologie,* 1913, *8* (Supplement).

Murdock, B. B. Signal detection theory and short-term memory. *Journal of Experimental Psychology,* 1965, *70,* 443–447.

Murdock, B. B. *Human memory: Theory and data.* Potomac, Md.: Lawrence Erlbaum Associates, 1974.

Murdock, B. B. Methodology in the study of human memory. In W. K. Estes (Ed.), *Handbook of learning and cognitive processes* (Vol. 4). Hillsdale, N.J.: Lawrence Erlbaum Associates, 1976.

Murdock, B. B. Recognition memory. In C. R. Puff (Ed.), *Handbook of research methods in human memory and cognition.* New York: Academic Press, 1982.

Murdock, B. B., & Anderson, R. E. Encoding, storage, and retrieval of item information. In R. L. Solso (Ed.), *Theories in cognitive psychology: The Loyola symposium.* Hillsdale, N.J.: Lawrence Erlbaum Associates, 1975.

Murdock, B. B., & Dufty, P. O. Strength theory and recognition memory. *Journal of Experimental Psychology,* 1972, *94,* 284–290.

Murphy, M. D. Measurement of category clustering in free recall. In C. R. Puff (Ed.), *Memory organization and structure.* New York: Academic Press, 1979.

Murphy, M. D., & Puff, C. R. Free recall: Basic methodology and analyses. In C. R. Puff (Ed.), *Handbook of research methods in human memory and cognition.* New York: Academic Press, 1982.

Nelson, T. O. Savings and forgetting from long-term memory. *Journal of Verbal Learning and Verbal Behavior,* 1971, *10,* 568–576.

Nelson, T. O. Detecting small amounts of information in memory: Savings for nonrecognized items. *Journal of Experimental Psychology: Human Learning and Memory,* 1978, *4,* 453–468.

Nelson, T. O., Fehling, M. R., & Moore-Glascock, J. The nature of semantic savings for items forgotten from long-term memory. *Journal of Experimental Psychology: General,* 1979, *108,* 225–250.

Nelson, T. O., & Rothbart, R. Acoustic savings for items forgotten from long-term memory. *Journal of Experimental Psychology,* 1972, *93,* 357–360.

Nelson, T. O., & Smith, E. E. Acquisition and forgetting of hierarchically organized information in long-term memory. *Journal of Experimental Psychology,* 1972, *95,* 388–396.

Nelson, T. O., & Vining, S. K. Effect of semantic versus structural processing on long-term retention. *Journal of Experimental Psychology: Human Learning and Memory,* 1978, *4,* 198–209.

Newtson, D. Attribution and the unit of perception of ongoing behavior. *Journal of Personality and Social Psychology,* 1973, *28,* 28–38.

Newtson, D. Foundations of attribution: The perception of ongoing behavior. In J. Harvey, W. Ickes, & R. Kidd (Eds.), *New directions in attribution research* (Vol. 1). Hillsdale, N.J.: Lawrence Erlbaum Associates, 1976.

Nickerson, R. S. Short-term memory for complex meaningful visual configurations: A demonstration of capacity. *Canadian Journal of Psychology,* 1965, *19,* 155–160.

Nickerson, R. S. A note on long-term recognition memory for picture material. *Psychonomic Science,* 1968, *11,* 58.

Nickerson, R. S., & Adams, M. J. Long-term memory for a common object. *Cognitive Psychology,* 1979, *11,* 287–307.

Norman, D. A., & Rumelhart, D. E. A system for perception and memory. In D. A. Norman (Ed.), *Models of human memory,* New York: Academic Press, 1970.

Norman, D. A., & Rumelhart, D. E. *Explorations in cognition.* San Francisco: Freeman, 1975.

Norman, D. A., & Wickelgren, W. A. Short-term recognition memory for single digits and pairs of digits. *Journal of Experimental Psychology,* 1965, *70,* 479–489.

Norman, D. A., & Wickelgren, W. A. Strength theory of decision rules and latency in retrieval from short-term memory. *Journal of Mathematical Psychology,* 1969, *6,* 192–208.

Osgood, C. E. On the whys and wherefores of E, P, and A. *Journal of Personality and Social Psychology,* 1969, *12,* 194–199.

Osgood, C. E., Suci, G. J., & Tannenbaum, P. H. *The measurement of meaning,* Urbana: University of Illinois Press, 1957.

Ostrom, T. M. Between-theory and within-theory conflict in explaining context effects in impression formation. *Journal of Experimental Social Psychology,* 1977, *13,* 492–503.

Ostrom, T. M., Lingle, J. H., Pryor, J. B., & Geva, N. Cognitive organization of person impressions. In R. Hastie, T. M. Ostrom, E. B. Ebbesen, R. S. Wyer, D. L. Hamilton, & D. E. Carlston (Eds.), *Person memory: The cognitive basis of social perception.* Hilldale, N.J.: Lawrence Erlbaum Associates, 1980.

Ostrom, T. M., Pryor, J. B., & Simpson, D. D. The organization of social information. In E. T. Higgins, C. P. Herman, & M. P. Zanna (Eds.), *Social cognition: The Ontario symposium on personality and social psychology.* Hillsdale, N.J.: Lawrence Erlbaum Associates, 1981.

Pachella, R. G. The interpretation of reaction time in information-processing research. In B. H. Kantowitz (Ed.), *Human information processing: Tutorials in performance and cognition.* Hillsdale, N.J.: Lawrence Erlbaum Associates, 1974.

Paivio, A. Imagery in recall and recognition. In J. Brown (Ed.), *Recall and recognition.* London: Wiley, 1976.

Parks, T. E. Signal detectability theory of recognition-memory performance. *Psychological Review,* 1966, *73,* 44–58.

Peabody, D. Trait inferences: Evaluative and descriptive aspects. *Journal of Personality and Social Psychology Monograph,* 1967, *7,* Whole No. 644.

Peabody, D. Evaluative and descriptive aspects in personality perception: A reappraisal. *Journal of Personality and Social Psychology,* 1970, 16, 639–646.

Pellegrino, J. W., & Hubert, L. J. The analysis of organization and structure in free recall. In C. R. Puff (Ed.), *Handbook of research methods in human memory and cognition.* New York: Academic Press, 1982.

Pellegrino, J. W., & Ingram, A. L. Processes, products, and measures of memory organization. In C. R. Puff (Ed.), *Memory organization and structure.* New York: Academic Press, 1979.

Peterson, L. R. Search and judgment in memory. In B. Kleinmuntz (Ed.), *Concepts and the structure of memory.* New York: Wiley, 1967.

Pollack, I., & Decker, L. R. Confidence ratings, message reception, and the receiver operating characteristic. *Journal of the Acoustical Society of America,* 1958, *30,* 286–292.

Pollack, I., & Norman, D. A. A non-parametric analysis of recognition experiments. *Psychonomic Science,* 1964, *1,* 125–126.

Posner, M. I. *Chrometric explorations of mind.* Hillsdale, N.J.: Lawrence Erlbaum Associates, 1978.

Postman, L. Inference theory revisited. In J. Brown (Ed.), *Recall and recognition.* London: Wiley, 1976. (a)

Postman, L. Methodology of human learning. In W. K. Estes (Ed.), *Handbook of learning and cognitive processes* (Vol. 3). Hillsdale, N.J.: Lawrence Erlbaum Associates, 1976. (b)

Pryor, J. B., & Kriss, M. The cognitive dynamics of salience in the attribution process. *Journal of Personality and Social Psychology,* 1977, *35,* 49–55.

Pryor, J. B., & Ostrom, T. M. The cognitive organization of social information: A converging-operations approach. *Journal of Personality and Social Psychology,* 1981, *41,* 628–641.

Raaijmakers, J. G. W., & Shiffrin, R. M. SAM: A theory of probabilistic search of associative memory. In G. H. Bower (Ed.), *The psychology of learning and motivation* (Vol. 14). Academic Press, 1980.

Raaijmakers, J. G. W., & Shiffrin, R. M. Search of associative memory. *Psychological Review,* 1981, *88,* 93–134.

Reder, L. M., Anderson, J. R., & Bjork, R. A. A semantic interpretation of encoding specificity. *Journal of Experimental Psychology,* 1974, *102,* 648–656.

Reed, A. V. Speed-accuracy trade-off in recognition memory. *Science,* 1973, *181,* 574–576.

Reed, A. V. The time course of recognition in human memory. *Memory & Cognition,* 1976, *4,* 16–30.

Reitman, J. S., & Reuter, H. H. Organization revealed by recall orders and confirmed by pauses. *Cognitive Psychology,* 1980, *12,* 554–581.

Reyes, R. M., Thompson, W. C., & Bower, G. H. Judgmental biases resulting from differing availabilities of arguments. *Journal of Personality and Social Psychology,* 1980, *39,* 2–12.

Robinson, J. A. Category clustering in free recall. *Journal of Psychology,* 1966, *62,* 279–285.

Roenker, D. L., Thompson, C. P., & Brown, S. C. Comparison of measures for the estimation of clustering in free recall. *Psychological Bulletin,* 1971, *76,* 45–48.

Rogers, T. B. A model of the self as an aspect of the human information processing system. In N. Cantor & J. F. Kihlstrom (Eds.), *Personality, cognition, and social interaction.* Hillsdale, N.J.: Lawrence Erlbaum Associates, 1981.

Rogers, T. B., Kuiper, N. A., & Kirker, W. S. Self-reference and the encoding of personal information. *Journal of Personality and Social Psychology,* 1977, *35,* 677–688.

Rosch, E. Cognitive reference points. *Cognitive Psychology,* 1975, *7,* 532–547. (a)

Rosch, E. Cognitive representations of semantic categories. *Journal of Experimental Psychology: General,* 1975, *104,* 192–233. (b)

Rosch, E. Human categorization. In N. Warren (Ed.), *Advances in cross-cultural psychology* (Vol. 1). London: Academic Press, 1977.

Rosch, E. Principles of categorization. In E. Rosch & B. B. Lloyd (Eds.), *Cognition and categorization*. Hillsdale, N.J.: Lawrence Erlbaum Associates, 1978.

Ross, L. The intuitive psychologist and his shortcomings: Distortions in the attribution process. In L. Berkowitz (Ed.), *Advances in experimental social psychology* (Vol. 10). New York: Academic Press, 1977.

Ross, M. Self-centered biases in attributions of responsibility: Antecedents and consequences. In E. T. Higgins, C. P. Herman, & M. P. Zanna (Eds.), *Social cognition: The Ontario symposium on personality and social psychology*. Hillsdale, N.J.: Lawrence Erlbaum Associates, 1981.

Rothbart, M., Evans, M., & Fulero, S. Recall for confirming events: Memory processes and the maintenance of social stereotypes. *Journal of Experimental Social Psychology*, 1979, *15*, 343–355.

Rothbart, M., Fulero, S., Jensen, C., Howard, J., & Birrell, P. From individual to group impressions: Availability heuristics in stereotype formation. *Journal of Experimental Social Psychology*, 1978, *14*, 237–255.

Rubin, D. C. Very long-term memory for prose and verse. *Journal of Verbal Learning and Verbal Behavior*, 1977, *16*, 611–621.

Runkel, P. J., & McGrath, J. E. *Research on human behavior: A systematic guide to method*. New York: Holt, Rinehart, and Winston, 1972.

Sachs, J. S. Recognition memory for syntactic and semantic aspects of connected discourse. *Perception and Psychophysics*, 1967, *2*, 437–442.

Salzberg, P. M. On the generality of encoding specificity. *Journal of Experimental Psychology*, 1976, *2*, 586–596.

Santa, J. L., & Lamwers, L. L. Encoding specificity: Fact or artifact? *Journal of Verbal Learning and Verbal Behavior*, 1974, *13*, 412–423.

Santa, J. L., & Lamwers, L. L. Where does the confusion lie? Comments on the Wiseman and Tulving paper. *Journal of Verbal Learning and Verbal Behavior*, 1976, *15*, 53–58.

Schank, R. C. The structure of episodes in memory. In D. G. Bobrow & A. Collins (Eds.), *Representation and understanding: Studies in cognitive science*. New York: Academic Press, 1975.

Schneider, D. J., Hastorf, A. H., & Ellsworth, P. C. *Person perception* (2nd ed.). Reading, Mass.: Addison-Wesley, 1979.

Schouten, J., & Bekker, J. Reaction time and accuracy. *Acta Psychologica*, 1967, *27*, 143–153.

Schwartz, R. M., & Humphreys, M. S. Recognition and recall as a function of instructional manipulations of organization. *Journal of Experimental Psychology*, 1974, *102*, 517–519.

Schwartz, S., & Witherspoon, K. D. Decision processing in memory: Factors influencing the storage and retrieval of linguistic and form identification. *Bulletin of the Psychonomic Society*, 1974, *4*, 127–129.

Shepard, R. N. Recognition memory for words, sentences and pictures. *Journal of Verbal Learning and Verbal Behavior*, 1967, *6*, 156–163.

Sherman, R. C., & Titus, W. Covariation information and cognitive processing: Effects of causal implications on memory. *Journal of Personality and Social Psychology*, 1982, *42*, 989–1000.

Shiffrin, R. M. Short-term store: The basis for a memory system. In F. Restle, R. M. Shiffrin, N. J. Castellan, H. R. Lindman, & D. B. Pisoni (Eds.), *Cognitive theory* (Vol. 1). Hillsdale, N.J.: Lawrence Erlbaum Associates, 1975.

Shiffrin, R. M. Capacity limitations in information processing, attention, and memory. In W. K. Estes (Ed.), *Handbook of learning and cognitive processes* (Vol. 4). Hillsdale, N.J.: Lawrence Erlbaum Associates, 1976.

Shoben, E. J. Theories of semantic memory: Approaches to knowledge and sentence comprehension. In R. J. Spiro, B. C. Bruce, & W. F. Brewer (Eds.), *Theoretical issues in reading comprehension: Perspectives from cognitive psychology, linguistics, artificial intelligence, and education.* Hillsdale, N.J.: Lawrence Erlbaum Associates, 1980.

Shuell, T. J. On sense and nonsense in measuring organization in free recall-oops, pardon me, my assumptions are showing. *Psychological Bulletin,* 1975, *82,* 720–724.

Singer, M. A replication of Bransford and Franks' (1971) "The abstraction of linguistic ideas." *Bulletin of the Psychonomic Society,* 1973, *1,* 416–418.

Smith, E. E. Theories of semantic memory. In W. K. Estes (Ed.), *Handbook of learning and cognitive processes* (Vol. 6). Hillsdale, N.J.: Lawrence Erlbaum Associates, 1978.

Smith, E. E., Adams, N., & Schorr, D. Fact retrieval and the paradox of interference. *Cognitive Psychology,* 1978, *10,* 438–464.

Smith, E. E., & Medin, D. L. *Categories and concepts.* Cambridge, Mass.: Harvard University Press, 1981.

Smith, E. E., Shoben, E. J., & Rips, L. J. Structure and process in semantic memory: A featural model for semantic decisions. *Psychological Review,* 1974, *81,* 214–241.

Snyder, M. Seek, and ye shall find: Testing hypotheses about other people. In E. T. Higgins, C. P. Herman, & M. P. Zanna (Eds.), *Social cognition: The Ontario symposium on personality and social psychology.* Hillsdale, N.J.: Lawrence Erlbaum Associates, 1981.

Snyder, M., & Cantor, N. Testing hypotheses about other people: The use of historical knowledge. *Journal of Experimental Social Psychology,* 1979, *15,* 330–342.

Solso, R. *Cognitive psychology.* New York: Harcourt Brace Jovanovich, 1979.

Sperling, G. The information available in brief visual presentations. *Psychological Monographs,* 1960, *74,* 1–29.

Spiro, R. J. Remembering information from test: The "State of Schema" approach. In R. C. Anderson, R. J. Spiro, & W. E. Montague (Eds.), *Schooling and the acquisition of knowledge.* Hillsdale, N.J.: Lawrence Erlbaum Associates, 1977.

Spiro, R. J. Accomodative reconstruction in prose recall. *Journal of Verbal Learning and Verbal Behavior,* 1980, *19,* 84–95.

Srull, T. K. Person memory: Some tests of associative storage and retrieval models. *Journal of Experimental Psychology: Human Learning and Memory,* 1981, *7,* 440–463.

Srull, T. K. Organizational and retrieval processes in person memory: An examination of processing objectives, presentation format, and the possible role of self-generated retrieval cues. *Journal of Personality and Social Psychology,* in press.

Srull, T. K., & Brand, J. F. Memory for information about persons: The effect of encoding operations on subsequent retrieval. *Journal of Verbal Learning and Verbal Behavior,* in press.

Srull, T. K., & Wyer, R. S. Progress and problems in cognitive social psychology. *Annals of Theoretical Psychology,* in press.

Standing, L. Learning 10,000 pictures. *Quarterly Journal of Experimental Psychology,* 1973, *25,* 207–222.

Standing, L., Conezio, J., & Haber, R. N. Perception and memory for pictures: Single-trial learning of 2500 visual stimuli. *Psychonomic Science,* 1970, *19,* 73–74.

Sternberg, R. J., & Tulving, E. The measurement of subjective organization in free recall. *Psychological Bulletin,* 1977, *84,* 539–556.

Sternberg, S. High-speed scanning in human memory. *Science,* 1966, *153,* 652–654.

Sternberg, S. Two operations in character recognition: Some evidence from reaction-time measurements. *Perception and Psychophysics,* 1967, *2,* 45–53.

Sternberg, S. The discovery of processing stages: Extensions of Donder's method. *Acta Psychologica,* 1969, *30,* 276–315. (a)

Sternberg, S. Memory-scanning: Mental processes revealed by reaction-time experiments. *American Scientist,* 1969, *57,* 421–457. (b)

Sternberg, S. Memory scanning: New findings and current controversies. *Quarterly Journal of Experimental Psychology,* 1975, *27,* 1–32.

Swets, J. A. Indices of signal dectability obtained with various psychophysical procedures. *Journal of the Acoustical Society of America*, 1959, *31*, 511–513.

Swets, J. A. (Ed.). *Signal detection and recognition by human observers*. New York: Wiley, 1964.

Taylor, S. E. Developing a cognitive social psychology. In J. S. Carroll & J. W. Payne (Eds.), *Cognition and social behavior*. Hillsdale, N.J. Erlbaum, 1976.

Taylor, S. E., & Crocker, J. Schematic bases of social information processing. In E. T. Higgins, C. P. Herman, & M. P. Zanna (Eds.), *Social cognition: The Ontario symposium on personality and social psychology*. Hillsdale, N.J.: Lawrence Erlbaum Associates, 1981.

Taylor, S. E., & Fiske, S. T. Salience, attention, and attribution: Top of the head phenomena. In L. Berkowitz (Ed.), *Advances in experimental social psychology* (Vol. 11). New York: Academic Press, 1978.

Taylor, S. E., & Fiske, S. T. Getting inside the head: Methodologies for process analysis in attribution and social cognition. In J. H. Harvey, W. Ickes & R. F. Kidd (Eds.), *New directions in attribution research* (Vol. 3). Hillsdale, N.J.: Lawrence Erlbaum Associates, 1981.

Teichner, W. H., & Krebs, M. J. Laws of visual choice reaction time. *Psychological Review*, 1974, *81*, 75–98.

Thomson, D. M., & Tulving, E. Associative encoding and retrieval: Weak and strong cues. *Journal of Experimental Psychology*, 1970, *86*, 255–262.

Thorndyke, P. W., & Bower, G. H. Storage and retrieval processes in sentence memory. *Cognitive Psychology*, 1974, *5*, 515–543.

Thurstone, L. L. Psychophysical analysis. *American Journal of Psychology*, 1927, *38*, 368–389.

Titchner, E. B. Relearning after 46 years. *American Journal of Psychology*, 1923, *34*, 468–469.

Tsujimoto, R. N. Memory bias toward normative and novel trait prototypes. *Journal of Personality and Social Psychology*, 1978, *36*, 1391–1401.

Tsujimoto, R. N., Wilde, J., & Robertson, D. R. Distorted memory for exemplars of a social structure: Evidence for schematic memory processes. *Journal of Personality and Social Psychology*, 1978, *36*, 1402–1414.

Tulving, E. The effects of presentation and recall of material in free-recall learning. *Journal of Verbal Learning and Verbal Behavior*, 1967, *6*, 175–184.

Tulving, E. Cue-dependent forgetting. *American Scientist*, 1974, *62*, 74–82.

Tulving, E. Ecphoric processes in recall and recognition. In J. Brown (Ed.), *Recall and recognition*. London: Wiley, 1976.

Tulving, E., & Bower, G. H. The logic of memory representations. In G. H. Bower (Ed.), *The psychology of learning and motivation* (Vol. 8). New York: Academic Press, 1974.

Tulving, E., & Pearlstone, Z. Availability versus accessibility of information in memory for words. *Journal of Verbal Learning and Verbal Behavior*, 1966, *5*, 381–391.

Tulving, E., & Psotka, J. Retroactive inhibition in free recall: Inaccessibility of information available in the memory store. *Journal of Experimental Psychology*, 1971, *87*, 1–8.

Tulving, E., & Thomson, D. M. Retrieval processes in recognition memory: Effects of associative context. *Journal of Experimental Psychology*, 1971, *87*, 116–124.

Tulving, E., & Thomson, D. M. Encoding specificity and retrieval processes in episodic memory. *Psychological Review*, 1973, *80*, 352–373.

Tulving, E., & Watkins, M. J. Structure of memory traces. *Psychological Review*, 1975, *82*, 261,276.

Underwood, B. J. Interference and forgetting. *Psychological Review*, 1957, *64*, 49–60.

Underwood, B. J. Attributes of memory. *Psychological Review*, 1969, *76*, 559–573.

Underwood, B. J., & Freund, J. S. Errors in recognition learning and retention. *Journal of Experimental Psychology*, 1968, *78*, 55–63.

Upshaw, H. S. The personal reference scale: An approach to social judgment. In L. Berkowitz (Ed.), *Advances in experimental social psychology* (Vol. 4). New York: Academic Press, 1969.

Upshaw, H. S. Social influence on attitudes and on anchoring of congeneric attitude scales. *Journal of Experimental Social Psychology*, 1978, *14*, 327–339.

Voss, J. F. Organization, structure, and memory: Three perspectives. In C. R. Puff (Ed.), *Memory organization and structure*. New York: Academic Press, 1979.

Wallace, W. P., & Underwood, B. J. Implicit responses and the role of intralist similarity in verbal learning by normal and retarded subjects. *Journal of Educational Psychology*, 1964, *55*, 362–370.

Watkins, M. J. Engrams as cuegrams and forgetting as cue overload: A cueing approach to the structure of memory. In C. R. Puff (Ed.), *Memory organization and structure*. New York: Academic Press, 1979.

Watkins, M. J., & Gardiner, J. M. An appreciation of generate-recognize theory of recall. *Journal of Verbal Learning and Verbal Behavior*, 1979, *18*, 687–704.

Watkins, M. J., & Gardiner, J. M. Cued recall. In C. R. Puff (Ed.), *Handbook of research methods in human memory and cognition*. New York: Academic Press, 1982.

Watkins, M. J., & Tulving, E. Episodic memory: When recognition fails. *Journal of Experimental Psychology: General*, 1975, *1*, 5–29.

Weimer, W. B. *Notes on the methodology of scientific research*. Hillsdale, N.J.: Lawrence Erlbaum Associates, 1979.

Wickelgren, W. A. Acoustic similarity and intrusion errors in short-term memory. *Journal of Experimental Psychology*, 1965, *70*, 102–108. (a)

Wickelgren, W. A. Distinctive features and errors in short-term memory for English vowels. *Journal of Acoustical Society of America*, 1965, *38*, 583–588. (b)

Wickelgren, W. A. Speed-accuracy tradeoff and information processing dynamics. *Acta Psychologica*, 1977, *41*, 67–85.

Wickelgren, W. A., Corbett, A. T., & Dosher, B. A. Priming and retrieval from short-term memory: A speed-accuracy tradeoff analysis. *Journal of Verbal Learning and Verbal Behavior*, 1980, *19*, 387–404.

Wickelgren, W. A., & Norman, D. A. Strength models and serial position in short-term recognition memory. *Journal of Mathematical Psychology*, 1966, *2*, 316–347.

Wickens, D. D. Encoding categories of words: An empirical approach to meaning, *Psychological Review*, 1970, *77*, 1–15.

Wickens, D. D. Characteristics of word encoding. In A. W. Melton & E. Martin (Eds.), *Coding processes in human memory*. Washington, D.C.: V. H. Winston, 1972.

Wiseman, S., & Tulving, E. A test of confusion theory of encoding specificity. *Journal of Verbal Learning and Verbal Behavior*, 1975, *14*, 370–381.

Woll, S. B., & Graesser, A. C. Memory discrimination for information typical or atypical of person schemata. *Social Cognition*, in press.

Woodworth, R. S. *Experimental psychology*. New York: Holt, 1938.

Wyer, R. S. *Cognitive organization and change: An information-processing approach*. Potomac, Md.: Lawrence Erlbaum Associates, 1974.

Wyer, R. S., & Carlston, D. E. *Social cognition, inference, and attribution*. Hillsdale, N.J.: Lawrence Erlbaum Associates, 1979.

Wyer, R. S., & Gordon, S. E. The recall of information about persons and groups. *Journal of Experimental Social Psychology*, 1982, *18*, 128–164.

Wyer, R. S., & Srull, T. K. The processing of social stimulus information: A conceptual integration. In R. Hastie, T. M. Ostrom, E. B. Ebbesen, R. S. Wyer, D. L. Hamilton, & D. E. Carlston (Eds.), *Person memory: The cognitive basis of social perception*. Hillsdale, N.J.: Lawrence Erlbaum Associates, 1980.

Wyer, R. S., & Srull, T. K. Category accessibility: Some theoretical and empirical issues concerning the processing of social stimulus information. In E. T. Higgins, C. P. Herman, & M. P.

Zanna (Eds.), *Social cognition: The Ontario symposium on personality and social psychology.* Hillsdale, N.J.: Lawrence Erlbaum Associates, 1981.

Wyer, R. S., Srull, T. K., & Gordon, S. E. *The effects of initial judgments of a person on subsequent ones.* Unpublished manuscript, University of Illinois at Urbana-Champaign, 1982.

Zajonc, R. B. Feeling and thinking: Preferences need no inferences. *American Psychologist,* 1980, *35,* 151–175.

Zanna, M. P., & Hamilton, D. L. Further evidence for meaning change in impression formation. *Journal of Experimental Social Psychology,* 1977, *13,* 224–238.

2 The Cognitive Representation of Social Information

Robert S. Wyer, Jr.
Sallie E. Gordon
University of Illinois at Urbana-Champaign

Contents

INTRODUCTION

Complex memory structures, formed through past experience, are typically assumed to guide the comprehension, organization, and recall of new information (for a review of theory and research bearing on this assumption, see Lachman, Lachman, & Butterfield, 1979). The implications of this assumption for the processing of information one receives about one's social environment have been a major impetus to research and theory in social cognition (cf. Cantor & Kihlstrom, 1981; Hastie, Ostrom, Ebbesen, Wyer, Hamilton, & Carlston, 1980; Higgins, Herman, & Zanna, 1981.) Extensive reviews of the possible role of knowledge structures in social information processing are already available (e.g., Hastie, 1981; Taylor & Crocker, 1981), and several theoretical formulations explicitly assume their existence (Ostrom, Lingle, Pryor, & Geva, 1980; Wyer & Carlston, 1979; Wyer & Srull, 1980). Much of this work has been interpreted within a more general ''schema'' theory of social cognition (cf. Taylor & Crocker, 1981). In so doing, however, the cognitive representations assumed to mediate social judgments have often been lumped under a common heading (e.g., ''schemata'') without considering possible differences in the structure of these representations.[1] This may hide some important differences between the types of representations that exist in memory and their effects on recall and judgment. An objective of this chapter is to call attention to these possible differences.

One may of course question whether the postulation of complex representations of information in memory is necessary at all. However, several phenomena identified in both cognitive and social research are difficult to account for without assuming the existence of organized bodies of knowledge that are retrieved from memory as units and are brought to bear on the comprehension and organization of new information. Three sets of findings are of particular relevance.

1. Effects of Prior Knowledge on Memory for New Information.   People's prior knowledge about objects and events in general affects their ability to learn and recall new information about particular objects and events (See Brewer &

---

[1]The tendency has been to define ''schemata'' in terms of the effects they are postulated to have rather than the structural properties of the representations that produce these effects. To this extent, the utility of schemata as explanatory constructs is limited (Wyer, 1979).

Nakamura, this volume). For instance, previously acquired knowledge about the characteristics of objects and events may intrude on the recall of details of new information about them, producing tendencies to report that features were described in this information when in fact they were not (Spiro, 1977; see also Brewer & Nakamura, this volume).

In addition, studies using recognition memory techniques have shown that people's prior knowledge about persons and events affects their ability to identify correctly aspects of new information about those persons or events (Graesser, Gordon, & Sawyer, 1979; Woll & Graesser, 1980).

Finally, while the knowledge required to comprehend new information may sometimes consist of a large number of interrelated concepts, the entire set of concepts can often be activated by only a short word or phrase. This has been demonstrated effectively by Bransford and his associates. For example, subjects in one study (Bransford & Johnson, 1972) read sentences that out of context appeared nonsensical and were extremely hard to learn and remember (e.g., "The notes were sour because the seam was split.") However, these sentences became immediately comprehensible, were given meaning, and therefore were recalled better, when they were preceded by a short word or phrase (e.g., a story title).

2. Effects of Construct Accessibility. People may form representations of persons and events either in the course of comprehending new information as it is presented, or when using the information later on to attain some more specific objective. Once formed, these representations serve as bases for subsequent judgments and decisions independently of the original information that led to their construction. Support for these assumptions comes from category accessibility research (for reviews, see Higgins & King, 1981; Wyer & Srull, 1981). In this research, subjects are typically stimulated to use a set of trait concepts in the course of performing some initial task. Then, ostensibly as part of a different experiment, they receive information about a target person's behavior that can be interpreted as exemplifying either these or other, less recently activated traits. Subsequent judgments of the target are biased toward the implications of the particular traits activated by the initial task. More important, the magnitude of this bias increases with the time interval between presentation of the behavioral information and the judgment of the target (Higgins, Rholes, &

---

[2]An alternative interpretation might be that once subjects have activated a trait concept, they use this concept to describe the target quite independently of the information presented (e.g., if "hostility" is activated, they may judge the target as hostile regardless of the implications of the information or their interpretation of it.) However, if this were the case, activating a concept *after* the information about the target is presented would also affect the judgment. In fact, "priming" effects do not occur unless a concept relevant to interpreting the information is activated *before* the information is received (Higgins, Rholes, & Jones, 1977; Srull & Wyer, 1980). This supports the hypothesis that the encoded representation of the original information is used as a basis for judgments, and that primed trait concepts affect these judgments only to the extent they influence the interpretation of the information at the time it is received.

Jones, 1977; Srull & Wyer, 1980). This suggests that subjects initially interpret the behavioral information in terms of whatever trait concepts happen to be activated at the time it is presented, and form a representation of the target based on this interpretation.[2] The implications of this representation are then used as the basis for judging the target later on. Moreover, the tendency to use this representation rather than the original information becomes greater as time goes on.

Using a different research paradigm, Carlston (1980) found that when subjects receive behavioral information with implications for two different traits (e.g., kind and dishonest) and then judge the target with respect to one of them (kind), their subsequent judgments of the second trait (honesty) are based on the evaluative implications of their first judgment as well as the descriptive implications of the original information. Making the first judgment presumably leads subjects to form a general impression of a person with the trait being judged (i.e., a kind person), and subsequent judgments are based on the implications of this representation (i.e., on attributes typical of a kind person) as well as the (dishonest) behaviors that led to its construction (for an elaboration of this process, see Wyer, Srull, & Gordon, 1984). Moreover, in Carlston's study, as in the priming studies described above, the effect of this representation appears to increase over time in relation to that of the original behavioral information.

Outside the domain of impression formation, Ross, Lepper, Strack, and Steinmetz (1977) showed that once subjects have generated an explanation for a hypothetical, arbitrarily selected event, they are likely to predict that the event will occur. In a more recent study (Sherman, Skov, Hervitz, & Stock, 1981), not only subjects' predictions of their own success on a task but also their actual performance were affected by arbitrarily asking them beforehand to explain why they might succeed on such a task or why they might fail. These studies also suggest that the implications of representations formed in the course of attaining some initial objective were then used as a basis for subsequent judgments and predictions, independently of the factors that led these representations to be formed.

3. Relation Between Recall and Judgments.   Research on social judgment and decision processes has repeatedly failed to obtain strong relationships between the judgments one makes of a stimulus and the amount and implications of recalled information that bears on these judgments. These failures have occurred using a variety of research paradigms. For example, evaluative judgments of a person who is described by a series of personality adjectives are most influenced by the first adjectives presented, whereas the last adjectives presented are more easily recalled (Anderson & Hubert, 1963; Dreben, Fiske, & Hastie, 1979). More complex differences between the effects of presentation order on the recall of success and failure information and its effects on ability and effort judgments were also detected by Hartwick (1981). Experimental manipulations of subjects' imagined perspective when receiving verbal information about an event have successfully affected both the amount of information recalled about different aspects of the event (Abelson, 1976; Fiske, Taylor, Etcoff, & Laufer, 1979) and explanations given for the event (Bower, 1978). Nevertheless, the correlation between the amount of information recalled about a participant in an event and attributions of responsibility to this person has typically been low (Fiske et al., 1979; Moore, Sherrod, Liu, & Underwood, 1979). Equally low relations have been found between attitudinal and behavioral intention judgments on one hand, and the implications of recalled judgment-relevant information on the other (B. Anderson, 1981). The above research has primarily employed verbal stimulus materials. However, subjects who observe ongoing behavior sequences with the intention of forming impressions of the participants subsequently make judgments of these participants that are minimally related to the implications of the behavior they have observed (d'Andrade, 1974; Cohen & Ebbesen, 1979). This suggests that judgments are independent of recalled information in this stimulus domain as well.

Perhaps the most direct evidence of the need to distinguish between the implications of recalled information and the cognitive mediators of judgments has come from research on communication and persuasion. Here again, there is typically little relationship between the recall of information contained in a persuasive communication and the influence of the communication on beliefs and attitudes (for a review, see McGuire, 1968). However, Greenwald (1968) has shown that the influence of a communication *is* related to subjects' recall of the thoughts they had while the information was being presented. These thoughts presumably could include elaborations of the information, counterarguments, or content-irrelevant cognitions ("Gee, I wish I could get out of this experiment early," etc.). In any event, some representation of one's thoughts about information during the course of receiving it appears to be the best predictor of its influence. (For a review of more recent demonstrations of the role of cognitive mediators in persuasion, see Petty & Cacioppo, 1981.)

The literature cited above suggests that study of information recall as an end in itself has few implications for judgmental processes per se, particularly when people receive the information with some particular objective in mind. On the other hand, an understanding of the structure and content of the cognitive representations formed on the basis of information, and of which aspects of these representations are most apt to be used to make judgments, may provide considerable insight into the determinants of social inferences and decisions. The present chapter reviews some of the central issues associated with the representation of social information in memory and discusses certain of their implications for judgments. This review will be somewhat limited in scope (for a more comprehensive review, see Hastie, Park, & Weber, this volume). As noted previously, research on the *effects* of complex knowledge structures on social inferences and decisions is extensive, and at least two thorough reviews are available elsewhere (Taylor & Crocker, 1981; Wyer & Srull, 1980). In contrast, we focus in this chapter on those issues that concern the structural properties of different types of cognitive representations and discuss the literature bearing on their postulated effects only insofar as it has implications for these structural considerations.

SEMANTIC SIMILARITIES, CATEGORIES AND SCHEMATA

Before discussing how particular types of social knowledge are represented in memory, some general distinctions are worth noting between various types of representations and their potential implications for information processing. First, a distinction should be made between the representations of persons, objects and events, each of which presumably functions as a cognitive unit that is stored in and retrieved from memory as a whole, and a more general ''semantic network'' of concepts that do not necessarily refer to a particular object or event and are related on the basis of their similarity in meaning. Thus, we know that ''honest'' and ''trustworthy'' are related without referring to a person who possesses these attributes. Other, more remote associations (e.g., between ''hardworking'' and ''aggressive,'' or between ''talkative'' and ''extraverted'') may be of the same character. The strength of such associations may not reflect the likelihood that the same person has the traits, but rather, how likely it is that the trait descriptions have the same behavioral referent (i.e., that a behavior exemplifying one trait would also exemplify the other). Similarly, two behaviors (''stealing'' and ''lying,'' for example) may be related to the extent that they both exemplify the same concept (i.e., ''dishonest behaviors''). For a detailed analysis of the role of such a ''semantic structure'' and its possible relation to concepts about particular persons, see Wyer and Carlston (1979).

Attributes may *also* be associated by virtue of their co-occurrence in the same person or type of person, their coexistence in a particular situation, or their temporal contiguity in an event sequence. However, to the extent that different representations of persons, objects, and events exist in memory as separate cognitive units, the strength of association between a particular pair of attributes (and therefore the likelihood that thinking about one stimulates recall of the other) may depend on which of several representations containing these variables is activated. For example, ''friendly'' and ''sincere'' may be more closely associated in one's representations of a priest or a lover than in one's representation of a used-car salesman. Moreover, in many cases, we may have different representations of the same person. In such instances, the extent to which calling attention to one attribute of the person stimulates recall of a second may depend upon which representation of the person is activated at the time the first attribute is mentioned. In any event, note that the associations among attributes in a representation of this sort may not be direct. Rather, they may exist only by virtue of the common relation of these attributes to a central concept or category.

The question is how these representations are structured. In considering this matter, Jean Mandler (1979) has distinguished between two types of representations: *categories* and *schemata*. As this distinction is not typically made in the social cognition literature, the characteristics of each are worth some discussion.

Categories

A *category* is theoretically denoted by a verbal or nonverbal symbol (i.e., a "name") and is represented by a set of features that serve as bases for inferring membership in it. These features are themselves not necessarily organized or interrelated except by virtue of their mutual presence in the set that is common to category members. Thus, a lawyer may be characterized as someone who prepares briefs, questions witnesses, is well educated, middle-class, persuasive, articulate, and ambitious. While some of these characteristics may be more typical of a lawyer than others, there are no inherent spatial, temporal, or logical relations among them. Rather, the features may be conceptualized metaphorically as comprising a list of attributes regarded as typical of category members. Alternatively, in terms of an associative network model (Collins & Loftus, 1975; Wyer & Carlston, 1979), the attributes may be viewed as concept nodes, connected by pathways to a central node denoting the category itself. In this representation, the length of these pathways would reflect the strength of the association between the feature and the category.

An attribute that is used to infer membership in a category may of course itself be viewed as a category. For example, "ambitious," an attribute of lawyers, may be conceptualized as a category of behaviors that has its own criteria for inclusion. However, a distinction should be made between a category of *behaviors* that are denoted by a particular adjective and a category of *persons* who are described by this same adjective. The characteristic features of these categories may differ considerably. For example, the characteristics of an "ambitious" behavior may be limited to those that serve as criteria for describing a particular behavior as ambitious. In contrast, the characteristics of an "ambitious" person may include attributes that, while not denotatively related to "ambitious," are nevertheless considered typical of ambitious people (e.g., "energetic," "conniving," "back-stabbing," etc.). Although this distinction is necessary in order to interpret several social judgment phenomena (for examples, see Wyer & Srull, 1980, 1981), it is often overlooked by social cognition researchers. This oversight has led to ambiguities in interpreting the results of their research, as we will see.

Categories may be related to one another, and this relationship may be either hierarchical or not. For example, "surgeon" and "pediatrician" may be subclasses of the general category "doctor," which is in turn a subcategory of "professional." However, categories at any given level of generality are not ordered. Moreover, many other categories ("female," "professional," "lover," etc.) may be overlapping and impossible to organize in any meaningful hierarchy whatsoever.

Schemata

A schema is theoretically a cognitive representation whose features, unlike those of a category, are organized according to specifiable a priori criteria. These criteria may be spatial, temporal, or logical. An example of a spatially organized schema is a human face, and of a temporally organized schema, the events involved in eating at a restaurant. As in categories, the features or elements of a schema may vary in the degree to which they are typical of the schema. (For example, in a "restaurant" schema, paying the bill may be more typical or "necessary" than buying a mint.)

Schemata may vary in abstractness, complexity, and function. One of the simplest types of schemata, conceptualized by Abelson and Reich (1969) as an "implicational molecule," may be a set of logically or "psycho-logically" related propositions that in combination represent a generalization about one's social world (e.g., "people with similar values usually like one another," "people generally get what they deserve," etc.). A molecule is applied to specific experiences in order to understand and draw inferences about them. (For an elaboration of this possibility, see the following section.) Other schemata, such as "scripts" (Schank & Abelson, 1977), may describe lengthy sequences of events involving people or objects that are themselves complexly represented. Some schemata may contain plans or procedures for attaining certain objectives (e.g., how to get food when one is hungry, how to prepare a journal article, etc.). In such cases, there may be several different "tracks," each representing an alternative way of attaining a particular goal (cf. Rumelhart & Ortony, 1977; Schank & Abelson, 1977). (For example, a representation of "eating at a restaurant" may be one track of a general procedural schema for getting food.) Under these conditions, the track that is activated and used is the one whose features can be exemplified, or "instantiated," in terms of the more specific features of the particular situation at hand.

As Rumelhart (1980) and others have maintained, schemata may play a central role in the comprehension of verbal information. This is particularly true in the case of actions or events. Indeed, Rumelhart notes that schemata may underlie the interpretation of most verbs that describe actions. For instance, the verb "pound" may be interpreted by invoking a schema that not only denotes an action but also contains references to an agent, an object, and an implement, all of which are organized in relation to one another in a specified way. These schema elements are essentially *variables* that are instantiated in terms of *values* specified in the information to which it is applied. Thus, the presence of "pound" in the sentence "John pound(ed) the nail into the wall" may activate the "pound" schema, and this may lead other components of the sentence to be interpreted as instantiations (values) of schema variables; that is, "John" is interpreted as the "actor," "nail" as the "object," and so forth.

The above example calls attention to two important characteristics of schematic processing. First, there are constraints on the types of elements that can instantiate the variables of a schema. (In other words, there are limits to the values that these variables can have.) Violations of these constraints can make information difficult to interpret. For example, the sentence "The nail pounded John into the wall" would be interpreted as bizarre. This is because "nail" has a position in relation to "pounds" that would lead it to be interpreted as an instantiation of the actor in the "pound" schema, and yet it is not within the range of acceptable values of "actor."

Second, certain variables are necessary features of a schema, and when the information to be interpreted does not provide explicit values of these variables, they may be spontaneously assigned "default" values. In our example, the "implement" is a variable of the "pound" schema that cannot be instantiated on the basis of the sentence "John pounded the nail into the wall." However, the default value of "implement" in this schema may be "hammer." Thus, this instantiation may be made spontaneously and may become part of the representation of the information stored in memory.

Relation Between Schemata and Categories.   Although categories and schemata are conceptually different types of cognitive representations, they are nevertheless intimately related. For one thing, the variables of a schema may often be categories. Therefore, the instantiation of schema variables in terms of a given set of information is essentially a process of assigning features of this information to categories specified in the schema. Moreover, attributes that serve as criteria for assigning an object to a category may sometimes be represented schematically. For example, attributes of a lawyer such as "questions witnesses" and "prepares briefs" refer to events that are presumably understood by invoking schemata pertaining to these events. Thus, not only may "lawyer" be a variable in the "questions witness" schema, but "questions witness" may function as an attribute that serves as a criterion for membership in the category "lawyer." The implications of this relationship become apparent below.

Some Theoretical Distinctions

The effects of categorical and schematic representations on information processing may differ in several respects. First, Mandler (1979) questions the extent to which categorical representations are spontaneously activated in the course of interpreting new information. Information about a subset of the attributes possessed by members of a particular category may not spontaneously activate this category unless either (a) the attributes are very strongly and uniquely associated with it, (b) one has a specific objective that leads the object being described to be classified, or (c) a category and its characteristic features are already activated at the time information is received. In general, the category to which an object belongs must be identified through data-driven, bottom-up processing (Norman & Bobrow, 1976). This processing may often be difficult and therefore may not occur spontaneously. One reason for this is that although a set of attributes *in combination* may uniquely define a category, the attributes considered individually or in subsets may not uniquely describe category members. Thus, we may believe that college professors are typically hardworking, intellectual, and idealistic (among other things), and these attributes may quickly come to mind when we learn that someone is a professor. Moreover, we may even report that these attributes in combination characterize a college professor if we are asked explicitly to guess what type of person they might describe. However, we may nevertheless not *spontaneously* think of a college professor when we hear someone described in this way. (In other words, we may spontaneously think of "intellectual" when we learn that someone is a college professor, but may *not* often think of a college professor when we hear someone described as "intellectual.")

In contrast, information that describes the characteristic features of a schema may be more inclined to activate the schema spontaneously. As Schank and Abelson (1977) note, the process of associating features of information with the variables contained in one or more previously formed schemata is an integral part of comprehension that often occurs automatically. Thus, the statement that "Bill was still looking at the menu when she asked him for his order" may automatically activate an event schema of eating at a restaurant, leading "Bill" and "she" to be interpreted as instantiations of the variables "customer" and "waitress," respectively. Once this occurs, the schema may guide the interpretation of subsequent information in ways we elaborate later on (see also Rumelhart, 1981).

The more fundamental role of schemata than of categories in comprehending information may be conveyed intuitively through the above examples. That is, in reading the statement "Bill was still looking at the menu when she asked him for his order," it is very difficult *not* to assume spontaneously that Bill is a customer in a restaurant. This is true despite the fact that the same statement could also describe a man and his wife placing a telephone order for a home delivery. In contrast, the description of Bill as "intelligent, hardworking, liberal, and idealistic," attributes that may be typical of a college professor, does not require the assignment of Bill to the "college professor" category (or, for that matter, to any category) in order to understand the information. That is, the category assignment is not an integral part of the comprehension process.

This is not to say that people do not attempt to identify a person's category membership when they know little else about the person. They may do this as a heuristic device in attempting to understand what a person is apt to be like. Thus, we may often ask someone we meet for the first time what his occupation is, or what part of the country he comes from, because we intuitively believe that knowledge of these category memberships will help us infer something about the person's attitudes, traits, or interests (i.e., attributes typical of members of these categories). Note, however, that in these cases, a person's membership in a general category is of interest primarily because it helps us to infer characteristics of this person, and not as an end in itself. Therefore, although people may seek information about a person's category membership in order to infer the person's attributes, they may not spontaneously use information about these attributes as bases for inferring the person's category membership.

There is one condition in which a category assignment *will* be made spontaneously. This is when the assignment is required in order to comprehend an action of the sort to which a *schema* is applied. For example, a person who reads the sentence "After preparing a brief, Bill went home" may spontaneously assign Bill to the category "lawyer." However, this is because the action "prepare(d) a brief" is comprehended by activating a schema containing the variable "lawyer," and "Bill" is taken as an instantiation of this variable. Or, a person who observes Bill kick a dog may assign Bill to the category "sadist" in the course of comprehending this action in terms of an "abusing animals" schema in which the actor is designated a "sadist." In some instances, it may not be clear which of several variables is instantiated by a component of information. For example, the statement "After Bill had finished speaking, the judge dismissed the case," may activate a trial schema. However, since Bill could be an instantiation of several variables in such a schema (witness, defendant, lawyer, etc.), the interpretation of the statement is ambiguous, and the recipient may therefore seek additional information that permits a category assignment to be made. Thus, if Bill is described elsewhere as "persuasive," and this is an attribute of "lawyer" but not "defendant" or "witness," this category assignment may be made rather than one of the alternatives. However, when a category assignment is not helpful for comprehension, it may occur only under the conditions described earlier; that is, only if the attributes specified in the information are strongly associated with the category ("absent-minded," in the case of a "professor"), if the recipient of the information has a specific a priori objective that requires categorization of the information, or if a category that is applicable for encoding the information is already activated at the time the information is received.

Other important differences exist between the effects of categories and the effects of schemata on comprehension and inference making. We have noted that when the assignment of values to certain schema variables is necessary for the comprehension of information but potential values of these variables are not specified, the variables may be assigned default values, which then become part of the representation being formed. For example, suppose someone says that he "went to a seafood restaurant yesterday evening." To understand this statement, we may activate a "restaurant" schema and, as a result, infer that the person looked at the menu, ate dinner, and ultimately paid the bill. Moreover, we assume that he did so in the order stated rather than the reverse.

The possibility that default values of schema variables are assigned spontaneously in the process of comprehending information has two implications. First, we may respond to this information by asking questions that imply the existence of these default values without verifying their actual existence. For example, we may ask the person who said he "went to a seafood restaurant" whether the restaurant served steak as well as seafood, what he decided to eat, or whether his meal was expensive, without first verifying that the person actually looked at the menu, ate, and ultimately paid the bill. Second, if asked to recall the speaker's statement later on, certain of the added default values may intrude on the information recalled. For example, we may recall that the person said he "ate at a seafood restaurant" rather than that he simply "went" there. Or, in the previous example, we may recall that "John pounded the nail into the wall with a hammer" even though the "hammer" was not mentioned. Evidence of such intrusion errors has been obtained by Bransford, Barclay, & Franks (1972).

Comparable effects are unlikely to occur as a result of categorization. For example, if we are told that a person is an "extravert," we may not spontaneously infer that the person has attributes that serve as criteria for membership in the category. Rather, we may ask (if anything) about the particular features that led to this description. That is, we may ask if the person likes parties, or more generally, *why* the speaker thinks the person is extraverted, rather than questions based on the assumption that these features exist. While we of course *could* make inferences about the behavior or characteristics of the person described *if asked* (cf. Cantor & Mischel, 1977), this may not be done automatically. Moreover, we may not spontaneously add these features if we are asked to recall information about the person. That is, intrusion errors analogous to those resulting from schematic processing may not occur.[3]

To summarize, categories are less likely than schemata to be activated spontaneously on the basis of information that describes features of this representation. Moreover, once activated, categories are less likely than schemata to lead to the spontaneous inference of features that were not contained in the information

---

[3]Intrusion errors in free recall of the sort discussed here should not be confused with false recognition errors (i.e., reports that a particular test item was contained in the information when it was not). The latter errors may often be attributable to a guessing bias that occurs at the time of judgment, independently of memory for the information. We will elaborate on this point in Section III.

presented, and are less likely to lead to intrusion errors in the subsequent recall of this information.

With these considerations in mind, we now turn to a more detailed discussion of the representation of five different types of social knowledge: (a) beliefs and opinions, (b) event and behavioral sequences, (c) persons, (d) groups and (e) oneself. While representations of the first two types of knowledge may be schematic, the others may be primarily categorical in nature.

COGNITIVE RULES: THE REPRESENTATION OF BELIEFS

People may acquire certain rules or principles as a result of their past experience, and may apply them in understanding their social environment and predicting future events. These rules may often have the form of generalizations about the world in which we live and may be equivalent to general beliefs (e.g., "smoking causes lung cancer," "persons with similar values are apt to like one another," etc.) The cognitive representation of these rules and their role in social information processing are most clearly stated in the implicational molecule theory proposed by Abelson and Reich (1969). As this theory is able to incorporate most rules and principles that have been postulated by social psychologists to affect social inferences, it is worth considering in some detail.

Theoretical Considerations

Abelson and Reich note that a generalization about one's social environment is conceptually equivalent to a set of two or more general, logically or psychologically related propositions about persons, objects, or events. For example, the two generalizations described above are equivalent to the sets

[A smokes; A will get(has) lung cancer]

and

[A likes X; B likes X; A and B like each other]

The elements of these propositions (A, B, C, likes, etc.), or *variables*, may be either quite general or fairly circumscribed. In combination, the propositions in each set of the sort described above comprise an *implicational molecule*.

Note that the propositions comprising a molecule are either logically or temporally related. For example, one proposition may describe an event that either precedes (causes) or follows (results from) the event described in another. The theoretical role of these molecules in comprehension and inference may therefore be similar to that postulated for schemata more generally. That is, if features of new information exemplify the variables contained in a molecule, this molecule may be activated and its variables used to encode the information. If features of the information exemplify all variables in a given proposition of the molecule, the proposition is said to be *instantiated*. When only a subset of the molecule's propositions can be instantiated on the basis of the information available, instantiations of the remaining propositions may be inferred. Thus, suppose we learn that Mary wants to go to Europe and is trying to save money. "Mary," "saves money" and "goes to Europe" may exemplify the general variables (concepts) A, X, and Y, respectively, in a "purposive behavior" molecule of the form:

[A wants Y; X causes Y; A does X].

The first and third propositions of the molecule are both instantiated on the basis of the information given, and so an instantiation of the second proposition may be inferred to be true as well; that is, we may infer that Mary's saving money may allow her to go to Europe. This general process is governed by what Abelson and Reich refer to as a *completion* principle. That is, if all but one proposition in a molecule are instantiated in terms of features of the information presented, an instantiation of the remaining proposition will also be inferred to be valid.

In our example, the unspecified proposition may be inferred nearly automatically in the course of comprehension. This is partly because no alternative molecule is equally applicable. This may not always be the case. For example, someone who learns that John works 10 hours a day may interpret this information as an instance of the general proposition "A does X." However, this proposition may be contained in not only the purposive behavior molecule noted above but also a "servitude" molecule, of the form

[B bosses A; B wants X; A does X],

and a "hedonic" molecule, of the form

[A likes X; A does X].

In such a case, the molecule that is actually applied may depend on several factors, including (a) the availability of other information bearing on the propositions contained in these molecules and (b) the relative accessibility of alternative molecules in memory. We return to these considerations presently.

In other instances, the applicability of a molecule may depend on the manner in which the particular features of the information presented are encoded. To borrow an example from Wyer and Carlston (1979), suppose a person with a "similarity-attraction" molecule of the form [A likes X; B likes X; A and B like one another] learns that Bob likes the Rolling Stones and Mary likes Beethoven sonatas. If "the Rolling Stones" and "Beethoven sonatas" are encoded as instances of "rock" and "classical music" respectively, and thus as members of different categories, the molecule would not be applied, and no inference about Bob's and Mary's attraction to one another would occur. However, if the features are both encoded as instances of the more general category "music," and if "music" is an instantiation of X, the molecule might be applied, and Bob and Mary might be inferred to have positive feelings toward one another. Thus, situational factors that fortuitously predispose persons to interpret information in different ways may have a substantial effect on the manner in which cognitive representations are activated, and therefore on which inferences are made on the basis of the information.

The implicational molecules that one forms and uses to comprehend one's social environment may often be idiosyncratic, resulting from one's unique past experiences. However, several molecules may be common to members of a given culture as a result of similar socialization. Although implicational molecule theory per se has not been applied widely in social psychology, many better known formulations of the organization of beliefs and attitudes may be conceptualized as specific applications of this broader theory, based on the assumption that certain common molecules exist. Therefore, although the primary focus of this chapter is on the structural properties of cognitive representations rather than their effects, it may be useful in this case to consider these traditional formulations in terms of implicational molecules, thereby clarifying some of the ambiguities that surround them and research bearing on their validity as models of cognitive organization.

Cognitive Balance

One of the first formal theoretical statements concerning the cognitive representations that mediate the comprehension and retention of social information was cognitive balance theory (Heider, 1946, 1958). This formulation and its derivatives (Abelson & Rosenberg, 1958; Cartwright & Harary, 1956) has decreased in popularity in recent years. However, it has nevertheless had a major influence on social psychological research.[4] Balance theory is well known, and reviews and critiques of it are numerous (e.g., Wyer, 1974; Zajonc, 1968). In this paper, we consider only the fundamental aspects of the theory within the conceptual framework outlined above and will note both its strengths and weaknesses from this perspective.

Heider's original conceptualization focused on relations between two persons (P and O), among three persons (P, O and Q) or among two persons and an object (P, O and X). He postulated a general tendency to believe that people's feelings toward one another are similar (that is, either both favorable or both

---

[4]Abelson's early work on symbolic psychologic (Abelson & Rosenberg, 1959), an extension of balance theory principles, contains the conceptual seeds of his later work on implicational molecules and ultimately scripts (Abelson, 1981; Schank & Abelson, 1977).

unfavorable). Moreover, he postulated that one person (P) is believed to have positive feelings (sentiments) toward another (O) when their feelings toward a third person (Q) or object (X) are similar, but to have negative feelings toward another when their feelings toward the third element differ. Assuming for the moment that positive and negative feelings can be represented in terms of the affective verb categories "likes" and "dislikes," respectively, these hypotheses essentially imply the existence of the following sets of implicational molecules:

1. [P likes O; O likes P]; [P dislikes O; O dislikes P]
2. [P likes (dislikes) Q or X; O likes (dislikes) Q or X; P likes O]; [P likes (dislikes) Q or X; O dislikes (likes) Q or X; P dislikes O]

These molecules may be used to make inferences in much the same manner described previously. Suppose a person learns that Bill supports Ronald Reagan but George opposes him. Suppose further that Bill, George, Reagan, "supports" and "opposes" can be interpreted as instances of the general categories P, O, Q, "likes" and "dislikes," respectively. If these interpretations are made, the first two propositions of the molecule

[P likes Q; O dislikes Q; P dislikes O]

may be instantiated, and an instantiation of the remaining proposition (i.e., "Bill dislikes George") may then be inferred. Alternatively, information that Bill supports Reagan and dislikes George may lead the first and third propositions in this molecule to be instantiated, leading to the inference that George opposes Reagan.

The dynamics that theoretically underlie the influence of cognitive balance principles on judgments are therefore very similar, if not identical, to those that presumably underlie the influence of other types of schematic representations on judgments. However, despite numerous applications of balance principles in predicting interpersonal attraction, the empirical support for their generality as cognitive mediators of judgments has not been impressive (for detailed reviews and critiques of balance research, see Wyer, 1974; Zajonc, 1968). Nevertheless, two studies provide strong evidence that when balance principles are applicable, they do have schematic properties of the sort implied by implicational molecule theory. In one (Picek, Sherman, & Shiffrin, 1975), subjects read stories describing four different persons' liking for one another. In some cases, not all relations were actually stated in the story. However, the relations that were specified were such that the entire set could either be balanced by inferring the appropriate missing relations or was impossible to balance regardless of the relations inferred. Later on, subjects were asked to recall the stories. When it was possible to balance the set of relations, subjects not only recalled the presented relations more accurately but made intrusion errors that were consistent with a balance principle. However, when the set was not possible to balance, these intrusion errors did not occur. These data not only suggest that a balance principle was used to organize the information in memory, but also indicate that the organization resulting from its application had schematic properties.

In a quite different type of study (Sentis & Burnstein, 1979), subjects read information describing several sets of relations, each set consisting of two persons and an object. In some cases, the set of relations was balanced, and in other cases it was not. Subsequently, subjects were given a recognition task in which they were asked to verify that either (a) a single relation was presented, (b) two of the three relations in combination were presented, or (c) all three relations in combination were presented. When the set was imbalanced, the time required to respond increased with the number of relations to be verified, suggesting that in this case, each relation was judged independently. When the set was balanced, however, response time *decreased* as the number of relations to be verified increased. In this case, the information was apparently organized into a single conceptual unit, and it took less time to verify the unit as a whole than to verify any of its individual components.

These successes notwithstanding, the inconsistent support for balance principles as bases for organizing information suggests that their general applicability is much more limited than often assumed. These limitations may be of two types. First, balance principles may apply to only certain classes of persons and objects. Second, situational factors may affect the ways in which a specific set of information activates a balance principle. A consideration of balance principles as implicational molecules helps to understand the nature of these contingencies.

a. Encoding of Person, Object and Verb Categories. In traditional applications of balance theory, little distinction was made between the alternative verbs that might be used to describe positive and negative sentiments between persons and objects. For example, "likes," "loves," "admires," "wants," "supports," and so forth, were all viewed as conveying positive sentiment relations, and therefore as functionally equivalent, whereas "dislikes," "hates," "opposes," and so on, were all treated as equivalent descriptions of negative sentiments. However, as Abelson and his colleagues (Abelson & Kanouse, 1966; Abelson & Reich, 1969) point out, these concepts are applied in different situations and contexts, and thus may be involved in different molecules, not all of which are consistent with balance principles. For example, the second set of balance molecules described above is essentially equivalent to the "similarity-attraction" molecule postulated earlier. However, Abelson and Reich suggest two additional molecules that might be applied to the same elements. One, a "competition" molecule, is based on the general notion that people who compete for the same goal grow to dislike one another, and has the general form

[P wants X; O wants X; P dislikes O].

A second, "jealousy" molecule is based on the general principle that people are envious of those who have what they want, and has the form

[P wants X; O has X; P dislikes O].

Since both "wants X" and "has X" imply a positive relation to X, these latter two molecules, if applied, would lead to inferences that differ from those predicted by balance theory.

The applicability of a balance molecule, and the likelihood of activating it, may also depend on the nature of the person or object categories involved and the manner in which they are encoded. To give a common example, someone who is told that Bob and John both love tennis are apt to infer that Bob and John like one another. However, if the person is told that Bob and John both love Mary, the "love" relation may be interpreted as an instantiation of "want," a competition molecule may be activated, and the inference that Bob likes John may be less likely. Alternatively, as data reported by Zajonc and Burnstein (1965) suggest, a balance molecule is less apt to be applied if the object to which P's and O's sentiments pertain is of little importance (e.g., Newsweek) than if its importance is high (e.g., racial integration). The failure to conceptualize a priori the nature of the categories to which balance molecules refer and the conditions under which these particular molecules are apt to be activated has undoubtedly contributed to the inconsistent support for balance principles obtained in social inference research (cf. Gollob, 1974; Wyer & Lyon, 1970; Zajonc, 1968). In reviewing this research, Wyer (1974) speculated that the more abstractly the persons, objects, and relations conveyed in information are described, the more likely it is that a balance principle will be used as a basis for inferences. That is, given no other information, one is more apt to infer that two people like one another if they have similar attitudes toward something than if they do not. However, the addition of specific descriptions of the persons and attitude objects involved may activate more restricted subsets of real world knowledge that are considered to be more applicable than a balance principle for interpreting the information presented, and thus this principle may not be invoked.

   b. Encoding of the Configuration.   In conceptualizing balance principles as a special case of implicational molecules, we assumed that the relations involving P, O and Q(X) are instantiated as three separate propositions, and that inferences of any one were based upon the nature of the remaining two. In many instances, however, two of the three relations may be encoded in terms of a single concept. For example, consider again the relations contained in the general balance molecule

[P likes X; O likes X; P likes O]

These three relations would also be consistent with at least three other 2-proposition molecules:

[P and O agree about X; P likes O]

[P likes O; P conforms to O's attitude toward X]

[P likes O; P influences O to agree with him about X]

The latter three alternative representations all convey the same set of three relations among P, O, and X. However, the social situations to which they apply clearly differ. For example, P's liking for O in the first molecule is presumably a consequence of P's and O's similar sentiments toward X, whereas P's liking for O in the second and third molecules is a determinant of P's similarity to O. Moreover, the behavior attributed to P in the second and third molecules differs. It seems intuitively likely that the three molecules are relevant to different classes of objects. To this extent, the consistency of inferences with predictions of balance theory may depend upon which two relations are given and which is to be inferred (cf. Wyer & Lyon, 1970).

Attribution Processes

When people are asked to explain a particular person's behavior (or a specific event in which the person is involved), they may attempt to retrieve from memory a subset of their prior knowledge about the type of behavior/event and why it has occurred in the past. They may then infer, on the basis of this general knowledge, why the behavior/event occurred again. However, the knowledge that people retrieve in such instances may not necessarily consist of specific events or behaviors they have experienced previously. Rather, it may consist of generalizations concerning why people typically engage in certain types of behaviors in certain types of situations. Although these generalizations may originally be formed by summarizing a set of specific experiences, they may come to be used independently of the experiences that led to their construction.

   To this extent, implicational molecules may govern many attribution phenomena. The possible existence of three such molecules, reflecting the general notions that people do things (a) to obtain a desired outcome, (b) because they are forced to do them by someone else, and (c) because they intrinsically like to do them, were suggested previously (see page 86, regarding the purposive behavior, servitude and hedonic molecules, respectively). As speculated elsewhere (Wyer & Carlston, 1979), much of attribution theory and research (e.g., Bem, 1972; Jones & Davis, 1965) can be viewed as concerned with the conditions that determine which one of these molecules is invoked in understanding a person's behavior in a given situation, and therefore which type of explanation is generated on the basis of the completion principle.

   However, an implicational molecule conceptualization has broader implications when placed in the more general context of cognitive functioning. Wyer and Srull (1980, 1981) postulated that when people are called upon to comprehend information and/or make a judgment, they are likely to retrieve and use only that concept or knowledge structure that is most easily available in memory, ignoring others that may be equally or more relevant. This may be the knowledge structure whose features have been most recently activated in the past. Thus, suppose several different implicational molecules are potentially applicable for comprehending and explaining a given behavior. Then, the one that is applied, and therefore the explanation that is generated on the basis of the completion principle, may depend in part on whether aspects of one's past experiences "prime" the concepts contained in this molecule (for evidence of priming effects in other situations, see Higgins & King, 1981; Wyer & Srull, 1981). Thus, a person who has recently observed someone else engage in a behavior out of pure enjoyment may be more likely to apply a hedonic molecule in interpreting his *own* behavior in a subsequent situation than will a person who has not recently made this observation, even if other molecules are in principle just as applicable.

The effects of taking a perspective on attributions (Jones & Nisbett, 1971) are also worth noting in this regard. That is, persons typically explain events in terms of persons and objects that were salient to them from their real or imagined point of view at the time they learn about them (for a summary, see Taylor & Fiske, 1978). Thus, in an interaction between two persons, A and B, persons in the real or imagined role of A are more likely to explain events in the interaction in terms of characteristics of B, whereas those in the role of B attribute these same events to characteristics of A (Regan & Totten, 1975). Although the perspective manipulations affect the attention paid to specific aspects of the situations that have direct implications for the attributions being made, there is often little correlation between these attributions and the amount of information remembered about the person to whom the explanation pertains (Fiske et al., 1979). It therefore seems equally reasonable to suppose that the judge's perspective affects the general rule of thumb (molecule) that is activated at the time of judgment, and that the implications of this molecule, rather than the details of the information itself, are used to generate explanations.[5]

Abstract Rules and Procedures

Many cognitive rules that may have the form of implicational molecules are not content specific. Several of these may function as judgmental "heuristics" (Nisbett & Ross, 1980; Tversky & Kahneman, 1974; see Sherman & Corty, this

---

[5]A variety of more abstract rules have been suggested as mediators of explanations, notably by Kelley (1967, 1971). For example, one general rule may be that is a behavior generalizes over exemplars of a given class (i.e., over persons, objects, or situations), it is unlikely to be due to a characteristic that is unique to any particular member of this class. (Thus, if a particular actor's behavior is also manifested by others, it is unlikely to be due to an attribute that is idiosyncratic to the actor, and therefore is relatively more apt to be due to either a situational factor or a characteristic of the object toward whom the behavior is directed.) More complex rules have also been suggested

volume). For example, subjects may often assume that the more frequently an event occurs, the easier it is to remember. This could be represented by the molecule

[X occurs frequently; X is easy to remember].

To the extent they apply this rule, subjects may infer the frequency of an event from the ease with which they can think of an instance of it.

Other rules may be the result of socially learned principles of reasoning. For example, people may learn to apply syllogistic rules in drawing conclusions about their social environment. Such rules may come to function as molecules of the form

[A; if A, then B; B]

or

[A implies B; B implies C; A implies C],

where A, B, and C are general concepts about social events. To this extent, propositions whose concepts exemplify those contained in two propositions of such a molecule may activate it. As a result, an instantiation of the remaining proposition may be constructed.

One aspect of this conceptualization that distinguishes it from the simpler assumption that people reason syllogistically is its implication that an instantiation of *any one* of the propositions in a "syllogism" molecule may be inferred from information bearing on the other two. Thus, not only may a "conclusion" be inferred from two "premises," but a "premise" may be nonlogically inferred from a conclusion and the other premise. These inferences may occur spontaneously, simply as a result of considering the propositions in close temporal contiguity, and the entire set of given and inferred propositions may then be stored in memory as a unit, in much the same form as the general syllogism molecule that was applied in comprehending them. This implies that subjects who have previously considered two propositions in a syllogistically related set (e.g., as a result of being asked to report their beliefs in them) may subsequently be unable to distinguish between the propositions they considered and the third, unmentioned proposition. Results of a recent study by Loken and Wyer (1983) provide some support for this possibility.

Procedures.   Not all cognitive rules may have the form of molecules. Some may be procedures for arriving at inferences based upon certain types of information. For example, Wyer and Hartwick (1980) hypothesize that a conditional

---

pertaining to configurations of generalizability information and the conditions in which a behavior or event is attributed to more than one cause (Kelley, 1972; Orvis, Cunningham & Kelley, 1975). Unfortunately, however, research has not strongly supported their validity (cf. Surber, 1981; Wyer & Carlston, 1979).

inference rule is often used to evaluate the validity of information one receives. That is, people who are asked the likelihood that a (target) proposition is true but who have not recently considered this proposition may first search memory for another "informational" proposition that bears on it. Their judgment of the target may then be arrived at by subjectively averaging the implications of the informational proposition's being true and the implications of its being false, weighting each by the strength of their beliefs that the proposition is, in fact, true and false, respectively. Syllogistic and algebraic rules of inference have also been suggested (cf. Anderson. 1974; McGuire, 1960, 1981). Since these rules have been discussed at length elsewhere (Wyer & Carlston, 1979; Wyer & Hartwick, 1980), they will not be elaborated here. The conditions under which people resort to such complex and abstract cognitive principles in making judgments have not been circumscribed and may be more limited than often assumed (Abelson, 1976; Wyer & Carlston, 1979). However, that such rules are applied in some conditions seems undeniable.

Conclusions

People often invoke fairly simple rules of thumb, derived from their past experience, in understanding their social environment and making inferences about it. Indeed, these rules may be invoked more frequently than the more complex representations of the sort we consider in the remainder of this chapter. However, the postulation of such rules in accounting for social judgments and decisions is of limited value without a complete understanding of the conditions in which a given rule is likely to be activated and used. Moreover, with few exceptions (e.g., Bear & Hodun, 1975; Picek et al., 1975; Sentis & Burnstein, 1979), no direct attempt has been made to show that rules, once constructed, operate in the ways suggested. In particular, the implications of their schematic nature have not usually been explored. It is unclear, for example, whether molecules are activated spontaneously in the course of comprehending information when it is first received, and whether subsequent intrusion errors occur of a sort implied by these molecules when the information is spontaneously recalled later on.[6] Research that investigates these possibilities, that differentiates among the effects of applying different rules, and that specifies a priori the conditions in which one or

---

[6]In early research investigating the role of balance principles in the organization of information (Zajonc & Burnstein, 1965; Zajonc & Sherman, 1967), subjects were typically asked to recall the relations between pairs of objects in sets that were originally either balanced or imbalanced. They found that subjects often made errors in a manner consistent with balance rules. However, subjects in this research were typically given the two elements involved in the relation and asked to infer whether the relation was positive or negative. Thus, results could well have been due to guessing biases that occurred at the time of output rather than to the organization of the information at the time of input. In fact, these biases may have had little if anything to do with cognitive balance principles per se (for an elaboration, see Wyer, 1974).

another rule is activated may bring coherence to what is presently a somewhat disorganized body of research.

THE REPRESENTATION OF EVENT SEQUENCES

Interest in the cognitive representation of events and the implications of these representations for social judgments has been stimulated in large part by Abelson and Schank's script-processing formulation (Abelson, 1976, 1981; Schank & Abelson, 1977). While script theory has been applied most rigorously in the area of prose comprehension (Bower, Black, & Turner, 1979; Graesser, Gordon, & Sawyer, 1979; Schank & Abelson, 1977), it has equally important implications for the representation of observed behavior and for the role of oneself and one's own subjective reactions in the representation of one's social environment (Abelson, 1976, 1981; Wyer & Carlston, 1979). The original theory contained several ambiguities, most of which are recognized by the theorists themselves (cf. Abelson, 1981), and alternative formulations have been suggested (cf. Rumelhart & Ortony, 1977). Because the general script conceptualization has been directly applied to social information processing (Abelson, 1976, 1981), it will provide the basis of much of our discussion. However, most of our remarks are equally applicable to event schemata as more broadly conceptualized. First, we outline generally the theoretical notions underlying the formation and use of event schemata. Then we discuss in detail some of the theoretical and empirical work bearing on the representation of events in memory.

General Considerations

Definition and General Characteristics.   Many characteristics of event schemata have already been noted in our more general discussion of schemata earlier in this chapter, and the examples of schemata we drew upon in this discussion (e.g., eating in a restaurant, pounding a nail, etc.) were largely of this type. Broadly conceived, an event schema is an organized representation of a series of temporally related events.[7] It may vary in specificity. For example, it may describe the general sequence of events involved in eating at a restaurant (entering, ordering, eating, leaving) or more detailed events that comprise each of these general ones (getting a menu, reading it, deciding what to eat, telling the

---

[7]In his script formulation, Abelson (1981) distinguishes between "strong" scripts, in which the events have a clear temporal order, and "weak" scripts, where the order is not clearly specified. (An example of the latter may be a "circus" script, which contains representations of specific circus acts, but in no particular sequence.) "Weak" scripts have the characteristics of categories rather than schemata. In this discussion, therefore, we focus primarily upon "strong" scripts, in which a temporal order is implied.

waiter, etc.). Or, it may be more abstract, covering general classes of behaviors or events that occur in response to general motives or desires. (Schank and Abelson refer to the former representations as *scripts*, and to the latter as *plans*.) Many schemata refer to events that occur frequently in everyday life and are experienced by most members of a given culture or society. However, some are undoubtedly quite idiosyncratic, resulting from encounters one has had with particular acquaintances in specific situations (Abelson, 1976).

In this regard, it may in some cases be useful to distinguish between the representation of a prototypic sequence of events that is used to interpret and organize new information (e.g., the representation of eating at a restaurant) and the representation of a particular experience that results from this cognitive activity. The latter representation is obviously itself a schema, but at a more concrete level. Once such a schema is formed, it may *also* be used as a basis for interpreting subsequent events and making predictions. (Certainly, an experience we have had with a particular person may be used to predict and interpret events involving that same individual in similar situations later on. It may also be used as a basis for interpreting a new experience involving a different person that we read or hear about. For example, we often respond to others' descriptions of an event they have experienced by recalling a similar experience of our own and using it as a basis for understanding why the first event occurred or what is likely to happen as a result of it.) It seems reasonable to assume that the structure of both general (prototypic) and specific event schemata is similar, and that these schemata differ primarily in the level of generality at which the variables contained in them are specified. Therefore, our discussion of the structural characteristics of event schemata in this chapter borrows from literature pertaining to both general and specific representations of events, and often does not distinguish between them in terms of their implications for information processing.

An event schema may consist of a series of frames, each of which refers to a particular action or event. The content of each frame may include verbal and nonverbal representations of both the action and the persons involved in it. In his original conceptualization, Abelson (1976) drew an analogy between the frames of a script and those of a comic strip. That is, each may have a caption denoting the event, but also a "picture" conveying many details about the people, objects and events involved. These details may conceivably be coded visually (for a discussion of this possibility, see Klatzky, this volume). Moreover, they may often include characteristics of oneself as a participant or observer in the situation, such as one's behavior, or even one's subjective reactions or thoughts that occur while the events take place. When applying script and schema theories to prose comprehension (Rumelhart, 1981; Schank & Abelson, 1977), the role of "self" in the construction of event schemata has not been considered in any detail. However, it is a more important consideration in the processing of information that one receives in social situations.

Although we have referred to event schemata as representations of entire sequences of events, the representation depicted in a single frame is of course itself a schema. (For example, "pounds a nail into the wall" may be one frame of a sequence associated with "hanging a picture.") Thus, an event schema composed of several frames may alternatively be conceptualized as consisting of several temporally related subschemata that are bound together into a single cognitive unit.

Role of Event Schemata in Social Information Processing.   The use of an event schema to interpret information and make inferences is theoretically governed by processes similar to those that underlie the use of implicational molecules. That is, if aspects of the information one receives about an event instantiate variables in a frame of an event schema, this schema may be activated for use in interpreting the specific event described. In the process, other schema-related features may be inferred to exist in the situation. These inferred features either may pertain to the same event that led the schema to be activated (default values), or may be instantiations of entire events that are depicted in frames that temporally precede or follow the one activated by the information presented. Thus, suppose one enters a room and finds someone on the floor in a pool of blood, with a knife lying nearby. The features of this observed event may instantiate variables in a "murder" schema, and therefore may activate this schema for use in interpreting the information. In the process, "weapon," a variable in the schema, may be instantiated in terms of "knife." Once this instantiation is made, subsequent inferences may be drawn (e.g., that John is dead, that the blood came from a knife wound rather than an injury incurred while falling, etc.). Moreover, additional information (e.g., that the door to the wall safe was open) may be interpreted in terms of prototypic events leading up to murders, giving rise to an inference that John was killed in the course of a robbery. Future events (e.g., that the police will be called to the scene of the crime) may be inferred or, if one is a participant in the event, may actually occur as a result of schema-implied courses of action. Inferences about events that precede the one described in the information may often constitute explanations of the event, whereas information about events that follow it may be consequences of it. Thus, event schemata may be used both to *explain* what has happened in the past, to *predict* what will happen in the future, and to guide one's own present and future behavior.

In some instances, of course, no single previously formed event schema may be sufficient to interpret the information one receives. For example, if one learns that George, in a restaurant, realizes he has forgotten his reading glasses, and if a "restaurant" schema is activated, the content of the "reading the menu" frame of this schema (plus a subschema pertaining to the act of reading) may be sufficient to generate the inference that John made this discovery while preparing to read the menu and now finds he is unable to do so. However, if one learns that George, in a restaurant, realizes he has forgotten his tennis racquet, an interpretation of the information in terms of a restaurant schema is more difficult. In such instances, one would either invoke a different schema or incorporate "forgot tennis racquet" into the representation being formed as an "exception" or "correction" (Woodworth & Schlosberg, 1954). This possibility will be elaborated presently.

While much work has been done on the representation and use of event schemata in comprehending and organizing new information and also in behavioral decision making (see Black, this volume; Brewer & Nakamura, this volume), some ambiguities remain concerning the precise nature of these representations and the conditions in which they are accessed. Although many of these ambiguities have been pointed out by Ebbesen (1980) and Abelson (1981), issues of particular relevance to social information processing may nonetheless be worth noting in the present context as well. Two general questions receive attention. One concerns which particular aspects of a continuous stream of events are retained in the representation formed of these events. The other concerns the structure of event schemata.

What Information is Retained?

The information we receive about events may be conveyed either verbally (through written or oral communications) or through direct experience. In the latter case, of course, a variety of sense modalities may be involved simultaneously. Moreover, the information is received in a continuous stream rather than as a series of discretely described episodes. Thus, while some of the issues associated with what information is actually encoded into memory are similar in the two cases, others are unique to the processing of observed event sequences. More general issues are considered first.

Encoding of Consistent, Inconsistent and Irrelevant Information. As we have noted, aspects of the information one receives are often not interpretable in terms of the event schema one uses to comprehend it. Some aspects may be irrelevant to those contained in the schema, whereas others may actually be incongruent. Still others may be so redundant with the content of the schema that they receive little attention once the schema is activated. Several conceptualizations of the processing of these different types of information have been proposed, two of which are of particular interest.

The first was stated in general terms many years ago by Woodworth and Schlosberg (1954). They postulated that once a schema is used to interpret information, features that are inconsistent with the implications of this schema are appended to the representation of the information as "corrections." Thus, if information about a person's behavior at a restaurant includes a statement that the person left without paying the bill, this latter event ("did not pay the bill") is regarded as a correction that qualifies the encoding of the information as simply "eating at a restaurant."

The second, related notion is the "script-pointer-plus-tag" formulation proposed by Graesser, Gordon and Sawyer (1979; see also Bower, Black, & Turner, 1979; Graesser, 1981). These authors suggest that when people receive information that is interpretable in terms of a prototypic event schema (script), they do not retain the information itself. Rather, they retain only a "pointer" to the generic script, along with an indication of the values of the information that instantiate the script variables. If features of the information do not match attributes of the generic script, and thus cannot be reconstructed later on by applying it, they are appended to the representation as "tags." This formulation differs from Woodworth and Schlosberg's primarily in its assumptions about the representation of schema-consistent features. Suppose one is told that John went to the Boar's Head, ordered a steak, paid his bill and left. All of this information is redundant with events specified in a prototypic "restaurant" script. It is therefore unnecessary to store representations of these individual events in order to reconstruct what happened later on. Rather, one need only remember that the events in combination were those that typically occur when eating at a restaurant (along with an indication that "John," "steak," and "the Boar's Head" are instantiations of variables in the restaurant script ("customer," "meal," and "restaurant," respectively). Only features of the information that are *not* able to be reconstructed from the prototypic schema used to encode it need to be retained. Thus, information that John went to a restaurant, ordered a steak, took off his clothes, paid the bill and left could be stored in memory in terms of a "pointer" to the restaurant script plus a "tag" representing the information that "John took off his clothes before eating." (The representation of this "tag" may of course also have the form of an event schema, or frame, as conceptualized earlier.)

There are several implications of this general notion. For example, suppose subjects who are asked to recall a sequence of events do not access a representation of the actual events themselves, but only a script pointer that permits the events to be reconstructed. This reconstruction is apt to contain instantiations of script-related variables that were not actually specified in the original information received (i.e., default values). In other words, it may contain intrusions of script-relevant attributes, and perhaps even entire events. On the other hand, many details of the original information may not be able to be reconstructed from the prototypic script but are not sufficiently important for understanding what occurred to warrant a "tag". These details may not be recalled at all. Support for these hypotheses was obtained by Bower et al. (1979) as well as Graesser, Woll, Kowalski, and Smith (1980). Moreover, in the former study, information that was presented in a different order than the one dictated by the script tended to be misrecalled in the script-consistent sequence rather than in its original order.

Finally, the frequency of script-consistent intrusion errors increased with the number of sets of information presented that were interpretable in terms of the same script. In other words, errors increased with the likelihood that a general script was in fact activated and used to interpret the information.

A second set of predictions concerns the relative recall of schema-consistent and inconsistent information. That is, inconsistent information may be processed more extensively than script-consistent information in an attempt to interpret it. If this is so, it should be recalled relatively better a short period of time after the information is presented (Craik & Lockhart, 1972). However, if this discrepant information is ultimately not integrated into the representation, but is instead treated as a "tag" or "correction," it may become dissociated from the central representation and therefore may become more difficult to retrieve as time goes on (Woodworth & Schlosberg, 1954; see also Wyer & Srull, 1980). Support for this hypothesis was obtained by Smith and Graesser (1980). That is, they found that inconsistent information was recalled better than consistent information initially; however, the recall of consistent information did not appreciably decrease over time, whereas the recall of inconsistent information eventually dropped to a level below that of the consistent information. Note that these results could also occur if the accessibility of both consistent and inconsistent aspects of the original information decreases at equal rates over time, but the consistent information can be reconstructed accurately whereas the inconsistent information cannot. Either interpretation is consistent with the general implications of the script-pointer-plus-tag hypothesis.

However, two qualifications should be made in considering the generality of this conclusion. First, the predicted decrease in recall of schema-inconsistent over time relative to schema-consistent information is based on the assumption that the inconsistent information is not effectively integrated into the representation, but is peripheral to the central theme. However, it is conceivable that in some cases, inconsistent features of the information *are* integrated into the unified representation being formed. When this occurs, these features should be retained as well as or better than consistent features even after considerable time has elapsed. While this has not been demonstrated in research on the effects of event schemata, it has frequently been found when trait and behavioral information about persons is presented (Hastie & Kumar, 1979; Srull, 1981)—that is, under conditions in which categorical rather than schematic representations are likely to be formed. We elaborate on these conditions in the next section.

Second, circumstances may arise in which information is retained in long-term memory despite the fact it can be reconstructed from the schema applied to it. One such instance may occur when the information is so completely redundant with script-based expectancies that it normally goes without saying. An example might be a statement that John picked up a piece of steak with his fork, opened his mouth, placed the steak into it, and chewed. Such a mundane account of John's eating behavior violates a fundamental axiom of communication, to be informative (Grice, 1975). Therefore, the information may stimulate cognitive activity in an attempt to understand why the communicator is bothering to provide it. This cognitive activity may lead the information to be retained *better* than information that is less consistent with script-based expectancies. Evidence supporting this possibility is provided by Graesser et al. (1980). Note, however, that this effect would probably *not* occur in the processing of visual information such as a videotape of John eating. In this instance, it would be impossible to show that John ate steak without pictorially representing these details. Thus, no communication axiom is violated, and the details may not become part of the representation for reasons implied by the script-pointer-plus-tag hypothesis. Thus, whereas the considerations raised above usually apply to the processing of both visual and verbal information, this is one case in which somewhat different representations would result from information presented in the two modes.

The Encoding of Ongoing Behavior.   Although the script-pointer-plus-tag hypothesis has been formally applied only to the processing of verbal information, it potentially is equally applicable to the representation of events that one learns about through direct observation. In this case, limitations on human processing capacity make it virtually impossible to attend to and remember all of the details of a continuous stream of events and the situational context in which they occur. Moreover (as in the case of verbal information about familiar events), it is usually unnecessary to do so in order to understand what occurred and to reconstruct the events later on with sufficient accuracy to describe them to others or answer questions about them. Rather, one may only need to extract fragments of the continuous event sequence that, if themselves remembered, serve as "pointers" to previously formed event schemata or subschemata that permit one to reconstruct what took place.

In some cases, these fragments may be higher level verbal or symbolic encodings of the information, made at the time of observation ("got a glass of water," "read his mail," etc.). However, it is not necessary that a pointer be verbal. In the absence of external incentives to encode information verbally at the time it is received, the pointers may be static visual frames (e.g., "images") extracted from the continuous action sequence, each containing sufficient features in common with the frame of a previously formed event schema to permit this schema to be activated subsequently and used to reconstruct what went on. Note that in this case, unlike the examples in which verbal information is presented, the instantiations of schema variables in terms of values specified in the information received are inherent parts of the pointer rather than additions to it.

Thus, suppose we see someone get up from his chair, walk to the refrigerator, get a beer and open it, take a drink, and return to his seat. To understand and recall this sequence of actions, we obviously do not need to retain all of the bodily movements that entered into them. All we would need in many cases is a visually or verbally coded "pointer" to the "getting a beer" schema. If for some reason we wished to be sure that we could reconstruct a more detailed representation of the event sequence, we might retain pointers to specific subschemata involved in the general act ("getting up," "walking to the refrigerator," etc.). However, the actual value of these latter pointers over and above a pointer to the more general "getting a beer" schema may be negligible unless some intervening actions occur that are not derivable from this schema. For example, if the person happened to have hopped rather than walked to the refrigerator, or fell over a table on the way, pointers to schemata representing these events would be required. (Alternatively, representations of these events would need to be added as "tags.")

To the extent that a continuous stream of events is not coded verbally, the question remains as to precisely *which* frames in this stream are retained for use as pointers. In the example given above, no single visual frame is sufficient to capture the entire sequence of events. At a minimum, an understanding of what went on would require frames representing an initial state (getting up from the chair), an intermediate event (e.g., the person at the refrigerator in the act of taking out a beer), and a terminal state (the person back in his chair, beer in hand). But which specific frames are in fact extracted, and how can they be identified a priori?

The answer to this question is somewhat controversial. The first systematic investigations of this matter were performed by Newtson and his colleagues (for a summary, see Newtson, 1976). Newtson argued that ongoing behavior is analyzed into action units, each of which is bounded by breakpoints that serve as transitions between the end of one action unit and the beginning of another. The number and size of units into which a given sequence of behavior is analyzed may depend on instructions or other situational factors that lead persons to attend more or less carefully to the information or, alternatively, to believe that they will need to remember the information in more or less detail in order to obtain the objectives for which it is to be used. Thus, subjects may analyze behavior into larger (and hence fewer) units when they are told to form a general impression of the actor or situation described than when they are told to remember the details of the information (Newtson, 1976). (Note that to the extent that each unit refers to a different event schema or subschema, this means that subjects interpret behavior sequences in terms of more abstract subschemata in the first case than in the second.)

In some instances, the number of units into which behavior is analyzed may affect the ability to recall certain aspects of the information. For example, subjects with an impression set (where large units are formed) may sometimes not remember details of the events in the observed sequence as do subjects with a memory set (where smaller units are formed) (Cohen & Ebbesen, 1979). However, this does not mean that a decrement in recall will *always* occur when the behavioral sequence is analyzed into large units. Theoretically, this should depend on whether or not the particular details of the information to be recalled are likely to be inferred from the prototypic schemata that are accessed by features contained in the breakpoint frames.

While the conceptualization underlying Newtson's work seems plausible and evidence reported in support of it is impressive (for reviews, see Ebbesen, 1980; Newtson, 1976; Wyer & Carlston, 1979), a number of ambiguities surround the interpretation of this research (for an extensive critique, see Ebbesen, 1980). Several of these ambiguities result from the procedures used by Newtson to identify breakpoints. Specifically, subjects view videotape of a person's behavior under instructions to press a button whenever one meaningful action ends and another begins. Subjects can obviously perform this task on demand, and the number of units defined on the basis of their button presses may be correlated with the amount of attention they pay to details of the stimulus information. However, as Ebbesen (1980) argues, the breakpoint data provided by the task may be an epiphenomenon, created by the task itself. That is, the breakpoints, or the units of behavior they define, may not necessarily reflect the manner in which the observed events are actually encoded into memory.

To evaluate this possibility, consider two types of evidence that are used to support the assumption that the button-pushing task actually taps a basic cognitive process. First, subjects who have viewed one of two halves of an action sequence can more easily identify the half from which a particular static frame was drawn when this frame occurs near a breakpoint than when it occurs near a nonbreakpoint (Newtson & Engquist, 1976). However, as Ebbesen (1980) notes, this might be due to differences in the inherent discriminability of the frames at these points in the action sequence, and not to differences in the recipient's initial perception or encoding of the information at these points into memory (see Newtson, Engquist, & Bois, 1977).

Second, the number and location of breakpoints appear to vary both with instructional set (Cohen & Ebbesen, 1979) and with the perspective given subjects concerning what the observed event sequence is about (Massad, Hubbard, & Newtson, 1979). These findings are consistent with the assumption that differences in unitizing reflect differences in the interpretation of the actions observed (i.e., differences in the event schemata used to interpret these actions). However, the data do not show a *direct* relation between differences in the units defined on the basis of button presses and differences in interpretation. In fact, this relation may not exist. Rather, a third variable, influenced by the experimental manipulations, could be having simultaneous but independent effects on both. Within-condition analyses performed by Cohen and Ebbesen (1979) suggest that this is the case. Specifically, the number of breakpoints generated by subjects in their study was not correlated with either (a) recognition memory for behavioral details, (b) the extremity of personality ratings of the persons observed, or (c) the confidence expressed about the validity of these ratings. In other words, the number of breakpoints identified was not directly related either to the amount of information extracted from the sequence or to the extremity of impressions formed on the basis of it.

Ebbesen (1980) suggests that although subjects may indeed be "chunking" ongoing event sequences in ways that permit them to understand and reconstruct it, these chunks may not necessarily be represented in memory by transition points between successive actions. It is equally reasonable to assume that each action is represented in memory by a *single* frame that contains its most typical features, that is, features that in combination activate a prototypic schema associated with the action. Thus, in the sequence of events associated with getting up from one's chair, walking to the refrigerator and getting a beer, and so on, the act of walking may not be represented in terms of its boundaries (i.e., a frame of the individual in front of his chair and another of him standing by the refrigerator about to open it). Rather, it may be represented by a frame of the person *in the act* of walking, midway to his destination. This could account for the results described above. That is, instructional sets that increase the attention paid to the stimuli may well affect both the identification of transition points and the number of discrete events that subjects believe to be important, interpret in terms of schemata or subschemata, and encode into memory in terms of visual pointers to these schemata. Therefore, these sets may simultaneously influence both the number of breakpoints and the material retained in memory. However, there may be no inherent relation between these two variables that is independent of the situational factors that affect both.

It is worth noting in this context that the videotaped action sequences used by Newtson in his research typically show relatively simple acts, often single individuals engaged in routine activities. In more complex social situations, such as an interaction between two or more persons, Newtson's approach is difficult to apply both conceptually and empirically. For example, it is unclear whether an interchange between two persons is interpreted as two separate action sequences, each of which pertains to a different one of the individuals and is encoded independently of the other, or whether the interaction is encoded as a single action sequence, with units often defining events that involve both persons in combination. In the latter case, the assumption that successive breakpoints define the boundaries of an interpretable event would not always be valid. That is, a breakpoint that signifies the onset of one person's behavior (e.g., shouting angrily) may be followed temporally by a breakpoint that defines the onset of a different behavior of the other (e.g., walking out of the room) that was initiated before the first person's behavior terminated. Note, however, that the alternative conceptualization, that the events in an ongoing event sequence are each represented in terms of a frame that is *typical* of the action but does not necessarily occur at a transition point, would avoid this dilemma. That is, an observer may encode a frame of the first person in the course of shouting at the second, followed by a frame of the second in the course of leaving the room, followed perhaps by a frame of the first person in the act of throwing something after the second as he exits. These frames, each a pointer to a different event schema, could easily be used to reconstruct the action sequence in terms of the schemata they exemplify without knowing the beginning and endpoints of these individual acts.

What Makes an Action Important?   The postulate that people encode and remember "important" frames in an event sequence is of course rather vacuous unless one can specify a priori *why* something is "important." Presumably a major factor is the extent to which the frame activates a prototypic schema at the time it is experienced. However, not all frames that are capable of activating a schema are likely to be retained. This is presumably because all discrete actions, although individually interpretable, are not equally relevant to an understanding of the overall sequence of events being observed.

A more formal theoretical statement of this possibility, along with empirical data bearing on its implications, is provided by Lichtenstein and Brewer (1980). They argue that behaviors are better remembered if they can be interpreted as instrumental to some objective of the actor, and therefore can be conceptualized in terms of a general "plan-goal" schema. (Such a schema may be conceptually equivalent to a purposive behavior molecule of the sort described in the previous section; that is, [A wants Y; X causes Y; A does X].) In support of this claim, Brewer and Dupree (1983) constructed videotapes of an actress engaged in a series of behaviors in her apartment. Under some conditions, certain target behaviors (e.g., taking a ruler from the drawer of a desk) were instrumental to some goal (setting the clock). In other conditions, however, the frames of the sequence that conveyed this goal were omitted. Observers were subsequently better able to recall the target behaviors if they were ostensibly goal-relevant than if they were not. This superiority in memory was also apparent on a delayed recognition task although not on a recognition task administered immediately after the sequence was observed. This latter finding suggests that not only are goal-irrelevant events less accessible in memory than goal-relevant ones a short time after they occur, but they may drop out of memory completely after a period of time has elapsed.

In summary, it seems reasonable to suppose that observed event sequences, perhaps like verbal descriptions of behavior, are encoded into memory in terms of frames or chunks, and that these frames, if recalled later on, serve as visual pointers to schemata that can be used to reconstruct details of the event sequence. However, it is unclear whether these frames define boundaries of meaningful actions, as postulated by Newtson's unitizing data, or whether they reflect a typical component of the action that permits it to be understood within the sequence of others that precede and follow it. The weak relation of unitizing measures to other indices of recall and interpretation of the information suggest that the latter possibility should be explored more fully.

The Organization of Event Schemata

People can often reproduce both prototypic event sequences and specific series of events they observe in temporal order. It might therefore seem reasonable to assume that the representation of these events in memory reflects this order. That is, the frames comprising an event schema may be stored in a linear, temporally ordered sequence, and people who access one frame cognitively progress through intermediate frames sequentially in order to access others that are temporally distant from it. Thus, if asked where I was at 4 p.m. yesterday afternoon, I am likely not to remember immediately. However, I may nonetheless be able to infer where I must have been by reconstructing the series of events that took place after eating lunch. This suggests that the episodic information we obtain in the course of everyday life seems to be preserved in its natural order. At least, inter-event associations are automatically formed that permit us to reconstruct the order in which events occur, one event serving as a retrieval cue for others that temporally precede or follow it.

Unfortunately, the assumption that event schemata are organized in a "comic-strip," linear fashion runs into difficulty empirically, at least when these schemata are prototypic. In a study by Nottenberg and Shoben (1980), for example, subjects were presented pairs of temporally related events taken from a prototypic script (e.g., the events involved in eating at a restaurant). In some conditions, they were asked in each case to indicate which of the two events came first, and in other conditions, to indicate which came last. A linear "comic-strip" organization would imply that the greater the temporal distance between the two events, the longer it would take to search from one to the other, and therefore the longer it would take to decide their relative position. In contrast, Nottenberg and Shoben obtained typical linear order effects (Banks, 1977). Specifically, response times were shorter when the events were temporally distant than when they were close together. Moreover, pairs of events that occurred early in the sequence were responded to more rapidly when subjects were asked which came first, whereas pairs that occurred later in the sequence were responded to faster than when subjects were asked which came last. These various response time differences were not attributable to differences in the salience or vividness of the individual items involved.

Additional evidence against a linear organization of schema-related events was obtained by Reder and Abelson (see Abelson, 1981). Priming research (e.g., Meyer & Schvaneveldt, 1971, 1976) demonstrates that if two concepts are closely associated, the time required to respond to one of them should decrease when the order has been activated (i.e., "primed") a short time before. However, no evidence of this was obtained by Reder and Abelson when the stimuli involved were schema-related events at different temporal distances from one another.

Thus, neither of two quite different empirical methodologies has yielded support for the hypothesis that events are organized in a temporal order. This conclusion is bolstered by some conceptual ambiguities that arise when one assumes such an organization. These concern the level of abstractness or generality at which prototypic event schemata are typically accessed, and therefore the level at which new event information is encoded and retained. The events involved in eating at a restaurant, for example, may be encoded in terms of general actions such as entering the restaurant, ordering the meal, eating, and leaving. On the other hand, each of these general events (e.g., ordering the meal) consists of more specific acts (asking for the menu, receiving it, deciding what to eat, telling the waiter, etc.) and these, in turn, may be further subdivided. The assumption that an event schema is temporally organized would require that all of these detailed events be represented in the sequence, and that individuals wade through all of them in order to decide whether asking for the bill occurred before asking for the menu. This seems unlikely. It seems necessary to postulate an organization that allows the cognizer to enter the representation at any level of abstractness and to process information at this level without being required to access more specific levels.

Most of the problems noted above could be handled by postulating a hierarchical representation of events and subevents of the sort depicted in Figure 2.1, where each element is "tagged" to denote its temporal location at each level of the hierarchy. Representations of events at the most general level (i.e., entering the restaurant, eating, leaving) may carry tags that denote the general point in the sequence at which they occur (e.g., "early," "middle," "late"). Representations at more specific levels, which are subordinate to the general ones, may have not only these tags but also a tag denoting their temporal position among those within the more general event. Still more specific representations may have additional tags that differentiate them from others at even lower levels of abstractness, and so on. Now, when two events are to be compared, subjects may

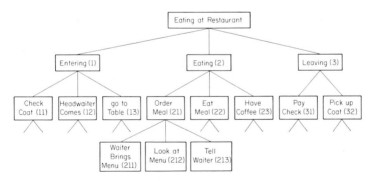

FIG. 2.1.   Hierarchical organization of "eating at a restaurant" schema. Numbers in parentheses denote time tags. The first tag denotes the temporal position of the event at the highest level of abstractness, the second denotes its temporal position at the next highest level, and so on.

first check their tags referring to the most general level. If these are different, a decision can be made immediately. If they are the same, the second tag of each event (indicating its position at the next lower level of abstractness in the hiarchy) is compared, and so on until a point is reached at which the tags being compared differ.

The above conceptualization could account for the general linear order effects obtained by Nottenberg and Shoben, and yet would allow for the possibility of reconstructing sequences in temporal order. That is, events that are temporally closer together generally require a greater number of comparisons in order to be distinguished, and thus the time required to make the discrimination will be greater. If the coding of the tags reflects their relative temporal position ("early," "late," etc.), a "translation" is required when the question asked (e.g., "which comes later . . .") carries a description ("later") that differs from the tags associated with the events being compared ("early"). If the translation takes time, the other results reported by Nottenberg and Shoben can also be predicted. In addition, because the tags at any given level of abstractness are temporally ordered, it is possible to construct the sequence of events at any given level by comparing the tags corresponding to this level, bypassing events at more specific levels. Finally, a hierarchical representation that allows for different strengths of association between concepts can account for the fact that certain events in the sequence may be more accessible in memory than others, and that the most accessible events are not always at the beginning. Thus, thinking about a restaurant may not activate events at the start of the sequence (i.e., frames concerned with entering) as quickly as those at some intermediate point (i.e., eating the meal) that are more closely associated with the central concept.

The above conceptualization has additional implications. For example, it implies that temporally adjacent events will be compared less quickly if they are part of the same superordinate event (i.e., "waiter bringing the menu" vs. "reading the menu") than if they are equally close temporally but are part of different superordinate events (e.g., "sitting down at the table" vs. "waiter bringing the menu"). Moreover, the time required to compare one event with a second at the same level of generality (e.g., to compare "entering the restaurant" with "ordering the meal") should be the same as that required to compare the first event with a more specific one that is subordinate to the second (e.g., to compare "entering the restaurant" with "reading the menu"). These and other implications of the conceptualization should of course be tested before the proposed conceptualization can be taken too seriously.

Caution should also be taken in concluding that the representation of newly acquired event information is also hierarchical. The interpretation of a sequence of observed events often requires several different and perhaps unrelated schemata, the order of which is not predictable from any previously formed schema. In fact, however, there are some intuitive reasons to suppose that a temporally ordered representation of such event sequences is unlikely. For example, if such a representation existed, the ability to recall the temporal order of occurrence of events should be maintained over time. However, whereas one can often recall accurately the order of one's activities at work yesterday (e.g., working on a paper, speaking to a student, teaching class, making a phone call, etc.) if asked today, this accuracy is unlikely to be very great a month from now, even if one is reminded of the individual events that occurred. The assumption of a linear organization of the information in memory would have difficulty accounting for such a phenomenon. In contrast, a hierarchical model could account for it by assuming that memory for the "time tags" associated with events in the sequence decay more rapidly than does memory for the events themselves. However, no research has yet been done to demonstrate that results comparable to Nottenberg and Shoben's would occur in responding to a newly experienced event sequence that requires several independent schemata to interpret it. This is a matter worth investigating.

Search Processes in Inference Making

Research bearing on the organization in memory of newly acquired event sequences that involve the use of multiple schemata was performed by Allen and Ebbesen (1981) in the context of investigating the memory search processes underlying judgments. Suppose that after witnessing a sequence of events, one is asked unexpectedly to judge the intelligence of one of the persons observed. In the absence of any a priori reason to do so, this judgment is unlikely to have been made spontaneously in the course of initially processing the information. Consequently, one must retrieve one's representation of the information in memory and search it for relevant material, at the time the judgment is requested. The question is whether this search is linear or hierarchical. A second question is whether the search is exhaustive, or whether it stops once information sufficient to make a judgment has been retrieved.

To investigate these matters, subjects observed a videotaped segment of ongoing behavior. The sequence varied in length (either 30, 60, 90, or 180 seconds). However, pooled over subjects, its content was controlled within each segment length. Afterwards, subjects were asked either behavioral detail questions (e.g., "did she hold the spoon in her hand?") or trait questions ("was she critical?"). Consider first the verification of behavioral details. The mean position of a given detail in a segment increases with its length. Therefore, the assumption that subjects search serially through a linear, temporally ordered representation implies that the mean time required to verify the event will increase with segment length, or with the amount of material in memory that one must search through before coming upon the detail to be verified. This is in fact what happened.

In the case of trait inferences, predictions are potentially more complicated. More than one event in the observed segment may have implications for the trait, and so the average position of the *first* relevant event may be similar regardless of overall segment length. Therefore, if observers perform a serial search only until they find the first relevant piece of information, and use this information without looking further, response time should not be a function of segment length. On the other hand, suppose subjects perform an exhaustive search, attempting to identify all relevant information before making an inference. Then, an increase in response time with segment length would be expected. It seems intuitively reasonable that whether the search is partial or exhaustive will depend on the type of trait being inferred. Based on normative data, Allen and Ebbesen divided stimuli into "concrete" traits, or those typically inferred from a single sample of behavior (e.g., argumentative, cheerful, etc.), and "abstract" traits, requiring many samples to verify (e.g., objective, noncommittal, etc.). As expected, the time required to infer "abstract" traits increased markedly with segment length, whereas the time to infer "concrete" traits was quite independent of segment length.

These data are therefore consistent with the assumption of a temporally ordered representation of an event sequence with subjects searching serially through successive frames either to verify details or to make inferences. Unfortunately, they are consistent with a hierarchical organization of the information as well. That is, suppose the events are organized as in Figure 2.1, and subjects engage in a top-down search (beginning at the central node and working down). Assume further that (a) the number of paths emanating from the central node increases with segment length, (b) each pathway contains some information relevant to the trait being inferred, and (c) pathways are searched sequentially in random order. Then, in the verification task, the average number of pathways one must search in order to find a particular behavioral detail, and thus the average time required, will increase with segment length. In the trait inference task, this would also be true when traits are abstract, since inferences of these traits require a sequential search of all pathways. However, concrete traits would be identified quickly on the basis of information contained in a single pathway, regardless of which one is traversed first, and so the time required would therefore not depend on segment length.

Therefore, Allen and Ebbesen's data are consistent with either a linear representation of event sequences or a hierarchical representation. As noted previously, the data reported by Nottenberg and Shoben (implying a nonlinear organization of events within a prototypic schema) do not preclude the possibility that a series of newly experienced events is organized in memory linearly, in the order they occur. However, in the absence of data to the contrary, the assumption that a hierarchical organization underlies the representation of both prototypic events and specific, newly experienced event sequences seems most parsimonious.

Conclusions

Research and theory on the representation of event sequences suggest two general conclusions. First, new information, presented either visually or verbally, may be represented as a series of "pointers" to prototypic event schemata that can be used to understand and reconstruct the events described, accompanied when necessary by "tags" denoting objects or events that cannot be derived from the event schemata alone. When the information is verbal, these pointers may also be coded verbally, consisting of the name of the schema used to interpret the event and an indication of the particular features of the information that instantiate schema variables. When the information is presented visually, as when one observes ongoing behavior, these pointers may be static, visually coded frames ("images") extracted from the stream of events observed, the features of which can be instantiated in terms of prototypic schemata and are sufficient to activate these schemata for use in reconstructing the original event sequence.

Second, the organization of prototypic event schemata may not be linear (temporal). Rather, the frames comprising the representation may be organized hierarchically, with frames denoting concrete or specific actions nested within frames pertaining to more general ones, and with tags appended to denote the relative point in time at which the events occur. A similar hierarchical organization may govern the representation of specific event sequences one experiences through observation. However, this possibility has not been empirically investigated and so a linear representation of this latter information cannot be discounted.

One important qualification should be placed on these various conclusions. That is, most of the research and theory considered in this section is based on assumptions that subjects receive and process the information with the objective of comprehending the information or remembering it, and not with any more specific goal in mind. When subjects receive event information with the objective of evaluating the persons participating in these events, or forming an impression of these persons, the nature of the representation formed may be quite different. We consider this possibility in the next section.

THE COGNITIVE REPRESENTATION OF INDIVIDUAL PERSONS

The manner in which information about persons and groups is represented in memory, and the effect of this representation on judgments, have been of concern in social psychology for decades, beginning with the traditional interest in stereotyping (for a review, see Hamilton, 1979) and Asch's (1946) seminal work on person impressions. Although it is almost universally assumed that integrated representations of both specific individuals and prototypic ones exist in memory, the precise nature of this representation has remained elusive. Several different types of representations may be formed, of the same or different individuals, and the activation of any given type may depend on the purpose for which the recalled material is to be used. In this section, we outline alternative types of representations of persons that may exist. Then, we review research bearing on the conditions in which the representations are apt to be formed.

General Considerations

The information we acquire about people is obviously of several types and comes from a variety of sources. One source may be interactions we have had with these persons, or observations of them interacting with others. Such information has the form of an event sequence of the sort described in the preceding section. However, when someone has the a priori objective of forming an impression of a person in a given situation, or of judging a particular characteristic of that person, the representation formed from this sequence may not necessarily have the structure and content of an event schema. It may nevertheless include a visual representation of the person's appearance as well as behavioral characteristics and codings of what the person said. Moreover, it may include subjective affective reactions to the person, or thoughts one has had during the course of the interaction. (We elaborate on this latter possibility later in this chapter when we discuss the representation of oneself.)

Information about persons is also obtained from written and oral communications. This information may include verbal descriptions of behavior, abilities or general personality characteristics, social roles or group memberships. Because verbal stimulus materials are generally easier to present in laboratory situations than are visual descriptions of ongoing behavior, and since their characteristics are easier to control or manipulate, the bulk of research on the representation of persons has employed these materials. It is legitimate to ask whether the representations formed from verbal stimulus information are similar to those formed on the basis of personal encounters with people outside the laboratory. The working assumption of researchers in this area seems to be that information, whatever the form in which it is received, is transformed into a common code and, once coded, is organized similarly in memory. A related assumption is that information about people that is obtained through direct observation and experience is spontaneously encoded in terms of traits, behavioral descriptions, or subjective reactions (e.g., "this person is making me nervous"), and that these encodings are then organized in much the same manner as verbal descriptions presented by an experimenter. If this is so, research on person memory using verbal materials is simply tapping a second stage of the overall process of person impression formation. Still a third stage may involve the combining of the implications of different verbal encodings into a single evaluation of the person, although there is some controversy as to whether existing models (e.g., Anderson, 1971, 1974) can actually capture this process (see Wyer & Carlston, 1979).

In the discussion to follow, we consider first the manner in which representations of persons are formed on the basis of observations of ongoing behavior, and then the nature of representations formed from verbal information. As we will see, the implications of these two bodies of research are inconsistent.

However, a major limitation of the following discussion should be noted at the outset. That is, we will concentrate on the representations formed from trait and behavioral information, largely because most of the existing literature focuses on this type of information. In doing so, we will ignore a major type of representation, namely, of a person's physical appearance. This is unfortunate for several reasons. First, an "image" of a person's appearance may well be a central ingredient of the overall representation of a person, around which other types of information are organized. Second, such a representation is inherently schematic, and thus represents an important exception to the general conclusion we draw in this section, that representations of individual persons are primarily categorical in nature. However, because there is a dearth of research and theory bearing directly on the representation of appearance information, we forego a consideration of this topic in the hope that this conspicuous gap in existing knowledge will ultimately be filled.

Representations Formed from Observed Behaviors

The cognitive representation of observed events under conditions in which subjects' objective is simply to comprehend these events was discussed at length in the preceding section. However, when the observer's objective is to form an impression of a person who is involved in the events, the representation formed may be quite different. That is, it may consist in part of trait descriptions of the person, or a general evaluation (e.g., as a "nice guy" or a "jerk"). Some of these traits may be implied directly by the person's behavior and may be assigned to the person at the time this behavior is observed. Others, however, may be inferred indirectly, based on assumptions about what traits are typically interrelated (Rosenberg & Sedlak, 1972).

It is conceivable, of course, that both types of representations—a representation of an observed event sequence and one of the person involved in the events—may be formed simultaneously and may coexist in memory. Ebbesen (1980) also suggests that the information obtained through direct observation of event sequences is subject to dual coding under conditions in which the observer wishes to form an impression of the actor. One code may be concrete and episodic in nature, whereas the other may be abstract and semantically based, consisting of traits and general behaviors and with a structure similar to that we will consider in a moment. Moreover, these representations are stored and reactivated independently.

Results reported by Cohen and Ebbesen (1979) are consistent with this possibility. Subjects viewed a videotaped sequence of an actor's behavior under instructions either to form an impression of the actor's personality (impression set conditions) or to remember what the actor did (memory set conditions). Subsequently, both groups made trait ratings of the actor, and the intercorrelations of these ratings were then determined under each instructional condition separately. In addition, the authors obtained normative co-occurrence estimates (i.e., estimates of the likelihood that a person with one trait would have the other). These latter estimates presumably reflect the semantic associations among the traits that are independent of any specific observations. (In fact, they appear to be based largely on general evaluative considerations; traits that are similar in favorableness are believed more likely to co-occur than traits that differ; see Rosenberg & Sedlak, 1972.)

The intercorrelations of trait ratings made under memory set conditions were relatively low, and moreover were unrelated to the corresponding correlations obtained under impression set conditions ($r = .08$). On the other hand, the pattern of intertrait correlations under an impression set, unlike that under a memory set, was similar to the pattern of normative co-occurrence estimates. In combination, these data suggest that the ratings made under memory set conditions (when subjects had not expected to evaluate the actor's personality) were based on a review of the representation formed of the original behavioral sequence, as suggested earlier in this chapter. Thus, their trait ratings were each based on different behaviors in the sequence and so they were not highly correlated. In contrast, subjects with an impression set may have attempted to form an abstract impression of the person at the time they observed the events. In doing so, they may have assigned the person to a general evaluative category (i.e., "nice guy") or may have assigned the person a particular trait that was applicable for encoding a behavior that seemed representative of the sequence observed. This general characteristic, along with the subjects' implicit personality theories, may then have been used to make other trait inferences quite independently of the specific implications of the original behaviors they observed. This interpretation suggests that the representation formed from observed behaviors under person impression conditions may be relatively simple. That is, it may be centered around one or two traits, inferred from a small subset of behaviors that are particularly favorable or unfavorable. Later on, other attributes of the person may be inferred indirectly from this representation on the basis of general semantic considerations. This is consistent with conclusions drawn by Srull and Wyer (1979) using another research paradigm (see also Wyer et al., 1984).

Representations Formed from Verbal Information

The research by Ebbesen and his colleagues suggests that subjects with the objective of forming an impression of a person construct an abstract representation of the person that is used to make trait inferences independently of the original information presented. However, it does not indicate the precise nature of the representation that is formed. Nor does it suggest the conditions in which behavioral information about a person is spontaneously encoded in terms of trait concepts. Research on the nature of representations formed from verbal descriptions of traits and behaviors provides some insight into these matters. First, we outline some of the alternative structural representations of a person that might be formed on the basis of trait and/or behavioral information. After this, we review the literature bearing on the formation of each.

Theoretical Considerations.   The behaviors and traits comprising the representation of a person are likely to have little if any spatial or temporal relationship. Rather, they may simply be a list of features, and the representation of them in memory may therefore be categorical rather than schematic. Although associations among these features (traits and behaviors) may sometimes be formed, the nature of these associations and the conditions in which they occur are not as obvious as one might expect.

Theoretical formulations of the representation of trait and behavioral information have typically made use of concepts suggested by associative network models of semantic memory (Anderson & Bower, 1973; Collins & Loftus, 1975; see Hastie, 1980; Srull, 1981, and Wyer & Carlston, 1979, for applications of such a model to social information processing). That is, they assume a central concept of the physical referent (e.g., person) denoted by the name of the person and perhaps a representation of the person's physical appearance (i.e., a visual image). This concept, representated by a node, is connected by pathways to "feature" nodes representing various traits or behaviors of the person.[8] The pathway between two nodes is presumably formed as a result of thinking about the concepts or features denoted by these nodes in relation to one another, thus establishing an association between them. The length or width of the pathway is assumed to reflect the strength of this association.

In this regard, feature nodes may be connected not only to the central person node, but also to one another. As we shall see, whether or not these latter connections exist has important theoretical and empirical implications for the type and number of features that are recalled, and much of the research conducted to date may be viewed as bearing on the conditions in which these connections are formed.

Given this general approach, several alternative structures for describing the representation of trait and behavioral information are possible. Each reflects somewhat different assumptions about how the information is processed at the time it is received. To convey these differences, assume that one receives information about a series of behaviors a person has manifested in various situations. On a priori grounds, any of the following alternative possibilities seem reasonable.

1. The behaviors may first be spontaneously interpreted as instances of traits that they exemplify, and these traits may then be integrated into an overall

---

[8]The name of the person, and a visual image of his/her appearance, may of course also constitute features. They therefore should technically be separated from the central object node, being connected to it by pathways in much the same manner as other features (see Anderson & Bower, 1973). However, for simplicity in the present discussion, this distinction will not be made.

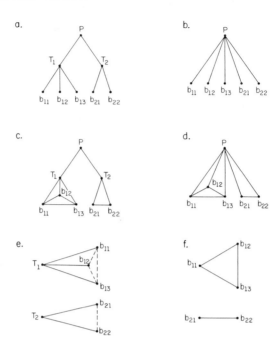

FIG. 2.2.   Alternative types of organization of trait and behavioral information in memory. T_i denotes trait i, and b_{ij} denotes the jth ·behavior exemplifying i.

representation (or "impression") of the person.[9] Such a representation could be described in network terms in the manner shown in Figure 2.2a, where P is the central person node, T_i is one of the traits assigned to P, and b_{ij} is the jth behavior associated with T_i.

2. The assumption that traits are fundamental ingredients of impressions has been pervasive in the social psychological literature from the time of Asch (1946), and underlies much of the early work by Anderson and others on impression formation (for reviews, see Anderson, 1974; Wyer & Carlston, 1979). However, this assumption may not always be correct. Gordon (1982) suggests that in many cases, behavioral information about persons may be organized according to the situational context in which it occurs (i.e., at home, in the office, etc.) rather than in terms of more general, cross-situational trait categories. Moreover, it is conceivable that in many instances, behavioral information will not be interpreted in terms of *any* higher order trait concept unless there is

---

[9]In some instances, this organization is assumed to be with reference to a prototypic person who possesses the configuration of traits described. However, the empirical evidence bearing on the validity of this assumption (e.g., Cantor & Mischel, 1977, 1979) is unimpressive, for reasons we indicate presently.

some explicit or implicit demand to do so. This notion is of course not new. Self-perception theory (Bem, 1972) is based on the assumption that people do not spontaneously attribute traits to themselves unless they are asked to do so, at which time they use their most recent relevant behavior as a basis for these judgments. Similar tendencies may exist in responding to information about others. That is, in the absence of explicit information about a person's traits, one may interpret the person's behavior without spontaneously identifying it as relevant to a particular trait. To this extent, the representation of a person described by a set of behaviors (manifested in a particular situation) might be similar to that shown in Figure 2.2b.

3. In the representations described in Figures 2.2a and 2.2b, the behaviors are associated with one another only through a more central node denoting either a trait (Fig. 2.2a) or the person who manifests them (Fig. 2.2b). This implicitly assumes that the behaviors are not thought about in relation to one another. In many instances, however, subjects may spontaneously recognize the semantic similarity of the behaviors. In such an event, the representation formed would be similar to that shown in Figures 2.2c or 2.2d, where each cluster indicates a set of semantically related behaviors that have been thought of in relation to one another. (In some conditions, subjects may also form associations between behaviors that are *not* semantically related, or do not exemplify the same trait. These possibilities are considered presently.)

4. The above representations all assume that information is organized around a central ''person'' node, with pathways connecting this node to specific attributes of the person being described. This implies that subjects attempt to form a single integrated impression of the person. However, it is conceivable that although subjects think about semantically related behaviors in relation to one another, or in relation to the traits they exemplify, they do not attempt to organize the information into an integrated impression. If this is true, sets of related behaviors, or trait-behavior clusters, may be formed and stored independently in memory as separate units, without any inherent organization of the units themselves. Such an assumption would be consistent with the information-processing model proposed by Wyer and Srull (1980, 1981). They conceptualize long-term memory as consisting of a set of content-addressable storage bins, each containing information about a particular person or object. Each unit of information in a bin (which may be either a judgment, a single behavior or trait description, or an interrelated set of traits and/or behaviors) is stored and retrieved independently. According to this conceptualization, the representation formed on the basis of the behavioral information might be similar to that shown in Figure 2.2e (if behaviors are spontaneously encoded in terms of traits) or Figure 2.2f (if they are not).

The various representations described in Figure 2.2 differ in three general respects. One concerns whether or not a single representation is formed, with traits and behaviors connected through a central person node, or whether trait-behavior clusters are formed, stored, and retrieved independently of one another. The second is whether or not behaviors are in fact encoded and organized in terms of traits. The third is whether behaviors are connected to one another only through their common association with a higher order trait or person node, or whether more direct interitem associations are formed as well (cf. Ross & Bower, 1981). The question is how to distinguish among these various possibilities.[10]

The first question is the easiest to evaluate. That is, if subjects form a single representation of a person described by information (see Fig. 2.2a), instructions to recall information about this person should lead the entire representation to be retrieved as a unit, and consequently should lead to better memory for all features of the representation relative to conditions in which a single representation is not constructed. On the other hand, if clusters of related features (e.g., trait-behavior clusters such as those shown in Fig. 2.2e) are formed and stored independently, without being connected to a central person node, instructions to recall the information should not have these general effects. Rather, memory for particular features should be facilitated only if other items in the particular cluster containing them happen to be recalled.

Whether behaviors are organized in terms of trait categories can be determined directly only under conditions in which trait as well as behavioral information has been presented. That is, suppose behaviors are associated with traits in the manner described by Fig. 2.2a or 2.2e. Then, the trait adjectives describing these traits (if recalled themselves) should serve as retrieval cues for recall of the behaviors connected to them. If this is the case, the likelihood of recalling a behavior should be greater if a trait adjective associated with it is recalled than if it is not.

Whether behaviors are associated with one another only by virtue of their common relationship to a higher-order trait or person node, or whether direct interbehavior connections are formed, is more difficult to evaluate. However, theoretical and empirical work by Anderson and Bower (1973) and Rundus (1971) provides a possible solution. That is, once a network is formed, components of the representation are presumably accessed (and therefore recalled) by

---

[10]As others (e.g., Anderson, 1976) have noted, an inherent problem exists in distinguishing between (a) differences in the manner in which information is organized in memory (structure) and (b) differences in the process of accessing or retrieving it. This is particularly true when recall data are used as a basis for inferring these differences. For every interpretation of a difference is recalled information in terms of a difference in its organization in memory (assuming a given process of accessing it), there is likely to be an equivalent interpretation in terms of differences in the process of retrieving the information (assuming a given organization). In fact, Raaijmakers and Shiffrin's (1981) model of retrieval processes, which has been applied successfully to a variety of recall phenomena, may be able in principle to account for much of the data to be reported in this chapter. Nonetheless, it seems conceptually useful to consider the data in terms of its implications for structure, with the caveat that a process model may also be applicable.

traversing the pathways connecting them. If no interbehavior connections exist, as in Fig. 2.2a, behaviors can be accessed only by traversing the pathways to each from a higher-order node, returning each time to this node before continuing the search. Under these conditions, the theoretical formulations proposed by Rundus and by Anderson and Bower imply that the greater the number of items connected to a given node, the less likely it is that any particular item in the set will be recalled. (For the theoretical bases for these predictions, see Anderson & Bower 1973; Rundus, 1971.)

In contrast, suppose interbehavior associations do exist, such that every behavior added to a set makes connections to others in the same set. This implies that the number of pathways connected to any given behavioral node increases with the number of items in the set. If the likelihood of recalling a given behavior is a function of the number of ways of accessing it, the likelihood of recalling a given behavior should *increase* with the number of behaviors in the set. If this conceptualization is valid, the extent to which interbehavior connections are formed under a given set of experimental conditions can be evaluated by varying the number of behaviors exemplifying each trait in the overall sample of those presented. That is, a negative effect of set size would imply the absence of these associations, whereas a positive effect would indicate their existence.

Each of the structures described in Fig. 2.2 may characterize the representation formed of a person on the basis of trait and/or behavioral information. In the discussion to follow, we attempt to identify the conditions, if any, in which each type of representation is likely, based upon the criteria outlined above and the empirical evidence reported to date.

The Organization of Trait Information

Studies in which behavioral information about persons is presented are most germane to the issues outlined above. However, two studies in which only trait information was provided are nonetheless worth noting. While both have implications of the extent to which trait information is organized around a central node, one primarily concerns the use of person prototypes as bases for organizing the information, and the second concerns the role of evaluative factors in this organization.

The Use of Prototypes as Bases for Organization. It is often assumed that when information about a person contains features that characterize a particular type of person (i.e., a "prototype"), this prototype will be activated and used as a basis for organizing the information presented and making inferences about the person described. It is certainly reasonable to assume that representations of prototypic individuals (e.g., the "typical" reactionary or college professor) do exist in memory. However, the extent to which such representations that are *spontaneously* activated by information pertaining to individual persons is unclear both theoretically and empirically. On the theoretical side, prototypic representations are likely to be categorical rather than schematic, and therefore are unlikely to be spontaneously activated by features that exemplify them for reasons noted earlier in this chapter. On the empirical side, the only studies that bear directly on this matter, by Cantor and Mischel (1977, 1979), are equivocal. In one study, for example (Cantor & Mischel, 1977), subjects read a series of trait adjectives that conveyed either extraversion or introversion under instructions that they described a particular person. The authors assumed that these adjectives would activate a representation of either a prototypic extrovert or a prototypic introvert, and that this prototype would then guide both subjects' inferences about the person and their memory for the original information. Consistent with predictions, subjects inferred the target to have characteristics that were consistent with the assumed prototype, and made errors on a recognition memory task that were biased in a manner implied by this prototype.

However, these data are not diagnostic with respect to the cognitive mediators of the effects obtained. In fact, data pertaining to both inferences and recognition errors could be based on the semantic similarity between the stimulus adjectives originally presented and the recognition items. For example, subjects who remember that the target person was described by adjectives that had something to do with extroversion may infer that other adjectives conveying extroversion are also applicable, based solely on the semantic similarity of these adjectives to one another. Moreover, when they are uncertain about whether a particular adjective was actually presented, they may make a guess, based upon their recollection that most of the adjectives presented had something to do with extroversion. However, this does not mean that a representation of a prototypic *person* (e.g., a "typical extravert") was activated and used to organize the information presented. Nor does it indicate that an integrated representation of the person described by the information was even formed. In fact, explicitly telling subjects that the target was an extravert or an introvert, which should have activated any prototypic representation that exists for organizing the information, had no effect on either inferences or recognition errors over and above the trait objective information.

Organization Around an Evaluative Concept.   One general basis for organizing trait information may be evaluative. That is, subjects with the objective of forming an impression of someone may focus on the evaluative aspects of the information in order to decide whether or not they would like the person. The evaluative (favorable or unfavorable) theme that emerges may then be used to organize subsequent information. A study by Hartwick (1979) bears on this possibility. Subjects received information under instructions either to form an impression of the person described by the information (impression set) or simply to remember the information (memory set). The information presented consisted of a series of ten trait adjectives. After receiving this information, subjects were given a recognition memory task containing nonpresented items (distractors) that varied systematically in both their descriptive and their evaluative consistency with the original ones. (Thus, if the trait adjectives presented were favorable and denoted honesty, some distractor items in the recognition task were similar to those presented in both respects. However, others either conveyed honesty but were unfavorable, conveyed dishonesty and were favorable, or conveyed dishonesty and were unfavorable.) Subjects were less able to distinguish presented items from distractors that were either evaluatively or descriptively consistent with them than from distractors that were inconsistent with them in one or both respects. More important, telling subjects to form an impression of the person increased the effect of evaluative consistency on discriminability but did *not* affect the influence of descriptive consistency. These findings suggest that instructions to form an impression of a person on the basis of trait adjectives led subjects to extract a general indication of the person's likeableness from the evaluative implications of these adjectives, but did not increase their sensitivity to the adjectives' descriptive implications. We return to this possibility later.

Although Hartwick's results are provocative, his study, like Cantor and Mischel's, does not necessarily indicate that the trait information presented was organized in memory around a more general concept of the person described. Subjects under an impression set may simply extract the evaluative implications of the information and combine them mechanistically into an evaluative judgment of the person in a manner similar to that proposed by Anderson (1971). Then, having done this, they may use the evaluative implications of this implicit judgment as a basis for guessing what items were presented in the recognition task. In other words, the difference identified by Hartwick could reflect an output bias rather than a difference in the organization of the original information in memory. (While signal detection procedures were employed in this study, the design did not allow effects on sensitivity (d') and effects on the criterion (β) to be separated.)

The Organization of Behavioral Information

In general, recognition measures are less likely to reflect differences in the organization of information than are free recall or cued recall measures. This is because they do not reflect the relative difficulty of retrieving information from memory and therefore are insensitive to differences in the relative accessibility of information that is organized in a hierarchical network of the sort described in Fig. 2.2. The most definitive research on the organization of behavioral information has therefore typically employed free recall procedures.

One of the first and most provocative studies of this sort was performed by Hamilton, Katz, and Leirer (1980). Subjects were exposed to a series of behaviors under both person impression and memory set conditions. Despite the fact that impression set subjects were not given any indication that they would have to remember the information at the time they first received it, their subsequent recall of these behaviors was significantly greater than that of subjects who were explicitly told to remember them.

One interpretation of this finding is that subjects with an impression set tended to organize the behaviors into an integrated representation of the person being described, and this organization facilitated their recall later on. However, the results are undiagnostic with respect to the nature of this representation. On one hand, the behaviors could be spontaneously encoded and organized in terms of the categories they exemplified, with these categories then being organized around a central person node in the manner described in Figure 2.2a. Alternatively, each behavior could be independently connected to the central person node as in Figure 2.2b. Or, a person impression set, unlike a memory set, may lead subjects to attend to the semantic similarities among the behaviors, leading to interitem associations of the sort shown in Figure 2.2e. Any of these representations, if retrieved as a single unit, could produce a general increase in the recall of the behaviors over and above that occurring under memory set conditions. On the other hand, none of these representations may underlie the effects reported. That is, subjects may simply engage in a deeper level of semantic processing of the individual items under an impression set than under a memory set, and this may facilitate recall of the items (Craik & Lockhart, 1972) even if interitem associations are not formed.

A more recent study (Wyer & Gordon, 1982, Experiment 1) is somewhat more diagnostic. In this study, subjects run under both memory set and person impression conditions first received a series of trait adjectives describing a person, followed by behaviors of the person that varied in both their evaluative and descriptive consistency with these adjectives. They subsequently recalled more behaviors under person impression than under memory set conditions, consistent with Hamilton et al.'s findings. However, they did *not* recall more trait adjectives under person impression conditions. This combination of findings argues against a representation of the sort described in Fig. 2.2a. That is, since the only access to behaviors in such a representation is through the traits associated with them, the formation of such a representation should facilitate the recall of *both* traits and behaviors. This was not the case.

Thus, the results seem more consistent with a representation of the sort shown in Figure 2.2e. That is, a person impression set may stimulate subjects to attend to the semantic implications of the information, and therefore to associate behaviors with the traits that they exemplify. Thus, to the extent that the traits are recalled, they may be more likely to serve as retrieval cues for the behaviors under these conditions than under a memory set. However, the traits themselves may be stored and retrieved independently of one another under both instructional conditions, and therefore may be recalled equally well in each.

Supplementary analyses of Wyer and Gordon's data provided further support for the above conclusion. That is, the extent to which a trait serves as a retrieval cue for a behavior may be indicated by the difference between (a) the conditional probability of recalling the behavior given that a descriptively consistent trait adjective was recalled and (b) the conditional probability of recalling the behavior given that such an adjective was not recalled. This difference was .26 under person impression conditions, but was only .01 under memory set conditions.[11]

The Formation of Interbehavior Associations.   The above retrieval cue effects provide evidence that when trait and behavior information are both provided, behaviors are organized in terms of the traits. This organization could account for Hamilton et al.'s results. However, these results could also be due to the formation of direct connections among semantically similar behaviors that occur instead of or in addition to the organization of these behaviors in terms of trait concepts. The existence of these interitem connections may be evaluated on the basis of considerations described earlier. That is, if the items in a trait category are not thought of in relation to one another (or, in network terms, if items are connected to a central node alone), the likelihood of recalling any given item should decrease as the number of items in the category increases. On the other hand, if direct associations exist among the items in a category, the likelihood of recalling a given item may *increase* with the number of items presented in the same trait category.

Several studies provide an indication of the conditions in which direct interitem connections are likely to be formed. Two factors seem intuitively important to consider, and their influence has been demonstrated empirically. First, it seems reasonable to suppose that when subjects are explicitly or implicitly encouraged to organize behaviors in terms of trait concepts, they may do so without thinking about the behaviors in relation to one another, and so interbehavior associations are unlikely. Two studies, by Gilligan and Bower (Bower, personal communication, March 1978) and by Gordon (1982) support this possibility. In Gilligan and Bower's study, subjects were explicitly asked to sort 16 behaviors into trait categories. The behaviors varied over conditions such that either eight behaviors pertained to each of two traits, four behaviors pertained to each of four traits, or two behaviors pertained to each of eight traits. Subjects' subsequent recall of the behaviors decreased as the number of behaviors per trait increased. This suggests that the behaviors were associated only through their common relation to the trait they exemplified.

---

[11]In addition, the probability of recalling a behavior under person impression conditions was unexpectedly facilitated by recalling a trait adjective with which it was descriptively inconsistent, provided it was *evaluatively* consistent with this adjective (i.e., similar in favorableness). Perhaps when a person's behavior is descriptively inconsistent but evaluatively consistent with a trait of the person, it is treated as an "exception" but is nonetheless connected to the trait node around which the behavior is organized. Consequently, the trait may serve as a retrieval for these behaviors as well as descriptively consistent ones, although not for behaviors that are *both* evaluatively and descriptively inconsistent.

In the study by Gordon (1982), subjects with a person impression set were first given trait adjective descriptions of a person, followed by different numbers of behaviors that exemplified these traits. Again, the likelihood of recalling a given behavior decreased as the number of behaviors exemplifying the same trait increased. This suggests that when subjects with an impression set are given expectancies for the traits of the person being described, they encode the person's behaviors in terms of traits without thinking about the behaviors in relation to one another, producing negative set size effects of the sort obtained by Gilligan and Bower.

However, now suppose subjects are not given explicit information about the traits of the person being described, but only a description of his/her behaviors. In these conditions, it is less clear (1) whether subjects will spontaneously encode the behaviors in terms of traits and (2) whether they will form direct associations among the behaviors themselves. The answer to the first question appears to be affirmative. The answer to the second depends on whether the traits to which the behaviors pertain are similar in favorableness. In two additional experiments, Gordon (1981) presented subjects with behaviors of a person without previously specifying the traits to which they pertained. However, in one study, all of the traits exemplified by these behaviors were favorable, whereas in the second study, the traits differed in favorableness. When the traits were similar in favorableness, the likelihood of recalling a behavior decreased with trait category set size, as in the previous studies. This effect suggests that subjects spontaneously encoded and organized the behaviors in terms of traits, even when the trait categories were not explicitly stated in the information provided them. (If this were not the case, no set size effects of any sort would have occurred.) However, when the traits exemplified by the behaviors differed in favorableness, the likelihood of recalling a behavior *increased* with trait category set size. This suggests that under this condition, direct associations among the behaviors were formed, the effects of which overrode the effects produced by organizing them in terms of traits.

The implications of Gordon's study may be summarized simply. When subjects form an impression of a person on the basis of behavioral information, they encode and organize the behaviors in terms of traits. Furthermore, when *either* (a) adjectives describing these traits are explicitly assigned to the target before the behaviors are presented, or (b) the traits exemplified by the behaviors are similar in favorableness, they perform this organization without engaging in the additional cognitive work required to form associations among the behaviors themselves (i.e., without thinking about the behaviors in relation to one another). In contrast, when trait adjective descriptions of the target person are *not* provided *and* the traits exemplified by the behaviors differ in favorableness, subjects do think about the behaviors in relation to one another, and so the interitem associations that produce positive set size effects are established.

Considered from the point of view of the subject, these contingencies make intuitive sense. That is, subjects with the goal of forming an impression of a person on the basis of behaviors may attempt to identify the traits exemplified by these behaviors. If they have explicit indications of the person's traits before receiving the behavioral information (e.g., if adjectives describing the traits are presented), subjects may simply encode the behaviors in terms of these traits without thinking about them in relation to one another. When they do not have these a priori expectancies, subjects may infer the person's traits from the behaviors and organize the behaviors into these inferred trait categories. If the traits they infer are similar in favorableness, subjects may not question the validity of their inferences. However, suppose the traits that the behaviors appear to exemplify differ in favorableness. Then, subjects may wonder if they have interpreted the behaviors correctly, and may think about them in relation to one another in order to determine if alternative trait encodings are possible. In this latter condition, unlike the others, interitem connections are formed within each trait category that lead to the positive set size effects obtained by Gordon.

While this possibility seems reasonable, it should be noted that the evaluative differences between behaviors that existed in Gordon's studies were always across trait categories; the behaviors *within* each trait category were always similar in favorableness. When the behaviors pertaining to any given trait of a person are evaluatively inconsistent, attempts to reconcile these inconsistencies may occur even when the traits of the person are explicitly stated. Evidence bearing this possibility is summarized below.

Effect of Trait-Behavior Inconsistency

When people have a prior expectancy for how someone is apt to behave, they may learn about behaviors of the person that are inconsistent with this expectancy. As we speculated above, it seems reasonable to suppose that when this occurs, they will attempt to reconcile these behaviors with previous information they have received about the person. This increased cognitive activity may lead to greater recall of the behaviors later on. In support of this contention, Hastie and Kumar (1979) found that when subjects had previously been told that a target person had general characteristics implying intelligence, the probability of recalling trait-incongruent behaviors of this person (i.e., behaviors implying lack of intelligence) was greater than the probability of recalling trait-congruent ones.

In these studies, inconsistency was often confounded with set size (i.e., there were generally fewer incongruent behaviors *presented* than congruent ones). However, a subsequent study by Srull (1981) found similar results under conditions in which trait-incongruent behaviors were even more frequent than trait-congruent ones.

Although the relatively greater recall of trait-incongruent information can be predicted on the basis of general amount-of-processing considerations (cf. Craik & Lockhart, 1972; Wyer & Hartwick, 1980), further and less intuitively obvious predictions can be generated by applying an extension of the conceptualization outlined earlier. Hastie (1980; see also Srull, 1981) postulated that when subjects with a person impression set receive behavioral information that is consistent with the traits attributed to a person, they recognize these behaviors as exemplifying the traits but do not think about their relation to one another. Thus, the behaviors are simply connected to a central trait (or person) node, and no interitem connections are formed. However, when subjects learn of a behavior that is incongruent with the trait, they attempt to reconcile it with previous information they have received. That is, they consider it in relation to other behaviors of the person. As a result, associations are established between the incongruent behavior and others. The implications of this can be seen with reference to Figure 2.3. This figure shows a simplified network representation of three behaviors consistent with trait T and three behaviors inconsistent with this trait. Each inconsistent behavior is assumed to stimulate cognitive activity that leads it to become connected at random to two other behaviors (which may be either consistent or inconsistent). In contrast, each consistent behavior does not stimulate this activity. Consequently, there are typically more pathways leading to inconsistent behaviors than to consistent ones. For reasons noted earlier, this should produce relatively better recall of the inconsistent behaviors, as found empirically both by Hastie and Kumar and by Srull. However, note that inconsistent behaviors may be connected either to consistent behaviors or to other inconsistent behaviors, whereas consistent behaviors are connected only to inconsistent behaviors. If recall of successive items proceeds by traversing the pathways connecting them, this implies that the conditional probability of recalling an inconsistent behavior immediately after recalling a consistent one should be greater than the probability of recalling a consistent behavior immediately after

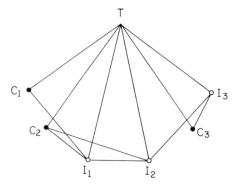

FIG. 2.3.   Representation of a person with trait T, three behaviors (C_1, C_2 and C_3) consistent with T, and three behaviors (I_1, I_2 and I_3) inconsistent with T. Behaviors are assumed to be presented in the order $C_1C_2I_1I_2C_3I_3$. The presentation of each inconsistent behavior is assumed to establish an association between it and two others that preceded it in the presentation sequence.

recalling an inconsistent one. In fact, Srull (1981, Experiment 1) found this to be the case, the two probabilities being .79 and .32, respectively.

A second implication of the general conceptualization concerns the effect of differences in the number of behaviors presented of one type on the recall of behaviors of the other type. Specifically, holding the number of consistent behaviors constant, the number of associations between inconsistent and consistent behaviors should increase as the number of inconsistent behaviors presented becomes greater. Therefore, the number of pathways leading to the consistent behaviors should also increase. In contrast, holding the number of inconsistent behaviors constant, an increase in the number of consistent behaviors presented should have no effect on the number of pathways to inconsistent ones. This implies that the recall of consistent behaviors should increase with the number of inconsistent behaviors presented, whereas recall of inconsistent behaviors should be independent of the number of consistent behaviors presented. Additional studies reported by Srull (1981, Experiments 3 and 4) confirmed this prediction as well.

The support for these two nonintuitive implications of the general formulation proposed adds strength to its plausibility as a description of how person information is represented in memory. However, it is important to note that the model assumes that no direct pathways are established among trait-consistent behaviors under the conditions being investigated (i.e., when behaviors are relevant to only one trait). In fact, since the predictions derived by Srull require this assumption, his findings provide indirect evidence for its validity under the conditions investigated. An additional experiment reinforces this contention. Moreover, it supports the assumption that the interitem connections involving inconsistent behaviors occur as a result of cognitive activity that is performed at the time these behaviors are presented. If this latter assumption is correct, the recall advantage of inconsistent behaviors should be eliminated when subjects are distracted from performing this cognitive activity during stimulus presentation. To test this hypothesis, Srull asked subjects to repeat each behavior aloud either 0, 1, 2, or 3 times as it was presented. The recall of inconsistent behaviors decreased substantially as the number of times that subjects repeated these items increased, whereas the recall of consistent behaviors was not appreciably affected. This suggests that repeating the items interfered with subjects' attempts to reconcile the inconsistent behaviors with the consistent ones, and so the recall advantage of these behaviors was eliminated. In addition, the fact that the recall of consistent items was not greatly affected by the manipulation suggests that direct associations among these behaviors were unlikely to be formed, even in the absence of distraction.

Effects of Time on the Recall of Consistent and Inconsistent Behaviors.   The evidence that inconsistent behaviors are remembered better than consistent ones may seem to contradict the notion that information is better recalled if it is better able to be integrated into a representation of the person or object described. Note, however, that the conceptualization proposed by Hastie and Srull assumes that incongruent information *is* in fact integrated into the representation, perhaps to an even greater extent than is consistent information. Further evidence supporting this assumption comes from data on the recall of information over time. That is, if inconsistent information is not integrated into the representation being formed, these "exceptions" may tend to be forgotten as time goes on, and only the more "central" behaviors (those consistent with the overall theme of the representation) may be retained. This implies that the advantage of inconsistent over consistent information should only be pronounced in the time interval immediately after the information is presented. As noted previously, this does appear to be the case when event sequences are involved (cf. Graesser et al., 1980). However, neither Hastie and Kumar nor Srull found any evidence for this in their research on person memory; the superior recall of inconsistent over consistent behavior was maintained over a period of several days. It therefore seems reasonable to conclude that trait-consistent and trait-inconsistent behaviors are both contained in the representation of a person that is initially formed on the basis of trait information. Both types of behavior should therefore be recalled better than behaviors that are irrelevant to the traits assumed to characterize the person being described, and therefore are not strongly associated with the representation being formed. In fact, this was true both in Hastie and Kumar's study and in Srull's.

Descriptive Versus Evaluative Consistency.   In most of the research described thus far, the differences in the descriptive implications of the information presented about a person—that is, whether it implies a particular trait (e.g., honest) or its bipolar opposite (dishonest)—were confounded with differences in its evaluative implications (i.e., its favorableness). In Hastie and Kumar's study, for example, when the original trait descriptions reflected intelligence (a presumably favorable attribute), the consistent behaviors were both favorable and implied intelligence whereas the inconsistent ones were unfavorable and conveyed lack of intelligence. A similar confound existed in Srull's (1981) study. It is therefore unclear from these studies whether the cognitive activity that presumably underlies the greater recall of inconsistent information is stimulated by attempts to reconcile descriptive inconsistencies between behaviors and traits of the person being described or attempts to reconcile evaluative inconsistencies.

Two studies that investigated this question directly (Wyer & Gordon, 198a, Experiment 1; Wyer, Bodenhausen & Srull, 1983) show that in fact, *evaluative* inconsistency is the critical factor. In the first study (Wyer & Gordon, 1982), the descriptive and evaluative consistency of behaviors with trait adjectives describing a target person were manipulated independently. Behaviors were recalled better if they were evaluatively inconsistent with the trait adjectives (i.e., if their implications differed in favorableness) than if they were evaluatively consistent with the adjectives. However, they were if anything recalled better if they were descriptively *consistent* with these adjectives (presumably because of the retrieval cue affects noted earlier).

In the second study (Wyer et al., 1983), subjects read trait adjective descriptions of a person implying one trait (e.g., intelligent) followed by behaviors that pertained either to this trait or to a second, unmentioned trait that was only evaluatively related to the first (e.g., kind). Subjects with a person impression set subsequently recalled more behaviors that were evaluatively inconsistent with the trait adjective description of the person than behaviors that were consistent with it, regardless of whether the behaviors pertained to the same trait described by the adjectives or a different one.

A Conceptual Integration

The various findings summarized above have implications both for an understanding of impression formation processes in general and for the nature of person representations in particular. In general, they indicate that instructions to form an impression of a person lead subjects to extract a general evaluation of the person as either "good" or "bad," and to organize the information around this evaluative concept. Interbehavior connections of the sort postulated by Hastie and Srull result primarily from attempts to reconcile behaviors of a person that are evaluatively inconsistent with this overall evaluation, independently of whether the behaviors are denotatively consistent or inconsistent with specific traits of this person.

In addition, trait-based representations of the person are formed in which behaviors are encoded and organized in terms of the traits they exemplify. However, the nature of this representation may depend on whether the traits are (a) stated explicitly or (b) must be inferred from the behaviors. In the former case, behaviors are simply encoded in terms of the traits they exemplify and are not considered in relation to one another. In the latter case, interbehavior associations *may* be established among the behaviors exemplifying each trait, provided the inferred traits differ in favorableness.

The question is whether these latter, trait-based representations are part of the same general, evaluation-based representation of the person described in the first paragraph of this section. At least these pieces of evidence argue against this possibility.

1. The evaluation of a person described by trait adjectives alone is often unrelated to the recall of these adjectives: for example, evaluations of a person described by trait adjectives are influenced most by the first adjectives presented, whereas the last ones presented are best remembered (Anderson & Hubert, 1963; Dreben, Fiske, & Hastie, 1979). This suggests that any trait-based representation formed of the person is independent of the more general, evaluatively encoded representation that underlies these liking judgments.

2. Whereas subjects with an impression set recall behaviors of a target person better than do subjects with a memory set, they do *not* recall better the traits that these behaviors exemplify (Wyer & Gordon, 1982); this also suggests that subjects do not form a single representation of the person that includes traits as well as behaviors.

3. Although trait adjectives serve as retrieval cues for behaviors that are either evaluatively *or* descriptively consistent with these adjectives (see Footnote 9), these adjectives do *not* cue the recall of behaviors that are inconsistent in *both* respects (Wyer & Gordon, 1982). This contradicts the conclusion that evaluatively inconsistent behaviors (although recalled better overall than consistent behaviors) are integrated into trait-based clusters of the sort implied by Wyer and Gordon's data.

To reconcile these various findings, it seems necessary to postulate a dual coding of the information presented (for a similar conclusion, see Ebbesen, 1980). That is, subjects who receive behavioral information about a person with the goal of forming an impression of the person may do two things. First, they may attempt to encode and classify behaviors in terms of the traits they exemplify, thus forming trait-behavior clusters of the sort described in Fig. 2.2e. If they have already formed trait-based expectancies for the person before receiving the behavioral information (e.g., if the person has been explicitly described in trait terms), or if the traits implied by the behaviors presented are similar in favorableness, subjects may perform these encodings without thinking about the behaviors in relation to one another, and so no direct associations are formed among the behaviors themselves. If, on the other hand, subjects do not have a priori expectancies, and if some behaviors appear to exemplify a trait that differs in favorableness from the others possessed by the person, subjects may question whether their interpretations of the behaviors are correct, and therefore may think about the behaviors in relation to one another in an attempt to decide if they have been incorrectly encoded. This leads interitem associations among the behaviors to be formed.

In addition, subjects with a general impression set may extract the evaluative implications of the information presented in order to form an overall judgment of the person as, for example, likeable or dislikeable. This evaluation may function as a central node around which behaviors that are evaluatively consistent or inconsistent with it are organized, with interitem links being established among these behaviors as a result of efforts to reconcile those that are evaluatively inconsistent with the central theme.

Thus, each behavior is represented twice, once in each type of representation.

As an example, suppose subjects are told that a person, P, has two favorable traits, $T_{A,F}$ and $T_{B,F}$, and that the person has manifested two favorable behaviors that are descriptively consistent with T_A (each denoted $b_{A,F}$), one favorable and one unfavorable behavior descriptively consistent with T_B ($b_{B,F}$ and $b_{B,U}$), and one favorable and one unfavorable behavior descriptively *in*consistent with T_B

($b_{\bar{B},F}$ and $b_{\bar{B},U}$). The representation of this information under person impression conditions would then be similar to that indicated in Figure 2.4. That is, two trait-behavior clusters would be formed in which the behaviors that are either evaluatively or descriptively consistent with the relevant traits are connected to nodes comprising these traits, but without any direct associations among the behaviors themselves. (Note that the behavior that is both descriptively and evaluatively inconsistent with T_B is represented in isolation.) Finally, since the majority of the behaviors and traits describing P are favorable, a favorable overall impression of the person may be extracted. This impression may be represented by a person node to which are connected all six behaviors, with direct paths connecting evaluatively inconsistent (unfavorable) behaviors to others as a result of the cognitive activity postulated by Hastie and Srull.

While the sort of dual representation exemplified in Figure 2.4 seems complex and cognitively inefficient, it provides the best account of the results reported to date. For example, it accounts for findings that trait adjectives serve as retrieval cues for consistent but not inconsistent behaviors, while preserving the notion that evaluatively inconsistent behaviors as well as consistent ones are integrated into a representation of the actor of the sort necessary to account for Srull's and Wyer and Gordon's findings. Second, note that although this formulation implies that behaviors are organized around a central node representing the overall evaluation of the target, there is no reason to suppose that the evaluative implications of the particular behaviors recalled are systematically related to the favorableness of this evaluation. Finally, to the extent that the behaviors in this latter representation are directly connected to a node representing the overall

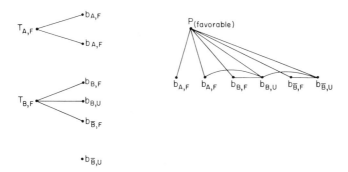

FIG. 2.4.   Hypothetical representation of person P in memory, based on information consisting of two favorable traits ($T_{A,F}$ and $T_{B,F}$) two behaviors that are both evaluatively and descriptively consistent with $T_{A,F}$ (each denoted $b_{A,F}$) one favorable and one unfavorable behavior that is descriptively consistent with $T_{B,F}$ ($b_{B,F}$ and $b_{B,U}$), and one favorable and one unfavorable behavior that is descriptively inconsistent with $T_{B,F}$ ($b_{\bar{B},F}$ and $b_{\bar{B},U}$).

evaluation of the target and not to trait adjectives, the finding that recall of behaviors but not of traits is increased under person impression conditions can be explained.

Conclusions

Despite a few loose ends, the research reported to date appears to be converging on several general conclusions concerning the representation of trait and behavioral information about a person.

1. Subjects with the objective of forming an impression of a person, in contrast to those whose goal is to remember the information presented about the person, attend to both the descriptive and the evaluative implications of the information. If subjects have a priori trait-based expectancies for what the person is like, they are apt to encode the behaviors in terms of the traits described by these adjectives without thinking of the behaviors in relation to one another. As a consequence, trait-behavior connections are formed that lead the trait descriptors, if recalled themselves, to serve as retrieval cues for the behaviors that exemplify them. When subjects do not have a priori trait-based expectancies before behaviors are presented, and the traits that these behaviors exemplify differ in their evaluative implications, subjects not only may encode the behaviors in terms of traits but may form direct associations among the behaviors within each category. However, the trait-behavior clusters may not themselves be organized into a single configural representation of the target. Instead, they may be stored as separate units, and retrieved independently of one another when information about the target person is being recalled.

2. Subjects with a person impression set also attempt to extract a general evaluation of the person as "good" or "bad." Once this is done, behaviors that are evaluatively in consistent with this evaluation may stimulate attempts to reconcile them with other available information about the person, leading interbehavior associations to be established between the behaviors involved. These associations facilitate the recall of the behaviors later on. However, this representation of information about the target person, in which behaviors are organized around a central evaluation of the target, is independent of the trait-behavior or interbehavior clusters formed on the basis of primarily descriptive considerations.

3. There is no evidence to date that the information presented about individual persons is spontaneously organized with reference to a prototypic representation of a person with characteristics similar to those described. This is not to say that prototypes do not exist. Moreover, associating the features of information about an individual person with features of a prototype may facilitate the recall of this information (for evidence suggesting this possibility, see Bower & Gilligan, 1979; Rogers, Kuiper, & Kirker, 1977). Moreover, subjects with the

objective of deciding whether a person exemplifies a particular prototype may selectively search new or previously acquired information for features that are contained in this prototype (Snyder & Cantor, 1979). However, prototypes presumably consist of a list of features that are not themselves organized. That is, they may be categorical rather than schematic in form, and therefore may not be elicited *spontaneously* by the information presented. Thus, their role in organizing information about persons may be rather limited.

4. The conceptualization proposed in this section implies that the representations formed of individual persons on the basis of trait and/or behavioral information are categorical rather than schematic in nature. While we have not provided direct evidence bearing on the categorical versus schematic properties of these representations, it should be noted that in virtually all of the studies in which free recall data were obtained (e.g., Hastie & Kumar, 1979; Srull, 1981a; Wyer & Gordon, 1982), the number of intrusion errors was negligible. This is in contrast to research on the representation of events, where intrusion errors are abundant (cf. Bower et al., 1979; Spiro, 1977). These data are therefore consistent with the assumption that these representations are categorical, although more direct tests of this assumption would be desirable.

THE REPRESENTATION OF GROUPS OF PERSONS

The research described above typically focused on the representation of a single person, based on information about this person alone. A question arises concerning the way in which *groups* of persons are represented based on information about different members of the group. There are two somewhat different aspects of this question. First, is the representation of information about a person the same when this information is presented in the context of information about other persons as it is when the information is presented alone? Second, is the representation of a single person formed from several pieces of information about the person similar to the representation of a group formed from comparable information about several different members of this group? We consider each question in turn.

Representations of Information about Several Different Individuals

As noted in the preceding section, information about an individual person is apparently not organized into a single configural representation of this person. Nevertheless, when information about several different persons is presented simultaneously, it seems likely that information will be categorized according to the person to whom it refers. A study by Ostrom, Pryor and Simpson (1981) raises questions about the generality of this conclusion. In this study, subjects in some conditions were given nine pieces of information, three of which pertained to each of three fictitious persons. Moreover, the information about each person pertained to three different characteristics (occupation, hometown, and hobbies). Subjects typically received the information under instructions that implicitly required comparative judgments (e.g., to "form an impression of what person would least fit in as a roommate"). After doing so, they recalled the information. Clustering analyses of subjects' free recall protocols suggested that the information tended to be organized in terms of attributes but not in terms of persons. Other studies showed that only when the persons described were familiar (e.g., well-known public figures) did significant organization of information by persons occur. However, the failure to find organization by persons in the former conditions may be an artifact of the comparative judgment instructions typically given subjects in these conditions. That is, such instructions may predispose subjects to compare the three target persons with respect to each attribute separately rather than integrating the attributes of each person into a representation of the individual as a whole.

In two more recent studies (Srull, 1983; Srull & Brand, 1983), strong evidence that information is organized by persons was obtained. In the study by Srull and Brand, subjects read a series of behaviors of several different persons. The number of behaviors describing each person was systematically varied. The information was presented both under instructions to form impressions of the persons described and to remember the information. Under memory set conditions, the recall of a given behavior decreased with both the number of other behaviors describing the same person and the number describing other persons. This general negative set size effect suggests that under a memory set, subjects learned the behaviors as a single list, undifferentiated by person. The results were quite different under an impression set. Here, the recall of behaviors decreased with the number presented about the same person, but was independent of the number of behaviors presented about others. These results suggest that the behaviors were organized into "person" categories, and that the information in one category had no influence on the recall of information in another. Srull's (1983) study yielded similar conclusions using different research procedures.

Additional factors to consider may be (a) the number of persons about whom information is presented, and (b) the amount and diversity of this information. A study by Rothbart, Fulero, Jensen, Howard, and Birrell (1978) bears on this question. Subjects were given information about the behavior of individual group members under conditions in which the number of persons described, the number of pieces of information about each person, and the favorableness of this information were systemically varied. Both recall and judgment data suggested that when relatively little information was presented (low memory load conditions), group impressions were a function of the proportion of persons whose attributes were desirable or undesirable. When a large amount of information was presented, however (high memory load conditions), group impressions tended to be based on the frequency with which favorable and unfavorable descriptions were presented, independently of whether these descriptions pertained to the same person or to different persons. In other words, representations upon which impression judgments were based appeared to be organized around individual persons under low memory load conditions, but around traits under high memory load.

The Representation of Groups

Rothbart et al.'s study leads to the second general question to be considered, concerning the manner in which groups are represented in memory. In research bearing directly on this matter, subjects are typically given information about individual members of a group and told to form impressions of the group. Srull (1981) found that the effect of inconsistency obtained under person impression conditions generalized to group impression conditions as well; that is, when the group was characterized as being composed of persons with a particular trait, the behaviors of individual members were recalled better when they were inconsistent with this group description than when they were consistent with it. Moreover, information that was consistent with the group description was recalled better than behaviors that were irrelevant to this general group characterization. Results reported by Rothbart, Evans, and Fulero (1979) also support this conclusion.

On the other hand, Wyer and Gordon (1982) identified some differences between the effects of these characteristics under group impression conditions and their effects under person impression conditions. Specifically, subjects who formed impressions of a single person described by trait and behavioral information recalled best those behaviors that were evaluatively inconsistent but descriptively consistent with the trait adjectives describing the person. In contrast, subjects who formed an impression of a group recalled *fewer* behaviors of this type than behaviors representing other combinations of descriptive and evaluative consistency. This study differs from both Srull's and Rothbart et al.'s in that the trait adjectives presented did not describe the group as a whole, but rather described individual group members. Under these conditions, subjects apparently did *not* try to reconcile the evaluative inconsistencies of the behaviors of some group members with the traits characterizing other members, provided the behaviors and traits were descriptively consistent. Rather, they ignored these behaviors in attempting to construct an overall group impression, with the result that very few were subsequently remembered. In contrast, individual members' behaviors that were *both* evaluatively and descriptively inconsistent did stimulate attempts to reconcile them with the overall group impression, and therefore *were* recalled well later on.

A critical factor in considering the organization of information about groups may be whether the group is a closely knit body of interacting individuals, or is simply a collection of persons who do not interact and have little in common other than their group membership. In other conditions of Srull's (1981) study and a more recent study by Wyer et al. (1983), subjects formed impressions of groups that shared a common trait but otherwise did not necessarily interact. The inconsistency effects noted above disappeared under these conditions. In fact, there was evidence that under these conditions, consistent behaviors were recalled better.

It therefore appears that a critical factor underlying the organization of information about groups of persons is whether the nature of the group being described, or characteristics of the information itself, leads subjects to try to reconcile evaluative inconsistencies among the behaviors of different group members, and consequently to think about the behaviors in relation to one another. Under these conditions, individual members' behaviors may be recalled better if they are inconsistent with the general group impression than if they are consistent with it. When this cognitive activity is not likely, however, members' behaviors that are consistent with the group impression may be better recalled.

Stereotyping.   Much of the work on group impression formation has been stimulated by an interest in stereotyping, that is, the tendency to apply characteristics of a group as a whole to individual group members. A common assumption underlying this theory and research is that stereotypes bias the perception of individual members of the stereotyped category, leading to better recall of instances that confirm the stereotype than those that disconfirm it. However, if the conclusions drawn from group impression formation research are generalizeable, they place qualifications on this assumption. That is, it may only be true when the members of the stereotyped category do not form a cohesive group; that is, when they do not interact, and have little in common other than their category membership. In contrast, when the stereotype pertains to a closely knit group of persons who commonly interact with one another, behaviors of individual members that are inconsistent with the stereotype may be recalled best. The tendency to recall "exceptions" better than nonexceptions presents a challenge for many theories of stereotyping (for a review, see Hamilton, 1979).

In addition to the effects of stereotyping, a question arises as to how stereotypes are formed. Perhaps the most provocative work bearing on this question was reported by Hamilton and Gifford (1976). These authors argue that low frequency (novel) events are more available in memory than common ones, and thus are easier to recall. On the other hand, when asked to estimate the frequency of occurrence of an event, subjects are likely to base their estimates on the ease with which individual instances of the event come to mind, assuming that the easier it is to recall such an instance, the more common these instances may be (Tversky & Kahneman, 1973). This should lead them to overestimate the frequency of relatively novel events. In applying this notion to stereotyping, Hamilton et al. argue that minority group members and undesirable social behaviors are both relatively infrequent. Therefore, instances of minority group members engaging in these behaviors should be easily available in memory. Consequently, the frequency of their behaviors is overestimated, leading to a negative bias in perceptions of the minority group. A series of studies reported by Hamilton et al. confirm this hypothesis.

Despite this research, much more needs to be learned about the process of forming stereotypes and the extent to which it differs, if at all, from the processes of group and individual impression formation outlined earlier in this chapter. In this regard, it would be desirable to explore more systematically not only the effects of a stereotype on judgments of individuals, but the influence of information about individual group members on previously formed group stereotypes. The nature of these influences, and their cognitive bases, are presently unclear.

THE REPRESENTATION OF SELF

The determinants and effects of one's self-concept have long been of concern to personality and social psychologists. However, this concern has focused primarily on the content of self-concepts rather than their structural properties. The structure of one's representation of self (or perhaps more accurately, representations) has rarely been investigated with any degree of rigor. Nor have the alternative ways in which self may be represented cognitively been conceptualized with much precision. Yet it is almost self-evident that one's conception of self occupies a central role in information processing (for a more detailed review and analysis, see Greenwald & Pratkanis, volume 3, this Handbook). In his original presentation of script theory, Abelson (1976) conceptualized a script as a sequence of events "involving the individual as either participant or observer." This conceptualization acknowledges that most if not all information is acquired episodically. That is, it is received in a social context, and cognitions associated with the act of receiving it in this context may often be important components of the episode that cue its retrieval. Thus, my recall of information about someone else may be cued by my recall of episodic information about my own behavior toward this person, and my judgments of the person may be based in part upon thoughts and reactions to this person that I recall having had during the course of interacting with him. More generally, the events in one's life that are easy to remember may provide a mechanism for organizing the information one acquires in the course of experiencing these events and therefore may facilitate its recall. Thus, by thinking back over what I did yesterday morning and remembering that I read the student newspaper, I may recall information about a newly instituted federal program that was described in this newspaper, or a movie I wanted to see that is now playing in town.

Not all self-relevant information remains episodic. That is, the substantive aspects of this information may often become separated from the situational cues associated with its acquisition, and therefore may become a more general part of one's self-representation. Thus, we may think of ourselves as hardworking, as drinking too much, as afraid of snakes, and as disliking attempts by big business to exploit the public, but we may not have any idea what specific events led to these self-descriptions. Moreover, we may acquire general notions of how we behave in certain types of situations, why we behave in these ways, and how others react to this behavior. These notions, which may have the form of event schemata of the sort described earlier, guide our behavioral decisions and are used to interpret the consequences of our actions.

Information we have about ourselves may be used as a basis not only for decisions about how we personally should behave in various situations, but also for interpreting and predicting others' behavior toward us or toward someone else (cf. Ross, 1977). Also, as Rogers et al. (1977) indicate, information about others is better recalled when it has been considered with reference to one's own characteristics. This suggests that the process of comparing characteristics of another person to features of one's self-representation establishes connections between these features and those of the other, leading these features to serve as retrieval cues for recalling the other's characteristics later on. [12]

These various examples suggest the possibly important role of self-representations in social information processing. However, neither the empirical nor the theoretical work available at this writing provides much insight into the structure of these representations. While the remarks to follow will unfortunately not fill this important gap in our understanding of the cognitive representation of social information, they point to some considerations that must be taken into account in any formulation of self-representations.

1. Most obviously, it is misleading to speak of a single representation of self. In fact, there may be many representations that are stored independently of one another. They may also be retrieved independently, depending on the situational factors that elicit them or objectives that make one or another representation useful. That is, we may have representations of ourselves in different social roles (professor, radical, lover, etc.) or in different situations (on a date, speaking in

---

[12]There are, of course, other interpretations; for example, comparing others to oneself may involve deeper and more extensive semantic processing than other uses of the information, and may facilitate its recall for this reason (Craik & Lockhart, 1972).

front of an audience, etc.). Each such representation may contain a different cluster of features that are in some instances likely to be inconsistent. (That is, we may consider ourselves to be confident and self-assured when speaking to an audience, but to be nervous and tongue-tied when out on a date.) Indeed, we may have unique representations of ourselves interacting with particular individuals who make us think of ourselves as either attractive or unattractive, intelligent or stupid, and witty or dull. These representations may be elicited at different times, depending on situational cues that make them salient. Thus, whether I describe myself as confident or shy may depend on whether I happen to be thinking about giving a lecture or going to dinner with someone for the first time. In this regard, McGuire and his colleagues (McGuire, McGuire, Child, & Fujioka, 1978; McGuire, McGuire, & Winton, 1979) have demonstrated in a series of studies that the attributes one uses to describe oneself are often those that are distinctive, either in the particular context in which one generates these descriptions or more generally. Thus, a black woman is more apt to describe herself spontaneously as a woman when in the company of black men, and as black when in the company of white women. A formulation of how self is represented in memory must take these possibilities into account, and a methodology must be developed for investigating them.

2. Two additional considerations are highly related to the previous one. First, the various representations one has of oneself may differ not only in content but in structure. The research by McGuire, for example (see also Rogers et al., 1977, and Markus, 1977) implicitly assumes that self-representations are categorical in nature, consisting of a list of features that are retrieved independently, depending on their typicality, distinctiveness, situational cues that activate them, and so forth. However, some information we have about ourselves is clearly schematic, consisting of representations of either unique experiences we have had (e.g., the time I made a fool of myself at the company Christmas party), or more general ones (a typical day at work). Moreover, as noted above, both individual features (trait descriptors, etc.) and event schemata may be restricted to certain social or vocational roles that we happen to occupy. How these various roles, schemata, and individual features are interconnected is unclear.

It may be possible to conceptualize the organization of self-relevant information in terms of (a) a set of categories, each referring to a different social or vocational role or situation in which one often finds oneself ("the office," "at home," "at parties," etc.) with (b) each category being characterized by features that include both trait descriptors and event schemata. These categories themselves may not be organized, but may in combination comprise a "super-list" of self-descriptors that may be activated either independently or in combination, depending on situational cues that make them salient.

One problem with this conceptualization is that it seems to preclude the activation or recall of a particular feature (i.e., a trait, behavior, or event schema) without first activating the role or situation-defined category that contains it. Although I am most likely to recall making a fool of myself at last year's Christmas party when I am asked whether I will go to this year's party, I may also do so if asked about whether I have ever behaved stupidly, or about my most embarrassing experience. Conceivably the same event schema is stored in different locations and can be activated in different ways. The "bin" model of social information processing proposed by Wyer and Srull (1980) takes this possibility into account. However, the details of this model remain to be worked out.

3. The second question is raised by self-perception theory (Bem, 1967, 1972). That is, the traits that people use to describe themselves are presumably a result of either descriptions of them by others or inferences they make about themselves on the basis of their own behavior and its consequences. However, these latter inferences may not be made spontaneously unless they are necessary in order to obtain some objective (e.g., to decide whether to apply for a job that requires a certain attribute) or to comply with another's request for information. Moreover, even after these self-descriptions have been made and are presumably stored as part of one's self-representation, they may not always be retrieved when one is asked to describe oneself. Rather, we may construct totally new descriptions from episodic information about ourselves that we believe to be relevant (i.e., schematic representations of our behavior in particular situations). Furthermore, this episodic information may be only a subset of the previously acquired relevant material that happens to be most easily available in memory. In many instances, this may be the information that was most recently acquired and/or used (Wyer & Srull, 1980).

Evidence on these possibilities comes not only from Bem's own work on self-perception effects on reported beliefs and attitudes (for a review, see Bem, 1972), but from work demonstrating that subjects' descriptions of themselves are substantially affected by the specific subset of relevant past experience they happen to be thinking about. Two studies by Salancik and his colleagues are noteworthy in this regard. In one (Salancik & Calder, 1974), subjects were asked how religious they were either before or after reporting the frequency with which they engaged in a series of behaviors associated with religiousness. They also reported demographic data concerning the religiousness of their parents and friends. Self-judgments of religiousness were much more highly correlated with the implications of their reported behavior when these behaviors were reported before self-judgments were made than when they were reported afterwards. Moreover, they were much less highly correlated with demographic variables in the first case than in the second. Finally, when behaviors were reported first, their relation to self-judgments of religiousness showed a serial position effect; that is, the first and the last sets of behaviors reported (the ones that are presumably the most easily recalled) were more highly correlated with self-judgments than were those in the middle. (This effect was not apparent when self-judgments were reported first.) Thus, the data suggest that subjects do not have stable conceptions of their attributes but tend to use whatever episodic information happens to be salient to them to infer these attributes.

A second study (Salancik, 1974) tested this possibility more directly. In this case, subjects first reported their agreement or disagreement with statements about religious behavior that contained either the phrase "on occasion" (i.e., "I go to church on occasion") or "frequently" ("I go to church frequently"). Since a statement of the first type can be verified on the basis of a few positive instances of the behavior described, subjects presumably search for such instances, find them, and agree with the statements. However, since the second type can easily be discredited with a few negative instances of the behavior, subjects presumably search for these instances, often find them, and disagree. As a result, more positive instances of religious behavior are salient to subjects in the first case than in the second. Consistent with this assumption and the considerations raised above, subjects reported themselves to be more religious in the first condition than in the second.

Bem's and Salancik's research suggests that subjects' reported self-concepts may be quite unstable, and that they may often be reconstructed anew each time they are reported. This possibility raises questions concerning several current approaches to investigating the nature of self-representations. For example, several studies by Rogers, Markus, and their colleagues (for reviews, see Markus & Smith, 1981; Rogers, 1981) have used recognition and reaction time procedures to diagnose the content of self-representations. For example, it should take less time to decide whether a given adjective applies to oneself if it is either highly self-descriptive or highly non–self-descriptive than if it is moderately so. However, whether an item is self-descriptive may depend upon which of several reprsentations of self happens to be activated at the time the task is performed. Presumably the pattern of reaction times to a given set of descriptors could be altered, simply by inducing conditions that make different representations salient.

As an example, Markus (1977) provided evidence that people who have previously labeled themselves either extremely independent or extremely dependent, and also attach importance to these characteristics, take less time to decide that adjectives describing the characteristic they apply to themselves are "like them" than to decide that adjectives describing the opposite characteristic are "like them." In contrast, subjects who have described themselves as moderate along an independence/dependence dimension do not differ in the time they take to make these decisions. Markus interpreted these results as indicating that the former subjects have "self-schemata" associated with independence or dependence whereas the latter subjects do not. There are some problems with the conclusion that these responses are in any way mediated by a "schema" as conceptualized in this paper. Indeed, it is hardly surprising that subjects who have already indicated themselves as having an extreme amount of an attribute take a short time to confirm that adjectives describing the attribute apply to them.

Since extremity of ratings and confidence in them are highly correlated (Wyer, 1973), this may simply indicate that subjects respond more quickly when they are confident of their judgments than when they are not.[13,14]

But be that as it may, a question arises as to whether the representation of self that underlies these judgments is consistent over situations, or is simply one that is typically elicited under conditions in which subjects perceive themselves in a "student" role and report information to faculty members or experimenters they don't know very well. The reaction time procedures used by Rogers and Markus may ultimately provide a useful tool in diagnosing the stability of different self-descriptions over situations. However, this possibility has not been explored to date.

4. A person may be more apt to remember his/her own behavior or reactions in a given situation than the behavior or reactions of others. An intuitive example is provided by Abelson (1976), who described his reaction to a speech as "I can't remember what he said, but I remember that I didn't like it." One possible reason for this difference is that thinking *about* the behavior of others, and about one's emotional reactions to it, involves cognitive elaboration, and thus requires a deeper level of processing than simply coding the behavior itself. Alternatively, one's own behavior and reactions may be more closely connected to other concepts in one's cognitive system, and are better recalled for this reason.

While the relatively better recall of internally generated cognitive and emotional reactions than of the events that produced them has not been empirically established, there are indirect indications of it. For example, in investigations of

---

[13]In fact, a closer scrutiny of Markus' data (p. 68, Fig. 2.1) calls into question the generality of her findings and the interpretation she gives to them. That is, subjects who had previously classified themselves as dependent responded more quickly when indicating that dependent adjectives were like them and independent adjectives were not like them than when indicating that dependent adjectives were not like them or independent ones were like them. However, subjects who had previously labeled themselves independent tended to respond more quickly when judging independent adjectives, regardless of whether these adjectives were like them or not. Moreover, they took less time to report that adjectives were like them than that adjectives were not like them, regardless of whether they conveyed independence or dependence. Finally, although statistical tests are not reported, the response times of "independent" schematics under various conditions do not appear to differ appreciably from those of subjects labeled as "aschematic" (i.e., as neither independent nor dependent).

[14]Another feature of Markus's work may be worth noting. That is, "schematics" in her study were defined as persons who not only described themselves extremely with respect to independence (or dependence) but also reported considering this characteristic to be important. Persons who attach importance to a characteristic are apt to think more about it, and also are likely to behave in ways that exemplify it. Moreover, they are apt to be sensitive to differences in this characteristic when manifested by others. It is therefore reasonable to speculate that differences between "schematics" and "aschematics" reported by Markus may be more fundamentally due to differences in the importance attached to the attribute being investigated, which affects both self-descriptions and perceptions of others, than to the mediating effects of self-representations per se.

the effect of taking a perspective on the recall of prose material, both Abelson (1976) and Fiske et al. (1979) found that persons in the imagined perspective of an actor recalled better what the actor subjectively experienced (e.g., body sensations) and said, but not what the actor looked like, than did persons with other perspectives. To the extent that imagined and real perspectives have similar effects on information processing, these findings would be consistent with the hypothesis noted above. Also, Moore, Sherrod, Liu, and Underwood (1979) found that subjects tended to recall fewer details of a situation in which they participated as time went on, but did not show a corresponding decrease in the recall of their own behavior; moreover, their attributions for the events that occurred in the situation became more dispositional over time. Finally, Carlston (1980) found that subjects' recall of verbal descriptions of a stimulus person's behavior decreased over time, whereas memory for their prior trait ratings of this person did not.

The possibility that self-generated responses (which are essentially part of one's self-representation) are better remembered than the events that gave rise to them is of importance is understanding the representation of events and other persons as well as of oneself. That is, it raises the possibility that in many social interaction situations, the features that one recalls later on may consist largely of one's own reactions to the person(s) with whom one interacted. These recalled reactions, rather than the person's own characteristics or behavior, may therefore provide the basis for later judgments of the person. For example, if I am asked to describe a colleague I have recently met for the first time, I may characterize him as intelligent. However, this may not be because I recall particularly insightful things he said. Rather, I may recall "feeling stupid" when I was talking to him. Or, I may describe a recent acquaintance as warm and friendly, not because I remember particular warm and friendly behaviors of this person, but because I remember "feeling good" when I talked with her at dinner. Once trait and behavior descriptions of a person have been generated for some reason, these cognitions may of course become part of the representation of the person and therefore may be used subsequently as a basis for future judgments and decisions concerning him/her (Carlston, 1980). However, the possibility that the most fundamental representation we form of a person is in fact a representation of ourselves in the course of interacting with this person is worth pursuing both conceptually and empirically.

CONCLUDING REMARKS

In our review of theory and research in this chapter, we have attempted to provide some coherence to existing literature bearing on the way in which different types of social information are represented in memory. In doing so, we have distinguished between categorical and schematic representations, arguing that whereas the representation of general beliefs about one's social environment and also of events one experiences in the course of interacting in this environment are schematic in nature, the representations of persons and/or groups are primarily categorical. The nature of these latter representations may nevertheless be relatively complex and moreover may depend upon both the particular type of information presented and subjects' a priori objectives for using the information at the time they receive it.

In trying to bring together the implications of different bodies of research, we have engaged in many untested speculations about the nature of the representations formed. Thus, many of the conclusions drawn in this chapter should be treated with caution. Despite this, the research reported to date potentially provides some insight into the organization of social information in memory and provides a conceptual framework within which specific formulations of social information processing can be refined and tested.

ACKNOWLEDGMENTS

This research was supported by National Science Foundation grant BNS 76-240001. Thanks are extended to Doug Medin and Thom Srull for perceptive comments on an earlier version of the manuscript.

REFERENCES

Abelson, R. P. Script processing in attitude formation and decision-making. In J. S. Carroll & J. W. Payne (Eds.), *Cognition and social behavior.* Hillsdale, N.J.: Lawrence Erlbaum Associates, 1976.

Abelson, R. P. The psychological status of the script concept. *American Psychologist,* 1981, *36,* 715–729.

Abelson, R. P., & Kanouse, D. E. The acceptance of generic assertions. In S. Feldman (Ed.), *Cognitive consistency: Motivational antecedents and behavioral consequents.* New York: Academic Press, 1966.

Abelson, R. P., & Reich, C. M. Implicational molecules: A method for extracting meaning from input sentences. In D. E. Walker & L. M. Norton (Eds.), *Proceedings of the International Joint Conference on Artificial Intelligence,* May, 1969.

Abelson, R. P., & Rosenberg, M. J. Symbolic psycho-logic: A model of attitudinal cognition. *Behavioral Science,* 1958, *3,* 1–13.

Allen, R. B., & Ebbesen, E. B. Cognitive processes in person perception: Retrieval of personality trait and behavioral information. *Journal of Experimental Social Psychology,* 1981, *17,* 119–141.

Anderson, B. J. *Information and instructional effects on beliefs and attitudes about persons and behavior.* Unpublished Ph.D. dissertation, University of Illinois. 1981.

Anderson, J. R. *Language, memory and thought.* Hillsdale, N.J.: Lawrence Erlbaum Associates, 1976.

Anderson, J. R., & Bower, G. H. *Human associative memory.* Washington, D.C.: V. H. Winston, 1973.

Anderson, N. H. Integration theory and attitude change. *Psychological Review,* 1971, *78,* 171–206.

Anderson, N. H. Information integration theory: A brief survey. In D. H. Krantz, R. C. Atkinson, R. D. Luce, & P. Suppes (Eds.), *Contemporary developments in mathematical psychology* (Vol. 2.) New York: Academic Press, 1974.

Anderson, N. H., & Hubert, S. Effects of concomitant verbal recall on order effects in personality impression formation. *Journal of Verbal Learning and Verbal Behavior*, 1963, *2*, 379–391.

Asch, S. E. Forming impressions of personality, *Journal of Abnormal and Social Psychology*, 1946, *41*, 258–290.

Banks, W. P. Encoding and processing of symbolic information in comparative judgments. In G. H. Bower (Ed.), *The psychology of learning and motivation,* (Vol. 2.) New York: Academic Press, 1977.

Bear, G., & Hodun, A. Implicational principles and the cognition of confirmatory, contradictory, incomplete and irrelevant information. *Journal of Personality and Social Psychology*, 1975, *32*, 594–604.

Bem, D. J. Self-perception: An alternative interpretation of cognitive dissonance phenomena. *Psychological Review*, 1967, *74*, 183–200.

Bem, D. J. Self-perception theory. In L. Berkowitz (Ed.), *Advances in experimental social psychology* (Vol. 6). New York: Academic Press, 1972.

Bower, G. H. Experiments on story comprehension and recall. *Discourse Processes*, 1978, *1*, 211–231.

Bower, G. H., Black, J., & Turner, T. Scripts in text comprehension and memory. *Cognitive Psychology*, 1979, *11*, 177–220.

Bower, G. H., & Gilligan, S. G. Remembering information related to oneself. *Journal of Research in Personality*, 1979, *13*, 420–432.

Bransford, J. D., Barclay, J. R., & Franks, J. J. Sentence memory: A constructive versus interpretative approach. *Cognitive Psychology*, 1972, *3*, 193–209.

Bransford, J. D., & Johnson, M. K. Contextual prerequisites for understanding: Some investigations of comprehension and recall. *Journal of Verbal Learning and Verbal Behavior*, 1972, *11*, 717–726.

Brewer, W. B., & Dupree, D. A. Use of plan schemata in the recall and recognition of goal-directed actions. *Journal of Experimental Psychology: Learning, Memory and Cognition*, 1983, *9*, 117–129.

Cantor, N., & Kihlstrom, J. (Eds.). *Cognition, social interaction, and personality*. Hillsdale, N.J.: Lawrence Erlbaum Associates, 1981.

Cantor, N., & Mischel, W. Traits as prototypes: Effects on recognition memory. *Journal of Personality and Social Psychology*, 1977, *35*, 38–48.

Cantor, N., & Mischel, W. Prototypicality and personality: Effects on free recall and personality impressions. *Journal of Research in Personality*, 1979, *13*, 187–205.

Carlston, D. E. The recall and use of traits and events in social inference processes. *Journal of Experimental Social Psychology*, 1980, *16*, 303–328.

Cartwright, D., & Harary, F. Structural balance: A generalization of Heider's theory. *Psychological Review*, 1956, *63*, 277–293.

Cohen, C. E., & Ebbesen, E. B. Observational goals and schema activation: A theoretical framework for behavior perception. *Journal of Experimental Social Psychology*, 1979, *15*, 305–329.

Collins, A. M., & Loftus, E. F. A spreading-activation theory of semantic processing. *Psychological Review*, 1975, *82*, 407–428.

Craik, F. I. M., & Lockhart, R. S. Levels of processing: A framework for memory research. *Journal of Verbal Learning and Verbal Behavior*, 1972, *11*, 671–684.

d'Andrade, R. G. Memory in the assessment of behavior. In H. H. Blalock, Jr. (Ed.), *Measurement in the social sciences*. Chicago: Aldine, 1974.

Dreben, E. K., Fiske, S. T., & Hastie, R. The independence of evaluative and item information: Impression and recall order effects in behavior-based impression formation. *Journal of Personality and Social Psychology*, 1979, *37*, 1758–1768.

Ebbesen, E. B. Cognitive processes in understanding ongoing behavior. In R. Hastie, T. Ostrom, E. Ebbesen, R. Wyer, D. Hamilton, & D. Carlston (Eds.), *Person memory: Cognitive basis of social perception*. Hillsdale, N.J.: Lawrence Erlbaum Associates, 1980.

Fiske, S. T., Taylor, S. E., Etcoff, N. L., & Laufer, J. K. Imaging, empathy, and causal attribution. *Journal of Experimental Social Psychology*, 1979, *15*, 356–377.

Gollob, H. F. The Subject-Verb-Object approach to social cognition. *Psychological Review*, 1974, *81*, 286–321.

Gordon, S. E. *Alternative organizations in memory for trait-relevant behaviors*. Unpublished Ph.D. dissertation, University of Illinois, 1981.

Gordon, S. E. *Alternative organizations in memory for trait-relevant behaviors*. Unpublished manuscript, Wright State University, 1982.

Graesser, A. C. *Prose comprehension beyond the word*. New York: Springer-Verlag, 1981.

Graesser, A. C., Gordon, S. E., & Sawyer, J. D. Memory for typical and atypical actions in scripted activities: Test of a script pointer + tag hypothesis. *Journal of Verbal Learning and Verbal Behavior*, 1979, *18*, 319–332.

Graesser, A. C., Woll, S. B., Kowalski, D. J., & Smith, D. A. Memory for typical and atypical actions in scripted activities. *Journal of Experimental Psychology: Human Learning and Memory*, 1980, *6*, 503–515.

Greenwald, A. G. Cognitive learning, cognitive responses to persuasion and attitude change. In A. G. Greenwald, T. Brock, & T. M. Ostrom (Eds.), *Psychological foundations of attitudes*. New York: Academic Press, 1968.

Grice, H. P. Logic and conversation. The William James Lectures, Harvard University, 1967–68. In P. Cole & J. L. Morgan (Eds.), *Syntax and semantics, (Vol. 3): Speech acts*. New York: Academic Press, 1975.

Hamilton, D. L. A cognitive-attributional analysis of stereotyping. In L. Berkowitz (Ed.), *Advances in experimental social psychology* (Vol. 12). New York: Academic Press, 1979.

Hamilton, D. L., & Gifford, R. K. Illusory correlation in interpersonal perception: A cognitive basis of stereotypic judgments. *Journal of Experimental Social Psychology*, 1976, *12*, 392–407.

Hamilton, D. L., Katz, L. B., & Leirer, V. O. Cognitive representation of personality impressions: Organizational processes in first impression formation. *Journal of Personality and Social Psychology*, 1980, *39*, 1050–1063.

Hartwick, J. Memory for trait information: A signal detection analysis. *Journal of Experimental Social Psychology*, 1979, *15*, 533–552.

Hartwick, J. *Presentation and chronological order effects in memory and judgments*. Unpublished Ph.D. dissertation, University of Illinois, 1981.

Hastie, R. Memory for information which confirms or contradicts and general impression. In R. Hastie, T. Ostrom, E. Ebbesen, R. Wyer, D. Hamilton, & D. Carlston, *Person memory: Cognitive basis of social perception*. Hillsdale, N.J.: Lawrence Erlbaum Associates, 1980.

Hastie, R. Schematic principles in human memory. In E. T. Higgins, C. P. Herman, & M. P. Zanna (Eds.), *Social cognition: The Ontario symposium on personality and social psychology*. Hillsdale, N.J.: Lawrence Erlbaum Associates, 1981.

Hastie, R., & Kumar, P. A. Person memory: Personality traits as organizing principles in memory for behaviors. *Journal of Personality and Social Psychology*, 1979, *37*, 25–38.

Hastie, R., Ostrom, T. M., Ebbesen, E. B., Wyer, R. S., Hamilton, D. H., & Carlston, D. E. *Person memory: Cognitive basis of social perception*. Hillsdale, N.J.: Lawrence Erlbaum Associates, 1980.

Heider, F. Attitudes and cognitive organization. *Journal of Psychology*, 1946, *21*, 107–112.

Heider, F. *The psychology of interpersonal relations*. New York: Wiley, 1958.

Higgins, E. T., Herman, C. P., & Zanna, M. P. (Eds.). *Social cognition: The Ontario symposium on personality and social psychology*. Hillsdale, N.J.: Lawrence Erlbaum Associates, 1981.

Higgins, E. T., & King, G. Accessibility of social constructs: Information processing consequences of individual and contextual variability. In N. Cantor & J. Kihlstrom (Eds.), *Cognition, social interaction and personality.* Hillsdale, N.J.: Lawrence Erlbaum Associates, 1981.

Higgins, E. T., Rholes, W. S., & Jones, C. R. Category accessibility and impression formation. *Journal of Experimental Social Psychology,* 1977, *13,* 131–154.

Jones, E. E., & Davis, K. E. From acts to dispositions: The attribution process in person perception. In L. Berkowitz (Ed.), *Advances in experimental social psychology.* New York: Academic Press, 1965.

Jones, E. E., & Nisbett, R. E. The actor and the observer: Divergent perceptions of the causes of behavior. In E. E. Jones, D. E. Kanouse, H. H. Kelley, R. E. Nisbett, S. Valins, B. Weiner (Eds.), *Attribution: Perceiving the causes of behavior.* Morristown, N.J.: General Learning Press, 1971.

Kelley, H. H. Attribution theory in social psychology. In D. Levine (Ed.), *Nebraska Symposium on Motivation,* 1967, *15,* 192–238.

Kelley, H. H. Causal schemata and the attribution process. In E. E. Jones, D. E. Kanouse, H. H. Kelley, R. E. Nisbett, S. Valins, & B. Widner (Eds.), *Attribution: Perceiving the causes of behavior.* Morristown, N.J.: General Learning Press, 1971.

Lachman, R., Lachman, J. L., & Butterfield, E. C. *Cognitive psychology and information processing.* Hillsdale, N.J.: Lawrence Erlbaum Associates, 1979.

Lichtenstein, E., & Brewer, W. F. Memory for goal-directed events. *Cognitive Psychology,* 1980, *12,* 412–445.

Loken, B. J., & Wyer, R. S. The effects of reporting beliefs in syllogistically-related propositions on the recognition of unmentioned propositions. *Journal of Personality and Social Psychology,* 1983.

Mandler, J. Categorical and schematic organization in memory, In C. R. Puff (Ed.), *Memory, organization and structure.* New York: Academic Press, 1979.

Markus, H. Self-schemata and processing information about the self. *Journal of Personality and Social Psychology,* 1977, *35,* 63–78.

Markus, H., & Smith, J. The influence of self-schema on the perception of others. In N. Cantor & J. Kihlstrom (Eds.), *Cognition, social interaction and personality.* Hillsdale, N.J.: Lawrence Erlbaum Associates, 1981.

Massad, C. M., Hubbard, M., & Newtson, D. Perceptual selectivity: Contributing process and possible cure for impression perseverance. *Journal of Experimental Social Psychology,* 1979, *15,* 513–532.

McGuire, W. J. A syllogistic analysis of cognitive relationships. In M. J. Rosenberg, C. I. Hovland, W. J. McGuire, R. P. Abelson, & J. W. Brehm (Eds.), *Attitude organization and change.* New Haven: Yale University Press, 1960.

McGuire, W. J. The nature of attitudes and attitude change. In G. Lindzey & E. Aronson (Eds.), *Handbook of social psychology.* Reading, Mass.: Addison-Wesley, 1968.

McGuire, W. J. The probabilogical model of cognitive structure and attitude change. In R. E. Petty, T. M. Ostrom, & T. C. Brock (Eds.), *Cognitive responses in persuasion.* Hillsdale, N.J.: Lawrence Erlbaum Associates, 1981.

McGuire, W. J., McGuire, C. V., Child, P., & Fujioka, T. A. Salience of ethnicity in the spontaneous self-concept as a function of one's ethnic distinctiveness in the social environment. *Journal of Personality and Social Psychology,* 1978, *36,* 511–520.

McGuire, W. J., McGuire, C. V., & Winton, W. Effects of household sex composition on the salience of one's gender in the spontaneous self-concept. *Journal of Experimental Social Psychology,* 1979, *15,* 77–90.

Meyer, D. E., & Schvaneveldt, R. W. Facilitation in recognition between pairs of words: Evidence of a dependence between retrieval operations. *Journal of Experimental Psychology,* 1971, *90,* 227–234.

Meyer, D. E., & Schvaneveldt, R. W. Meaning, memory structure and mental processes. In C. N. Cofer (Ed.), *The structure of human memory*. San Francisco: W. H. Freeman, 1976.

Moore, B. S., Sherrod, D. R., Liu, T. J., & Underwood, B. The dispositional shift in attribution over time. *Journal of Experimental Social Psychology*, 1979, *15*, 553–569.

Newtson, D. A. Foundations of attribution: The perception of ongoing behavior. In J. Harvey, W. Ickes, & R. Kidd (Eds.), *New directions in attribution research* (Vol. 1). Hillsdale N.J.: Lawrence Erlbaum Associates, 1976.

Newtson, D. A., & Engquist, G. The perceptual organization of ongoing behavior. *Journal of Experimental Social Psychology*, 1976, *12*, 436–450.

Newtson, D. A., Engquist, G., & Bois, J. The objective basis of behavior units. *Journal of Personality and Social Psychology*, 1977, *35*, 847–862.

Nisbett, R. E., & Ross, L. *Human inference: Strategies and shortcomings of social judgment.* Englewood Cliffs, N.J.: Prentice-Hall, 1980.

Norman, D. A., & Bobrow, D. G. On the role of active memory processes in perception and cognition. In C. N. Cofer (Ed.), *The structure of human memory*. San Francisco: W. H. Freeman, 1976.

Nottenburg, G., & Shoben, E. J. Scripts as linear orders. *Journal of Experimental Social Psychology*, 1980, *16*, 329–347.

Orvis, B. R., Cunningham, J. D., & Kelley, H. H. A closer examination of causal inference: The roles of consensus, distinctiveness and consistency information. *Journal of Personality and Social Psychology*, 1975, *32*, 605–616.

Ostrom, T. M., Lingle, J. H., Pryor, J. B., & Geva, N. Cognitive organization of person impressions. In R. Hastie, T. Ostrom, E. Ebbesen, R. Wyer, D. Hamilton, & D. Carlston (Eds.), *Person memory: Cognitive basis of social perception*. Hillsdale, N.J.: Lawrence Erlbaum Associates, 1980.

Ostrom, T. M., Pryor, J. B., & Simpson, D. D. The organization of social information. In E. T. Higgins, C. P. Herman, & M. P. Zanna (Eds.) *Social cognition: The Ontario Symposium on personality and social psychology*. Hillsdale, N.J.: Lawrence Erlbaum Associates, 1981.

Petty, R. E., & Cacioppo, J. T. *Attitudes and persuasion: Classic and contemporary approaches.* Dubuque, Iowa: W. C. Brown, 1981.

Picek, J. S., Sherman, S. J., & Shiffrin, R. M. Cognitive organization and coding of social structures. *Journal of Personality and Social Psychology*, 1975, *31*, 758–768.

Raaijmakers, J. G. W., & Shiffrin, R. M. Search of associative memory. *Psychological Review*, 1981, *88*, 93–134.

Regan, D., & Totten, J. Empathy and attribution: Turning observers into actors. *Journal of Personality and Social Psychology*, 1975, *32*, 850–856.

Rogers, T. B. A model of the self as an aspect of the human information processing system. In N. Cantor & J. Kihlstrom (Eds.), *Cognition, social interaction and personality*. Hillsdale, N.J.: Lawrence Erlbaum Associates, 1981.

Rogers, T. B., Kuiper, N. A., & Kirker, W. S. Self-reference and the encoding of personal information. *Journal of Personality and Social Psychology*, 1977, *35*, 677–688.

Rosenberg, S., & Sedlak, A. Structural representations of implicit personality theory. In L. Berkowitz (Ed.), *Advances in experimental social psychology* (Vol. 6). New York: Academic Press, 1972.

Ross, B., & Bower, G, H. Comparisons of models of associative recall. *Memory & Cognition*, 1981, *9*, 1–16.

Ross, L. The intuitive psychologist and his shortcomings. In L. Berkowitz (Ed.) *Advances in experimental social psychology*, vol. 10. New York: Academic Press, 1977.

Ross, L., Lepper, M. R., Strack, F., & Steinmetz, J. Social explanation and social expectation: Effects of real and hypothetical explanations on subjective likelihood. *Journal of Personality and Social Psychology*, 1977, *35*, 817–829.

Rothbart, M., Evans, M., & Fulero, S. Recall for confirming events: Memory processes and the maintenance of social stereotypes. *Journal of Experimental Social Psychology,* 1979, *15,* 343–355.

Rothbart, M., Fulero, S., Jensen, C., Howard, J., & Birrell, P. From individual to group impressions: Availability heuristics in stereotype formation. *Journal of Experimental Social Psychology,* 1978, *14,* 237–255.

Rumelhart, D. Schemata: The building blocks of cognition. In R. J. Spiro, B. C. Bruce, & W. F. Brewer (Eds.), *Theoretical issues in reading comprehension: Perspectives from cognitive psychology, linguistics, artificial intelligence and education.* Hillsdale, N.J.: Lawrence Erlbaum Associates, 1980.

Rumelhart, D. E., & Ortony, A. The representation of knowledge in memory. In R. C. Anderson, R. J. Spiro, & W. E. Montague (Eds.), *Schooling and the acquisition of knowledge.* Hillsdale, N.J.: Lawrence Erlbaum Associates, 1977.

Rundus, D. Analysis of rehearsal processes in free recall. *Journal of Experimental Psychology,* 1971, *89,* 63–77.

Salancik, G. R. Inference of one's attitude from behavior recalled under lingu-stically manipulated cognitive sets. *Journal of Experimental Social Psychology,* 1974, *10,* 415–427.

Salancik, G. R., & Calder, B. J. *A non-predispositional information analysis of attitude expressions.* Unpublished manuscript, University of Illinois, 1974.

Schank, R. C., & Abelson, R. P. *Scripts, plans, goals and understanding.* Hillsdale, N.J.: Lawrence Erlbaum Associates, 1977.

Sentis, K. P., & Burnstein, E. Remembering schema-consistent information: Effects of a balance schema on recognition memory. *Journal of Personality and Social Psychology,* 1979, *37,* 2200–2212.

Sherman, S. J., Skov, R. B., Hervitz, E. F., & Stock, C. B. The effects of explaining hypothetical future events: From possibility to probability to actuality and beyond. *Journal of Experimental Social Psychology,* 1981, *17,* 142–158.

Smith, D. A., & Graesser, A. C. *Memory for actions in scripted activities as a function of typicality, retention interval and retrieval task.* Unpublished manuscript, California State University, Fullerton, 1980.

Snyder, M., & Cantor, N. Testing hypotheses about other people: The use of historical knowledge. *Journal of Experimental Social Psychology,* 1979, *15,* 330–342.

Spiro, R. J. Remembering information from text: The "state of schema" approach. In R. C. Anderson, R. J. Spiro, & W. E. Montague (Eds.), *Schooling and the acquisition of knowledge.* Hillsdale, N.J.: Lawrence Erlbaum Associates, 1977.

Srull, T. K. Person memory: Some tests of associative storage and retrieval models. *Journal of Experimental Psychology: Human Learning and Memory,* 1981, *7,* 440–463.

Srull, T. K. Organizational and retrieval processes in person memory: An examination of processing objectives, presentation format, and the possible role of self-generated cues. *Journal of Personality and Social Psychology,* 1983, *44,* 1157–1170.

Srull, T. K., & Brand, J. F. Memory for information about persons: The effect of encoding operations on subsequent retrieval. *Journal of Verbal Learning and Verbal Behavior,* 1983, *22,* 219–230.

Srull, T. K., & Wyer, R. S. The role of category accessibility in the interpretation of information about persons: Some determinants and implications. *Journal of Personality and Social Psychology,* 1979, *37,* 1660–1672.

Srull, T. K., & Wyer, R. S. Category accessibility and social perception: Some implications for the study of person memory and interpersonal judgment. *Journal of Personality and Social Psychology,* 1980, *38,* 841–856.

Surber, C. F. Necessary versus sufficient causal schemata: Attributions for achievement in difficult and easy tasks. *Journal of Experimental Social Psychology,* 1981, *17,* 569–586.

Taylor, S. E., & Crocker, J. Schematic basis of social information processing. In E. T. Higgins, C. P. Herman, & M. P. Zanna (Eds.), *Social cognition: The Ontario symposium on personality and social psychology*. Hillsdale, N.J.: Lawrence Erlbaum Associates, 1981.

Taylor, S. E., & Fiske, S. T. Salience, attention and attribution: Top of the head phenomena. In L. Berkowitz (Ed.), *Advances in experimental social psychology* (Vol. 2). New York: Academic Press, 1978.

Tversky, A., & Kahneman, D. Availability: A heuristic for judging frequency and probability. *Cognitive Psychology*, 1973, *5*, 207–232.

Tversky, A., & Kahneman, D. Judgment under uncertainty: Heuristics and biases. *Science*, 1974, *85*, 1124–1131.

Woll, S. B., & Graesser, A. C. *Memory for information typical or atypical of person schemata*. Unpublished manuscript, California State University, Fullerton, 1980.

Woodworth, R. S., & Schlosberg, H. *Experimental psychology*. New York: Holt, 1954.

Wyer, R. S. *Cognitive organization and change: An information-processing approach*. Hillsdale, N.J.: Lawrence Erlbaum Associates, 1974.

Wyer, R. S. *The nature and use of schemata about persons*. Invited address, Midwestern Psychological Association Convention, Chicago, Ill., 1979.

Wyer, R. S. Category ratings as "subjective expected values": Implications for attitude formation and change. *Psychological Review*, 1973, *80*, 446–67.

Wyer, R. S., Bodenhausen, G. V., & Srull, T. K. The cognitive representation of persons and groups and its effect on recall and recognition memory. Unpublished manuscript, Univ. of Illinois, 1983.

Wyer, R. S., & Carlston, D. E. *Social cognition, inference and attribution*. Hillsdale, N.J.: Lawrence Erlbaum Associates, 1979.

Wyer, R. S., & Gordon, S. E. The recall of information about persons and groups. *Journal of Experimental Social Psychology*, 1982, *18*, 128–164.

Wyer, R. S., & Hartwick, J. The role of information retrieval and conditional inference processes in belief formation and change. In L. Berkowitz (Ed.), *Advances in Experimental Social Psychology* (Vol. 13). New York: Academic Press, 1980.

Wyer, R. S., & Lyon, J. A test of cognitive balance theory implications for social inference processes. *Journal of Personality and Social Psychology*, 1970, *16*, 598–618.

Wyer, R. S., & Srull, T. K. The processing of social stimulus information: A conceptual integration. In R. Hastie, T. Ostrom, E. Ebbesen, R. Wyer, D. Hamilton, & D. Carlston (Eds.), *Person memory: Cognitive basis of social perception*. Hillsdale, N.J.: Lawrence Erlbaum Associates, 1980.

Wyer, R. S., & Srull, T. K. Category accessibility: Some theoretical and empirical issues concerning the processing of social stimulus information. In E. T. Higgins, C. P. Herman, & M. P. Zanna (Eds.), *Social cognition: The Ontario symposium* on personality and social psychology. Hillsdale, N.J.: Lawrence Erlbaum Associates, 1981.

Wyer, R. S., Srull, T. K., & Gordon, S. E. The effects of predicting a person's behavior on subsequent trait judgments. *Journal of Experimental Social Psychology*, 1984.

Zajonc, R. B. Cognitive theories in social psychology. In G. Lindzey & E. Aronson (Eds.), *Handbook of social psychology* (Vol. 1). Reading, Mass. Addison-Wesley, 1968.

Zajonc, R. B., & Burnstein, E. The learning of balanced and unbalanced social structure. *Journal of Personality*, 1965, *33*, 153–163.

Zajonc, R. B., & Sherman, S. J. Structural balance and the inducation of relations. *Journal of Personality*, 1967, *35*, 635–650.

3 Social Memory

Reid Hastie
Bernadette Park
Reneé Weber*
Northwestern University

Contents

---

*Order of authorship for second and third authors was determined by a coin toss.

INTRODUCTION

The most fundamental questions for the field of social cognition concern the nature of social information, its acquisition, and the manner in which it is represented in the mind. Almost all current theories of cognition are based on the notion that physical events in the outside world are represented in a mental code that resides in the head. This chapter is a review of the empirical literature concerned with the mental representation of information about people.

We have selected the person as the basic object of social cognition to facilitate connections with closely related fields of psychology and to provide definitional convenience and precision. Developmental, personality, and clinical psychologists have been concerned with the mental representation of the person for far longer than social psychologists. Enduring questions concerning the differences in perception of animate and inanimate objects by children (Piaget, 1929, 1954), the representation of significant others in memory and fantasy (Monroe, 1955; Freud, 1935) and the gradual acquisition of self- and personological-concepts across the lifespan are central in these fields (Adler, 1956; Sullivan, 1953; Laing, 1967; Kelly, 1955; Allport, 1961; Bandura & Walters, 1963). The present review should be useful to theoreticians who wish to integrate empirical and conceptual results from social psychology and these neighboring fields. Furthermore, the person is a relatively well-defined, easily identifiable entity with clear "borders" and a finite measurable existence, unlike some alternate social units (see chapter by Ostrom this Handbook for further discussion). Finally, we believe that the individual is truly one of the basic organizational units of memory and we will review empirical evidence for the salience, stability, and centrality of the person in mental life. We emphasize that the focus of the review is on empirical results or facts relevant to these social memory processes. Of course, it is not possible to talk about facts in an "atheoretical" language. We have made decisions about which articles to include based on theoretical considerations and there are many low-level theoretical commentaries scattered throughout the review. Nevertheless, our emphasis is on methods and results rather than theoretical issues and we do not deal directly with general models for person memory. Many of the other chapters in the present handbook (e.g., those by Wyer, and others) provide more substantial treatments of theoretical problems.

Hastie and Carlston (1980) noted that a "minimal cognitive model" for person memory would have to include at least five components: (a) a vocabulary to describe the stimulus environment; (b) a characterization of the encoding transformations of stimulus information that occur during acquisition; (c) a description of the mental representation that is created and retained in memory; (d) a characterization of the decoding function that operates on the mental representation to generate a response during retrieval; and (e) a vocabulary to describe the response and its alternatives. We use this general framework to organize our review of empirical results in the present paper. In addition we have included a short review of individual differences in memory for information about people.

THE STIMULUS

Stimulus materials in research on memory for information about people have included photographs of faces, tape recordings of voices, movies and videotapes of people acting and interacting, staged and natural interactions, and (most frequently) verbal materials in the form of sentences describing people's behavior or trait adjectives attributed to people. Two stimulus environments must be considered in any evaluation of "the stimulus" in social memory research. First, there is the stimulus structure of the natural social world outside the laboratory; second, there is the structure of the stimulus materials presented in the laboratory research task. It is a cliché in research on perception, although a profound cliché, that "the stimulus" can only be defined with reference to the set of events of which it is a part (Garner, 1974; Gibson, 1960). Thus, the "perception" of a stimulus in a laboratory task will be determined by the set of alternative events that a subject conceives of but knows did not occur. This set of alternative events is controlled both by the context defined by the experimental task in the laboratory and by the larger context of possible events in the natural world. It would be hard to overestimate the significance of this point for research on social judgment and social memory, particularly when we consider the fact that most social psychology experimental tasks are designed to mimic naturally occurring tasks. In fact, many social psychology experiments take place under conditions where subjects are unaware that they are in an artificial, experimenter-controlled environment.

Unfortunately, there are very few studies of the structure of the real social world and almost no research that provides analyses of the structure of ordinary social stimulus events and relates that structure to structure in the subject's responses in a memory task. Most of the research that does attempt to look at the structure of the natural social stimulus is associated with traditions of research concerned with verbal and nonverbal communication (e.g., Krauss, Apple, Morency, Wenzel, & Winton, 1980; Kraut, 1978). This area of research provides the most sophisticated analyses of natural social stimulus structure in psychology, but as yet there are no published reports of research studying memory processes. Research on memory for faces and voices (Clifford, 1980; Davies, Ellis, & Shepherd, 1981) has also been accompanied by more careful analyses of stimulus domains, both in laboratory and in natural environments.

One example of research that attempted to analyze the contribution of the structure in a sequence of natural stimulus events to the structure in memory-based responses is provided in the literature on behavioral observation techniques. D'Andrade (1974) reports the results of reanalyses of behavioral rating data generated by trained observers who watched and rated the members of small groups. D'Andrade found that the relationships between the observers' delayed ratings of group members' behavioral tendencies and the observer's semantic concepts for behavior were much stronger than the relationships between the delayed ratings of group members' behavioral tendencies and observational ratings of the group members' actual rated behaviors. Schweder and D'Andrade (1979) have interpreted this differential strength of relationships as evidence for biased guessing processes when memory-based judgments of behavioral tendencies were made long after the original behaviors were observed. Assuming that the original observers' ratings of the behaviors of members of the groups were a useful measure of stimulus structure, D'Andrade concluded that a major source of the inter-response structure in delayed ratings of behavioral tendencies was derived from mental structure that the observers bring to the observation situation and not from stimulus structure.

We have also noted, in previous reviews, that some researchers (e.g., Beach & Wertheimer, 1961; Fiske & Cox, 1979; Ostrom, 1975) have used information in subjects' open-ended descriptions of other people to form categories to classify person stimulus information. For example, Fiske and Cox suggested that categories for physical attributes, behavioral information, social relations, characteristic situations, origins, and functional properties could be applied to classify information about people as stimulus entities. However, no memory researchers have tried to explore the rates at which personal attributes and behaviors occur in the real world, and perhaps more important, the correlations or constraints among attributes.

The point of this short comment is that we know virtually nothing about the structure of the natural social stimulus in person memory research. The failure to include considerations of the natural stimulus domain structure has been noted by recent critics of the information-processing approach to social memory and social perception processes (e.g., Baron, 1980; Forgas, 1979; McArthur & Baron, 1983; Neisser, 1980). Many of the theoretical advances catalogued in the present handbook have occurred at the expense of developments in our knowledge of the structure of the real social world and its phenomena outside the laboratory. One of the major functions served by the interstitial field of social psychology is to connect results from artificial stimulus environments with their analogues in naturally occurring phenomena. Furthermore, given the natural appearance of many of social psychology's research tasks, an understanding of the extra-laboratory social world is essential for an adequate characterization of the psychologically effective laboratory stimulus. Finally, knowledge of the relationships between laboratory and real-world environments is a necessary condition for the integration of social psychological findings with results from field observation and participant research (e.g., Goffman, 1959, 1967).

ENCODING

Units of Perception

In an effort to understand how individuals break up a sequence of incoming information into meaningful chunks, Newtson (1973) developed a procedure, referred to as unitization, in which a subject is asked to press a button whenever he or she perceives a "unit" of social information has been completed within an ongoing social interaction. One study that attempted to relate subjects' unitization of information to memory for that information was conducted by Newtson and Engquist (1976). They showed subjects one half of a film, and then asked them to determine whether each of a series of slides was part of the presented half of the film or part of the unpresented half. On the basis of judgments from a separate group of subjects, these slides were taken from consensually defined breakpoints at the end or beginning of a unit as well as from nonbreak points centrally located within a unit. Subjects were better able to recognize both presented and nonpresented breakpoint events than nonbreakpoint events. Newtson and Engquist concluded that memory for the film information was stored in a form structured according to the perceptual units identified in the button-pressing task.

Ebbesen (1980) has criticized the Newtson and Engquist study by noting that the types of behaviors that occurred at breakpoints and nonbreakpoints were systematically different. Hence differential recognition may be due to the nature of the stimulus behaviors, rather than because of their locations relative to perceptual breakpoints. Ebbesen argued that within the Newtson and Engquist videotape, behaviors that occurred at breakpoints were objectively more distinctive than the behaviors that occurred within the units.

Ebbesen also pointed out that Newtson's hypothesis that sequences of actions would be segmented and stored in memory according to breakpoint information appeared to diverge from principles of memory in other stimulus domains. In many cases (memory for word lists, sentences, narrative discourse, photographs), the gist or prototypical characteristics of a to-be-remembered event appear to be stored (or to endure longer) in memory than other surface features of the event. Thus, it would be natural to hypothesize that the prototypical characteristics of a behavior segment, usually found in central rather than breakpoint locations, would dominate memory representation.

It is possible that the same mechanism (i.e., distinctiveness) is the underlying determinant of both recall and judgments of breakpoint location. Nevertheless, research by Cohen and Ebbesen (1979) indicates that subjects with different task orientations (i.e., goals) unitize the same stimulus sequence differently. There is a suggestion that unitization and memory are related in the Cohen and Ebbesen study. Subjects given the task of learning to perform the actions of the videotaped character reported smaller action units and more accurately recognized details concerning the filmed actress's behavior than subjects instructed to form an impression.

Massad, Hubbard, and Newtson (1979) found that assigning different social roles to cartoon figures affected unitization judgments and the impressions formed of the "actors" in a cartoon "block world." Interpretive set may affect memory for some aspects of stimulus episodes and it is plausible that perceptual unitization is a related or even mediating process in the larger cognitive system. However, memory measures were not obtained in these experiments and additional research is needed to explore the unitization-memory relationship.

A fundamental methodological problem is raised by our review of the Cohen and Ebbesen (1979) and Massad et al. (1979) studies. Hypotheses concerning the role that perceptual unitization plays in the comprehension and memory of person information require sophisticated research designs and analyses for their investigation. Converging operational measures of the hypothesized intervening cognitive processes and sophisticated statistical models (cf. Kenny, 1979; Smith, 1982) are necessary to tease apart alternate hypotheses for these relationships. To date, adequately powerful methods have not been applied in this area.

Encoding Task

There are a number of studies of social memory in which the encoding task is varied in instructions to the subject. We have divided these studies into three sets according to the generality of the task manipulation. Some instructions were designed to change the subject's definition of the experimental task and general *performance goals.* For example, some subjects may be led to expect a memory test, producing the goal of remembering as much information as possible, while other subjects may be instructed to form an impression of a stimulus character producing the goals of attending to, comprehending, and integrating relevant stimulus information. Research on subjects' strategies in memory and impression formation tasks is usually cited to provide a bridge between the experimenter's instructions and the subject's (hypothesized) cognitive processes.

In some cases, more indirect relationships exist between the experimenter's instructions and the subject's processing goals. For example, subjects may be instructed that they will actually meet the stimulus character at some later point in time. For the most part the effects of the "future interaction" instruction on subjects' cognitive processes have not been studied. Research by Srull and Brand (1983) is the best example of an investigation of the effects of expected future interaction on cognitive processing and person memory. These researchers found that subjects were able to recall more information about a character with whom they expected to interact and that they were likelier to organize the relevant information around the individual in memory if future interaction was expected as compared to no future interaction. However, in most research a chain of speculations links the instruction to the subject's behavior.

A second set of studies involves variations in the subject's *perspective* but not changes of the more general processing goals. In these studies, instructions vary the subject's assigned social role, spatial perspective, mood, or empathetic identification. The third set of studies involves variations of the specific *focus* of evaluation within a social judgment task. For example, subjects might be asked to evaluate a stimulus character's degree of extraversion or intelligence, thus, varying judgment focus while holding task and perspective constant.

Performance Goals.   Most research that explores the influence of goals on the organization of information has contrasted instructions to remember an event or person with instructions to form an impression of the event or person. Subjects with an impression set appear to organize information by impression-relevant trait concepts (Cohen & Ebbesen, 1979; Hoffman, Mischel, & Mazze, 1981; Jeffrey & Mischel, 1979). However, the effects of memory set instructions on memory organization are less clear. Several studies have found that information is organized by traits to a lesser extent when subjects are told to memorize the information rather than to form an impression (Cohen & Ebbesen, 1979; Hamilton, 1981). Wyer and Gordon (1982) concluded that a subtle difference existed between memory structures created under impression and memory set instructions. In the relevant conditions of their experiments large numbers of behaviors and traits were attributed to a single character under either memory set or impression set instructions. Under memory set instructions the distinctiveness or unexpectedness of behavioral information at encoding appeared to be the primary determinant of later recall and memory structures because recall of behaviors did not reflect the organization of traits attributed to the character. Under impression set instructions, a trait-based organizational structure appeared plausible, and evaluative inconsistency between behaviors and traits was correlated with recall. This result was supported by Hartwick's (1979) finding that a general instruction to form an impression would focus attention on evaluative (good–bad) dimensions of meaning in stimulus materials. Thus, evaluative features would be especially likely to appear in memory representations and affect recall.

Wyer and Gordon included a modification of the standard impression set instruction in which subjects were instructed that the behaviors and traits should be attributed to different individuals and that an impression should be formed of the group to which these individuals belonged. Under this group impression instruction, trait information (rather than behavioral information) appeared to be primary in the impression judgments and in structuring memory. Interestingly, evaluative inconsistency was not directly related to recallability (as in the case of the individual impression set); instead, behaviors that were evaluatively inconsistent with trait adjectives were relatively poorly recalled.

The major focus of research on goals and memory has been on the completeness of recall memory (i.e., proportion of to-be-remembered events recalled) under Memory and Impression instruction sets. Several researchers have found evidence of more complete recall under Impression task instructions. Hamilton and his associates (Hamilton, Katz, & Leirer, 1980) found that subjects recalled more information if they received impression formation instructions prior to reading behavioral descriptions about a person than if they were told to memorize the information. (See also Pryor, Simpson, Mitchell, Ostrom, & Lydon, 1982; Srull, 1981; Wyer & Gordon, 1982).

Some evidence suggesting that more complete recall may be obtained under Memory goals than Impression goals has been reported. However, the two relevant studies (Hoffman et al., 1981; Jeffrey & Mischel, 1979) used different procedures from those previously mentioned. In these studies, one group (sorters) was given a goal (impression, memory, prediction, empathy) and asked to sort episodes about a person into categories. Subjects in a second group (recallers) were each yoked to a member of the first (sorters) group and were given a set of episodes sorted by their yoked-partner and told to infer what categorization criteria had been used. On a subsequent recall test, more episodes were recalled by recallers who were given the episodes originally sorted under Memory-set instructions. However, the results from the yoked-subject designs are not directly relevant to conditions under which *one* subject "organizes" and retrieves information.

Researchers have found that goals affect the recall of particular types of information. Cohen and her associates (Cohen & Ebbesen, 1979; Cohen, Ebbesen, & Allen, 1981) have suggested that each goal activates a cluster of schemas. These schemas direct attention to certain features of a situation and consequently affect what information can be recalled. Consistent with this speculation, subjects who were told to learn to perform a task while watching an instructional videotape recognized task-related details more accurately than those told to form an impression of the actor performing the task.

Before further progress can be made, a typology of goals must be developed. It is unclear which goals should be regarded as distinct and which are coordinate or subordinate to one another. In addition to providing a system for classifying goals, the typology should also specify how goals are activated. Experimental instructions vary considerably from laboratory to laboratory, and they may be comprehended by subjects quite differently than intended. Finally, the generality of research examining the relationship between perceivers' goals and the organization and retrieval of information is limited. Most studies have focused on the influence of Impression formation or Memory goals that are induced through instructional sets. Future research should also examine the influence of perceivers' naturally instigated goals and the conditions under which different goals are invoked.

Perspective. A series of studies has investigated the effects of the perceiver's perspective at the time of encoding on later retrieval of information. The visual, emotional, or cognitive perspective from which individuals experience social stimuli influences the way that information is encoded and retained.

1. Role-Taking. Several studies have explored the effects of taking the role of a character in a narrative on later recall for information contained in the narrative. For example, Anderson and Pichert (1978) found that when a subject was instructed to read a prose passage from the perspective of a burglar or of a home buyer, and later asked to recall information from the same perspective, a larger proportion of perspective-relevant information was retrieved than when encoding and retrieval perspectives did not match. However, if a second recall followed a shift in perspective, the subject recalled additional perspective-relevant information with the new perspective. Fass and Schumacher (1981) extended Anderson and Pichert's design by including a 24-hour recall condition. With immediate recall, a subject recalled more information relevant to the perspective taken at the time of recall, regardless of the encoding perspective. However, with a delay the subject recalled more perspective-relevant information only when the retrieval and encoding perspective were the same.

Fass and Schumacher hypothesized that immediately after reading the story a great variety of perspective-relevant and irrelevant details are available in memory. The availability of encoding-perspective-irrelevant details (which are relevant to alternate perspectives) enables a novel retrieval-perspective to access additional information in memory. As time passes, details that are not relevant to the encoding perspective are lost and the potential advantage of a novel retrieval-perspective also decreases.

Wyer, Srull, Gordon, and Hartwick (1982) conducted an experiment that included conditions replicating the basic Anderson and Pichert design and included delayed recall conditions similar to Fass and Schumacher. They found that information relevant to encoding perspective was better recalled than irrelevant information. But, the slight differences in recall as a function of an altered retrieval perspective did not reach conventional levels of statistical significance. Unlike Fass and Schumacher, they failed to find clear effects of the retrieval perspective on either immediate or delayed recall. A conservative summary of the findings from research on the Anderson and Pichert role-perspective is that encoding perspective has sizeable, replicable effects on memory for perspective relevant material. However, postpresentation perspective has at most small, unreliable effects on memory.

The concept of role-defined perspective is close to the notion of empathic identification (e.g., Regan & Totten, 1975). Harvey, Yarkin, Lightner, & Town (1980) manipulated empathic set by instructing subjects to take the role of a close friend of a couple who were engaged in an intimate conversation; other subjects were instructed to take an objective, detached role. All subjects then viewed a videotaped conversation that ended unpleasantly or pleasantly. Empathic set subjects recalled more details from the conversation than did detached set subjects. These authors also varied several other task or set factors and obtained effects on the memory measures: (a) subjects expecting a memory test while viewing the film showed superior recall compared to subjects who did not expect the test; (b) subjects expecting to interact with a person on the videotape recalled more than subjects who did not expect future interaction; and subjects who were told that one person on the videotape was emotionally disturbed recalled more than subjects who were not so instructed.

Harvey et al. interpreted all of these findings as evidence for the mediation of a single "interpretive involvement" process. It is plausible that the effects on recall memory were produced by subjects' thoughts while "trying to understand the bases of the events observed." More empathic, involved roles or sets would instigate more reasoning about the causes of other people's behavior and causal reasoning has been shown to increase memorability of events in several other experimental investigations (Black & Bern, 1981; Bradshaw & Anderson, 1982; Hastie, 1980).

2. Spatial Perspective. Taylor and Fiske (1975) report that a person who is visually salient during a conversation is later judged as having been more causally relevant in determining the nature of the conversation. However, they found no evidence for differential recall of verbal or visual information relevant to the character who was visually salient.

Fiske, Taylor, Etcoff, and Laufer (1979) report that subjects recalled a greater proportion of verbal statements made by the character whose perspective they were instructed to take while reading a story. The research provided a comparison of the effects of subject perspective (physical vantage point attributed to a character) and subject role (actor or observer) and found that the visual perspective produced much larger effects on recall memory for verbal material than subject role in a narrative about a traffic accident.

3. Mood. Bower, Gilligan, and Monteiro (1981) have studied the influence of the subject's mood at the time of reading a story on the information retained about the story. Following hypnotic induction of mood state (happiness or sadness), a subject read a passage that contained both happy and sad information. The subject later recalled as much information from the passage as possible while in a neutral mood state. Subjects were more likely to recall information congruent with their mood at the time of encoding. No differential recall was observed in a second study, in which subjects read the story in a neutral mood state and later retrieved the information in a hypnotically induced happy or sad state. Similarly, if mood at encoding is crossed with mood at retrieval, almost all the effects on recall are due to the mood at encoding. Finally, Bower et al. ruled out the possibility that a subject was simply identifying with the story character in a similar mood. Rather, the subjects were differentially attending to mood-congruent items across characters. After reading a story containing a happy and a

sad character in a hypnotically induced happy or sad mood, subjects recall more mood-congruent items, but do not recall more information overall for the mood-congruent character. (See chapter by Isen in this handbook for further discussion of mood and memory.)

4. Self-referent Processing. In 1977 Rogers, Kuiper, and Kirker published a provocative paper in which they concluded that the self-concept was a vast "cognitive schema" and that establishing relationships between information in memory and the self-schema would produce strong facilitating effects on later recall for that information. Their research used an incidental learning paradigm in which subjects initially made ratings of words (usually trait adjectives). In one condition the words were rated with reference to the cue question, "Describes you?" This self-reference encoding task, as compared to phonemic, structural, and semantic judgment tasks, produced high levels of recall on later memory tests. These researchers made strong claims for the power of the self-reference encoding task: "In the realm of human information processing it is difficult to conceive of an encoding device that carries more potential for the rich embellishment of stimulus input than does self-reference" (p. 687). In subsequent papers (e.g., Kuiper & Rogers, 1979) the authors demonstrated that the facilitative effects of the self-referent judgment were not duplicated with some other social judgments, for example, judgments with reference to an unfamiliar experimenter.

One response to the Rogers et al. demonstration was a series of papers that showed that there was nothing "unique" about the self-referent encoding task. For example, Bower and Gilligan (1979) demonstrated that semantic encoding judgments could produce incidental recall levels that were comparable to those produced by the self-referent encoding task (see also Ferguson, Rule, & Carlson, 1983, in press). Keenan and Baillet (1980) demonstrated that a series of person-referent judgments yielded incidental recall performances that were roughly ordered according to the familiarity of the referent persons (ordered from self, to best friend, to parent, to acquaintance, to teacher, and so forth). Kuiper and Rogers (1979, Experiment 4) had also explored some effects of familiarity. They found that judgments of trait adjectives with reference to a familiar experimenter yielded levels of recall that were at least as high as self-referent judgments. This finding parallels results of research concerned with the recall of information about characters varying in familiarity (see section on familiarity and memory below). Kendzierski (1980) also found relatively high levels of recall for trait adjectives given self-referent processing. Her design also included judgments of fittingness to a situation or behavioral script. Self-referent judgments and script-fittingness judgments produced comparably high levels of recall.

These results imply that it is the quantity of information available in memory about the self that produces the relatively high memory performances following self-referent encoding tasks. This interpretation is consistent with the original Rogers et al. account that emphasized the quantity of information about the self in long-term memory and the effects of quantity on the elaboration or embellishment of incoming information. However, other characteristics of self-referent processing or self-information in long-term memory may also be involved in the phenomenon. For example, the affective quality of information about the self could be responsible for the memory results. Or perhaps the distinctiveness rather than the elaboration of the to-be-remembered information in the context of the self-concept produces the obtained memory effects (cf. Jacoby & Craik, 1979).

In any event, the phenomenon is probably more complex than suggested by a simple familiarity or quantity of information account. For example, Lord (1980) replicated the Rogers et al. finding using trait adjectives as stimulus materials. However, when concrete noun stimulus items were presented, he found that other-referent mental images produced superior recall compared to self-referent mental images. These results were not anticipated by any of the theoretical accounts for the original self-referent encoding effect. Lord argued that verbal or propositional information may be especially easily linked to the self-concept, while visual information is more easily linked to representations of other people. While this may be an interesting possibility, a clear explication of what is meant by verbal and visual information is still needed, as well as additional research on the difference between memory for information related to self and other memory structures.

Markus and her colleagues (Markus, 1977; Markus, Crane, Bernstein, & Siladi, 1982) have explored individual differences in self-concept and memory processes. In her early research (1977) Markus classified her subjects with reference to the personality trait construct of independence-dependence. Using self-rating on an adjective checklist, subjects were classified as independent (subjects who rated themselves highly ''independent'' and who rated the trait as important), dependent, or aschematic (subjects who rated themselves in the middle range on the scales). Markus found correlations between self-schema and performance on self-description and prediction tasks. In a second series of experiments (Markus et al., 1982) subjects were classified as masculine, feminine, or androgynous, again using self-descriptive trait adjective checklists. In an incidental learning task, similar to those used by Rogers and his colleagues, subjects were likelier to recall traits that were congruent with their gender self-schema.

A number of other studies have obtained results consistent with the generalization that information consistent with one's self-concept is better remembered than information that is inconsistent. For example, Mischel, Ebbesen, and Zeiss (1973) found that subjects recalled information consistent with an experimentally induced positive or negative self-expectation. Swann & Read (1981, Study 3) obtained a similar result, selective recall of information consistent with the self-concept, for the subject's pre-experimental level of ''self-likeability''. Bem and McConnell (1970) and Wixon and Laird (1976) found that subjects ''recalled'' their original attitudes about university policy as consistent with their current attitudes rather than with their true (pre-experimental) original attitudes.

The "self-perspective" also appears to introduce certain self-serving biases in recall. Ross and Sicoley (1979) found that subjects performing a great variety of tasks recalled information about their own behaviors and about statements attributed to them at higher rates than they recalled information about their partners or teammates. This "self-information availability bias" appeared to be responsible for subjects' judgments of credit or responsibility for performance of group tasks. Changes in the numbers of own and other contributions to a task were correlated with changes in credit judgments. Rosenzweig (1943) and Glixman (1949) also found evidence for a self-serving memory bias in research on memory for completed or interrupted tasks. They observed that memory for specific tasks appeared to be related to whether or not the tasks signalled personal success. Successful tasks were better remembered than unsuccessful tasks. Greenwald (1981) provides a scholarly and provocative review of the autocratic, self-serving properties of memory.

Judgment Focus.   The cognitive representation of a person has traditionally been viewed as a set of "mental copies" of stimulus events. Past events involving the person, the person's behaviors or preferences, and other factual knowledge are copied from sensory representations and stored together in memory. However, it has also been argued that cognitive representations contain more than copies of sensory information; they are influenced by prior judgments or inferences. Whenever an inference, attribution, or assessment is made about a person, that judgment may also be incorporated into the mental representation of the person.

Several studies have examined the influence of judgments on recall for stimulus information. The most basic finding is that items relevant to judgments are more apt to be recalled than judgment-irrelevant items. In research by Lingle, Ostrom and their associates (Lingle, Geva, Ostrom, Leippe, & Baumgardner, 1979; Ostrom, Lingle, Pryor, & Geva, 1980), subjects examined trait information about a fictional character and judged his suitability for an occupation. On both immediate and delayed memory tests, subjects remembered more occupation-relevant traits than occupation-irrelevant traits and made fewer recognition errors (false alarms) for relevant than irrelevant traits. Using a similar paradigm, Carlston (1980) found that after reading an episode involving a character and making an inference about him on a positive (kindness) or negative (dishonesty) dimension, subjects recalled more inference-relevant episodes than irrelevant episodes.

Snyder and Cantor (1979) investigated the effects of goals defined by decision-relevant hypotheses on the utilization of information in a subsequent social judgment task. All subjects initially read a story about a woman who exhibited equal numbers of extraverted and introverted behaviors. They were later asked to evaluate her suitability for a job requiring extraversion (real estate salesperson) or for a job requiring introversion (research librarian). Subjects were asked to list information about the person that was relevant to testing their hypothesis. Subjects testing the woman's suitability as a real estate salesperson listed more extraverted then introverted behaviors, whereas those testing her suitability for a research librarian listed more introverted than extraverted behaviors. However, these findings merely demonstrate that the judgment affects the perceived relevance of types of information. The dependent variable measured *perceived relevance* of information, *not recall*.

Bower and Karlin (1974) used the trace elaboration concept to account for results of research studying recognition memory for faces. The encoding task was manipulated to vary the "depth of processing" that subjects allocated to the perception of faces. In some conditions subjects judged the likableness or honesty of faces and in others they judged the sex of the face. Consistent with a prediction from Craik and Lockhart's levels of processing framework (1972), subjects remembered photographs better when greater depths of processing had been allocated (the judgments of likableness or honesty). This result held whether subjects had been instructed to expect a recognition test (intentional learning) or not (incidental learning).

A second basic finding is that recalled stimulus information is distorted to be more consistent with the prior judgment. Ratings of episodes recalled in Carlston's (1980) study showed that episode descriptions by subjects in the positive inference condition were more positive than episode descriptions by subjects in the negative inference condition.

Theoretical Comment.   From the empirical evidence it is clear that a subject's task goal, perspective, or judgment focus influences memory for social information. One source of these effects is doubtless differential attention at the time of encoding. Almost all of the substantial, replicable effects of task variations can be explained in terms of differential attention or differential cognitive elaboration at the time of encoding. There is also some evidence for small state-dependent effects such that recall memory is highest when encoding perspective matches retrieval perspective. Our speculation is that these "perspective-dependent" effects will only be obtained when discrimination between presented and nonpresented events is a critical component of the retrieval process (cf. Bower, Monteiro, & Gilligan, 1978).

The phenomenon of increased access to events by assuming a novel goal, perspective, or focus at retrieval has not been demonstrated to be of substantial magnitude. Such effects, if substantial and replicable, would be of considerable theoretical significance because they would not be predicted from the principles underlying most current models of memory (see section on reconstruction processes below).

Semantic Interpretation Effects

Social psychologists have been interested in the effects of semantic context on the interpretation of information in a great variety of perception and judgment tasks. Research on the "halo effect" and "change of meaning effects" as well as research on assimilation and contrast effects has explored the influence of semantic context on the interpretation of new information. Two types of phenomena have been investigated that involve semantic interpretation effects on memory: the effects of semantic information on memory for faces and the effects of semantic context on memory for descriptions of behaviors.

Memory for Faces. Watkins, Ho, and Tulving (1976) studied the effect of presenting faces in the context of a second face or a descriptive phrase on recognition memory judgments. In contrast to an earlier study by Bower and Karlin (1974), Watkins et al. found that pictorial or verbal context from the time of study presented during the recognition test increased accuracy slightly but reliably on the recognition test (although reliable, the effects were small). Watkins et al. interpreted this result as evidence for the Encoding Specificity Principle (Tulving & Thomson, 1973).

Klatzky, Martin, and Kane (1982) presented photographs of faces in the context of occupational category labels. The faces were selected to represent either a typical example for a particular occupational category or a peripheral example of the same category. Presenting a typical face in the context of a congruent occupational category label increased subjects' tendencies to judge that they had seen the face before. Presentation at the time of test, paired with a congruent label, increased the tendency to identify the face as previously presented (higher "hit" rates for old faces and higher "false alarm" rates for new faces). Klatzky et al. (1982) interpreted their results as evidence for a "semantic code hypothesis" that assumes that the recognition memory effects were produced by the existence of relatively separate physical and semantic codes associated with each face. This hypothesis implies that there is no interaction between the verbal and the physical codes (e.g., the verbal label does not affect the amount or types of features included in the physical code); rather, the occupation label produces a distinct semantic code that has independent effects on the recognition memory judgment from the physical code. In one experiment forced-choice recognition judgments were required between physically similar "old" and "new" faces. In this experiment no effects of the semantic occupation category label were observed on recognition accuracy. This result offers further support for the "semantic code hypothesis" favored by Klatzky et al. Bahrick and Boucher (1968) had also concluded that visual storage codes carried information that enabled a subject to discriminate among instances of a generic concept whereas verbal codes did not support within-category discrimination. However, their interpretation was that the verbal code was dependent on the visual code (but not the reverse) rather than that the two codes were independent.

These results are especially important in the person memory area because they illustrate the effects of generic social information about physical characteristics (typical faces) associated with a conceptual category (occupation category). Furthermore, the investigation of the relationships between semantic and physical memory code information is important in evaluating fundamental assumptions in many cognitive theories.

Semantic Priming.   Priming refers to the process by which previous experience increases the general accessibility of a conceptual category, thereby increasing its likelihood of being used to encode new information. This process has been characterized as unconscious and has been studied by cognitive psychologists interested in lexical priming (e.g., Foss, 1982; McKoon & Ratcliff, 1979; Neely, 1977).

In social research on priming, subjects typically engage in a task designed to increase the accessibility of a specific personality trait concept. They then participate in a second task that appears unrelated to the first. During the second task subjects are given behavioral information about a stimulus character, some of which is ambiguous with respect to the primed trait category. Subsequent ratings of the character are made and analyzed to determine the influence of the primed trait on the subject's encoding of the character's behavior.

An example is provided by Higgins, Rholes, and Jones (1977) in an experiment that started with a "perception study" in which subjects were required to repeat several trait adjectives while viewing slides. The set of traits was either evaluatively positive or negative. During a second ostensibly unrelated study, subjects read information about a character whose behavior could be interpreted using traits repeated in the first "perception study." Higgins and his colleagues found that a stimulus character and his descriptions were rated more positively by subjects who had been previously exposed to positive traits than by subjects exposed to negative traits (and vice versa). These priming effects occurred only when the primed trait was applicable to the stimulus character's behavior and when priming materials were presented before the to-be-primed behaviors (Srull & Wyer, 1980). The primed trait affected judgments on both that trait and on others indirectly related to it through implicit personality theory. Bargh and Pietromonaco (1982) have demonstrated that conscious awareness of the priming material is not a necessary condition for priming effects to occur. Several additional factors have been found to influence the accessibility and likelihood of using a primed trait. The effects of priming on dimensions descriptively or evaluatively related to the primed trait are increased by: (a) increasing the number of trait-relevant items used during the priming task (Srull & Wyer, 1979, 1980); (b) decreasing the time interval between the priming task and the presentation of information about the target character (Srull & Wyer, 1979, 1980); (c) increasing time interval between target character's information (behaviors) and the judgment (Srull & Wyer, 1980) (d) increasing the ambiguity of the target character's behavior (Srull & Wyer, 1979); (e) increasing expectations that category-relevant events will occur (Higgins, Kuiper, & Olson, 1981); (f) increasing frequency of activation of the category (Wyer & Srull, 1980); and (g) increasing strength of semantic relationships between the category and other activated concepts (Collins & Loftus, 1975; Warren, 1972).

There are few studies of the effects of a primed trait on the reconstruction or recall of stimulus information. One study (Higgins et al., 1977) examining this relationship found no differences in recall by subjects who had received different priming traits (positive or negative). However, the authors noted that these results may be due to their instructions asking subjects to memorize the information.

Higgins, King, and Mavin (1982) assessed individual differences in personality trait concept accessibility. This individual difference was correlated with subjects' mention of material presented as a description of a hypothetical character in impression formation and on recall memory tasks. Traits that were "accessible" in individual subjects' conceptual systems were likelier to be cited or recalled than "inaccessible" traits. This finding closely parallels results from research on individual differences in self-concept (e.g., Markus, 1977). It is quite likely that prominence of a trait concept in an individual cognitive system is closely related to its significance in the individual's self-concept. Thus, Markus's research on construct accessibility and Higgins et al.'s research on trait accessibility may be studying a single phenomenon.

Most of the research on semantic priming has provided demonstrations of the existence of these phenomena and the conditions that produce semantic "assimilation" effects. One recent study by Herr, Sherman, and Fazio (1983) using animal names as materials identified some of the conditions that were necessary to produce assimilation effects such that an instance was seen as more characteristic of a primed category compared to an unprimed category. Contrast effects were obtained when unambiguous instances were presented and when ambiguous instances were presented in the context of an extreme, noncongruent category. Assimilation effects were only obtained when ambiguous instances were paired with moderate, congruent categories.

Theoretical accounts for the original priming results, predominantly assimilation effects, cited spreading activation processes in associative memory networks (Collins & Loftus, 1975; Higgins & King, 1981) or last-in-first-out memory bins (Wyer & Srull, 1980) as explanatory constructs. However, spreading activation accounts appear to be inadequate in light of the Herr et al. (1983) demonstrations of contrast effects and the bin-model account would need extension to explain these phenomena. A more elaborate account that prescribes both availability (e.g., concept activation) and judgment (e.g., perceptual dimension anchoring) processes would appear to be necessary. In fact, such a model has been favored by cognitive psychologists who are concerned with priming effects in the comprehension of discourse and isolated lexical items.

This model was first proposed by Posner and Snyder (1975) who argued that the effects of context on comprehension are due to two separate mechanisms. First is a fast, "spreading activation" mechanism that does not require attentional resources and leads to facilitation of processing related items. This mechanism seems likely to produce assimilation-priming effects. Second, there is a slow attentional mechanism that requires mental resources to effect priming and it can produce inhibition (i.e., contrast) as well as facilitation (i.e., assimilation) effects. There is considerable support for this model in empirical research by cognitive psychologists (Foss, 1982; Neely, 1977; Ratcliff & McKoon, 1981).

The comparison between lexical priming as studied by cognitive psychologists and trait concept priming in social judgment as studied by social psychologists creates at least one enigma. The puzzle involves the relative time frames associated with priming effects in the two domains. In research on lexical priming using materials from lists of unrelated English words, the decay of semantic activation (the duration of priming effects) was short, often not exceeding one or two words or a few seconds (e.g., Warren, 1972). Foss has recently demonstrated that the duration of priming-based facilitation in comprehension of sentences (in contrast to lists of unrelated words) was considerably longer than previously observed, extending up to a duration of about 12 words intervening between the prime and the primed items. However, there is no suggestion in the cognitive literature that semantic activation effects could endure for longer than a few sentences. In fact, there are logical arguments that suggest that semantic activation must be of exceedingly limited duration.

On the other hand, social psychologists have claimed priming effects that can be observed over durations of 24 hours (Srull & Wyer, 1979) or over many intervening sentences or lexical items. It is difficult to reconcile these two points of view on the priming phenomena: cognitive psychologists hypothesizing that semantic activation effects decay within the space of a few words or sentences and social psychologists who hypothesize that the activation duration is virtually unbounded, extending over hours and even days.

Experiments studying relatively short duration priming phenomena (e.g., Herr et al., 1983) and research studying relatively longer duration priming effects (Srull & Wyer, 1979) may actually be studying different but related phenomena. We suspect that there are two conditions associated with the social priming research tasks that are necessary to produce delayed priming effects. First, in these studies only one concept was extensively activated by the experimental manipulations. Second, the distinctive background context of the priming situation (i.e., elements of the experimental setting, the presence of the experimenter, the experimental room, etc.) were repeated during each phase of the experimental paradigm. In short, the experimental paradigm could produce a strong association between a single primed concept and the experimental context. Thus, the primed concept is likely to be cued by the experimental context every time the subject returns to it. This set of conditions is absent from the cognitive research paradigms in which dozens of concepts are presented as primes within the experimental context. An interesting question for future research concerns the extent to which the single-concept prime and association of the prime to experimental context are necessary conditions for many of the social priming effects.

Expected and Unexpected Events

Memory for expected and unexpected information has recently become a central issue in social cognition. In several experiments memory for expected, congruent, or schema-consistent events is compared to memory for unexpected, incongruent, or schema-inconsistent events (Hastie, 1980). The experiments by social psychologists can be separated into two sets according to the types of materials employed. One set of studies compares memory for expected information with memory for incongruent, inconsistent, or highly unexpected information, while a second set compares expected information to information that is simply "not expected" or irrelevant. Rather than addressing the knotty definitional issues raised by this distinction, we review some concrete examples of each type of experiment.

Memory for Inconsistent Information.   Several studies have investigated differential processing and memory for behaviors that are inconsistent, consistent, or neutral with respect to an expectancy based on a trait impression of a character. In some of the earliest studies, Hastie and Kumar (1979) examined this issue in the context of an impression formation task. Subjects were initially given a list of traits attributed to a stimulus character and told to form an impression. They were then shown a series of sentences describing behaviors of the character. These behaviors were either congruent, incongruent, or irrelevant with respect to the subject's initial impression. Finally, subjects were given a free recall task. The results showed that subjects recalled proportionally more incongruent than congruent behaviors (irrelevant behaviors were recalled least well). However, the higher recall for incongruent items was influenced by set size. The smaller the number of incongruent behaviors in a list, the higher the probability of recalling any single item.

Several studies have obtained similar results. Srull (1981) has replicated Hastie and Kumar's (1979) finding that subjects recall proportionally more items that are incongruent with an impression. Hamilton, Katz, and Leirer (1980) reported a higher probability of recall for a single behavior that was evaluatively inconsistent rather than consistent with a character's other behaviors. Hemsley and Marmurek (1982) replicated the Hastie and Kumar pattern of results for the recall of information where incongruent behaviors were in the minority in the total set of behaviors attributed to a character. They also extended the original design by including conditions in which the majority of behaviors presented in the list were incongruent with an initial trait description of the target character. Under these conditions set size effects again appeared such that the smaller the set size the greater the probability of recall of any specific behavior in the set. In other words, the relatively small numbers of trait-congruent behaviors were recalled at higher levels than the relatively large numbers of trait-incongruent behaviors. These authors also collected data on the study times that subjects allocated to different types of items presented in the lists. They found that unexpected items (items in the smaller set sizes) tended to receive more study time and were better recalled. They interpreted this result as consistent with the levels of processing interpretation suggested by Hastie (1980) and Hastie and Kumar (1979).

Rothbart, Evans, and Fulero (1979) found that subjects given an expectation about a group of individuals were later able to recall more behavioral items that were consistent with, rather than irrelevant to, the initial impression. On the surface this result appears to contradict the conclusions of Hastie and others who found higher proportions of inconsistent items recalled under comparable conditions. Rothbart et al. compared absolute frequencies of behaviors recalled, whereas Hastie and Kumar compared proportions of behaviors recalled. Moreover, while Rothbart et al. make direct comparisons only between consistent and irrelevant, and inconsistent and irrelevant, Hastie and Kumar make direct comparisons between consistent and inconsistent behaviors.

Srull (1981) was interested in the extent to which this apparent discrepancy was due to attributing information to a group in the Rothbart et al. experiments, but attributing information to an individual in the Hastie and Kumar experiment. Srull presented information about three different types of stimulus targets: an individual, a close-knit, coherent group of individuals, or a nonmeaningful group. Srull was able to replicate the Hastie and Kumar results for information about an individual and also about a meaningful, coherent group of individuals. The Rothbart et al. results were replicated in Srull's condition where a non-meaningful group of individuals was depicted (see also Wyer & Gordon, 1982). This suggests that there are different implicit expectations about the consistency of an individual versus the consistency of a group which perceivers apply in understanding information in the social world.

A few researchers have begun to investigate the limitations of this "incongruence effect." Srull (1981) predicted and found superior recall for incongruent information in free recall tasks but found no differences on a recognition memory task. However, ceiling effects caused by subjects' high levels of performance on the recognition test may have obscured actual memory differences. Wyer and Gordon (1982) found evidence that behaviors evaluatively inconsistent with the subject's impression were better recalled than evaluatively consistent behaviors. However, this pattern was not present for consistency/inconsistency defined on descriptive dimensions.

Srull (1981) and Hastie (1980) have developed a model that provides a general account for most of these phenomena related to memory for behaviors that are congruent and incongruent in the context of a trait impression. The model is closely related to earlier work by cognitive psychologists (e.g., Anderson & Bower, 1973) who used the concept of a simple associative network to characterize memory structure and undirected search and match mechanisms to characterize memory processes. The fundamental principle underlying the Srull-Hastie model is that unexpected behavioral information will instigate elaborative processing of the unexpected event; at least when the subject is attempting to integrate information about a person into a unified impression.

Hastie (1980) has suggested that causal reasoning processes instigated by the occurrence of unexpected events are involved in the elaboration of incongruent behavior information. He has reported empirical findings consistent with this speculation: Subjects are likelier to spontaneously explain why an incongruent behavior has occurred than a congruent behavior; there is a correlation between spontaneous explanation and subsequent recall; and when explanations are induced with an experimental manipulation explained items are better recalled than unexplained items.

Bradshaw and Anderson (1982) presented subjects with lists of facts attributed to famous historical characters. Four experimental conditions were defined by varying the context facts that were provided along with a target, to-be-remembered fact. In one case the context facts were plausible causes of the target fact; in a second case the context facts were plausible effects of the target fact; in a third case the context facts were conceptually unrelated to the target fact; and in the fourth case no context facts were presented. In a series of three experiments, Bradshaw and Anderson found that facts that were related to their context (caused-by or resulted-in relationships) were best remembered on recall tests whereas facts presented alone or in the context of unrelated facts were relatively poorly recalled. The authors interpreted these results as support for an elaboration explanation of depth-of-processing effects. According to their interpretation, when target facts were presented in the context of related facts additional connecting and elaborating inferences would be made and stored along with the to-be-remembered facts. This ensemble of presented and inferred facts would comprise a relatively rich bundle of associatively linked information. This high degree of elaboration would result in relatively high recall rates on later memory tests.

Crocker, Hannah, and Weber (1983) have examined the relationship between attributions and recall for inconsistent behaviors. To study this, they replicated Hastie and Kumar's procedure with one modification: Subjects were given either a dispositional or situational attribution for a target behavior. On a free recall task the targeted inconsistent behavior was more likely to be recalled than a consistent behavior only when subjects had attributed the inconsistent behavior to a dispositional cause (i.e., "within" the stimulus character).

Cohen (1981) noted several limitations on the paradigm used to study memory for expected and unexpected information and she advocated the use of a more naturalistic experimental task. In her study, subjects viewed a videotape of a woman identified as either a waitress or a librarian. After viewing the videotape, subjects were given a recognition memory test. The results indicated that subjects correctly recognized more characteristics and behaviors of the woman that were consistent with their stereotype of the character's occupation (waitress or librarian) than features that were inconsistent. However, Cohen only examined the number of correct responses (i.e., "hits"), and, thus, subjects' "better" recognition for stereotype-consistent information may be due to a response bias.

Most of the social research on memory for expected and unexpected events has been conducted in research paradigms where the experimenter determines what events are expected or unexpected by varying task instructions or the initial information presented about stimulus characters. As Cohen noted, only a few studies have explored memory for information that is unexpected in the context of normal extra-laboratory experiences. One example of research with natural stimulus materials is provided by studies of recognition memory for faces. Researchers have repeatedly found that unusual faces are better remembered than faces that are less unique (e.g., Cohen & Carr, 1975; Going & Read, 1974; Light, Kayra-Stuart, & Hollander, 1979). Light et al. suggest that the typical versus unusual face recognition memory difference occurs because typical faces are similar to more other faces than unusual faces. Thus, the interpretation of the results depends on an assumption about the structural characteristics of faces in a general population of naturally occurring faces.

Memory for Irrelevant Information. Graesser and his colleagues (Graesser, Gordon, & Sawyer, 1979; Graesser, Woll, Kowalski, & Smith, 1980; Smith & Graesser, 1981; Woll & Graesser, 1982) have conducted a series of studies examining memory for information that was consistent ("typical") or irrelevant ("atypical") with respect to a behavioral script (Abelson, 1981). An item was regarded as "typical" if it commonly occurred in the enactment of a "scripted" sequence of activities. An item was defined as "atypical" if it could logically occur in the script, but was not expected to occur. For example, "read the menu" would be labeled "typical" in the context of eating a meal in a restaurant; while "read a letter" would be labeled "atypical" in the same context. In Graesser's research, subjects read narrative passages that included scripted action sequences. The scripts were cued by evocative labels ("eating in a restaurant") and the sequences included "typical" and "atypical" actions. After reading the passage, subjects were given either a free recall test or a recognition test.

Several general findings have emerged from these studies. On a recognition test subjects either recognized more script-typical than script-atypical items (Graesser et al., 1980; Smith & Graesser, 1981) or recognized equal numbers of both (Graesser et al., 1979; Woll & Graesser, 1982). Subjects also exhibited higher "false alarm" rates for typical than atypical items. Further analyses were conducted on subjects' discrimination (d') scores which provide a measure of memory sensitivity based on both the "hit" and "false alarm" rates. Results showed that subjects more accurately distinguished between presented and non-presented atypical items than typical items (Graesser et al., 1979; Graesser et al., 1980; Smith & Graesser, 1981; Woll & Graesser, in press). In fact, in several studies subjects exhibited no memory discrimination for highly typical items (Graesser et al., 1979; Graesser et al., 1980). Analyses of free recall data revealed that subjects' intrusions included more script-consistent (similar to typical) than script-irrelevant items. There was an interaction between hit rates and delay. When there was s short delay between information presentation and testing, subjects recalled more irrelevant than consistent items. With a longer delay (one week), more consistent than irrelevant items were recalled (Graesser et al., 1980; Smith & Graesser, 1981).

Woll and Graesser (in press) have extended their atypicality effect research to schemata other than scripts including social roles (e.g., "man of the world"), occupation stereotypes (e.g., "truck driver"), and trait concepts (e.g., "aggressive male"). In these experiments the results from research using scripts were substantially replicated; "old" and "new" atypical items were discriminated at higher levels than typical items. Graesser and his colleagues (e.g., Graesser et al., 1980) have suggested that a "schema pointer plus tag" hypothesis can account for their results. They assert that when a memory trace is created to represent information from one of the scripted action sequences that the trace has a "pointer" to a generic script. The generic script includes "slots" for typical actions associated with that script and even "default" values as attributes for some acts, instruments, or actors. Atypical or irrelevant actions are retained as separate units and linked to the script with a special pointer ("tag") that is "labeled" to indicate the tagged item contrasts with script implications or default information. When the subject retrieves information about an event, it is difficult to determine which typical actions actually occurred and which were inferred as "default implications" of the script knowledge structure. However, atypical actions are stored separately, accessed through strong "tag" links, and are unlikely to be confused with nonrepresented inferred propositions stored in memory.

Bower, Black, and Turner (1979) reported a series of experiments studying comprehension and memory for scripted activities. In one experiment (Experiment 7) they compared recall memory for script relevant actions ("read the menu"), script irrelevant actions ("noticed the waitress's red hair"), and script interruptions ("couldn't read the French menu"). Recall performance was ordered with interruptions best recalled, then relevant actions, and irrelevant actions worst recalled.

If we accept an analogy between Bower et al.'s interruptions and Graesser's atypical actions, the results from these programs of research are consistent. However, an analogy between irrelevant and atypical actions seems more plausible from the descriptions of materials provided by the two groups of researchers. This would raise interpretive questions as Bower et al. found irrelevants worst recalled in immediate recall while Graesser et al. (1979, 1980) found atypicals best recalled under comparable conditions.

Bellezza and Bower (1981, 1982) have conducted a series of studies of recall and recognition memory for typical and atypical events in schemata. Their findings from recognition memory tasks essentially replicate Graesser's results showing greater discrimination for presented and nonpresented atypical items as compared to typical items. However, they suggest that their recall memory results pose problems for the general "schema pointer plus tag" model favored by Graesser. In particular, they obtained evidence for differential allocation of attentional resources to typical and atypical items during encoding, with atypical items receiving more attention. Furthermore, they found no evidence for item clustering at output by script or for groupings of typical and atypical items within recall from a single script. They argued that plausible interpretations of the "schema pointer plus tag" model would have predicted such output order effects.

A third relatively separate line of results on memory for irrelevant events has developed in the research by Hastie (Hastie, 1980; Hastie & Kumar, 1979) and Srull (1981) in their studies of memory for the behaviors of individuals. In these studies the relevant versus irrelevant contrast is defined with reference to the subject's personality impression of a character. Thus, a behavior such as "cheated at poker" would be labeled relevant (and congruent to the trait dishonest) and a behavior such as "ate a cheeseburger" would be labeled irrelevant to the personality impression.

Most of the research studying memory for this type of irrelevant events has utilized free recall tasks. The consistent finding has been low levels of recall for irrelevant as compared to relevant (either impression congruent or incongruent) events. Intrusion rates for all types of items are extremely low in these memory tasks, although there is a hint that congruent-relevant items are likelier to be fabricated than other types of items. In the one study that examined performance on recognition tests, all types of items were equally likely to be "hits" or "false alarms" (Srull, 1981, Experiment 2). However, we have noted that the possibility of ceiling effects keeps us from relying heavily on this experiment.

Theoretical Comment. Three explicit principles or process models to account for the relative memorability of consistent, inconsistent, and irrelevant information are in the current literature (see Hastie, 1980, and Graesser & Nakamura, 1982, for reviews). The simplest of these accounts is based on the principle that expected, schema-consistent, or impression-congruent events will be better remembered than unexpected or irrelevant events. This principle is explicit in the theoretical discussions by Cohen (1981), Cantor and Mischel (1977), Rothbart (1981), and Taylor and Crocker (1981). The basic problem for this principle is that it is too simple. Although it applies in some cases there are many empirical conditions under which it fails.

The second theoretical position emphasizes trace elaboration processes at encoding, and it postulates that events that receive more processing or are linked to many other events in memory will be relatively well recalled. This position assumes that the most informative events in the context of the subject's task at encoding (often unexpected or incongruent events) will produce the most elaborate and recallable memory representations (Hastie, 1980; Hastie & Kumar, 1979; Srull, 1981). The consistent finding of relatively high levels of recall for incongruent actions in impression formation tasks is the most frequently cited evidence for the trace elaboration position. The greatest problem for the position is its failure to provide an account of responses to nonpresented distractor items.

The "Schema Pointer Plus Tag" model developed by Graesser and his colleagues (see summary in Graesser & Nakamura, 1982) provides an explicit account of recognition test performance for typical and atypical events. This model is relevant when a well-formed schemata (e.g., script) is available to guide perception, and it has been applied to cases where somewhat less articulated concepts are invoked by the task materials (e.g., trait concepts and occupation stereotypes). This model assumes that a partial copy of a generic knowledge structure is written into episodic memory and serves as the scaffold that "supports" information about ongoing events (see also Bower et al., 1979, for a closely related model). When information is encoded that fits the knowledge structure (i.e., matches its default values), these "very typical" events are represented within their generic slots in the mental scaffold and are difficult to distinguish from generic event information that is included in the generic knowledge structure. Information about moderately typical and atypical events is written into memory outside of the generic structure and linked to that structure with special "tags": memory links that signify a contrast relationship. Graesser's model includes a number of principles concerning forgetting and retrieval of information stored in generic knowledge structures. In particular, two retrieval processes underlie recognition judgments, conceptually driven retrieval through the structure, and data-driven retrieval through the event representation (accessed by the recognition test probe). The major empirical problems for Graesser's model derive from its inability to account for output sequence ordering in recall and the effects of varying number of incongruent items on congruent item recall (Srull, 1981).

Doubtless there will be some rapprochement between encoding models that appear to account for attention allocation and recall memory in impression formation tasks where highly incongruent events occur and models that postulate partial copies of generic knowledge structures to account for recognition test performance.

RETENTION

Format of the Memory Trace

Discussions of possible formats for the representation of social information in memory have contributed little to the more general consideration of memory trace formats that has been produced by cognitive psychologists (see Kosslyn, 1980; Holyoak, this volume; and Klatzky, this volume, for reviews). Most social memory researchers have used stimulus information presented in verbal form either as single words (e.g., trait adjectives) or sentences (e.g., descriptions of behaviors). Consequently, virtually all discussions of the format of the memory trace have suggested that this information is stored in some propositional form similar to hypothesized representations for lexical memory or for sentence memory.

A few researchers have at least suggested that nonpropositional formats should be postulated to represent visual information. Swann and Miller (1982), Lord (1980), Fiske, Kenny, & Taylor (1982), and Fiske et al. (1979) have suggested that mental images are an important format for certain types of social information while Wyer and Srull (1980) and Wyer and Carlston (1979) include image formats in their general characterization of a social memory model.

A few experiments have focused on the difference between propositional and pictorial memory codes for different types of social stimulus information. For example, Klatzky et al. (1982) used results of their studies of face recognition to argue that there were two relatively independent memory codes, one pictorial and one semantic.

In an earlier review Hastie and Carlston (1980) identified the representation format for affect or evaluative information as an important problem in social psychology. Since that review several proposals for the representation of emotional or evaluative meaning have appeared. For example, Bower and Cohen (1982) suggest that such information is represented in semantic form in propositional networks. Thus, similar contents, formats, and structures would be hypothesized to represent "the dog is large," "the dog bites me," and "I fear the dog." Bower and Cohen have also outlined an elaborate processing system (closely related to other production system based models such as Anderson's

ACT, 1976) that includes both descriptive and emotional information processing procedures.

In contrast to Bower and Cohen, Zajonc, Pietromonaco, and Bargh (1982; Zajonc, 1980) argue that cognition and affect are handled in relatively independent processing systems and that different aspects of a stimulus control emotional and cognitive responses. They have suggested that evaluative and emotional information is stored in a motoric code. However they have not provided a specific characterization of the nature of formats for representation of information in the two independent systems.

At present both the Bower and the Zajonc proposals for the representation of emotion information are highly speculative and there are no empirical findings that strongly favor one position over the other. Bower's research program utilizes stimulus materials and manipulations of emotional state that are "loaded" to induce verbal or propositonal representations. Zajonc's research has not provided dramatic empirical demonstrations of process or representation independence and the concept of "independence" itself is difficult to define or demonstrate (Garner & Morton, 1969). Nonetheless, we anticipate the current activity in the emotion and memory area to yield important advances in the immediate future (see chapter by Isen, this volume and Clark & Fiske, 1982).

Structure of the Memory Trace for Individuals

Today all serious efforts to characterize the retention of social information assume that a mental representation is established during encoding and that the representation is carried in the mind until it is utilized at retrieval. Thus, central theoretical questions concerning retention will involve the contents and format of this representation and its structure. A number of difficulties confront researchers who are concerned with any type of mentalistic or cognitive theory. First, the structure of the stimulus in the experiment must be determined and represented in terms that are comparable to those that will be used to describe mental structures. Second, the relationship between the structure of stimulus events in the experiment and the structure of stimulus in the natural world must be identified in order to theorize about the perceptual process (cf. Garner, 1970; Gibson, 1960). The second task is especially important in social psychology where experimental situations are frequently designed to mimic natural environments.

A third point, which is implied by this discussion, is that the most convincing evidence for the existence and nature of mental structures will come from experiments in which subjects are forced to "go beyond the information given in the stimulus." That is, we can confidently conclude that mental structures in the head have contributed to structure in the responses when we have identified stimulus structure and find that it is not responsible (correlated with) the systematic structure in responses. Hochberg (1968; 1981) has provided the most compelling empirical demonstrations supporting the existence of mental structures underlying visual perception and Bransford and Franks and their colleagues (Bransford & Franks, 1971; Franks & Bransford, 1971) have provided demonstrations in support of comprehension structures in more traditional memory tasks. Although mental structures are routinely cited as explanatory constructs in social judgment and memory tasks, we know of no comparable demonstrations in the social domain.

The typical experiment on memory structures for social materials involves presenting the subject with structure in the to-be-remembered stimulus and then observing which portions of that structure are reflected in the subject's responses. Although presumably mental representational media "carry" the structure from the stimulus to the response, these experiments do not attempt to demonstrate that mental structures take us "beyond the stimulus structure."

One exception to this generalization may be provided in research by Hamilton, Ostrom, and their colleagues, who have studied the development of subjective organization in output sequences across trials in multitrial free recall learning tasks (e.g., Hamilton et al., 1980; Ostrom, Pryor, & Simpson, 1981). However, although these researchers have used subjective organization indices as dependent variables, they have not gone further to explore the nature of subject-generated organizations (cf. Friendly, 1979).

Several types of structures have been posited for the representation of information about individual people. At the simplest level, researchers have suggested that memory for information about individuals can be accounted for by assuming that a relatively undifferentiated associative network is characteristic of individual person representations. These researchers have almost all been concerned with explaining subjects' memory for actions or descriptive predicates that are attributed to an individual. For example, Hastie and Kumar (1979), Srull (1981), Anderson (1977), Hamilton et al. (1980), and Berman, Read, and Kenny (1982) have all suggested that relatively undifferentiated networks or graphs are sufficient to account for the structure of memory for individuals. These networks are actually somewhere between undifferentiated graphs and more constrained hierarchically ordered directed graphs. For example, researchers have identified certain nodes in the network as having special status (i.e., individual or person nodes) and have hypothesized that access to the network occurs only through certain node locations.

The next most complex structure that has been hypothesized to exist in mental representations of individuals is a hierarchical, directed-graph network. This is probably the most popular memory structure among theoreticians attempting to account for memory for virtually any verbal materials. Wyer and Gordon (1982), Rothbart et al. (1979), Jeffrey and Mischel (1979), Cohen (1981), Carlston (1980), and Higgins et al. (1977) have all suggested that a hierarchical structure is the basis for the representation of information about individuals. For most of these researchers the highest node in the hierarchy represents the person, and occasionally the suggestion is made that this node includes special indices that allow access to the information stored about the person, for example, a proper name, a visual image description, some definite descriptors (e.g., occupation category), and so forth. At the next most general level in the hierarchy, general organizing principles are postulated, for example personality traits, or categories of attribute information about the person (location of origin, occupation, intellectual and social abilities, and so forth). At the lowest level in the hierarchy, most researchers postulate that specific episodic information such as the descriptions of behaviors and situations in which the person has been observed is stored.

Some researchers (Cohen & Ebbesen, 1979; Ebbesen, 1980) have suggested that the distinction between relatively abstract information such as traits or inferred dispositions and relatively concrete information such as behavioral images is important, but that the ordering is not directional or hierarchical. Rather, both types of information are stored in memory, somewhat independently, and access to information about an individual can proceed from abstract to concrete, concrete to abstract, or to only one of the two.

Only a few researchers have considered memory structures that are more elaborate than the hierarchical graph structure when accounting for the results of research on person memory. Graesser and his colleagues (Graesser et al., 1979; Graesser et al., 1980) have suggested that more complex knowledge structures such as generic schemata or scripts are important in memory for information about a person's actions. The same point has been made by a number of other theoreticians (e.g., Abelson, 1981; Nisbett & Ross, 1980) although these later researchers have not conducted empirical studies to demonstrate the significance of the more elaborate memory structures in memory for information about individuals.

Wyer and Srull (Wyer & Srull, 1980, 1981) have put several of these organizational principles together into a general model for person information. Wyer and Srull have used an analogy to a very elaborate and flexible filing system that has "bins" for information of various types (the bins are analogous to physical receptacles in which information might be stored in a file cabinet) but have allowed for the existence of complex structures that order information stored within the bins. For example, in a bin storing information about a specific person there might exist schematic structures like scripts, hierarchies of information ordered according to traits and behaviors, action sequence molecules containing subject-verb-object information about actions, and relatively undifferentiated associative networks. Bins could also be set up for individual episodes or individual entities other than people and structures within these bins might exhibit a great variety of forms.

One type of stimulus that has received considerable study, particularly with reference to the question of mental representation, is the human face. There is suggestive evidence from developmental, physiological, and behavioral sources that human perceivers do have a relatively well specified, innately determined schema for the human face. Some investigators have concluded that there are special or unique properties of human recognition processes. For example, recognition memory for faces is particularly sensitive to changes in the orientation of the to-be-recognized stimulus (Yin, 1969; for a different view see Toyama, 1975); that the recognition process for faces involves considerable parallel, global, automatic processing (Smith & Nielsen, 1970); and that face recognition performance depends on specific neurophysiological structures and exhibits a distinctive developmental history (Carey, 1981). There are a number of researchers who have concluded that generic face concepts, prototypes, or schemata are involved in the face recognition process (Reed, 1972). However, other investigators (e.g., Ellis, 1981) have argued that prototype extraction processes are not involved, at least in learning individual faces.

Anderson and Paulson (1978) have argued that associative propositional networks provide acceptable format and structures for the representation of both verbal information (e.g., written descriptions of actions) and pictorial information (e.g., pictures of faces in a uniform mental medium). But, they also assume that Gestalt-like configural principles determine some features or constrain processing of the representation. Nonetheless, the notion of generic face types and of an even more general generic face schema seems very congenial in the context of empirical research (e.g., Klatzky et al., 1982; Light et al., 1979) and intuitions about face perception and face memory. Even investigators who are reluctant to accept the notion of prototype faces for categories of individuals (e.g., Ellis, 1981) accept the notion that a global "Is it a face?" decision stage precedes subsequent recognition memory processing of faces. This stage of processing would seem to be well served by a generic concept or schema for the human face. However, at present, views on the utility of a generic face schema appear to be mixed.

A substantial literature, much of it applied, exists on the topic of voice identification. Many of the theoretical issues and empirical research paradigms parallel those in the face recognition literature. Useful reviews of this literature are available elsewhere (e.g., Clifford, 1980).

Structure of the Memory Trace for Groups of Individuals

Individuals in the Context of Groups.   While the bulk of research concerning memory for social stimuli focuses on processes involved in memory for information about an individual, there is a collection of papers concerned with the individual in the context of a group. The evidence suggests that there are differences in memory processing when the to-be-remembered stimulus is a collection of individuals as opposed to a single individual.

Three studies have studied memory for ingroup and outgroup members. Howard and Rothbart (1980) examined subjects' memory for behavioral information associated with ingroup and outgroup members. Subjects were allegedly categorized into under-estimators and over-estimators of dots in a perceptual task, although in reality the classification was random. They were then asked to sort positive and negative behaviors according to whether they thought the actor was an over- or under-estimator. The results showed that subjects assigned more positive than negative items to ingroup members and more negative than positive items to outgroup members. In a second study, subjects were presented with behavioral information, both positive and negative, about their own group and the outgroup. In a subsequent memory test subjects' recognition memory for negative behaviors was better for outgroup than for ingroup members, whereas recognition memory for positive behaviors was equal for the two target groups. If subjects did not learn their own group membership prior to presentation of the behaviors, the recognition differences were not present. This suggests that an "ethnocentric" bias influenced memory for items associated with the outgroup. It is also possible to account for these recognition memory biases without distinguishing between memory for individuals and groups. In fact, it may be that these results provide another example of the influence of self-concept on memory. Subjects may simply infer that a member of the same group they belong to is like they are (i.e., "good") while an outgroup member is expected to be unlike them (i.e., "bad").

A second study by Park and Rothbart (1982) investigated subjects' memory for attributes associated with ingroup and outgroup members. Male and female subjects read news stories that contained information about the sex and occupation, as well as other attributes, associated with either a male or female character. Following a retention period of two days, subjects were asked to recall as much of the information in the news stories as they could. In addition, a cued recall test was completed in which subjects were specifically asked to recall the sex, occupation, and several other attributes of the main character. Although subjects were equally likely to correctly recall the sex of ingroup and outgroup members, they were more likely to recall the occupation of ingroup members than of outgroup members. The authors argued that a more complex memory structure exists for encoding information about ingroup members, and hence more detailed and differentiated attributes are stored for ingroup members as compared to outgroup members. In summary, these two studies provide evidence that memory for information concerning two groups of individuals may differ depending on whether the perceiver is or is not a member of the target group. The conclusion that ingroups are represented as more complex and heterogeneous than outgroups was also reached in a separate series of social judgment experiments conducted by Linville and Jones (1980), Linville (1982), Quattrone and Jones (1980).

In a third study on the effects of categorization, Taylor, Fiske, Etcoff, and Ruderman (1978) investigated the types of errors subjects made in attributing verbal statements to members of a group whose conversation they had previously heard. The conversation involved either males and females, or blacks and whites. Later subjects were asked to match statements from the conversation provided to them by the experimenter with the stimulus person who they believed had originally made each statement. Taylor et al. predicted and found that subjects were more likely to make within-category errors than between-category errors. That is, subjects were more likely to mistakenly attribute a statement made by a female to a second female than they were to attribute it to a male. Taylor and Falcone (1982) have replicated this finding. This suggests the information is not stored simply person-by-person but rather the group membership of the individuals also plays a role in the organization of the information. However, it is possible to account for most of these results with reference to a general notion of interindividual similarity, without claiming that memory organization is especially dependent on gender or race categories. Nonetheless, one might speculate that Rosch's notion of Basic Object Level defined on a vertical dimension of categories within a taxonomy for concrete objects (e.g., Murphy & Smith, 1982; Rosch, Mervis, Gray, Johnson, & Boyes-Braem, 1976) also applies to social categorization. Just as certain intermediate levels of category abstractness for everyday objects yield fastest classification times, certain social categories may be most accessible and likely to be applied to perceived individuals. For example, gender, racial, and occupational categories may be "basic" to much of social perception in a fashion analogous to categories such as "dog," "tree," or "chair" in object perception.

A second area of research involving memory processes for a group of individuals concerns the organization of information either by the individual members of the group or by undifferentiated association to the group itself. In a study by Rothbart, Fulero, Jensen, Howard, and Birrell (1978) subjects received pairs of names and trait-descriptors for individuals who comprised a group. Each member of the group was presented once or several times and the relative proportion of positive and negative trait-descriptors associated with the group members was varied. By assessing subjects' estimates of the proportion of positive and negative members in the group, the authors could determine whether subjects had retained the name-trait pairings in the organization of the information or had simply retained the trait pairing with the larger group. They found that under low-memory load conditions, subjects did retain the name-trait parings so that information for the group was organized around the individual members who comprised the group. Estimates of the proportion of positive and negative persons in the group therefore accurately reflected the actual numbers of those members within the groups. However, under high memory load conditions, subjects no longer retained the name-trait descriptor pairings and instead paired the trait descriptors only with the larger group. Thus, information was organized around the group as a whole rather than individual members of the group. Therefore, in the condition in which group members were presented several times, since the trait-descriptors were simply attached to the group as a whole rather than retained with the individual, these multiply-presented traits dominated the memory representation of the group. This research suggests that memory for a group of individuals is not simply the sum of memories associated with each of the individuals of that group but, under certain conditions (i.e., high memory load), information is no longer retained in a way which identifies it with individual group members. Rather, information is represented as attributes characterizing the group as a whole in an undifferentiated way, and a few members may dominate the impression of the group stored in memory.

There is a need for development of theoretical accounts for the memory processes which operate for groups relative to individuals. The majority of the memory structures that have been considered thus far are simple hierarchy or network models. It would be interesting to know how the phenomena cited earlier would be represented as memory constructs within a more complex theory of knowledge structures (e.g., Schank & Abelson, 1977). In developing a theory of representation of information associated with a group, one consideration is the multiplicity of group memberships, such that any given individual is a member of numerous groups at any one time. Research should address how these multiple memberships are represented and what determines the particular group member-ship that is used in encoding a given informational episode. In addition, the nature of social categories as studied by social psychologists is different from "categories" studied by experimental psychologists. The criteria for social group membership are frequently sharp and distinctive (e.g., a person *is* or *is not* a policeman) in contrast to membership in many other natural linguistic catego-ries where membership functions appear to shade off gradually from a prototype (e.g., the color red, the class of birds, etc.).

Interindividual Relationships.   A large number of social psychology experi-ments have investigated subjects' ability to remember relationships among indi-viduals. In some of the earliest experiments in this tradition, De Soto and his colleagues (De Soto, 1960; Henley, Horsfall, & De Soto, 1969) demonstrated that subjects were quicker to learn relationships among individuals if they con-formed to abstract principles defined by the semantic meanings of the relation-ships. For example, if a series of propositions was consistent with principles of asymmetry, transitivity, and completeness and the relation "influences" was specified in the propositions, then they would be learned relatively quickly. Other researchers have found that relational consistency yields faster, more confident, and more accurate learning (e.g., Tsujimoto, Wilde, & Robertson, 1978).

The universality of hereditary relationships and linguistic systems to describe them gives the topic of kinship a special status in anthropology and linguistics. However, there is little research by psychologists on the representation and processing of genealogical relationships. Rips and Stubbs (1980) have reported one of the few studies of cognition and kinship. They used reaction times to make inferences about kinship relations to study the structure of genealogical information in memory. Their general conclusions favored the application of a semantic network as a model for genealogical knowledge with parent-child and generational information providing structure.

One type of social relationship that has received a considerable amount of attention in the memory literature is concerned with social balance principles. Heider (1946, 1958) proposed the balance principle as defined on the sentiment relations among three people. He hypothesized that the triad of relationships was balanced if it contained three positive relations or one positive relation and two negative relations. He predicted that balanced relationship structures would be easier to learn and more accurately remembered than unbalanced structures. Early research using recognition (Delia & Crockett, 1973; Sherman & Wolosin, 1973) paired associate learning (Zajonc & Burnstein, 1965a, 1965b; Rubin & Zajonc, 1969; Zajonc & Sherman, 1967), and free recall (Gerard & Fleischer, 1967) did not obtain clear results consistent with Heider's predictions. Press, Crockett,& Rosenkrantz (1969) did obtain some support for the Heider predictions with subjects classified as low in cognitive complexity. Recently more sophisticated (and probably more sensitive) research methods have found more support for Heider's predictions. For example, Picek, Sherman, and Shiffrin (1975) gave subjects short stories describing relationships among four people. When subjects attempted to recall the relationships presented in each of the stories, balanced stories were better recalled than unbalanced stories. The authors were even able to localize the difficulty in recall at the third relationship which was the first unbalanced relationship in the unbalanced structures. Sentis and Burnstein (1979) found that the time required to recognize previously learned sets of relationships was greater when the sets were imbalanced than when the sets were balanced. Bear and Hodun (1975) taught subjects an explicit principle and found that information was less well recalled when it was inconsistent or irrelevant to the principle than when it was consistent with the principle.

Spiro (1980) used the balance principle to construct materials for a study of reconstructive memory processes. Subjects were given a story in which three concepts (Bob, Margie, and having children) were related to one another in a balanced (both Bob and Margie did not want children) or an imbalanced (Margie wanted children, Bob did not want children) manner. After hearing either a balanced or imbalanced version of the stories, subjects were given information that either Bob and Margie did get married and were living happily together or that Bob and Margie broke off their engagement and were not married. Spiro assumed that the married outcome was consistent with the balanced triad structure and the unmarried outcome was consistent with the imbalanced triad structure. He hypothesized that when the outcome was inconsistent with the triad (married-imbalanced and unmarried-balanced) that memory errors would tend to "reconcile" the inconsistencies. Thus, changes or distortions of the interrelationships, additions of relationships, or other changes in recall of the story would tend toward consistency with the outcome. These results were obtained, and Spiro interpreted them as evidence for reconstructive processes at the time of retrieval.

Learning New Information about a Familiar Individual

One area of importance to the topic of social memory concerns the effects of prior knowledge on the acquisition of new information about a concept or individual. Several studies of familiarity effects have been conducted by experimental psychologists whose focus was somewhat different from that of social psychologists. These experimental psychologists have investigated the effects of learning additional numbers of propositions about a concept on the speed with which any one proposition could be verified as true or false and the effects of prior knowledge about a concept on the speed with which new information about that concept was acquired.

A study by Lewis and Anderson (1976) addressed itself to the first of these two questions. Lewis and Anderson had subjects learn fantasy facts about famous persons and varied the number of fantasy facts learned for any one famous person. In a subsequent recognition test subjects were presented with the fantasy facts they had previously learned, true facts about the famous person, or fake facts they had never seen before. Subjects were to respond, "True," as quickly as possible to fantasy facts learned earlier and true facts, but to respond "False" to fake facts previously not seen. The greater the number of fantasy facts that had been previously learned, the slower the subject's reaction time either to an actual fact about that person or to one of the fantasy facts.

In a second study by Anderson (1981) subjects were first given either the proper name of a stimulus character or a sentence or paragraph that described the character. They then learned new but unrelated information about the stimulus character. Subjects who initially were given either a sentence or paragraph description learned the new but unrelated information more quickly than did those who were given the proper name. However, they also took longer to retrieve and identify this new information. Prior knowledge also resulted in smaller interference effects when more than one piece of new information was learned for the stimulus person.

Anderson was able to replicate these results both with fictitious characters and with actual well-known stimulus persons. However, when famous persons were used as the stimulus targets, reaction times were faster for retrieval of newly learned information as compared to characters for whom no previous knowledge existed (name only).

In a third study, Schustack and Anderson (1979) instructed subjects to read biographical sketches of fictitious persons that were analogous to famous persons. The famous person whom the biography was modeled after was mentioned either at both study and test times, at study time only, at test time only, or at neither time. Recognition of biographical information was better when he or she had been mentioned both at study and test than when the famous person had not been mentioned at all. Subjects showed better recognition when the famous person had not been mentioned at all than when he or she was mentioned only once at the study time only or at the test time only. This suggests that the prior knowledge associated with the famous persons facilitated learning new information about the fictitious target.

These three studies taken together imply that the more propositions one knows about a concept the slower one is to verify any one of those propositions as true or false. In addition, prior knowledge about a concept enhances the speed with which new information is acquired for that concept. Anderson argued that the evidence relating to prior knowledge about a stimulus person supports a spreading activation network theory (Anderson & Bower, 1973). This theory consists of a relatively undifferentiated network. The majority of the work on familiarity effects has supported this activation theory as applied to memory for relatively simple sets of information about a person (see Pryor & Ostrom, 1981 for some related conclusions).

Although these conclusions doubtless hold for many cases of person memory, there is one type of result in the literature that implies that there are limits on its generality. Under certain conditions the addition of related information to a set of propositions actually speeds access to all items of information in the set (e.g., Sentis & Burnstein, 1979; Smith, Adams, & Schorr, 1978). Such findings have not been reported for intra-individual information sets, but they could doubtless be obtained. Identifying the conditions that produce increased accessibility to larger information sets attributed to a single person is an important task for social researchers.

RETRIEVAL

Reconstructive Processes in Recall and Recognition

One of the hallmarks of the cognitive approach to human memory is the emphasis on the active character of encoding and retrieval processes. More specifically, there is an emphasis on the transformation of information as it flows from representation to representation or processing stage to processing stage. Thus, when we discussed encoding processes we emphasized the sometimes subtle influences of the perceiver's perspective, primed concepts, and experimental goals on the nature of memory traces that were produced by the encoding processes. The involvement of inferential processes in all phases of memory tasks has been a topic of great interest to researchers during the past 10 years. Most of the research on inferential processes in memory has focused on constructive inferences that occur closely upon perception of stimulus events during the memory stage we have labeled encoding. However, there are also experimental investigations of reconstructive processes that are hypothesized to occur at retrieval.

It seems undeniable that the memory traces produced following the perception of complex social events or social individuals are comprised of both attributes that are relatively reflective or veridical of the original stimulus events (we might call these copy attributes) and attributes that go far beyond the information given in the original stimulus (we might call these schematic attributes). We should note that we are referring to a continuum of attributes, all inferred from the fragments of reality available through the sensory systems, but some of these attributes (the copy attributes) can potentially be verified with relatively direct perceptual checks while others are very difficult to verify with perceptual tests.

The recent memory literature is replete with compelling demonstrations of inferential activity during encoding (e.g., Bransford, Barclay, & Franks, 1972; Owens, Bower, & Black, 1979; Sulin & Dooling, 1974). These demonstrations are all evidence for the existence of constructive processes in memory. Several experiments also provide evidence for reconstructive processes: inferences that occur at the time of retrieval and influence responding on memory tests. Bartlett (1932) used examples of distortions, intrusions, and reorderings of narrative stories at recall as evidence for reconstructive processes. Although his methods are subject to criticism (e.g., Gauld & Stephenson, 1967) his general theoretical treatment of the nature of reconstructive processes and his emphasis on their significance in everyday social memory are doubtless correct. More recently two types of research paradigms have been used to argue for the existence of reconstructive processes. Both of these methods depend on an analysis of errors in recall (intrusions or distortions of the original stimulus information) or recognition ("false alarm" responses).

One argument in support of reconstructive processes simply depends on the observation of increases in recall intrusion or recognition false alarm errors as the retention interval increases. For example, Spiro (1977) observed increases in recall intrusions with increasing time intervals between the original presentation of to-be-remembered information and recall memory tests. The logic underlying this argument is simple: As the delay interval increases, more of the original stimulus information (especially copy attributes) is forgotten. Subjects, motivated by the experimenter's instruction to recall as much information as possible, are forced to rely more heavily on reconstructive inferences than on retrieval of the original stimulus attributes and other memory traces. However, it is obvious that this logic is not irresistible. It is quite plausible that as forgetting occurs subjects rely more and more on constructed attributes stored in memory during initial encoding. Thus, what may be observed using these experimental methods is increased dependence on constructed (at encoding) information rather than reconstructed (at retrieval) information.

A second experimental procedure has been used to argue for the existence of reconstructive processes at retrieval. The logic of this method is based on the assumption that reconstruction proceeds by making inferences from "premise information" that has been retained in memory. The "conclusions" of these inferences, in addition to the original trace information, guide responding on a memory test. Researchers have hypothesized (Hasher & Griffin, 1978; Spiro, 1977) that if the "premise information" can be changed during the retention interval, new inferences should be generated at the time of retrieval and these can be measured as intrusions, distortions, or "false alarm" responses on a memory test. The application of this method to the study of reconstructive processes requires that the researcher know what types of information will serve as "premises" for the reconstruction inferences. Furthermore, the experimenter must be able to control this premise information with some manipulation that can be inserted during the retention interval. Using this procedure, the appearance of different types of intrusions, distortions, or false alarm errors in an experimental group (where "premise material" is changed) as compared to a group where no changes are made after initial encoding is evidence for reconstruction inferences during either the retention interval or at retrieval. In all research that we are aware of, the "premise" changes that have been made have involved changes in relatively abstract or thematic material. However, there is no reason to assume that inferences at retrieval are not also based on more specific stored perceptual information as well (perhaps Neisser's "bone chips," 1967).

Dooling and Christiaansen (1977) presented paragraphs describing the behavior of a person associated either with a common proper name (e.g., "Carol Harris") or with the name of a well-known person (e.g., "Helen Keller"). They also varied the name that was associated with the paragraph just before retrieval was requested. They found that association with the name of the famous person yielded false alarm responses to test statements on a recognition test that could be inferred to be true of the well-known person (e.g., "She was deaf, dumb, and blind") either when the label was presented at the time of study or at the test. Furthermore, they were able to produce "false alarm" inferences consistent with the well-known label when the label was presented at the time of test, even when the common proper name label had been associated with the paragraph at the time of study. Hasher and Griffin (1978) and Spiro (1977) used much more elaborate materials and thematic labels (descriptive titles) that varied at study or immediately preceding a recall test. These labels produced intrusions consistent with the theme even when the theme was presented at retrieval only.

Probably the most frequently cited recent study of reconstructive processes in memory by social psychologists is reported in a paper by Snyder and Uranowitz (1978). These researchers presented a three-page case history describing the life of a young woman to their subjects. A short descriptive sentence was appended to the case history that indicated, for some subjects, that the main character was currently living a heterosexual life-style and, for other subjects, that the main character was currently living a lesbian life-style. This descriptive material was provided either immediately after the paragraph was read or one week later. Subjects' memories for the case history material were tested on a multiple-choice test with response items that included lures and targets that were consistent with the lesbian life-style or the heterosexual life-style. Subjects' performance seemed to indicate that the types of errors subjects made on the multiple-choice test were influenced by which life-style label they received at the end of the retention period just before testing. Subjects given the heterosexual life-style description were less likely to correctly choose a lesbian information item that had actually been presented in the case history. Heterosexual description subjects also made fewer errors on target items that were consistent with the heterosexual description. Snyder and Uranowitz concluded that these results indicated that the life-style description label affected the types of information subjects were able to "remember" from the case history, even if the label was presented at the end of the retention interval. They hypothesized that the label and certain global characteristics of the young woman's life were retrieved as "veridical traces" and then served as "premises" to guide further reconstructive processes.

The Snyder and Uranowitz (1978) results and their theoretical conclusions have turned out to be controversial on a number of grounds. First, their dependent variables, response bias measures for various types of material presented on the multiple-choice test, are not conventional memory accuracy measures and the magnitudes of the effects that underlie their major theoretical conclusions are tiny. Second, several other researchers have failed to replicate the Snyder and Uranowitz results under similar experimental conditions (Bellezza & Bower, 1981; Clark & Woll, 1981). Third, Bellezza and Bower have demonstrated that an alternative interpretation of the Snyder and Uranowitz results, in terms of response or guessing biases, is at least as plausible as the reconstruction account favored by Snyder and Uranowitz.

One conceptual problem raised by a comparison of the Snyder and Uranowitz and Bower and Bellezza conclusions is that it is difficult to distinguish between "reconstruction process" and "response bias" (or "guessing") process accounts. Both accounts hypothesize that the subject uses relatively fragmentary memory traces as "premises" to infer ("reconstruct" or "guess") missing information. What may distinguish between the two accounts is the implication that when reconstruction processes operate, the inferred material is then stored in memory, either replacing older memory traces or adding to the collection of memory traces. There is no similar assumption of replacement or updating in the "response bias" model. However, none of the experiments we have reviewed above attempt to test empirical implications of the replacement or updating principle. Thus, although we find the Bower and Bellezza interpretation conceptually clearer and more closely connected to empirical findings than the Snyder and Uranowitz account, we also find both accounts and all relevant data consistent (but not uniquely consistent) with the concept of reconstructive memory.

In summary, two major advances in the study of reconstructive memory processes have occurred during the last 5 years. First, compelling empirical demonstrations using the changed "premise material" procedure have supported the hypothesis that reconstructive processes occur. Second, several accounts of the types of inferential processes that are fundamental to the traditional interpretation of reconstructive processes have been presented by Spiro (1977), Hasher and Griffin (1978), and Reder (1982).

Memory and Social Judgment

"Availability Effects". A priori expectations would perhaps lead one to imagine that a judgment or inference based on a collection of information should be related directly to the information that can be recalled or remembered from that collection. However, several studies have failed to find a relationship between the information that a subject can recall and a judgment or inference that in principle should be based on that same set of information.

The first of these studies is an investigation by Anderson and Hubert (1963) of the relationship between impression formation judgments and recall of the information on which those impressions are based. The subject was given a series of traits and asked to make an impression rating of the stimulus person as well as to recall the traits. Depending on the experimental condition (the subject may or may not have anticipated the recall task), Anderson and Hubert argued that the memory processes that underlie impression formation judgments and recall are distinct on the basis of three findings. First, large recency effects occurred in the recall of the traits, but large primacy effects in the impression formation ratings. Second, some of the trials consisted of lists of traits of length six and some of length eight. The impression ratings based on lists of these two lengths are essentially identical and show strong primacy effects. However, the serial position recall curves for the two list lengths are different. Third, following that trial on which the subject was first asked to recall the items (unexpectedly), the impression formation rating shows a large primacy effect, whereas recall shows a large recency effect. Thus, while one might predict that a subject's impression rating should be influenced by the traits he or she is able to recall, this does not seem to be the case in the Anderson and Hubert findings. Impression formation ratings show the traditional primacy effects (Asch, 1946), whereas the serial position curves for recall show recency effects.

Dreben, Fiske, and Hastie (1979) have replicated the basic Anderson and Hubert findings using sentences describing behaviors rather than traits, and more elaborate analyses of the data (see also Riskey, 1979; Rywick & Schaye, 1974). In addition, they found that a delay produced large changes in recall memory performance, but small changes in impression ratings and concluded that this difference was evidence for memory and impression independence.

In a separate line of research, Taylor and Fiske (1975, 1978) found that characters who were more visually salient during a conversation were judged to be more causally potent when rated on dimensions such as "setting the tone and direction" of the conversation. However, there was no evidence to suggest superior recall either for visual or verbal information associated with characters who were more visually salient. Thus, while subjects did judge visually salient characters as being more causally significant, this result was not reflected in differential recall for information associated with that salient character. Fiske et al. (1982) reported experiments that were designed to identify factors that mediate the effect of stimulus salience on attributions of causality. They evaluated a set of models through the use of path analysis and concluded that the major mediating factor was information that was recalled by subjects and also judged to be relevant in determining causality. Thus, they argued that while there is no overt relationship between subjects' recall for information associated with salient characters and judgments of causality attributed to those characters, information that was recalled and judged by subjects to be important in determining causality was a determinant of attributions of causality. However, it should be noted that Fiske et al. (1982) point out two alternative accounts of their data, neither of which depends on recall as a mediator, and neither of which is ruled out by their empirical results. Hence, there is only suggestive evidence that recall mediates the effects of salience on judgments of causality. In addition, the path analysis model favored by Fiske et al. accounts for a small proportion of the variance of the causal rating data.

Wyer and Frey (1983) have reported a study in which they argue for the independence of recall and judgment processes. They concluded that while a motivationally induced response-bias determines subjects' judgments of information relevant to the self, separate memory processes determine recall of that same information.

Reyes, Thompson, and Bower (1980) have conducted a frequently cited study of the relationship between judgments of guilt in a mock-juror decision and memory for evidence favoring and opposing the defendant's guilt. They manipulated the memorability of portions of the evidence by varying the relative vividness of statements with probative significance. They found that when they weighted each item of evidence that was recalled by subjects' postrecall judgment of the item's probative weight, summed all of the items rated as favoring guilt (weighted by the subjects' ratings), and then divided this weighted sum by the total weighted sum for all evidence, producing a "relative strength index of recall," this index was correlated with the subject's delayed judgments of apparent guilt. However, no relationship was found between recall or weighted recall and immediate judgments of apparent guilt. Thus, this availability correlation was only obtained for certain delayed conditions and only when subjects' post-judgment weights were included in the calculation of the recall index. Our evaluation is that the Reyes et al. results provide little evidence for clear or general "availability effects."

Finally, Zajonc (1980) argues that the processes associated with preference judgments and recognition memory judgments are distinct. Zajonc and his colleagues (Kunst-Wilson & Zajonc, 1980; Matlin, 1971; Moreland & Zajonc, 1977, 1979; Wilson, 1979) conducted a series of studies of the relationships among frequency of exposure, recognition memory judgments, and preference judgments. In several of these experiments, recognition ("old" versus "new") judgments were not sensitive to variations in frequency of presentation (for stimuli given extremely broad exposures), although preference judgments did reflect frequency of presentation. Although there are criticisms of the replicability and the interpretation of this research (cf. Birnbaum, 1981; Mandler, 1982), we believe that the work provides a substantial case for the independence of cognitive and affective processing systems.

There are two important conceptual points to be made with respect to the apparent failure to find strong relationships between the information subjects are able to recall and judgments based on that information. The first is that an explicit rule must be established that specifies the expected relationship between recall and ratings based on the same set of information. For example, Reyes et al. (1980) specified that the relationship would hold between a weighted recall index (a ratio of recalled items weighted by their probative significance) and the subjects' guilt ratings. Unfortunately, there is no explicit theory of judgment that applies similarly to all of the tasks in which recall or recognition memory has been related to judgment ratings. In fact, the most plausible models for juror decision making are not consistent with the simple weighted proportion model assumed in the Reyes et al. analysis (cf. Pennington & Hastie, 1981). Without an explicit, valid model of the judgment process, it is not possible to make strong predictions of the impact of information, whether retrieved from memory or perceived through the senses, on the judgment.

Second, the cited studies have failed to control or identify the point in time at which the judgment is made (see Fiske, 1982 for a similar view). In fact, it is plausible in all of the relevant experiments that subjects actually have made their judgments at the time when the stimulus information was perceptually available. Thus, when subjects are asked to recall items and make ratings, there is no necessary reason to expect that the judgment will depend on the items recalled. For example, in the Reyes et al. study there is no doubt that subjects were making their judgments concerning the defendant's probable guilt at the time that the mock-trial evidence was being presented. Thus, one could predict that perceptual availability at the time when the judgment was being "computed" might be reflected in the judgment, but that there would be no necessary relation between later recallability and impact on the (earlier) judgment.

This distinction between perceptually based and memory-based judgments and its implications for conditions under which "availability effects" may be expected can be expressed in an example. Imagine attending a conference and meeting a colleague. Then, on returning to your home university, you are asked to evaluate that colleague's record of accomplishments with reference to a promotion decision. In the perceptually based judgment condition you would have been informed of the judgment before meeting the colleague, and you would doubtless be "computing" parts of your judgment while talking to the colleague at the conference. Note that in this case substantial portions of the judgment process would occur "on line" and would not require retrieval of information from long-term memory. In fact, there may be no relationship between information recalled subsequently and your evaluation. However, consider the memory-based judgment condition. Here imagine that you had no inkling that an evaluative judgment of your colleague would be called for after you met at the conference. Under this condition your judgment must necessarily depend on the types of information that can be retrieved from long-term memory. In this case we would predict that a relationship between information recalled and the judgment would be found. Regrettably, according to the logic of this illustration, all research on availability and judgment (with which we are familiar) has studied perceptually based judgments; exactly the condition where the relationship between recall and judgment cannot be predicted.

Effects of Judgments on a Subsequent Judgment.   In making memory-based judgments, prior judgments and stimulus information may be combined in several alternative ways. Research has focused on three alternatives: the modified Fact Recall model, the Recalled Judgment model, and the Dual Memory model (Carlston, 1980; Lingle & Ostrom, 1979). The modified Fact Recall model posits that judgments are based on recalled stimulus information, although access to this information may be biased by a prior judgment. In the Recalled Judgment model, judgments are based exclusively on prior judgments or inferences. The Dual Memory model assumes that both recalled stimulus information and prior judgments contribute to subsequent judgments. Each of these models is regarded as optionally selectable by the "information processor." That is, a subject is able deliberately to choose among the alternate strategies when making different types of judgments.

Research has usually supported the Dual Memory model. Carlston's study (1980) found that subjects given episodes in which a person behaved in an honest and unkind manner rated the person as unkind and honest regardless of an interpolated judgment (positive or negative). These ratings suggest that subjects were using the original episodic information. (If they had relied solely on the interpolated judgment, the person would have been rated as kind and honest or unkind and dishonest.) However, subjects rated the person as less unkind and more honest after making a positive interpolated judgment than a negative one. Together, these results indicate that both the original episodic information and a prior judgment influenced subsequent judgments about the target person.

Studies conducted by Lingle, Ostrom and their associates (Leippe, Ostrom, Baumgardner, & Lingle, 1981; Lingle & Ostrom, 1979; Lingle et al., 1979; Ostrom, et al., 1980) have reached mixed conclusions. One study (Lingle et al., 1979) examined whether the original traits describing a character or an intervening judgment made about his suitability for an occupation determined subsequent trait ratings of the character. Using an elaborate paradigm in which the contributions of both sources could be inferred from the pattern of trait ratings, these researchers concluded that subjects were drawing upon their prior judgments. This conclusion favored the Recalled Judgment model over the Dual Process model. A systematic replication using open-ended impressions instead of rating scales to assess memory-based judgments (Leippe et al., 1981) found evidence that subjects retrieved both their initial judgment and a subset of the original trait information in describing their impression of the person. However, the generality of this finding is suspect, since explicit instructions telling subjects not to include original stimulus traits in their impressions may have focused attention on the inferred traits to an unusual degree.

Lingle and Ostrom (1979) studied the use of prior judgments and stimulus information in memory-based judgments by examining decision times for pairs of judgments. Across these judgments, the amount of stimulus information initially used to describe the person (i.e., set size), the similarity of the two judgments, and the stimulus information's homogeneity were varied. If the second judgment were based on the retrieval of stimulus information, decision times would be expected to increase with the amount of information initially used to describe the person and decision times should not be affected by similarity between the first and second judgments. Analysis of subjects' decision times failed to support either of these predictions. However, there was evidence that a portion of the stimulus information was selectively retrieved. When the stimulus information was homogeneously positive or negative, decision times for the second judgment increased more with increasing set sizes for positive than for negative information, suggesting that subjects selectively searched for disqualifying stimulus information. A subsequent paper by Lingle, Dukerich, and Ostrom (1983) clarifies this result, suggesting that it should be interpreted as evidence for a decision strategy in which incongruent evidence (disconfirming the hypothesis conveyed by the question) is selectively sought in memory. In sum, Lingle and his colleagues propose a variation on the Dual Memory model in which a prior judgment plus disqualifying stimulus information contribute to subsequent judgments.

To date, most evidence supports the Dual Process model. People probably do use some combination of prior judgments and stimulus evidence for the majority of their memory-based judgments, although the relative dependence on prior judgments over stimulus information may vary across conditions. However, a major limitation of this research is that plausible alternative models have not been considered and ruled out. For example, a model for judgment in which all stimulus information is retrieved but weighted differentially has been neglected. Finally, there are apt to be several judgment strategies or models that apply under different conditions. Given these alternatives, it is important to explore what determines the selection of a judgment strategy. Two likely determinants are (a) the time interval between exposure to decision-relevant information and the point at which a decision is rendered and (b) consequences of the decision. If many details of the original evidence are forgotten over time or if the judgment is inconsequential, a Recalled Judgment procedure may be preferred by subjects over more effortful memory retrieval alternatives.

Optional Retrieval Routes

Theoreticians have hypothesized that social information can be organized in many different ways. Often the same item of information is stored in memory so that it can be accessed with many alternate retrieval cues. Organizations based on personal attributes, individuals, environmental contexts, and reference group memberships represent a few of these alternatives. Encoding conditions and stimulus structure (e.g., heterogeneity of persons, length of interaction) influence the appropriateness and salience of different organizational structures, but the perceiver maintains considerable flexibility in organizing information in memory. For example, it is obvious that we can access memory for information about people using generic attributes (e.g., describe some of the Texans you know, describe some of the creative people you know, etc.), temporal and spatial context (e.g., describe some of the people you met at the party in Dallas, some of the people in your graduate school class, etc.), or individual attributes (e.g., describe James Bartlett). Research has focused on general organizational preferences, determinants of organizational strategy, and postorganizational flexibility.

Initial Organization. Several researchers have suggested that people have general preferences for particular organizations of social information. Both attribute-based organization and person-based organization have been studied. Pryor and his associates (Pryor et al., 1983) claim that people tend to structure social information around generic attributes. In a series of studies, subjects were given information about several individuals. Although this information could be organized around individuals or attributes, Pryor et al. found that items tended to be clustered at recall by generic attributes (e.g., religion) to a greater degree than by persons.

Pryor and Ostrom (1981) studied the organization of information as a function of familiarity with the target and concluded that a subject's tendency to organize information around the person (as opposed to around the trait construct) increases with the familiarity of the person. Anderson (Anderson, 1977, Anderson & Hastie, 1974) views the individual as the most common unit for the organization of social information. When learning about others, the perceiver tends to develop a distinct memory node for each individual and information associated with that individual. Anderson's work provides support for the pervasiveness of the individual as an organizing structure. In these studies subjects learned facts about several characters. Facts referenced characters either by name or by occupation label. Before learning the facts, some subjects were told that a name and occupation applied to the same character (Before Condition), whereas other subjects were told this only after learning the facts (After Condition). Subjects' reaction time to answer questions about the characters was the primary dependent variable in the research. Some of these questions required subjects to make simple deductive inferences and others did not. Subjects in the Before Condition responded to inference and noninference sentences similarly and they often made errors identifying the label (name or occupation) that had originally appeared with a particular fact. These results indicated that subjects stored all facts about the individual in a single structure. Subjects in the After Condition were slower to verify inference sentences and accurately recalled the original fact-label pairings, indicating that they initially created two structures for an individual. Taken together, these results suggest that social information frequently tends to be organized around a memory unit representing the individual.

Despite evidence for "preferred organizations," it is clear that subjects are able to strategically choose appropriate organizational structures. Two factors, the subject's goal and the organizational strength of alternative structures, have been cited as important determinants of organization (Pryor et al., 1982). The concept of organizational strength is based on the assumption that alternative structures have potentially quantifiable strengths and that the "strongest" structure is chosen to organize incoming information. Elements identified as contributing to organizational strength include the structure's discriminability from other memory structures, the association of the structure's features to a modal focus, and the degree of interfeature association.

The relationship between the strength factor and organizational preferences has not been systematically explored, although some evidence indirectly bears on the relevance of its elements. In one study Herstein, Carroll, and Hayes (1980) concluded that social information tended to be organized according to the format prominent at the time it was presented. Subjects were given information about several people. The information was either presented such that several traits appeared with each individual (trait focus) or several individuals appeared with each trait (person focus). Under the trait-focus condition, subjects organized information around traits, whereas in the person-focus condition, person-based organization was dominant. These findings lend some support to the idea that given alternative structures, the more discriminable one will be chosen. Studies by Pryor et al. (1983) made two alternative structures (temporal, individual) equally discriminable while manipulating the stimulus person's familiarity. From past research it was known that familiarity enhances the strength of interfeature associations and the association between features and person structures. Pryor et al. predicted that person-based organization would be used more for familiar than unfamiliar people. Analyses of free recall data showed that subjects tended to cluster information around the individual under familiar conditions, but tended to use an organization that matched the presentation sequence under unfamiliar conditions.

Studies that do examine more than a single basis for organization have found that organization is largely contingent on the structure of stimulus information. Subjects apparently strive to organize information in a way that facilitates retrieval. When a general theme such as the target person's intention (e.g., losing weight) is available, it is used to organize different episodes involving the person. In the absence of such themes, information appears to be organized by its most salient or central feature. For example, if given a series of episodes to memorize and one half of the episodes focus on the target person, whereas the others focus on situations, subjects organize some of the episodes by trait and some by setting (Hoffman et al., 1981; see also Jeffrey & Mischel, 1979).

Reorganization. Once social information has been organized around one structure, its organization is not necessarily static. In response to new information or task requirements, reorganization may occur. For example, in the experiments described above by Anderson and Hastie (1974), subjects were presented a dilemma in which facts pertinent to a single individual were stored in separate locations in memory. Analyses of subjects' reaction times and errors while answering inference and noninference questions showed that subjects were reorganizing the information such that eventually all factual information relevant to a single individual was accessible at one memory location. The most plausible mechanism to account for this pattern of reorganization was a "copy process" that "duplicated" facts initially stored at one memory location at the second location.

Herstein et al. (1980) also inferred reorganization from changes in subjects' reaction times to different cues. These researchers concluded that subjects copied information associated with a weaker dimension (i.e., name) onto a stronger dimension's location (i.e., occupation). If dimensions were of similar strength (i.e., nationality vs. occupation), each of the dimensions was equally likely to be used as the organizing principle.

Research on the optimal organization of social information has been relatively atheoretical. The only reference to theory is made by Anderson (1977; Anderson & Hastie, 1974) who was concerned with testing the assumption that social knowledge is organized around individuals. Several empirical limitations are also apparent. Those exploring preferred organizational structures have included very limited alternatives. Few conditions influencing the preference for different organizations have been discussed and even fewer empirically tested. Ostrom and Pryor (Ostrom et al., 1981; Pryor et al., 1982) have speculated about the manner in which organizational structures are chosen, but have not specified conditions maximizing the different elements of organizational strength. Finally, the fact that information may be reorganized raises a host of new issues. Perhaps the major issue concerns preference. Given more than one existing organization, which will be used?

INDIVIDUAL DIFFERENCES IN SOCIAL MEMORY

The study of individual differences is becoming a major basis for the evaluation of cognitive theories (Carroll & Maxwell, 1979; Underwood, 1975). There are only a few examples of the use of individual differences as a variable in research on social memory. Obvious candidates for important individual differences might be intelligence, social class, and gender. However, there is virtually no empirical research on the relationships between these individual difference factors and memory for information about people. Maccoby and Jacklin (1974) speculated that there might be differences between the completeness and accuracy of memory by men and women for social events. Stereotypes suggest that women might remember relatively more social information than men, although empirical evidence for this suggestion is not strongly supportive. Shepherd (1981) reviewed the literature on gender differences in face memory and concluded that women are marginally superior to men in face recognition memory.

Swann and Miller (1982) classified subjects as vivid or nonvivid imagers using a standard assessment procedure and then compared performance of subjects in these two groups on a social memory task. The task involved listening to a conversation between two characters. The vivid imagers outperformed the nonvivid imagers in remembering snatches of the conversation if they were allowed to visually observe the conversation taking place. However, the ordering was reversed if no visual information was provided, with the nonvivid imagers performing slightly better than the vivid imagers. One comment on the empirical findings in this study is that although statistically reliable, the differences were tiny in magnitude.

The one area in social psychology where there has been extensive research on individual differences has concerned construct accessibility and self-concepts. Higgins et al. (1982), Markus (1977), and Markus et al. (1982) studied the correlations between individual differences in the accessibility of social constructs and perception and memory task performance (see reviews above).

There have also been several studies that examined individual differences in recognition memory accuracy for faces. One fairly consistent difference that has been obtained in this literature involves cross-racial identification. Subjects are typically most accurate in recognizing faces from members of races with whom they have had extensive experience. Thus, in the United States, blacks exhibit relatively high recognition accuracy for either black or white faces, whereas white subjects exhibit higher levels of accuracy when recognizing white faces than black faces (Brigham & Barkowitz, 1978). Another difference that has received attention in the face recognition area involves the contributions of training in face recognition on accuracy (Baddeley, 1979). For the most part, although a number of sensitive experiments have been conducted in this area, there are no clear differences in recognition memory accuracy for faces as a function of individual difference in training or experience in face recognition tasks.

CONCLUSIONS

As a concluding discussion we list the major empirical and theoretical issues that have emerged from our review of the person memory literature. Although the subject of social memory has a long history, that history is a very quiet one. Only recently has there been a moderate volume of papers on the subject of memory for social information. Thus, most of our concluding remarks take the form of suggestions or imperatives for future research.

1. There is a paucity of research on the nature of natural social stimulus structure. Although the picture is somewhat brighter in the area of social perception, we were only able to identify a single study in which memory-based response structures were compared to stimulus structures in an effort to determine the contribution of "mental structure" to the final response structure (D'Andrade, 1974). Even this study used general measures of stimulus and response structures and the dependent variables were not conventional memory measures. We noted that an understanding of naturally occurring social stimulus structure was essential for the interpretation of laboratory experiment results as well as to form conceptual bridges between results from laboratory studies and results from field studies by psychologists and other social scientists.

2. Progress in research on memory organization is directly linked to advances in the study of stimulus structure. At present, lack of analysis of natural social stimulus structures has limited investigations of the organization of social information in memory. We can imagine that complex, loosely articulated generic knowledge structures, analogous to "scripts" for stereotyped behavior sequences, constrain the representation of information about individuals. Perhaps analyses of Implicit Personality Theories (e.g., Rosenberg & Sedlak, 1972; Schneider, 1973) can be extended to yield "implicit dynamic theories of individual personalities." For example, the theories of Freud, Erikson, Jung, Adler, or Sullivan may provide useful models for the perception and memory of person information by lay observers.

3. The analysis of human motivation in terms of goals and perception is potentially one of the greatest contributions of the cognitive approach (Bower, 1975; Miller, Galanter, & Pribram, 1960; Powers, 1973). These concepts have

been used extensively in theoretical analyses of certain problem-solving skills (e.g., Newell & Simon, 1972); however, they have only been applied to a few instances of social perception (e.g., Carver & Scheier, 1981). Our review of research studying the effects of variations in task definition, perspective, and attention focus concluded that a development of theoretical constructs for the analysis of social goals and goal effects in social tasks is an important priority for social psychology.

4. In several subareas of social memory we found that focal empirical questions concerned the uniqueness or distinctiveness of social memory processes in comparison with other perception and memory processes. This issue has been with social psychology throughout its short history (e.g., Asch, 1952; Berkowitz, 1960; Ostrom Chapter in this Handbook; Sherif & Cantril, 1945; Tagiuri & Petrullo, 1958) and it has been a central theme in the longer history of research on social development (see papers in Flavell & Ross, 1981). In research on memory for faces and on self-referent processing, investigators have suggested that there is something distinctive about these materials or these processes as compared to the materials and processes studied in other cognitive research. However, at present the terms "unique" and "distinctive" are still poorly defined and no strong case has been made to apply either adjective to social memory processes. Our own view is that there is probably nothing "special" about the elementary information processes involved in social judgment and social memory tasks. What is distinctive or "special" is the ordering of those elementary information processes into strategic sequences and the conditions that invoke them in natural or laboratory tasks.

The focus on the uniqueness issue may be an obstacle to fruitful research. Perhaps this obstacle derives from the ill-defined character of the concept of uniqueness. In some ways the almost logical intractability of the concept may have impeded solutions to similar arguments that have arisen in other areas of psychology (e.g., consider the imagery controversy that has been viable in psychology for centuries, [Anderson, 1978; Kosslyn, 1980, 1981; Pylyshyn, 1981]). Our suggestion is that it is premature to focus on the uniqueness of social phenomena. Rather, our goal should be a thorough theoretical analysis of social phenomena with the issue of uniqueness reserved until adequate theoretical characterizations are available. Then the uniqueness question may be decidable with reference to the emergent theoretical analyses.

5. A considerable amount of recent research has focused on the conditions that activate or invoke concepts and the effects of activating a general social concept on the processing of specific social information. We concluded that more empirical research is needed that relates the social priming results to priming and activation results obtained by cognitive researchers using nonsocial comprehension and judgment tasks. Furthermore, there is need for the development of a general theoretical analysis of mental activation or priming effects across social and nonsocial tasks.

6. From a review of research on memory for consistent, inconsistent, and irrelevant information, our major conclusion was that it is time to produce a general theoretical analysis to account for results from recall and recognition tasks as well as results from studies on memory for inconsistent information and irrelevant information. We believe that the ingredients for such an integration are available in the literature and that what is needed are experiments and theoretical developments to connect the two relatively independent areas of work.

7. Research on the so-called "availability effect" could be advanced by more explicit process models specifying the nature of the judgment process and the timing of information retrieval and utilization from memory. We think that the body of research that had studied the effects of a prior judgment on subsequent judgments could be advanced by further study of more natural judgment tasks.

8. Research on recognition memory judgments was frequently weakened by a failure to report measures of false alarm or guessing rates in recognition memory tasks. Some lines of research (e.g., the work of Graesser and his colleagues and the work of Bellezza & Bower) are exemplary in providing measures of both "hit" rates and "false alarm" rates as well as in manipulating the nature of false alarm eliciting lure items. However, many social psychologists appear to be unfamiliar with conventional methods of measuring recognition memory developed by cognitive psychologists (see chapter by Srull, this volume).

9. Finally, research on individual differences in social memory was limited and individual differences were not employed in tests of models for social memory. For the present, we can simply urge researchers to be more alert to the potential for using considerations of individual differences as bases for theoretical predictions and theoretical tests.

The study of social memory has had a very languid history since its energetic inception (Bartlett, 1932). However, the tempo has quickened during the past decade. Empirical research on memory for social information has virtually exploded during the past 5 years. A number of distinctly social phenomena have started to attract attention from cognitive psychologists within and outside of the field of social psychology: the structure of information about individuals and groups in memory; relationships between causal reasoning, affect, and memory; the influence of goals on memory processes; and many other topics.

Theoretical analyses in the area of social memory have been heavily dependent on developments in laboratory cognitive psychology. The central theoretical metaphor in research on social memory is the associative network with encoding elaboration and retrieval activation processes. The concept of a schema or "script" for stereotyped action sequences has also been utilized extensively although the strong empirical case for the necessity of such constructs has been made by traditional cognitive psychologists (Bower, Black, & Turner; 1979; Graesser & Nakamura, 1982), not by social psychologists. Finally, the "availability heuristic," a principle to account for judgment-memory relationships, has received extensive citation in the social memory literature (Tversky & Kahneman, 1973). In our view a large number of theoretical principles from cognitive psychology are underused in the interpretation of social memory findings: Rosch's (Rosch & Lloyd, 1978) analysis of the structure of natural categorical taxonomies; Tulving's (Tulving & Thomson, 1973) Encoding Specificity Principle; Posner's (1978) analysis of consciousness; Newell and Simon's (1972) models for goal-directed behavior, and Anderson's (1976) procedural models for inference, to name a few examples.

The future of the field of social memory is inviting. It is filled with fascinating empirical phenomena, intriguing theoretical puzzles, and the promise of rewarding practical applications.

REFERENCES

Abelson, R. P. The psychological status of the script concept. *American Psychologist*, 1981, *36*, 715–729.

Adler, A. *The individual psychology of Alfred Adler: A systematic presentation in selections from his writings*. In H. L. Ansbacher & R. R. Ansbacher (Eds.), New York: Harper, 1956.

Allport, G. *Pattern and growth in personality*. New York: Holt, Rinehart and Winston, 1961.

Anderson, J. R. *Language, memory, and thought*. Hillsdale, N.J.: Lawrence Erlbaum Associates, 1976.

Anderson, J. R. Memory for information about individuals. *Memory and Cognition*, 1977, *5*, 430–442.

Anderson, J. R. Arguments concerning representations for mental imagery. *Psychological Review*, 1978, *85*, 249–277.

Anderson, J. R. Effects of prior knowledge on memory for new information. *Memory and Cognition*, 1981, *9*, 237–246.

Anderson, J. R., & Bower, G. H. *Human associative memory*. Washington, D.C.: Winston, 1973.

Anderson, J. R., & Hastie, R. Individuation and reference in memory: Proper names and definite descriptions. *Cognitive Psychology*, 1974, *6*, 495–514.

Anderson, J. R., & Paulson, R. Interference in memory for pictorial information. *Cognitive Psychology*, 1978, *10*, 178–202.

Anderson, N. H., & Hubert, S. Effects of concomitant verbal recall on order effects in personality impression formation. *Journal of Verbal Learning and Verbal Behavior*, 1963, *2*, 379–391.

Anderson, R. C., & Pichert, V. W. Recall of previously unrecallable information following a shift in perspective. *Journal of Verbal Learning and Verbal Behavior*, 1978, *17*, 1–12.

Asch, S. E. Forming impressions of personality. *Journal of Abnormal and Social Psychology*, 1946, *41*, 258–290.

Asch, S. E. *Social psychology*. New York: Prentice-Hall, 1952.

Baddeley, A. Applied cognitive and cognitive applied psychology: The case of face recognition. In L. G. Nilsson (Ed.), *Perspectives on memory research*. Hillsdale, N.J.: Lawrence Erlbaum Associates, 1979.

Bahrick, H. P., & Boucher, B. Retention of visual and verbal codes of the same stimuli. *Journal of Experimental Psychology*, 1968, *78*, 417–422.

Bandura, A., & Walters, R. *Social learning and personality development*. New York: Holt, Rinehart and Winston, 1963.

Bargh, J. A., & Pietromonaco, P. Automatic information processing and social perception: The influence of trait information presented outside of conscious awareness on impression formation. *Journal of Personality and Social Psychology,* 1982, *43,* 437–449.

Baron, R. M. Contrasting approaches to social knowledge: An ecological perspective. *Personality and Social Psychology Bulletin,* 1980, *6,* 591–600.

Bartlett, F. C. *Remembering: A study in experimental and social psychology.* Cambridge, Eng.: Cambridge University press, 1932.

Beach, L., & Wertheimer, M. A free response approach to the study of person cognition. *Journal of Abnormal and Social Psychology,* 1961, *62,* 367–374.

Bear, G., & Hodun, A. Implicational principles and the cognition of confirmatory, contradictory, incomplete, and irrelevant information. *Journal of Personality and Social Psychology,* 1975, *32,* 594–604.

Bellezza, F. S., & Bower, G. H. Person stereotypes and memory for people. *Journal of Personality and Social Psychology,* 1981, *41,* 856–865.

Bellezza, F. S., & Bower, G. H. Remembering script-based text. *Poetics,* 1982, *11,* 1–23.

Bem, D. J., & McConnell, H. K. Testing the self-perception explanation of dissonance phenomena: On the salience of premanipulation attitudes. *Journal of Personality and Social Psychology,* 1970, *14,* 23–31.

Berkowitz, L. The judgmental process in personality functioning. *Psychological Review,* 1960, *67,* 130–142.

Berman, J. S., Read, S. J., & Kenny, D. A. *Processing inconsistent social information.* Unpublished manuscript, University of Texas, 1982.

Birnbaum, M. H. Thinking and feeling: A skeptical review. *American Psychologist,* 1981, *36,* 99–101.

Black, J. B., & Bern, H. Causal coherence and memory for events in narratives. *Journal of Verbal Learning and Verbal Behavior,* 1981, *20,* 267–275.

Bower, G. H. Cognitive psychology: An introduction. In W. K. Estes (Ed.), *Handbook of learning and cognitive processes* (Vol. 1). Hillsdale, N.J.: Lawrence Erlbaum Associates, 1975.

Bower, G. H., Black, J. B., & Turner, T. J. Scripts in memory for text. *Cognitive Psychology,* 1979, *11,* 177–220.

Bower, G. H., & Cohen, P. R. Emotional influences in memory and thinking: Data and theory. In M. S. Clark & S. T. Fiske (Eds.), *Affect and cognition.* Hillsdale, N.J.: Lawrence Erlbaum Associates, 1982.

Bower, G. H., & Gilligan, S. G. Remembering information related to one's self. *Journal of Research in Personality,* 1979, *13,* 420–432.

Bower, G. H., Gilligan, S. G., & Monteiro, K. Selectivity of learning caused by affective states. *Journal of Experimental Psychology: General,* 1981, *110,* 451–473.

Bower, G. H., & Karlin, M. B. Depth of processing pictures of faces and recognition memory. *Journal of Experimental Psychology,* 1974, *103,* 751–757.

Bower, G. H., Monteiro, K. P., & Gilligan, S. G. Emotional mood as a context for learning and recall. *Journal of Verbal Learning and Verbal Behavior,* 1978, *17,* 573–585.

Bradshaw, G. L., & Anderson, J. R. Elaborative encoding as an explanation of levels of processing. *Journal of Verbal Learning and Verbal Behavior,* 1982, *21,* 165–174.

Bransford, J. D., Barclay, J. R., & Franks, J. J. Sentence memory: A constructive versus interpretive approach. *Cognitive Psychology,* 1972, *3,* 193–209.

Bransford, J. D., & Franks, J. J. The abstraction of linguistic ideas. *Cognitive Psychology,* 1971, *2,* 331–350.

Brigham, J. D., & Barkowitz, P. Do "They all look alike?" The effect of race, sex, experience, and attitudes on the ability to recognize faces. *Journal of Applied Psychology,* 1978, *8,* 306–318.

Cantor, N., & Mischel, W. Traits as prototypes: Effects on recognition memory. *Journal of Personality and Social Psychology,* 1977, *35,* 38–48.

Carey, S. The development of face perception. In G. Davies, H. Ellis, & J. Shepherd (Eds.), *Perceiving and remembering faces.* New York: Academic Press, 1981.

Carlston, D. E. The recall and use of traits and events in social inference processes. *Journal of Experimental Social Psychology*, 1980, *16*, 303–328.

Carroll, J. B., & Maxwell, S. E. Individual differences in cognitive abilities. *Annual Review of Psychology*, 1979, *30*, 603–640.

Carver, C. S., & Scheier, M. F. *Attention and self-regulation: A control theory approach to human behavior.* New York: Springer-Verlag, 1981.

Clark, L. F., & Woll, S. B. Stereotype biases: A reconstructive analysis of their role in reconstructive memory. *Journal of Personality and Social Psychology*, 1981, *41*, 1064–1072.

Clark, M. S., & Fiske, S. T. (Eds.). *Affect and cognition.* Hillsdale, N.J.: Lawrence Erlbaum Associates, 1982.

Clifford, B. R. Voice identification by human listeners: On earwitness reliability. *Law and Human Behavior*, 1980, *4*, 373–394.

Cohen, C. Person categories and social perception: Testing some boundaries of the processing effects of prior knowledge. *Journal of Personality and Social Psychology*, 1981, *40*, 441–452.

Cohen, C., & Ebbesen, E. B. Observational goals and schema activation: A theoretical framework for behavior perception. *Journal of Experimental Social Psychology*, 1979, *15*, 305–329.

Cohen, C. E., Ebbesen, E. B., & Allen, R. B. *Remembering impressions and behavior: The effects of observational goals as time passes.* Unpublished manuscript. Rutgers University, 1981.

Cohen, M. E., & Carr, W. J. Facial recognition and the von Restorff effect. *Psychonomic Society*, 1975, *6*, 383–384.

Collins, A. M., & Loftus, E. A spreading activation theory of semantic processing. *Psychological Review*, 1975, *82*, 407–428.

Craik, F. I. M., & Lockhart, R. S. Levels of processing: A framework for memory research. *Journal of Verbal Learning and Verbal Behavior*, 1972, *11*, 671–684.

Crocker, J., Hannah, D. B., & Weber, R. Person memory and causal attributions, *Journal of Personality and Social Psychology*, 1983, *44*, 55–66.

D'Andrade, R. G. Memory and the assessment of behavior. In H. M. Blalock, Jr. (Ed.), *Measurement in the social sciences.* Chicago: Aldine, 1974.

Davies, G., Ellis, H., & Shepherd, J. (Eds.). *Perceiving and remembering faces.* New York: Academic Press, 1981.

Delia, J. G., & Crockett, W. H. Social schemas, cognitive complexity, and the learning of social structures. *Journal of Personality*, 1973, *41*, 414–429.

De Soto, C. B. Learning and social structure. *Journal of Abnormal and Social Psychology*, 1960, *60*, 417–421.

Dooling, D. J., & Christiaansen, R. E. Episodic and semantic aspects of memory for prose. *Journal of Experimental Psychology: Human Learning and Memory*, 1977, *3*, 428–436.

Dreben, E. K., Fiske, S. T., & Hastie, R. The independence of evaluative and item information: Impression and recall order effects in behavior-based impression formation. *Journal of Personality and Social Psychology*, 1979, *37*, 1758–1768.

Ebbesen, E. B. Cognitive processes in understanding ongoing behavior. In R. Hastie, T. M. Ostrom, E. B. Ebbesen, R. S. Wyer, D. L. Hamilton, & D. E. Carlston (Eds.), *Person Memory: the cognitive basis of social perception.* Hillsdale, N.J.: Lawrence Erlbaum Associates, 1980.

Ellis, H. D. Theoretical aspects of face recognition. In S. Davies, H. Ellis, & J. Shepherd (Eds.), *Perceiving and remembering faces.* New York: Academic Press, 1981.

Fass, W., & Schumacher, G. M. Schema theory and prose retention: Boundary conditions for encoding and retrieval effects. *Discourse Processes*, 1981, *4*, 17–26.

Ferguson, T. J., Rule, B. G., & Carlson, D. Memory for personally relevant information. *Journal of Personality and Social Psychology*, 1983, *44*, 251–261.

Fiske, S. T., & Cox, M. G. Person concepts: The effect of target familiarity and descriptive purpose on the process of describing others. *Journal of Personality*, 1979, *47*, 136–161.

Fiske, S. T., Kenny, D. A., & Taylor, S. E. Structural models for the mediation of salience effects on attribution. *Journal of Experimental Social Psychology*, 1982, *18*, 105–127.

Fiske, S. T., Taylor, S. E., Etcoff, N. L., & Laufer, J. K. Imagine, empathy, and causal attributions. *Journal of Experimental Social Psychology*, 1979, *15*, 356–377.

Flavell, J. H., & Ross, L. (Eds.) *Social cognitive development*. New York: Cambridge University Press, 1981.

Foos, P. W. Searching memory for congruent or incongruent information. *Journal of Verbal Learning and Verbal Behavior*, 1982, *21*, 108–117.

Forgas, J. P. *Social episodes: The study of interaction routines*. London: Academic Press, 1979.

Foss, D. J. A discourse on semantic priming. *Cognitive Psychology*, 1982, *14*, 590–607.

Franks, J. J., & Bransford, J. D. Abstraction of visual patterns. *Journal of Experimental Psychology*, 1971, *90*, 65–74.

Freud, S. *A general introduction to psycho-analysis*. London: Liveright, 1935.

Friendly, M. Methods for finding graphic representations of associative memory structures. In C. R. Puff (Ed.), *Memory organization and structure*. New York: Academic Press, 1979.

Garner, W. R. The stimulus in information processing. *American Psychologist*, 1970, *25*, 350–358.

Garner, W. R. *The processing of information and structure*. Potomac, Md.: Lawrence Erlbaum Associates, 1974.

Garner, W. R., & Morton, J. Perceptual independence: Definitions, models and experimental paradigms. *Psychological Bulletin*, 1969, *72*, 233–259.

Gauld, A., & Stephenson, G. M. Some experiments relating to Bartlett's theory of remembering. *British Journal of Psychology*, 1967, *58*, 39–49.

Gerard, H. B., & Fleischer, L. Recall and pleasantness of balanced and imbalanced cognitive structures. *Journal of Personality and Social Psychology*, 1967, *7*, 332–337.

Gibson, J. J. The concept of the stimulus in psychology. *American Psychologist*, 1960, *15*, 694–703.

Glixman, A. F. Recall of completed and uncompleted activities under varying degrees of stress. *Journal of Experimental Psychology*, 1949, *39*, 281–296.

Goffman, E. *The presentation of self in everyday life*. New York: Doubleday Anchor, 1959.

Goffman, E. *Interaction ritual*. New York: Doubleday Anchor, 1967.

Going, M., & Read, J. D. Effects of uniqueness, sex of subject, and sex of photograph on facial recognition. *Perception and Motor Skills*, 1974, *39*, 109–110.

Graesser, A. C., Gordon, S. E., & Sawyer, J. D. Recognition memory for typical and atypical actions in scripted activities: Tests of a script pointer and tag hypothesis. *Journal of Verbal Learning and Verbal Behavior*, 1979, *18*, 319–332.

Graesser, A. C., & Nakamura, G. V. The impact of a schema on comprehension and memory. In G. H. Bower (Ed.), *The psychology of learning and motivation* (Vol. 16). New York: Academic Press, 1982.

Graesser, A. C., Woll, S. B., Kowalski, D. J., & Smith D. A. Memory for typical and atypical actions in scripted activities. *Journal of Experimental Psychology: Human Learning and Memory*, 1980, *6*, 503–515.

Greenwald, A. G. The totalitarian ego: Fabrication and revision of personal history. *American Psychologist*, 1981, *35*, 603–618.

Hamilton, D. L. (Ed.). *Cognitive processes in stereotyping and intergroup behavior*. Hillsdale, N.J.: Lawrence Erlbaum Associates, 1981.

Hamilton, D. L., Katz, L. B., & Leirer, V. O. Organizational processes in impression formation. In R. Hastie, T. M. Ostrom, E. B. Ebbesen, R. B. Wyer, D. L. Hamilton, D. E. Carlston (Eds.), *Person Memory: The cognitive basis of social perception*. Hillsdale, N.J.: Lawrence Erlbaum Associates, 1980.

Hamilton, D. L., Katz, L. B., & Leirer, V. O. Cognitive representation of personality impressions: Organizational processes in first impression formation. *Journal of Personality and Social Psychology*, 1980, *39*, 1050–1063.

Hartwick, J. Memory for trait information: A signal detection analysis. *Journal of Experimental Social Psychology*, 1979, *15*, 533–552.

Harvey, J. H., Yarkin, K. L., Lightner, J. M., & Town, J. P. Unsolicited interpretation and recall of interpersonal events. *Journal of Personality and Social Psychology*, 1980, *38*, 551–568.

Hasher, L., & Griffin, M. Reconstructive and reproductive processes in memory. *Journal of Experimental Psychology: Human Learning and Memory*, 1978, *4*, 318–330.

Hastie, R. Memory for behavioral information that confirms or contradicts a personality impression. In R. Hastie, T. M. Ostrom, E. B. Ebbesen, R. S. Wyer, D. L. Hamilton, D. E. Carlston (Eds.), *Person Memory: The cognitive basis of social perception* Hillsdale, N.J.: Lawrence Erlbaum Associates, 1980.

Hastie, R., & Carlston, D. Theoretical issues in person memory. In R. Hastie, T. M. Ostrom, E. B. Ebbesen, R. S. Wyer, D. L. Hamilton, D. E. Carlston (Eds.), *Person Memory: The cognitive basis of social perception* Hillsdale, N.J.: Lawrence Erlbaum Associates, 1980.

Hastie, R., & Kumar, P. A. Person memory: Personality traits as organizing principles in memory for behaviors. *Journal of Personality and Social Psychology*, 1979, *37*, 25–38.

Heider, F. Attitudes and cognitive organization. *Journal of Psychology*, 1946, *21*, 107–112.

Heider, F. *The psychology of interpersonal relations*. New York: Wiley, 1958.

Hemsley, G. D., & Marmurek, H. H. C. Person memory: The processing of consistent and inconsistent person information. *Personality and Social Psychology Bulletin*, 1982, *8*, 433–438.

Henley, N. M., Horsfall, R. B., & De Soto, C. B. Goodness of figure and social structure. *Psychological Review*, 1969, *76*, 194–204.

Herr, P. M., Sherman, S. J., & Fazio, R. H. On the consequences of priming: Assimilation and contrast effects. *Journal of Experimental Social Psychology*, 1983, *19*, 323–340.

Herstein J. A., Carroll, J. S., & Hayes, J. R. The organization of knowledge about people and their attributes in long-term memory. *Representative Research in Social Psychology*, 1980, *11*, 17–37.

Higgins, E. T., & King, G. Accessibility of social constructs: Individual and interpersonal considerations. In N. Cantor & J. Kihlstrom (Eds.), *Personality, cognition, and social interaction*. Hillsdale, N.J.: Lawrence Erlbaum Associates, 1981.

Higgins, E. T., King, G. A., & Mavin, G. H. Individual construct accessibility and subjective impressions and recall. *Journal of Personality and Social Psychology*, 1982, *43*, 35–47.

Higgins, E. T., Kuiper, N. A., & Olson, J. M. Social cognition: A need to get personal. In E. T. Higgins, C. P. Herman, M. P. Zanna (Eds.), *Social cognition: The Ontario Symposium* (Vol. 1). Hillsdale, N.J.: Lawrence Erlbaum Associates, 1981.

Higgins, E. T., Rholes, W. S., & Jones, C. F. Category accessibility and impression formation. *Journal of Experimental Social Psychology*, 1977, *13*, 141–153.

Hochberg, J. In the mind's eye. In R. N. Haber (Ed.), *Contemporary theory and research in visual perception*. New York: Holt, Rinehart, & Winston, 1968.

Hochberg, J. Levels of perceptual organization. In M. Kubovy & J. R. Pomerantz (Eds.), *Perceptual organization*. Hillsdale, N.J.: Lawrence Erlbaum Associates, 1981.

Hoffman, C., Mischel, W., & Mazze, K. The role of purpose in the organization of information about behavior: Trait-based versus goal-based categories in person cognition. *Journal of Personality and Social Psychology*, 1981, *40*, 211–225.

Howard, J. W., & Rothbart, M. Social categorization and memory for in-group and out-group behavior. *Journal of Personality and Social Psychology*, 1980, *38*, 301–310.

Jacoby, L. L., & Craik, F. I. M. Effect of elaboration of processing at encoding and retrieval: Trace distinctiveness and recovery of initial content. In L. Cermack & F. Craik (Eds.), *Levels of processing in human memory*. Hillsdale, N.J.: Lawrence Erlbaum, Associates, 1979.

Jeffrey, K. M., & Mischel, W. Effects of purpose on the organization and recall of information in person perception. *Journal of Personality*, 1979, *47*, 397–419.

Keenan, J. M., & Baillet, S. D. Memory for personally and socially significant events. In R. S. Nickerson (Ed.), *Attention and performance*, VIII. Hillsdale, N.J.: Lawrence Erlbaum Associates, 1980.

Kelly, G. *The psychology of personal constructs,* Volume 1. New York: Norton, 1955.

Kendzierski, D. Self-schemata and scripts: The recall of self-referent and scriptal information. *Personality and Social Psychology Bulletin,* 1980, *6,* 23–29.

Kenny, D. A. *Correlation and causality.* New York: Wiley, 1979.

Klatzky, R. L., Martin, G. L., & Kane, R. A. Semantic interpretation effects on memory for faces. *Memory and Cognition,* 1982, *10,* 195–206.

Kosslyn, S. M. *Image and mind.* Cambridge: Harvard University Press, 1980.

Kosslyn, S. M. The medium and the message in mental imagery: A theory. *Psychological Review,* 1981, *88,* 46–66.

Krauss, R. M., Apple, W., Morency, N., Wenzel, C., & Winton, W. Verbal, vocal, and visible factors in judgments of another's affect. *Journal of Personality and Social Psychology,* 1980, *40,* 312–320.

Kraut, R. E. Verbal and nonverbal cues in the perception of lying. *Journal of Personality and Social Psychology,* 1978, *36,* 380–391.

Kuiper, N. A., & Rogers, T. B. Encoding of personal information: Self-other differences. *Journal of Personality and Social Psychology,* 1979, *37,* 499–514.

Kunst-Wilson, W. R., & Zajonc, R. B. Affective discrimination of stimuli that cannot be recognized. *Science,* 1980, *207,* 557–558.

Laing, R. *The politics of experience.* New York: Ballantine, 1967.

Leippe, M. R., Ostrom, T. M., Baumgardner, M. H., & Lingle, J. H. *Selective retrieval of stimulus information vs. thematic judgments in natural language inferences.* Unpublished manuscript, St. Norbert College, 1981.

Lewis, C. H., & Anderson, J. R. Interference with real world knowledge. *Cognitive Psychology,* 1976, *8,* 311–335.

Light, L., Kayra-Stuart, F., & Hollander, S. Recognition memory for typical and atypical faces. *Journal of Experimental Psychology: Human Learning and Memory,* 1979, *5,* 212–228.

Lingle, J. H., Dukerich, J. M., & Ostrom, T. M. Accessing information in memory-based impression judgments: Incongruity versus negativity in retrieval selectivity. *Journal of Personality and Social Psychology,* 1983, *44,* 262–272.

Lingle, J. H., & Ostrom, T. M. Retrieval selectivity in memory-based impression judgments. *Journal of Personality and Social Psychology,* 1979, *37,* 180–194.

Lingle, J. H., Geva, N., Ostrom, T. M., Leippe, M. R., & Baumgardner, M. H. Thematic effects of person judgments on impression formation. *Journal of Personality and Social Psychology,* 1979, *37,* 674–687.

Linville, P. W. The complexity-extremity effect and age-based stereotyping. *Journal of Personality and Social Psychology,* 1982, *42,* 193–211.

Linville, P. W., & Jones, E. E. Polarized appraisals of outgroup members. *Journal of Personality and Social Psychology,* 1980, *38,* 689–703.

Lord, C. G. Schemas and images as memory aids: Two modes of processing social information. *Journal of Personality and Social Psychology,* 1980, *38,* 257–269.

Maccoby, E., & Jacklin, C. *The psychology of sex differences.* Stanford: Stanford University Press, 1974.

Mandler, G. The structure of value: Accounting for taste. In M. S. Clark & S. T. Fiske (Eds.), *Affect and cognition.* Hillsdale, N.J.: Lawrence Erlbaum Associates, 1982.

Markus, H. Self-schemata and processing information about the self. *Journal of Personality and Social Psychology,* 1977, *35,* 63–78.

Markus, H., Crane, M., Bernstein, S., & Siladi, M. Self-schemas and gender. *Journal of Personality and Social Psychology,* 1982, *42,* 38–50.

Massad, C. M., Hubbard, M., & Newtson, D. Selective perception of events. *Journal of Experimental Social Psychology,* 1979, *15,* 513–532.

Matlin, M. W. Response competition, recognition, and affect. *Journal of Personality and Social Psychology*, 1971, *19*, 295–300.

McArthur, L. Z., & Baron, R. M. Toward an ecological theory of social perception. *Psychological Review*, 1983, *90*, 215–238.

McKoon, G., & Ratcliff, R. Priming in episodic and semantic memory. *Journal of Verbal Learning and Verbal Behavior*, 1979, *18*, 463–480.

Miller, G. A., Galanter, E., & Pribram, K. *Plans and the structure of behavior*. New York: Holt, Rinehart, & Winston, 1960.

Mischel, W., Ebbesen, E. B., & Zeiss, A. M. Determinants of selective memory about the self. *Journal of Consulting and Clinical Psychology*, 1973, *44*, 92–103.

Monroe, R. L. *Schools of psychoanalytic thought*. New York: Holt, Rinehart and Winston, 1955.

Moreland, R., & Zajonc, R. B. Is stimulus recognition a necessary condition for the occurrence of exposure effects? *Journal of Personality and Social Psychology*, 1977, *35*, 191–199.

Moreland, R. L., & Zajonc, R. B. Exposure effects may not depend on stimulus recognition. *Journal of Personality and Social Psychology*, 1979, *37*, 1085–1089.

Murphy, G. L., & Smith, E. E. Basic-level superiority in picture categorization. *Journal of Verbal Learning and Verbal Behavior*, 1982, *21*, 1–20.

Neely, J. H. Semantic priming and retrieval from lexical memory: Roles of inhibitionless spreading activation and limited capacity attention. *Journal of Experimental Psychology: General*, 1977, *106*, 226–254.

Neisser, U. *Cognitive psychology*. Englewood Cliffs, N.J.: Prentice-Hall, 1967.

Neisser, U. On "social knowing." *Personality and Social Psychology Bulletin*, 1980, *6*, 601–605.

Newell, A., & Simon, H. A. *Human problem solving*. Englewood Cliffs, N.J.: Prentice-Hall, 1972.

Newtson, D. Attribution and the unit of perception of ongoing behavior. *Journal of Personality and Social Psychology*, 1973, *28*, 28–38.

Newtson, D., & Engquist, G. The perceptual organization of ongoing behavior. *Journal of Experimental Social Psychology*, 1976, *12*, 436–450.

Nisbett, R., & Ross, L. *Human inference: Strategies and shortcomings of social judgment*. Englewood Cliffs, N.J.: Prentice-Hall, 1980.

Ostrom, T. M. *Cognitive representation of impressions*. American Psychological Association, Chicago, September, 1975.

Ostrom, T. M., Lingle, J. H., Pryor, J. B., & Geva, N. Cognitive organization of person impressions. In R. Hastie, T. M. Ostrom, E. B. Ebbeson, R. S. Wyer, D. L. Hamilton, D. E. Carlston (Eds.), *Person memory: The cognitive basis of social perception*. Hillsdale, N.J.: Lawrence Erlbaum Associates, 1980.

Ostrom, T. M., Pryor, J. B., & Simpson, D. D. The organization of social information. In E. T. Higgins, C. P. Herman, & M. Zanna (Eds.), *Social Cognition: The Ontario Symposium, Volume 1*. Hillsdale, N.J.: Lawrence Erlbaum Associates, 1981.

Owens, J., Bower, G. H., & Black, J. B. The "soap opera" effect in story recall. *Memory and Cognition*, 1979, *7*, 185–191.

Park, B., & Rothbart, M. Perception of out-group homogeneity and levels of social categorization: Memory for the subordinate attributes of in-group and out-group members. *Journal of Personality and Social Psychology*, 1982, *42*, 1051–1068.

Pennington, N., & Hastie, R. Juror decision-making models: The generalization gap. *Psychological Bulletin*, 1981, *89*, 246–287.

Piaget, J. *The child's conception of the World*. London: Routledge & Kegan Paul, 1929.

Piaget, J. *The construction of reality in the child*. New York: Basic Books, 1954.

Picek, J. S., Sherman, S. J., & Shiffrin, R. M. Cognitive organization and coding of social structures. *Journal of Personality and Social Psychology*, 1975, *31*, 758–768.

Posner, M. I. *Chronometric explorations of mind*. Hillsdale, N.J.: Lawrence Erlbaum Associates, 1978.

Posner, M. I., & Snyder, C. R. R. Attention and cognitive control. In R. L. Solso (Ed.), *Information processing and cognition*. Hillsdale, N.J.: Lawrence Erlbaum Associates, 1975.

Powers, W. T. *Behavior: The control of perception*. Chicago: Aldine, 1973.

Press, A. N., Crockett, W. H., & Rosenkrantz, P. S. Cognitive complexity and the learning of balanced and unbalanced social structures. *Journal of Personality*, 1969, *37*, 541–553.

Pryor, J. B., & Ostrom, T. M. The cognitive organization of social information: A converging-operations approach. *Journal of Personality and Social Psychology*, 1981, *41*, 628–641.

Pryor, J. B., Simpson, D. D., Mitchell, M., Ostrom, T. M., & Lydon, J. Structural selectivity in the retrieval of social information. *Social Cognition*, 1982, *1*, 336–357.

Pylyshyn, Z. The imagery debate: Analogue media versus tacit knowledge. *Psychological Review*, 1981, *88*, 16–45.

Quattrone, G. A., & Jones, E. E. The perception of variability within in-groups and out-groups: Implications for the law of small numbers. *Journal of Personality and Social Psychology*, 1980, *38*, 141–152.

Ratcliff, R., & McKoon, G. Automatic and strategic components of priming in recognition. *Journal of Verbal Learning and Verbal Behavior*, 1981, *20*, 204–215.

Reder, L. M. Plausibility judgments versus fact retrieval: Alternative strategies for sentence verification. *Psychological Review*, 1982, *89*, 250–280.

Reed, S. Pattern recognition and categorization. *Cognitive Psychology*, 1972, *3*, 383–407.

Regan, D., & Totten, J. Empathy and attribution: Turning observers into actors. *Journal of Personality and Social Psychology*, 1975, *32*, 850–856.

Reyes, R. M., Thompson, W. C., & Bower, G. H. Judgmental biases from differing availabilities of arguments. *Journal of Personality and Social Psychology*, 1980, *39*, 2–12.

Rips, L., & Stubbs, M. Genealogy and memory. *Journal of Verbal Learning and Verbal Behavior*, 1980, *19*, 705–721.

Riskey, D. R. Verbal memory processes in impression formation. *Journal of Experimental Psychology: Human Learning and Memory*, 1979, *5*, 271–281.

Rogers, T. B., Kuiper, N. A., & Kirker, W. S. Self-reference and the encoding of personal information. *Journal of Personality and Social Psychology*, 1977, *35*, 677–688.

Rosch, E., & Lloyd, B. B. (Eds.). *Cognition and categorization*. Hillsdale, N.J.: Lawrence Erlbaum Associates, 1978.

Rosch, E., Mervis, C. B., Gray, W. D., Johnson, P. M., & Boyes-Braem, P. Basic objects in natural categories. *Cognitive Psychology*, 1976, *8*, 382–439.

Rosenberg, S. E., & Sedlak, A. Structural representations of implicit personality theory. In L. Berkowitz (Ed.), *Advances in experimental social psychology*. (Vol. 6). New York: Academic Press, 1972.

Rosenzweig, S. An experimental study of "repression" with special reference to need-persistive and ego-defensive reactions to frustration. *Journal of Experimental Psychology*, 1943, *32*, 64–74.

Ross, M., & Sicoly, F. Egocentric biases in availability and attribution. *Journal of Personality and Social Psychology*, 1979, *37*, 322–336.

Rothbart, M. Memory processes and social beliefs. In D. L. Hamilton (Ed.), *Cognitive processes in stereotyping and intergroup behavior*. Hillsdale, N.J.: Lawrence Erlbaum Associates, 1981.

Rothbart, M., Evans, M., & Fulero, S. Recall for confirming events: Memory processes and the maintenance of social stereotypes. *Journal of Experimental Social Psychology*, 1979, *15*, 343–355.

Rothbart, M., Fulero, S., Jensen, C., Howard, J., & Birrell, P. From individual to group impressions: Availability heuristics in stereotype formation. *Journal of Experimental Social Psychology*, 1978, *14*, 237–255.

Rubin, Z., & Zajonc, R. B. Structural bias and generalization in the learning of social structures. *Journal of Personality*, 1969, *27*, 310–324.

Rywick, T., & Schaye, P. Use of long-term memory in impression formation. *Psychological Reports*, 1974, *34*, 939–945.

Schank, R. C., & Abelson, R. *Scripts, plans, goals, and understanding*. Hillsdale, N.J.: Lawrence Erlbaum Associates, 1977.

Schneider, D. J. Implicit personality theory: A review. *Psychological Bulletin*, 1973, *79*, 294–319.

Schustack, M. W., & Anderson, J. R. Effects of analogy to prior knowledge on memory for new information. *Journal of Verbal Learning and Verbal Behavior*, 1979, *18*, 565–583.

Schweder, R. A., & D'Andrade, R. G. Accurate reflection or systematic distortion? A reply to Block, Weiss, & Thorne. *Journal of Personality and Social Psychology*, 1979, *37*, 1075–1084.

Sentis, K. P., & Burnstein, E. Remembering schema-consistent information: Effects of a balance schema on recognition memory. *Journal of Personality and Social Psychology*, 1979, *37*, 2200–2211.

Shepherd, J. Social factors in face recognition. In G. Davies, H. Ellis, & J. Shepherd (Eds.), *Perceiving and remembering faces*. New York: Academic Press, 1981.

Sherif, M., & Cantril, H. The psychology of "attitudes": Part I. *Psychological Review*, 1945, *52*, 295–319.

Sherman, S. J., & Wolosin, R. J. Cognitive biases in a recognition task. *Journal of Personality*, 1973, *41*, 395–413.

Smith, D. A., & Graesser, A. C. Memory for actions in scripted activities as a function of typicality, retention interval, and retrieval task. *Memory and Cognition*, 1981, *9*, 550–559.

Smith, E. E., Adams, N., & Schorr, D. Fact retrieval and the paradox of interference. *Cognitive Psychology*, 1978, *10*, 438–464.

Smith, E. E., & Nielsen, G. D. Representations and retrieval processes in short-term memory: Recognition and recall of faces. *Journal of Experimental Psychology*, 1970, *85*, 397–405.

Smith, E. R. Beliefs, attributions, and evaluations: Nonhierarchical models of mediation in social cognition. *Journal of Personality and Social Psychology*, 1982, *43*, 248–259.

Snyder, M., & Cantor, N. Testing hypotheses about other people: The use of historical knowledge. *Journal of Experimental Psychology*, 1979, *15*, 330–342.

Snyder, M., & Uranowitz, S. W. Reconstructing the past: Some cognitive consequences of person perception. *Journal of Personality and Social Psychology*, 1978, *36*, 941–950.

Spiro, R. J. Remembering information from text: The "state of the schema" approach. In R. C. Anderson, R. J. Sprio, & W. E. Montague (Eds.), *Schooling and the acquisition of knowledge*. Hillsdale, N.J.: Lawrence Erlbaum Associates, 1977.

Spiro, R. J. Accommodative reconstruction in prose recall. *Journal of Verbal Learning and Verbal Behavior*, 1980, *19*, 84–95.

Srull, T. K. Person memory: Some tests of associative storage and retrieval models. *Journal of Experimental Psychology: Human Learning and Memory*, 1981, *7*, 440–463.

Srull, T. K., & Brand, J. F. Memory for information about persons: The effect of encoding operations on subsequent retrieval. *Journal of Verbal Learning and Verbal Behavior*, 1983, *22*, 219–230.

Srull, T. K., & Wyer, R. S. The role of category accessibility in the interpretation of information about persons: Some determinants and implications. *Journal of Personality and Social Psychology*, 1979, *31*, 1660–1672.

Srull, T. K., & Wyer, R. S. Category accessibility and social perception: Some implications for the study of person memory and interpersonal judgment. *Journal of Personality and Social Psychology*, 1980, *38*, 841–856.

Sulin, R. A., & Dooling, D. J. Intrusion of a thematic idea in retention of prose. *Journal of Experimental Psychology*, 1974, *103*, 255–262.

Sullivan, H. *The interpersonal theory of psychiatry*. New York: Norton, 1953.

Swann, W. B., Jr., & Miller, L. C. Why never forgetting a face matters: Visual imagery and social memory. *Journal of Personality and Social Psychology*, 1982, *43*, 475–480.

Swann, W. B., Jr., and Read, S. J. Self-verification processes: How we sustain our self-conceptions. *Journal of Experimental Social Psychology*, 1981, *17*, 351–372.

Tagiuri, R., & Petrullo, L. (Eds.). *Person perception and interpersonal behavior*. Stanford: Stanford University Press, 1958.

Taylor, S. E., & Crocker, J. Schematic bases of social information processing. In E. T. Higgins, C. P. Herman, M. P. Zanna (Eds.), *Social Cognition: The Ontario Symposium* (Vol. 1). Hillsdale, N.J.: Lawrence Erlbaum Associates, 1981.

Taylor, S. E., & Falcone, H. Cognitive bases of stereotyping: The relationship between categorization and prejudice. *Personality and Social Psychology Bulletin*, 1982, *8*, 426–432.

Taylor, S. E., & Fiske, S. T. Point of view and perceptions of causality. *Journal of Personality and Social Psychology*. 1975, *32*, 439–445.

Taylor, S. E., Fiske, S. T., Etcoff, N. L., & Ruderman, A. V. Categorical and contextual bases of person memory and stereotyping. *Journal of Personality and Social Psychology*, 1978, *36*, 778–793.

Toyama, J. S. *The effect of orientation on the recognition of faces: A reply to Yin*. Ph.D. thesis, University of Waterloo, Canada, 1975.

Tsujimoto, R. N., Wilde, J., & Robertson, D. R. Distorted memory for exemplars of social structure: Evidence for schematic memory processes. *Journal of Personality and Social Psychology*, 1978, *38*, 1402–1414.

Tulving, E., & Thomson, D. M. Encoding specificity and retrieval processes in episodic memory. *Psychological Review*, 1973, *80*, 352–373.

Tversky, A., & Kahneman, D. Availability: A heuristic for judging frequency and probability. *Cognitive Psychology*, 1973, *5*, 207–232.

Underwood, B. J. Individual differences as a crucible in theory construction. *American Psychologist*, 1975, *30*, 128–134.

Warren, R. E. Stimulus encoding and memory. *Journal of Experimental Psychology*, 1972, *94*, 90–100.

Watkins, M. J., Ho, E., & Tulving, E. Context effects in recognition memory for faces. *Journal of Verbal Learning and Verbal Behavior*, 1976, *15*, 505–517.

Wilson, W. R. Feeling more than we can know: Exposure effects without learning. *Journal of Personality and Social Psychology*, 1979, *37*, 811–821.

Wixon, D. R., & Laird, J. D. Awareness and attitude change in the forced-compliance paradigm: The importance of when. *Journal of Personality and Social Psychology*, 1976, *34*, 376–384.

Woll, S. B., & Graesser, A. C. Memory discrimination for information typical or atypical of person schemas. *Social Cognition*, 1982, *1*, 287–310.

Wyer, R. S., & Carlston, D. . *Social cognition, inference, and attribution*. Hillsdale, N.J.: Lawrence Erlbaum Associates, 1979.

Wyer, R. S., & Frey, D. The effects of feedback about self and others on recall and judgments of feedback-relevant information. 1983.

Wyer, R. S., & Gordon, S. The recall of information about persons and groups. *Journal of Experimental Social Psychology*, 1982, *18*, 128–164.

Wyer, R. S., & Srull, T. K. The processing of social stimulus information: A conceptual integration. In R. Hastie, T. M. Ostrom, E. B. Ebbesen, R. S. Wyer, D. L. Hamilton, & D. E. Carlston (Eds.). *Person memory: The cognitive basis of social perception*. Hillsdale, N.J.: Lawrence Erlbaum Associates, 1980.

Wyer, R. S., & Srull, T. K. Category accessibility: some theoretical and empirical issues concerning the processing of social stimulus information. In E. T. Higgins, C. P. Herman, M. P. Zanna (Eds.), Social cognition: The Ontario Symposium (Vol. 1) Hillsdale, N.J.: Lawrence Erlbaum Associates, 1981.

Wyer, R. S., Srull, T. K., Gordon, S. E., & Hartwick, J. The effects of taking a perspective on the recall of prose material. *Journal of Personality and Social Psychology*, 1982, *43*, 674–688.

Yin, R. K. Looking at upside-down faces. *Journal of Experimental Psychology*, 1969, *81*, 141–145.

Zajonc, R. B. Feeling and thinking: Preferences need no inferences. *American Psychologist*, 1980, *35*, 151–175.

Zajonc, R. B., & Burnstein, E. The learning of balanced and unbalanced social structures. *Journal of Personality*, 1965, *33*, 153–163. (a)

Zajonc, R. B., & Burnstein, E. Structural balance, reciprocity and positivity as sources of cognitive bias. *Journal of Personality*, 1965, *33*, 570–583. (b)

Zajonc, R. B., Pietromonaco, P., & Bargh, J. Independence and interaction of affect and cognition. In M. S. Clark & S. T. Fiske (Eds.), *Affect and cognition*. Hillsdale, N.J.: Lawrence Erlbaum Associates, 1982.

Zajonc, R. B., & Sherman, S. J. Structural balance and the induction of relations. *Journal of Personality*, 1967, *35*, 635–650.

4 Semantic and Episodic Memory

Edward J. Shoben
University of Illinois

Contents

Many theorists in cognitive psychology have adopted a distinction between semantic and episodic memory. According to this distinction, there are important differences in the storage and processing of our general (semantic) knowledge and particular, temporally marked (episodic) information. Although this distinction has been accepted by some theorists, it has been explicitly denied by others, and its utility is currently a matter of some controversy. Although I certainly cannot claim impartiality in this dispute, its resolution has important constraints on theory construction in all areas of memory. If it is decided that the distinction is not needed, then our theories will have to apply to a much wider range of phenomena than they now do. If, as I suspect, we find that the distinction is a necessary and valid one, then many theorists may be performing experiments that do not tap the memory system with which their theory is concerned.

For the most part, this distinction has had no influence on the work in social cognition. Although many writers distinguish between behaviors (and sometimes events) and traits (see Wyer & Srull, 1980), this distinction does not correspond to the difference between episodic and semantic memory. Hastie and Carlston (1980) come closest to the semantic episodic distinction when they develop a contrast between conceptual social memory and social event memory. However,

213

this distinction has not been widely adopted, and it does not correspond to the distinction between specific personal knowledge and shared general knowledge, as we demonstrate later.

Although the semantic/episodic distinction may seem an esoteric one that is of interest only to cognitive psychologists, it is argued here that this distinction is of profound importance to research in social cognition. If there really is a difference between episodic and semantic memory, then paradigms commonly employed to study social cognition may invoke different memory systems. For example, asking subjects to decide whether warm people are generous is a request for general information that is presumably stored in semantic memory. Asking people to judge if John is warm after learning that John helped an elderly person across the street is a request for information acquired in a psychological experiment that is presumably stored in episodic memory. If the two memory systems are governed by different (although similar) laws, then paradoxical experimental results are a virtually inevitable consequence.

One example of this kind of result is a pair of articles by Ebbesen and Allen (1979; Allen & Ebbesen, 1981). They sought to apply the feature comparison model of semantic memory (Smith, Shoben, & Rips, 1974) to social cognition. In the earlier paper, they reported two studies that clearly involve general semantic knowledge. In the first, they timed subjects as they decided if traits tended to go together, for example if cold people are stingy. Overall, the reaction times obtained in this task did not fit terribly well with those expected from the model. In particular, the correlations between similarity and RT (a critical prediction of the feature comparison model) were uniformly small, and generally not significant. A slight improvement in these results was obtained when the task was changed (in the second experiment) to timing subjects as they judged if two trait terms were similar, although the correlations were still much smaller than those typically obtained with nonsocial semantic stimuli.

Allen and Ebbesen (1981) attempted to fit the feature comparison model to a more typical social cognition task in which subjects were shown a videotape and then asked to make judgments on the basis of the information in the videotape. Although the design is quite complex and the results are complicated by other factors, the important result for the present discussion is that the model fit very well.

We thus have a circumstance where a semantic memory model fits the data from one experiment very well (ironically an episodic memory study) but fits the data from a semantic memory experiment quite poorly. Of course, it may be that the reason for the poor fit in the Ebbesen and Allen study is unrelated to the distinction proposed here. Ebbesen and Allen make just this sort of argument and they may be entirely correct. It is also possible that the good fit of the feature comparison model to the Allen and Ebbesen data is spurious. The merits of these arguments are not important here; the critical point is that this kind of disparity should alert us to the possibility that different social cognition experiments may be tapping different kinds of human memory.

In this chapter, we first consider the origins of the semantic/episodic distinction. We also try to indicate what kind of definition is appropriate and what kind is not. Subsequently, we examine the cognitive evidence and the experimental logic by which this evidence has been obtained. Lastly, we consider the implications of this distinction for theories of social cognition.

ORIGINS OF THE DISTINCTION

In his seminal paper, Tulving (1972) noted that the term semantic memory was initially employed to distinguish this kind of memory research from the more common type of memory research that existed at that time. Until the 1970s, the paradigmatic memory experiment asked subjects to learn some body of material, commonly a list of words or nonsense syllables. They then received a memory test (commonly free recall) on this information. The information on which subjects were tested was always specific to the psychological experiment. In contrast to this approach, researchers interested in semantic memory did not have subjects learn information for the purposes of the experiment. Instead, the memorial information that was subsequently tested was information that all people share: our general world knowledge. Moreover, the dependent measure for this information was usually the time subjects required to verify a single semantic fact.

Initially, Tulving restricted his description to knowledge of the language. He described semantic memory as the place where knowledge of the lexicon was stored, a kind of mental thesaurus. In addition, Tulving also ascribed to semantic memory the knowledge of the rules by which these terms could be used. Thus, Tulving's examples of information handled by the semantic memory system include basic definitions of concepts or inferences based on such definitions. For example, NaCl is the formula for common table salt, July follows June, and summers are usually hot in Katmandu are representative statements that Tulving claims are from the semantic system. Expanding semantic memory to include general world knowledge permits us to include general facts that are not true solely on the basis of the meaning of the words. For example, dessert need not follow the entree; in some cultures the order is reversed. Similarly, there is nothing in the meaning of the words that verifies the statement that warm people are usually helpful. Yet, both of these pieces of information are part of our knowledge of the world.

In contrast to semantic memory, episodic memory stores information about temporally dated episodes or events. This information is always stored in terms of an autobiographical reference. Moreover, Tulving makes the restrictive assumption that information can only be stored in terms of its perceptible properties. This assumption contrasts with the corresponding postulate that information in semantic memory is stored in terms of cognitive referents of input signals. Examples that Tulving provides involve information that has these distinctive qualities of being both personal and autobiographically marked. For example, I saw a flash of light a short while ago, followed by a loud sound a few seconds later; I have an appointment with a student at 9:30 tomorrow morning; one of the words I saw in the memory experiment was LEGEND, and the word that was paired with DAX was FRIGID; are all examples of episodic statements.

This distinction became a source of theoretical controversy very soon after the publication of Tulving's original article. Atkinson, Herrmann, and Wescourt (1974) adopted (with new names) the distinction, while Anderson and Bower (1973) denied it. Most important, perhaps, were the modifications that arose from the original distinction. Kintsch (1974), for example, did not like the restriction of semantic memory to the lexicon. He felt that general world knowledge should all be stored in the same place regardless of whether the information was about a single word or some more complicated activity. Schank (1974) raised a similar issue in an unpublished paper entitled "Is there a semantic memory?" (to which Schank's answer was "No") in which he argued that it was illogical to have a distinction between general knowledge about words and general knowledge about events. He placed all such information in a conceptual memory. Knowledge that ordering dessert follows eating the main course is difficult to classify according to Tulving's original formulation. This information is certainly not episodic because it is general knowledge and is consequently neither autobiographical nor temporally marked. It is similarly difficult to argue that this statement is semantic because it would be very difficult to deduce its truth on the basis of the meaning of the words alone.

One solution to this problem is to relax the definition of semantic memory to one that includes general world knowledge. In this way, we can include not only our knowledge of particular objects (such as robins have red breasts), but also knowledge about sequential events, such as what happens in flying to Europe, what happens in particular stories such as fairy tales, and what particular people, such as lawyers, are like. This broader definition of semantic memory has tacitly become accepted in later usage (Anderson & Ross, 1980; Shoben, 1980; Shoben, Wescourt, & Smith, 1978; Smith, 1978).

Interactions Between Semantic and Episodic Memory

It should be emphasized that semantic and episodic memory are not two fully independent systems that never communicate with each other. First, if one assumes that all information is initially both temporally marked and autobiographical, then information in semantic memory must have its origins in episodic memory. Second, as discussed later in this section, there is overwhelming experimental evidence that semantic memory organization can influence episodic memory performance.

The necessity of transferring information from episodic to semantic memory is best understood in the context of learning new information. For example, if one goes to a zoo and learns some facts about an oryx, then the information is certainly episodic in that one remembers the time and place that the information was acquired. Over time, however, the autobiographical and temporal aspects of this information may be lost and one's information that an oryx is a small African antelope may be stored in semantic memory along with the information that sparrows are small songbirds.

Information about events must be subjected to a related, but different, analysis. A child will probably learn about what goes on in a dentist's office through firsthand experience. From these personal experiences, the child will develop some general knowledge about events that occur when one goes to the dentist's office that is independent of any particular personal experience and will consequently be part of the child's general world knowledge stored in semantic memory. Thus, in this instance, the information in semantic memory will be a generalization of personal experiences in episodic memory.

There is abundant evidence that semantic organization can influence episodic memory. Clustering in free recall is probably the best known example of such influence. Words that are similar in meaning tend to be recalled together even if they are spread out throughout the list of to-be-recalled words (see Tulving, 1968, for a review of the early literature). In one of the nicest demonstrations of this phenomenon, Miller (1969) showed that similarity (as derived from Johnson's [1967] hierarchical clustering program) would predict temporal proximity in recall very well. In addition, Bower, Clark, Lesgold, and Winzenz (1969) showed that it was much easier to learn a categorized list than to learn an uncategorized list of similar words.

Thus, there is considerable evidence that episodic and semantic memory are not two fully independent systems that do not interact. The semantic system can clearly influence performance in episodic tasks, and there are strong logical reasons for believing that information can be transferred from episodic to semantic memory. However, at this juncture, we have not specified the differences in the two systems in terms of the form in which information is stored, or the types of cognitive operations that occur in the two systems. Similarly, although we have suggested some ways in which the two systems may make contact, we have not determined under what circumstances such contact may occur. Given the interrelations between the two systems, such specificity will not be achieved easily, and we will therefore review the available evidence for and against the semantic episodic distinction before we attempt such a specification.

EMPIRICAL STATUS OF THE SEMANTIC/EPISODIC DISTINCTION

Somewhat surprisingly, very few studies have been specifically concerned with the semantic-episodic distinction. Of these studies, half conclude that the distinction has merit and half reject the distinction. We first examine studies that support the distinction and then turn our attention to those that reject it.

Shoben, Wescourt, and Smith (1978) used the logic of selective factors in their attempt to find evidence for the distinction. According to this logic, two tasks are required, one that is clearly a semantic task and one that is clearly an episodic task. In addition, two independent variables are required such that the first affects semantic tasks, but not episodic ones, and the second affects episodic tasks but not semantic ones. If these conditions are met, then we have evidence for the distinction at issue. Similar logic has been used in arguing for the distinction between short-term and long-term memory. For example, one widely cited claim is that acoustic similarity impairs short-term memory performance but not long-term memory performance, whereas semantic similarity impairs long-term memory performance but not short-term memory performance (although see Shulman [1972] for evidence that short-term memory performance can be adversely affected by semantic similarity).

Shoben et al. used the sentence verification paradigm as their example of a semantic memory task. Subjects determined if sentences such as *cows have legs* were true or false. For the episodic task, Shoben et al. employed the sentence recognition paradigm, often used by Anderson and his colleagues (Anderson & Bower, 1973; Anderson & Ross, 1980). In this task, subjects learn a list of sentences to a criterion (usually one error-free trial). They are subsequently presented with a sentence for which they must decide whether it was present on the memorized list. Thus, to reuse the previous example, subjects might have to decide if *cows have legs* was on the memorized list.

The verification task is clearly a semantic one in that it asks us to determine from our world knowledge if cows have legs. There is nothing temporal or autobiographical about the statement, and it does not presuppose any prior personal contact with cows. We know that whooping cranes have legs and very few psychologists have ever seen a whooping crane. In contrast, the question about whether the sentence occurred on a particular memorized list is both temporal and autobiographical. The question of whether you saw it *in this experiment* refers by nature to one's personal experience at a particular time.

The two independent variables that Shoben et al. came up with were semantic relatedness and fanning. Semantic relatedness is the degree to which the subject and predicate of the sentence "go together" in meaning. For example, most would agree that *robins* and *have wings* are highly related, whereas *robins* and *have toes* are less so. Relatedness can also apply to false statements. The subject-predicate pair *cows* and *have horns* is judged more related than the pair *cows* and *have wings*. Fanning refers to the number of predicates paired with any subject noun. Thus, for example, in one of Shoben et al.'s experiments, subject nouns were paired with either four predicates (Fan-4) or two (Fan-2). Reaction time (RT) in a sentence recognition paradigm has been shown (Anderson & Bower, 1973; Anderson & Hastie, 1974) to depend on fanning. High degrees of fanning lead to slow RTs (see Smith, Adams, & Schorr, 1978, for a counterexample). Analogously, relatedness has been shown to have a large effect in sentence verification experiments. High levels of relatedness facilitate true judgments and inhibit false ones (Holyoak, 1974; Smith, Shoben, & Rips, 1974). Thus fanning is a variable that will affect episodic memory and relatedness is a variable that will affect semantic memory.

Shoben et al. found results consistent with the semantic/episodic distinction. Subjects first memorized the list of sentences and then performed either a verification or a recognition task. In the verification task, semantic relatedness had a large effect, with high relatedness facilitating true decisions and inhibiting false ones. However, the episodic variable of fanning had no effect; high fan statements were verified no more rapidly than low fan statements. Interestingly, the relatedness effect persisted even over a large number of repetitions. For both true and false statements, the size of the relatedness effect did not change over blocks. In the recognition task, Shoben et al. obtained the reverse result. Semantic relatedness had no effect on recognition latency. In contrast, fanning had a large effect, with high fan statements recognized more slowly than low fan ones. This fanning effect held for both true and false statements.

Thus, these results are consistent with the semantic-episodic distinction. Semantic relatedness affects verification (a semantic task) but not recognition (an episodic task). Conversely, fanning affects recognition but not verification.

A somewhat different approach has been adopted by Herrmann and his associates (Herrmann & Harwood, 1980; Herrmann & McLaughlin, 1973). Their examination of the semantic-episodic distinction has focused on the relative contributions of episodic and semantic priming on recognition. In the most conclusive of these experiments (Herrmann & Harwood, 1980), they argue that a close examination of these two types of priming will provide evidence for the semantic-episodic distinction. Their logic is quite complex and is detailed below.

Subjects in the Herrmann and Harwood study learned six categorized lists of 14 words each. Subsequently, they were presented with pairs of words and had to make a ternary decision. A positive response signified that both words were in the memorized set; a negative decision signified that neither word was in the memorized set; and a mixed decision indicated that only one word was in the set. The critical comparisons are among the negative decisions. Three of the categorical lists were *body parts, relatives,* and *countries.* There are four types of negative pairs. First, pairs such as *pelvis-elbow* and *niece-Bolivia* are from categories that were memorized, but the pairs differ in whether the individual items are from the same category. Pairs such as *mouse-donkey* and *nurse-tuba* are both from categories that were not memorized, but they also differ in whether the individual items are from the same category. Herrmann and Harwood reasoned that pairs whose items were from the same category were semantically associated. In addition, memorized categories were episodically associated.

If one denies the semantic/episodic distinction, then we would expect same category pairs to be faster than different category pairs. Because these pairs are already associated, they should be retrieved from memory more readily than pairs that are not semantically associated. It is possible that this difference may be larger for pairs that are drawn from memorized categories because the episodic associations within categories may overwrite some of the preexisting semantic associations (McKoon & Ratcliff, 1979). However, if same category judgments are faster when the categories are in the memory set, but same category judgments are not faster when the categories are not in the memory set, then we have evidence for the distinction. According to a single store model, faster retrieval presumably results from associations between the stimulus items. It would therefore seem difficult for such a proposal to explain why items from a single category (and thus associated) should not be faster than items from different categories when the categories are not previously memorized.

Herrmann and Harwood found results consistent with the semantic/episodic distinction. When negative pairs were from memorized categories, category origin had a large effect. Overall, pairs from the same category were judged 463 msec faster than pairs from different categories. However, when negative pairs were from categories that were not in the memory set, a quite different picture emerged. Items from the same semantic category were judged only a scant (and nonsignificant) 23 msec faster than items from different categories.

Although this research does provide some evidence that is consistent with the semantic/episodic distinction, a unitary view could account for the findings with an additional assumption. Specifically, if subjects first check to see if each test word is from a category that has been memorized, then the results are predictable. If the word is from a memorized category, subjects check the appropriate category to see if the item is on the list. Same category pairs are easier, because only one category needs to be examined whereas two category lists must be searched when the two items are from different categories. If the test items are not from memorized categories, then no further processing is required and a negative response can be made immediately. Thus, with this additional assumption, we should expect no difference between same category pairs and different category pairs when the categories have not been previously learned. Consistent with this assumption, the decision times for these negative pairs from nonmemorized categories were far and away the fastest in the study.

Thus, the empirical support for the semantic/episodic distinction is quite meager. Although the Herrmann and Harwood study provides some evidence, the addition of a reasonable extra assumption makes these results consistent with a unitary view. In addition, the Shoben et al. results have also been criticized, most thoroughly by Anderson and Ross (1980). They also provide experimental evidence for denying the distinction and we consider all of their arguments later.

Evidence Against the Semantic/Episodic Distinction

Researchers who have criticized the distinction have done so on the basis of finding interdependencies between the two hypothesized systems. Most of these studies show either a facilitative effect of semantic information on episodic decisions (McCloskey & Santee, 1981) or a facilitative effect of episodic information on semantic decisions (McKoon & Ratcliff, 1979). Before considering these pieces of evidence in greater detail, it is important to note that such results do not render the semantic/episodic distinction useless. Given the two systems, it would not be surprising if there were tasks in which both systems could play a role. What such results would rule out is a very strong view that there is a sharp dichotomy between the two systems where one and only one system is used for one set of tasks and one and only one system is used for another set.

The primary result obtained by McKoon and Ratcliff (1979) is the facilitative effects of episodic association on subsequent lexical decisions. In three experiments they presented subjects with pairs of words to learn for a subsequent cued recall test. The pairs of principal interest were those that were semantically associated (*green-grass*) and those that were not (*city-grass*). Subjects were then presented with a group of words for which a lexical decision was required. McKoon and Ratcliff found, as expected, the RT to the target word *grass* was faster when preceded by *green* than when preceded by an unassociated and unlearned word. In addition, there was also facilitation when *grass* was preceded by an experimentally associated word such as *city*. McKoon and Ratcliff argue that if semantic and episodic memory were two separate systems, then there should be no episodic facilitation in a task that taps only semantic memory.

This logic would be difficult to fault if we could be certain that subjects' strategies did not play a role in their performance in these experiments. If we assume that subjects learned the materials in the study phase of the experiment, then while making a lexical decision about *city*, they might be consciously thinking about its associate *grass*. Given that expectations clearly play a role in these sorts of tasks (Posner & Snyder, 1975a, 1975b), it is not surprising that facilitation for the associated word *grass* occurs. McKoon and Ratcliff consider this possibility, but they reject it because they claim that Neely (1977) found that 500 msec was required for the operation of strategic processing, and the interval they used was only 250 msec. The difficulty with this argument is that McKoon and Ratcliff required subjects to make a decision about the priming word. Because this decision required almost 550 msec (on average), the time between the onset of the priming word and the onset of the target word was close to 800 msec. Moreover, the evidence from Neely's study is not all that clear-cut, in that facilitation in RT is often accompanied by inhibition in error rates. Interestingly, Neely (page 241) interprets his two kinds of facilitation as supporting the semantic/episodic distinction. Thus it seems that a strategy account of these findings is both possible and consistent with the distinction.

There is also evidence that semantic variables can in some circumstances influence recognition judgments. Anisfeld and Knapp (1968) found evidence of synonym errors in recognition memory. More recently, McCloskey and Santee (1981) have observed a similar finding. They presented subjects with a list of sentences to memorize. The sentences consisted of a name and an occupation, such as *John is a rabbi*. In the recognition task, McCloskey and Santee created false items by a repairing of subjects and predicates. Some of these repairings formed related items (*John is a priest*) an some formed unrelated items (*John is a sailor*). McCloskey and Santee found that subjects took longer to determine that a sentence was not on the list if it was related than if it was unrelated. Thus, McCloskey and Santee demonstrated that semantic relatedness can affect episodic judgments.

Although McCloskey and Santee have provided additional evidence that semantic factors can, in some cases, influence episodic decisions, it is not clear what conclusion can be drawn about the semantic/episodic distinction as a result of this finding. In order to claim that this finding casts doubt on the validity of the distinction, one must assume that no semantic information at all is stored in episodic memory. In contrast to this extreme position, Shoben et al., for example, argued that episodic representations were incomplete copies of semantic representations. If one permits some semantic information in episodic memory, then it is not surprising that massive variations in relatedness will produce an effect in an episodic task. For example, one might reasonably assume that some surface information and the semantic information that John is religious is what is stored in the sentence *John is a rabbi.* A sentence like *John is a sailor* should be rejected rapidly, because it can be disconfirmed on the basis of either its surface information or its semantic content. In contrast, the semantic representation is likely not to provide the basis for rejection of *John is a priest,* and hence it must be rejected on other grounds. There is thus less evidence on which to base a negative decision in these semantically related statements.

The most thorough critique of the semantic/episodic distinction has been offered by Anderson and Ross (1980). They argue first that the evidence presented in favor of the semantic/episodic distinction is not inconsistent with Anderson's (1976) well-known model (ACT) that denies the distinction. Second, they present some evidence that the acquisition of certain episodic relationships can affect subsequent semantic decisions. Each of the arguments is considered in turn.

In terms of the evidence that purports to support the semantic/episodic distinction, Anderson and Ross contend that the ACT model corresponds fairly well to the existing data. In particular, they argue that this model is consistent with the apparent failure to find fanning effects in semantic memory and the apparent lack of relatedness effects in episodic memory (Shoben et al., 1978).

Working in the context of the earlier HAM model (Anderson & Bower, 1973), Shoben et al. (1978) argued that true statements should be subject to repetition effects. In terms of the HAM model, repetition of test items should tend to raise these items to near the top of the list of propositions to be searched. After repeated testing, tested items should occupy the top of the list, and consequently items that have little fanning should be verified more readily than items of high fanning where many tested items are competing for the top position on the list. As Anderson and Ross note, ACT makes similar predictions and predicts an interaction between "the number of facts tested about a concept and the number of times they are tested" (page 445). Only with repeated practice would ACT expect high fanning items to be verified more slowly than low fanning items. Although they also note that it is not clear according to ACT how many times an item must be tested for this interaction to occur, they go on to note that there was some effect in this direction in Shoben et al.'s second experiment.

The relevant data are displayed in Table 4.1. For the true items, the size of the fanning effect is 30 msec on average and it varies from a high of 115 msec in the third block to a low of 125 msec in the wrong direction in the first block. However, the pattern of results is quite different from what ACT would predict in that the difference between the low fanning and high fanning items does not increase with block. The most striking counter-example is in block five where the effect decreases quite sharply and in fact is below the average mean difference of 30 msec. The false data, however, do show an increasing fanning effect with successive blocks. The effect is 55 msec in the wrong direction in the first block and increases monotonically to 113 msec in the last block. Although this may be the tendency to which Anderson and Ross were referring, it is not clear how this result supports the ACT model in that the model does not really account for the disconfirmation of false statements. Because false information is not stored in ACT (at least under usual circumstances) it is not clear how ACT could talk about repetition strengthening preexisting links, and it is also clear that the ACT derivation of true RT (Anderson, 1976, chapter 8) would not be applicable. There is also no support for the ACT predictions in Shoben et al.'s other experiment where the mean difference between the two levels of fanning is in the wrong direction for the true statements and near zero for the false ones. More importantly, there is no hint of the interaction Anderson and Ross would like to see; the differences observed in the last block are, for both the true and false statements, below the averages for the entire experiment. Although the fanning

TABLE 4.1

Verification RTs (in msec) and Error Rates (in percent; in parentheses) as a Function of Truth Value, Blocks and Fanning

	True			False		
Block	*Lo Fan*	*Hi Fan*	*Difference*	*Lo Fan*	*Hi Fan*	*Difference*
1	1425(1.7)	1300(6.3)	−125(4.6)	1434(4.4)	1379(4.5)	−55(.1)
2	1058(.3)	1109(3.0)	51(−2.7)	1207(.9)	1200(4.2)	−7(3.3)
3	996(.5)	1111(3.1)	115(2.6)	1163(1.5)	1169(3.4)	6(1.9)
4	1014(2.2)	1112(3.6)	98(1.4)	1171(2.7)	1199(2.9)	28(.2)
5	1165(.5)	1177(3.0)	12(2.5)	1184(1.9)	1297(3.5)	113(1.6)
Mean	1132(1.0)	1162(3.8)	30(2.8)	1232(2.3)	1249(3.7)	17(1.4)

manipulation may not have been wholly successful in this experiment, it certainly provides no support for the ACT predictions.

Anderson and Ross also question the claim that relatedness has no effect on subsequent recognition judgments. According to ACT, relatedness should facilitate the learning of episodic relationships for both true and false statements. Anderson and Ross reviewed the evidence provided by Shoben et al. and noted that seven of the eight relevant comparisons were in the right direction. Although this summary is factually correct, it does not give an accurate picture of the results. The data are shown in Table 4.2. For the true statements, there is a 95 msec advantage for related statements, but this effect is qualified by a speed accuracy tradeoff, in that subjects made more errors with related statements. It is thus difficult to determine which condition is harder (Wickelgren, 1977). The data from the false statements are inconsistent with the predictions of ACT. There is no difference in RT between related and unrelated statements, and the direction of the difference in accuracy is opposite from what ACT would predict. It thus seems clear that these data do not confirm the predictions of the ACT model.

The data that Anderson and Ross present is designed to show transfer from episodic memory to semantic memory. Subjects learn a set of episodic facts and are then asked to verify categorical statements. Anderson and Ross argue that proponents of the semantic/episodic distinction predict no effect of prior training.

TABLE 4.2
Recognition RTS (in msec) and Error Rates (in percent; in parentheses) as a Function of Truth Value, Fanning, and Relatedness

True Statements		Related	Unrelated
Experiment 1	Low Fan	1089(7.5)	1171(10.8)
	High Fan	1143(7.1)	1156(7.1)
Experiment 2	Low Fan	1099(2.8)	1357(.5)
	High Fan	1406(4.8)	1432(1.4)
	Mean	1184(5.6)	1279(5.0)
False Statements			
Experiment 1	Low Fan	1215(6.7)	1274(6.7)
	High Fan	1258(10.0)	1265(5.0)
Experiment 2	Low Fan	1346(8.5)	1254(4.3)
	High Fan	1579(17.7)	1602(16.4)
	Mean	1350(10.7)	1349(8.2)

In their second experiment, for example, subjects were tested with 49 instance-category pairs of which half were true (*python-snake*) and half were false (*python-dog*). The manipulation of primary interest was the material learned by the subject in the study phase of the experiment. Prior to verifying these instance-category pairs, subjects learned one of the three types of sentences. In the practice condition, the sentence was simply the true category statement, for example, *An instance of a snake is a python*. In the interference condition, subjects learned an episodic statement that involved one of the nouns in the pair, such as *The python ate a fish*. Lastly, subjects in a control group learned no sentence at all; instead they rated the instance and the category on a pleasantness scale. For false pairs, subjects in the interference condition learned sentences similar (although not identical) to those in the interference condition for trues. Similarly, subjects in the practice condition rated the two nouns for pleasantness. Finally, subjects in the "spurious" condition learned episodic sentences that related the two critical nouns, such as *The python attacked the dog*.

Anderson and Ross claim that there are many examples in their study where one finds effects of episodic relationships on semantic verifications. More specifically, they cite four examples (1980, p. 459). First, practice facilitates true judgments. Even in later blocks, subjects who had received episodic practice were faster than subjects in the control condition. Second, subjects in the interference condition (for falses) were reliably slower than subjects in a control condition, suggesting that their episodic practice inhibited their semantic decisions. Similarly, subjects in the "spurious" condition were similarly slower than those in the control condition. Fourth, the effects of practice on the trues decreased with time.

There are several comments to be made both about the results themselves and about the assumptions that Anderson and Ross make about theories that espouse a dintinction between episodic and semantic memory. First, as Anderson and Ross themselves note (pp. 461–462), the size of their effects was very small (often as small as 20 msec), and some of their effects did not appear consistently across experiments. Second, the learning task itself would seem to have two effects. First, it would familiarize subjects with the stimulus materials, and familiarity can be important in semantic memory judgments (McCloskey, 1980). Second, it would lead subjects to expect a test on the materials they had learned. Thus for example, the subject who learned *The python attacked the dog* might reasonably expect to be tested on it, and might be confused when presented with the pair *python-dog* and have to response false. For one to think otherwise would require the assumption that episodic memory can be completely turned off like an electric light. This possibility seems very remote, particularly when subjects are learning episodic information in a situation in which they expect to be tested on it.

One might be tempted to look at these effects in terms of congruence. Items that are studied are old items (in terms of recognition) as compared to new items.

If one assumes that old is positive (yes, it is on the list) and new is negative (no, it is not on the list), then we might say that old and true are congruent responses because both are positive while new and false are also congruent because they are both negative. Old-false and new-true are incongruent pairs. If we also assume that congruent responses are facilitative and incongruent responses are inhibitory, then it provides us with an explanation of why Anderson and Ross observed facilitation in the practice condition and inhibition in the interference and spurious conditions. Shoben et al. found some support for this congruence principle in their data.

THE NATURE OF THE DISTINCTION

Anderson and Ross make a useful separation of functional distinctions and content distinctions. With reference to memory, a functional distinction describes a qualitatively different pair of systems that have different structures and processes. A content distinction refers to different types of materials that, by their nature, may invoke somewhat different processes from a single memory system. For example, chunking occurs in long-term memory for words but not for letters, yet no one wants to propose a $LTM_{words}/LTM_{letters}$ distinction

Although this distinction is conceptually useful, it is often difficult to apply. Moreover, as Anderson and Ross note, it may be more appropriate to consider the distinction as a continuum between function and content. For example, in the early 1960s, there was considerable controversy over the nature of the distinction between short- and long-term memory. It is not widely agreed what kind of experimental logic can be employed to determine which distinction is appropriate.

The most commonly used logic is the method of selective factors which has been employed in connection with both the short-term/long-term memory distinction and the semantic/episodic distinction. In this method, one finds two factors such that each affects one supposed memory system but not the other. For example, acoustic similarity affected short-term memory but not long-term memory. Analogously, semantic similarity affects long-term memory but not short-term memory. Although the empirical facts here have become less clear (Shulman, 1972), no one has criticized the logic explicitly. Similarly, Shoben et al. claimed evidence for the semantic/episodic distinction on the basis fo the findings that relatedness affected semantic memory but not episodic, and fanning affected episodic memory but not semantic.

At this juncture, it seems clear that the results from these selective factors experiments are not as unambiguous as one might have hoped. From the perspective of a unitary memory theory, there might be material for which one factor would have a large effect and another factor would have little effect. For a different set of material, however, the influence of these two factors might be reversed. Thus, even though we have only a content distinction between the two sets of material, we have results that are expected according to a functional distinction.

Although the method of selective factors may not be as diagnositc as originally thought, one should not conclude that it has no utility. With reference to the semantic/episodic distinction, for example, the selective factors result that relatedness affects semantic memory but not episodic memory and fanning affects episodic memory but not semantic memory places the burden on proponents of a unitary view to show how a single memory store could account for these findings. Anderson and Ross follow this pattern in that they argue that a single memory store model, ACT, can account for the selective factors findings that have been observed. The question then becomes how successful is this single store account. Do such models account for the relevant data, and do they make reasonable assumptions? Without some constraint on assumptions, one can always construct a single store model that will explain the results from selective factors experiments.

Although it may seem premature at this juncture, it is useful to ask how concepts are represented in the two systems. Shoben et al. suggested that episodic representations might be incomplete copies of semantic ones. An episodic representation will contain some surface information (such as its temporal marking) and some semantic information. It might also be suggested that the degree to which semantic information is included may be affected by instructions. For example, impression-set (as opposed to memory-set) instructions generally produce more semantically detailed representations in experiments on social cognition. One could also interpret the effects of processing depth in this manner.

The effects of instructions suggest that the episodic system is quite flexible. It may be that certain tasks may require that a large amount of semantic information is copied into the episodic system; in other circumstances, such extensive copying may not be necessary. If one admits this flexibility, then it is quite understandable that semantic relatedness will sometimes have an effect in episodic memory (Anisfield & Knapp, 1968; McCloskey & Santee, 1981) and sometimes will not (Shoben et al., 1978).

The effects of fanning are more difficult to explain. If one espouses a network model of semantic memory (Collins & Loftus, 1975; Collins & Quillian, 1969) then one should find fanning effects (given standard assumptions) in that concepts with many properties should take longer to verify than concepts with few properties, because more links would have to be searched. However, this kind of fanning effect has never been investigated (although see Lewis and Anderson [1976] for some hints on how such a study might be done). With repeated presentation in semantic memory, it is reasonable from the perspective of most models that experimental practice affects the strength of the relationship very little. In episodic memory, in contrast, practice can have a great deal of an effect on the strength of a relationship because the relationships here are transitory and temporally marked as opposed to permanent and not temporally marked in semantic memory.

It is difficult to be specific when fundamental theoretical choices remain to be made. More specifically, should our model of semantic memory emphasize comparison operations (McCloskey & Glucksberg, 1979) or should it emphasize retrieval (Glass & Holyoak, 1975)? Analogously, is an ACT-like representation with its emphasis on activation adequate as a framework for episodic memory, or is there something fundamentally wrong with this approach as Ratcliff and McKoon (1981) have suggested? Without answers to such questions, it is difficult to be more specific about the semantic and episodic memory system.

SEMANTIC AND EPISODIC SOCIAL COGNITIONS

In the work on social cognition, the semantic/episodic distinction has been largely ignored. One exception to this generality is the paper by Hastie and Carlston (1980) that distinguished bewteen conceptual social memory and social event memory. The former corresponds roughly to semantic memory in that it contains information about social entities and events and contains the lexicon of social concepts. It also contains the inference-making routines. Hastie and Carlston's definition of event memory is somewhat vaguer, and it could be argued that the term "event" is unfortunate in that it would seem to exclude certain kinds of personal information, such as John wears tank tops or John has long legs. Although this kind of information is not really an event (see the chapter by Wyer & Gordon, this volume), it is information about a particular individual that should be included in our episodic memory. Thus, like the distinction between semantic and episodic memory, the distinction between conceptual social memory and what Hastie and Carlston term social event memory is between general knowledge and personal knowledge. The knowledge that honest people are not usually liars would be stored in conceptual social memory, while the information that John Smith is both honest and a liar is stored in social event memory.

If one is willing to accept this distinction, then it may be that we have blurred two important issues. Our general social knowledge and our personal social knowledge may not be organized or processed in the same fashion. Nevertheless, researchers have for the most part ignored this distinction. Models such as the ones proposed by Hastie & Carlston (1980) and by Wyer and Srull (1980) are specifically concerned with information stored about particular individuals. Cantor and Mischel (1977, 1979), on the other hand, appear to be interested in the way in which people are categorized (1979, page 5). Despite these differing goals, all use similar research methods. If the analogy to the semantic/episodic distinction were apt, one might expect that memory for particular individuals might be tested by recall or recognition, and that more conceptual information might be tested in a verification paradigm. This kind of parallel does exist in the social domain. Ebbesen and Allen (1979) used a verification paradigm ("A _____ person is also a _____ person" where the blanks were trait adjectives) to study the relationships among trait concepts. When they shifted their attention to a sequencing of an individual's behavior (Allen & Ebbesen, 1981), they changed their research paradigm to one that asked about specific individuals rather than general questions. In fact, the questions employed (e.g., "Did she hold the spoon in her hand?") are quite close to the fact recognition paradigm employed by Anderson and Bower (1973) and Anderson and Hastie (1974).

Cantor and Mischel, in contrast, have used recognition measures seemingly to address conceptual questions. For example, one of their early findings was that people made more false recognitions to trait adjectives that were consistent with the prototype of the stimulus person. Although one can raise many questions about the Cantor and Mischel study, our concern is the drawing of conceptual conclusions from episodic data. More specifically, one could argue that subjects may use prototypes in learning new material and will certainly combine individual facts into more integrated wholes (Smith, Adams, & Schorr, 1978). Consequently, subjects are more willing to reject recognition foils that are inconsistent with their integrated units. At the same time, this analysis says nothing about how certain kinds of people are categorized. In the cognitive literature, there are numerous ways in which categorization could occur (see Smith & Medin, 1981, for a review); these recognition results based on a particular person do not constrain the alternatives. This is not to suggest that the recognition paradigm is never informative, only that it is not usually appropriate for studying general knowledge.

The problems at issue here are important and difficult ones. Many have taken the trouble to familiarize themselves with relevant portions of the cognitive literature. This approach is sensible, because it would be difficult to espouse a model that was cognitively implausible. The importance of the semantic/ episodic distinction is more difficult to assess, because cognitive psychologists cannot agree on its utility. Nevertheless, it would seem very premature to require a unitary theory of social knowledge.

REFERENCES

Allen, R. B., & Ebbesen, E. B. Cognitive processes in person perception: Retrieval of personality trait and behavioral information. *Journal of Experimental Social Psychology*, 1981, *17*, 119–141.

Anderson, J. R. *Language, memory, and thought*. Hillsdale, N.J.: Lawrence Erlbaum Associates, 1976.

Anderson, J. R., & Bower, G. H. *Human associative memory*. Washington, D.C.: Winston, 1973.

Anderson, J. R., & Hastie, R. Information and reference in memory: Proper names and definite descriptions. *Cognitive Psychology*, 1974, *6*, 495–514.

Anderson, J. R., & Ross, B. H. Evidence against a semantic-episodic distinction. *Journal of Experimental Psychology: Human Learning and Memory*, 1980, *6*, 441–465.

Anisfeld, M., & Knapp, M. Association, synonymity, and directionality in false recognition. *Journal of Experimental Psychology*, 1968, *77*, 171–179.

Atkinson, R. C., Herrmann, D. J., & Wescourt, K. T. Search processes in recognition memory. In R. L. Solso (Ed.), *Theories in cognitive psychology: The Loyola symposium*. Potomac, Md.: Lawrence Erlbaum Associates, 1974.

Bower, G. H., Clark, M. C., Lesgold, A. M., & Winzenz, D. Hierarchical retrieval schemes in recall of categorized word lists. *Journal of Verbal Learning and Verbal Behavior*, 1969, *8*, 323–343.

Cantor, N., & Mischel, W. Traits as prototypes: Effects on recognition memory. *Journal of Personality and Social Psychology*, 1977, *35*, 38–48.

Cantor, N., & Mischel, W. Prototypes in person perception. In L. Berkowitz (Ed.), *Advances in experimental social psychology* (Vol. 12). New York: Academic Press, 1979.

Collins, A. M., & Loftus, E. F. A spreading activation theory of semantic processing. *Psychological Review*, 1975, *82*, 407–428.

Collins, A., & Quillian, M. R. Retrieval time from semantic memory. *Journal of Verbal Learning and Verbal Behavior*, 1969, *8*, 241–248.

Ebbesen, E. B., & Allen, R. B. Cognitive processes in implicit personality trait inferences. *Journal of Personality and Social Psychology*, 1979, *37*, 471–488.

Glass, A. L., & Holyoak, K. J. Alternative conceptions of semantic memory. *Cognition*, 1975, *3*, 313–339.

Hastie, R., & Carlston, D. E. Theoretical issues in person memory. In R. Hastie, T. M. Ostrom, E. B. Ebbesen, R. S. Wyer, D. L. Hamilton, & D. E. Carlston (Eds.), *Person memory: The cognitive basis of social perception*. Hillsdale, N.J.: Lawrence Erlbaum Associates, 1980.

Herrmann, D. J., & Harwood, J. R. More evidence for the existence of separate semantic and episodic stores in long-term memory. *Journal of Experimental Psychology: Human Learning and Memory*, 1980, *6*, 467–478.

Herrmann, D. J., & McLaughlin, J. P. Effects of experimental and preexperimental organization on recognition: Evidence for two storage systems in long-term memory. *Journal of Experimental Psychology*, 1973, *99*, 174–179.

Holyoak, K. J. The role of imagery in the evaluation of sentences: Imagery or semantic factors. *Journal of Verbal Learning and Verbal Behavior*, 1974, *13*, 163–166.

Johnson, S. C. Hierarchical clustering schemes. *Psychometrika*, 1967, *32*, 241–254.

Kintsch, W. *The representation of meaning in memory*. Hillsdale, N.J.: Lawrence Erlbaum Associates, 1974.

Lewis, C. H., & Anderson, J. R. Interference with real world knowledge. *Cognitive Psychology*, 1976, *8*, 311–335.

McCloskey, M. The stimulus familiarity problem in semantic memory research. *Journal of Verbal Learning and Verbal Behavior*, 1980, *19*, 485–502.

McCloskey, M., & Glucksberg, S. Decision processes in verifying category membership statements: Implications for models of semantic memory. *Cognitive Psychology*, 1979, *11*, 1–37.

McCloskey, M., & Santee, J. Are semantic memory and episodic memory distinct systems? *Journal of Experimental Psychology: Human Learning and Memory*, 1981, *7*, 66–71.

McKoon, G., & Ratcliff, R. Priming in episodic and semantic memory. *Journal of Verbal Learning and Verbal Behavior*, 1979, *18*, 463–480.

Miller, G. A. A psychological method to investigate verbal concepts. *Journal of Mathematical Psychology*, 1969, *6*, 169–191.

Neely, J. H. Semantic priming and retrieval from lexical memory: Roles of inhibitionless spreading activation and limited-capacity attention. *Journal of Experimental Psychology: General*, 1977, *106*, 226–254.

Posner, M. I., & Snyder, C. R. R. Facilitation and inhibition in the processing of signals. In P. M. A. Rabbitt & S. Dornic (Eds.), *Attention and Performance* (Vol. 5). New York: Academic Press, 1975. (a)

Posner, M. I., & Snyder, C. R. R. Attention and cognitive control. In R. L. Solso (Ed.), *Information processing and cognition: The Loyola symposium*. Hillsdale, N.J.: Lawrence Erlbaum Associates, 1975. (b)

Ratcliff, R., & McKoon, G. Does activation really spread? *Psychological Review*, 1981, *88*, 454–462.

Schank, R. *Is there a semantic memory?* Castagnola, Switzerland: Istituto per gli Studi Semantici e Cognitivi, 1974.

Shoben, E. J. Theories of semantic memory: Approaches to knowledge and sentence comprehension. In R. J. Spiro, B. C. Bruce, & W. F. Brewer (Eds.), *Theoretical issues in reading comprehension*. Hillsdale, N.J.: Lawrence Erlbaum Associates, 1980.

Shoben, E. J., Wescourt, K. T., & Smith, E. E. Sentence verification, sentence recognition, and the semantic/episodic distinction. *Journal of Experimental Psychology: Human Learning and Memory*, 1978, *4*, 304–317.

Shulman, H. G. Semantic confusion errors in short-term memory. *Journal of Verbal Learning and Verbal Behavior*, 1972, *11*, 221–227.

Smith, E. E. Theories of semantic memory. In W. K. Estes (Ed.), *Handbook of learning and cognitive processes* (Vol. 6). Potomac, Md.: Lawrence Erlbaum Associates, 1978.

Smith, E. E., Adams, N., & Schorr, D. Fact retrieval and the paradox of interference. *Cognitive Psychology*, 1978, *10*, 438–464.

Smith, E. E., & Medin, D. L. *Categories and concepts*. Cambridge: Harvard University Press, 1981.

Smith, E. E., Shoben, E. J., & Rips, L. J. Structure and process in semantic memory: A featural model for semantic decisions. *Psychological Review*, 1974, *81*, 214–241.

Tulving, E. Theoretical issues in free recall. In T. R. Dixon & D. L. Horton (Eds.), *Verbal behavior and general behavior theory*. Englewood Cliffs, N.J.: Prentice-Hall, 1968.

Tulving, E. Episodic and semantic memory. In E. Tulving & W. Donaldson (Eds.), *Organization of memory*. New York: Academic Press, 1972.

Wickelgren, W. Speed-accuracy tradeoff and information processing dynamics. *Acta Psychologica*, 1977, *41*, 67–85.

Wyer, R. S., & Srull, T. K. Category accessibility: Some theoretical and empirical issues concerning the processing of social stimulus information. In E. T. Higgins, C. P. Herman, & M. P. Zanna (Eds.), *Social cognition: The Ontario symposium*. Hillsdale, N.J.: Lawrence Erlbaum Associates, 1980.

5 Visual Memory: Definitions and Functions

Roberta L. Klatzky
University of California,
Santa Barbara

Contents

This chapter is about visual memory and its information-processing functions. That statement may seem straightforward enough (albeit ambitious), but from the outset, the goal of the chapter is a problematic one. The first problem is to determine just what constitutes visual memory. The fact that we add the qualifying adjective "visual" to "memory" suggests that there must be something unique about the way we think about and remember visual objects and events, something that distinguishes this aspect of memory. But what?

In the first part of this chapter, I review three different answers to this question. I propose that attempts to specify what is uniquely visual about visual memory have variously focused on the specificity of its *content;* the *form* in which it stores information, and the *processes* by which visual-memory information is achieved. Moreover, each focus leads to a different conception of the principal functions of visual memory.

The three definitions of visual memory that will be considered in Part I, although differing in the assumed properties and functions of visual memory, nevertheless converge. Together, the definitions suggest that information in visual memory is highly specific, resembles the products of visual perception, and is unique to the visual modality. I call such a representation "pictoliteral." It is to be contrasted with more abstract, non–modality-specific, "conceptual" information in nonvisual memory. Part II of the chapter examines cognitive functions that straddle the pictoliteral/conceptual boundary. That is, where Part I looks at functions that are attributed specifically to visual memory, Part II considers the working of visual and nonvisual memory in tandem.

The topics discussed in this chapter are relevant to the work of cognitive and social psychologists with interests other than memory per se. To those who study thinking and reasoning, for example, visual memory is important because of its potential contributions to such intellectual activities as reading maps (Thorndyke & Stasz, 1980), making transitive inferences (DeSoto, London, & Handel, 1965), or mentally transforming objects in space (Shepard, 1978b). Visual memory may also have profound effects on the processing of social information. The visual context in which a social interaction occurs—the setting, the appearance of the actors, their movements—often conveys relevant social information, much of which may be subtle and inarticulable. Categorical information about visual events might color the original perception and interpretation of an interaction, and later memory for visual attributes of the event might have even more profound effects. Visual information might be remembered in greater detail and vividness than speech, so that the context of an interaction might be given greater credence in later interpretation than what was said. The process of retrieving the visual attributes of an interaction might in some sense resemble the replaying of the scene; it might lead to reinterpretation long after the original event had concluded. These ideas, although speculative, are derived from the theories of visual memory to be considered here.

PART I: THE NATURE OF VISUAL REPRESENTATIONS IN MEMORY

The structure of this part of the chapter is as follows: Three definitions of visual memory are considered, which focus on its content, form, and the processes by which it is achieved. These definitions are prefaced by a general comment on how memory representations can be differentiated. In conjunction with each definition of visual memory, there is a discussion of its function, as suggested by the given definition. The emphasis here is on what can be accomplished specifically with visual memory. Later, in Part II, how visual and nonvisual representations operate together is considered.

Differentiating Memory Representations

In information-processing terms, the search for a uniquely visual component of memory—a visual "mode," in the term of Pick and Saltzman (1978)—is a search for a uniquely visual *representation*. Palmer (1978) has described a representation in general as a mapping from some represented world—which consists of "objects" (elements) and the relations among them—into a representing world—with its own objects and relations. (See Fig. 5.1) In this framework, we can call two representations "different," if they represent (map onto) different objects and/or relations from the represented world, or if they represent the same objects but by different mappings. That is, representations can be distinguished either by *what* information they represent or how they represent it. I call these distinguishing aspects of representations *content* and *form,* respectively. When the representations under consideration are internal, or "memorial" mappings from an external world, there is a third means of distinguishing among them, and that is by the *processing* mechanisms by which the mapping is accomplished.

Using these terms, a uniquely visual mode of representation—a "visual memory"—might be defined, or identified, by the uniqueness of the content, form, or process of its mapping. In fact, psychologists have considered each of these three means of defining visual memory (although not necessarily using the present terminology). The first part of this chapter reviews their attempts.

Each of the definitions of visual memory to be considered will be formulated in terms of some criterial property. The idea is that some attribute of information represented in memory is designated as a criterion for calling that information a part of visual memory, or alternatively, a part of nonvisual memory. The criterion thus constitutes the definition of visual memory. In one case to be considered, the criterial property concerns what information from the external, represented world is preserved in the representing world of visual memory—its content. In another case, the property concerns the uniqueness of the objects and/or relations in the representing world of visual memory—its form. And in the third case, the property concerns the nature of the mapping process by which visual-memory information can be achieved. Of course, the three distinctions are not entirely independent; for example, the form of a representation might constrain the content it can represent. But the criteria can be distinguished according to their principal area of concern—content, form, or process. As was mentioned above, in addition to defining visual memory, each criterion links it to some principal

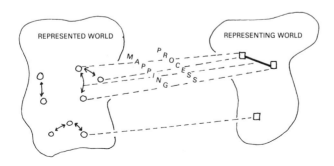

FIG. 5.1. A Representation depicted as a mapping.

function. The discussion to come will therefore include both definition and function.

Definition by Content: The Visual/Verbal Criterion

The Nature of the Definition

The visual/verbal criterion for defining visual memory stems from models of memory that emphasized encoding of information into long-term memory by a process of verbal rehearsal (e.g., Atkinson & Shiffrin, 1968). The models generally assumed that verbal stimuli were learned by a repetitive internal articulation, which strengthened a memorial representation of the words. The present definition of visual memory contrasts it with this verbally based representation. Visual memory is proposed to be specialized to represent nonverbal visual stimulation—scenes, pictures, and so on. (Note, however, one exception—visual memory might represent a word as a physical configuration, treating it like any other pictorial stimulus.) The essential criterion for a visual-memory representation is that it derive from nonverbal, visual stimulation—*unmediated* by verbal description of that stimulation.

Why call this a definition by content? It might appear instead that it adopts a criterion based on the external stimulus (word or nonword) or the process (verbalization or nonverbalization) that leads to a memory representation. While it is true that visual and verbal memory are distinguished by the type of stimuli they represent and the encoding process, the more critical distinction is between the representations themselves, and it is one of content. Because pictures are inherently more specific than words, a visual memory that is specialized for representing pictures will have a more specific content than verbal memory.

A brief digression is in order here: The level of specificity of a representation reflects the size of the set of objects in the external world that maps into a single object in the representing world. In a hierarchical system of categories, for example, if Category A is a superordinate of Category B, all objects that map into B, as well as additional objects, will map into A. Because the set of external objects that maps into B is smaller, B is the more specific representation. The two representations might be said to differ in how finely they discriminate among real-world objects.

Now, to relate this notion to the visual/verbal criterion: The internal representation derived from a verbal input must be inherently limited in its level of specificity. A word denotes a conceptual category. The internal representation of a verbal description, no matter how precise, is a representation of categories. For example, the representation of "my blue hat" maps onto all possible configurations of that object; it represents a large category of physical events. But scenes and pictures are particular physical configurations. In order to represent such stimuli, we need a uniquely visual memory, one that is capable of representing information from the external world more specifically than words can. So goes the argument for this definition of visual memory.

An obvious question arises at this point. According to the visual/verbal criterion, visual memory is that which makes possible a more specific memory representation than can be achieved by words. But is memory really that specific? Suppose we found that we can't remember any more about viewed stimuli than could be conveyed by a verbal description? Obviously, there would no longer be any need to talk about this definition of visual memory. The adequacy of this definition therefore relies on demonstrations that we can remember more about visual stimuli than would be expected if all we remembered was a verbal description.

Attempts to demonstrate that we can remember highly specific information about visual stimuli actually serve two purposes. As stated above, they help justify a visual/verbal criterion for defining visual memory, by suggesting that not all memory is based on verbalization. But such attempts also indicate the *function* of visual memory. That is, visual memory must exist in order to provide the detailed information that we remember about pictures and scenes.

The Function of Visual (Nonverbal) Memory

The general function of visual memory, as defined by the visual/verbal criterion, is to represent visual stimuli at a level of specificity that words cannot. Several particular phenomena in the memory literature have been attributed to such a representation. These phenomena include memory for minimally verbalizeable information and the "picture superiority effect."

Memory for "Nonverbalizeable" Attributes of Pictures.   If visual memory is specialized for the function of providing a highly specific content, and if we are to justify proposing such a memory in distinction from memory for words, then we should find that people can remember information about pictures that they cannot verbalize. In order to demonstrate that we remember more about a visual stimulus than can be captured in a verbal label, we must first consider what the relevant label for a picture might consist of. It is useful to consider several possibilities.

Take first a view of verbal labeling that adopts what will be called the "minimality principle." It states that the label to which a visual stimulus should be related is the simplest one. The simplest label may not generally be known, but one case seems reasonably clear: When the visual stimulus is a common object, the simplest description is the object's "basic-level" name, the one commonly given when people are asked what the object is called (e.g., "hammer," not "ball-peen hammer"—Rosch, Mervis, Gray, Johnson, & Boyes-Braem, 1976). Using this principle, it is easily demonstrated that more is remembered about a picture than its label (the simplest one) provides. People know, for example, whether they saw a picture of some object or its label, in a mixed-modality list (Snodgrass, Wasser, Finkelstein, & Goldberg, 1974). In fact, they can discriminate a particular object they saw earlier from visually similar members of the same basic-level class (Bahrick, Clark, & Bahrick, 1967).

Another type of evidence for storage of information other than the minimal verbal label comes from measures of the time required to make simple judgments about previously seen pictorial items. If all that is encoded about a picture is its simplest label, response time might be sensitive to manipulations of label-related variables, but it should not vary with manipulations of the physical attributes of the picture, holding its label constant. Yet, many studies indicate that the time required to determine that a given picture matches another, previously seen picture in name depends on their physical similarity (Bencomo & Daniel, 1975; Klatzky & Stoy, 1974). Also, the extent to which initial naming of a picture shortens naming latency to a subsequent one with the same name depends on the physical similarity of the two (Bartram, 1974), indicating physical features of the first are retained in memory.

Other supporting results have been obtained in nonspeeded memory tasks. Nelson and associates (Nelson & Brooks, 1973; Nelson & Reed, 1976) found that when pictures served as stimuli in a paired-associate learning task, the nominal similarity among the pictures had no disruptive effect—unless naming was induced. This indicates that memory for the pictorial stimulus item was not inevitably mediated by an acoustically or graphemically represented label.

In short, it is clear that we remember visual-attribute information about objects and not just simple verbal labels. But we have not entirely ruled out the possibility that labels provide the representations for pictures. It remains possible that *nonminimal* information about their physical attributes is verbalized, and that the memorial representation stems from this more complex verbal description. In fact, complex verbal labels have often been assumed to be used in order to account for recognition of visual stimuli (Glanzer & Clark, 1962).

A second principle for verbal labeling must be adopted to address this problem. Suppose we assume a "modified-minimality" principle, namely, that the verbal description to which a visual stimulus should be compared is that description which is normally sufficient for performance in the given context. Everyday experience presumably determines what a sufficient description should be. For example, the complexity of a description necessary to find a building on a street is not as great as that of the description needed to draw it.

Given this principle, in order to demonstrate the specificity of content of visual memory, we must show that more is remembered about visual stimuli than would be provided under the modified-minimality rule. One demonstration comes from studies showing that in a task which requires only that words be read, people may nevertheless remember their typeface (e.g., Kolers & Ostry, 1974). Since the sufficient verbal description for a word in this content would stop short of its physical appearance (presumably, it would be only the word itself), this finding raises the possibility that appearance information is stored in a visual representation. Another supporting demonstration comes from face-recognition studies. Performance on tests of face memory is generally quite high in laboratory situations (Goldstein, 1977), despite the fact that we are not very good at verbalizing descriptions of faces—and despite evidence that efforts at verbalization are irrelevant to performance (Baddeley, 1979; Goldstein & Chance, 1970).

Why, it might be asked, is any sort of minimality principle necessary? Why not simply determine what can be articulated about a visual stimulus, then see what can be remembered, and attribute the difference to a visual representation? In general, the point of adopting a minimality principle is to make *a priori* predictions. If more is remembered than is predicted by the principle, the existence of a visual memory might be said to be "proven" by the difference. Without the principle, if memory for some difficult-to-articulate stimulus attribute (such as typeface) is demonstrated, an adept user of the language might approximate it with a verbal description, rendering invalid the argument that "It can't be verbalized; therefore it's visual." The problem of pinning down just what verbal descriptions constitute is therefore an important one for the present definition of visual memory. To the extent that we can agree that at least some seemingly inarticulable information is retained, however, we can attribute retention to visual memory, under the present definition.

Picture Superiority. The "picture superiority effect," a second phenomenon attributed to a highly specific visual memory for pictures, consists of superior performance on tests of memory for pictorial stimuli, relative to memory for words (e.g., Paivio, Rogers, & Smythe, 1968; Shepard, 1967). One interpretation of this effect is that pictures are represented in visual memory (as well as, through labeling, in a verbal memory) and that this visual memory provides superior storage and retrievability.

Much of the literature on picture superiority has considered alternative explanations of the effect, especially in terms of stimulus differences per se, maintaining, for example, that pictures are better remembered because they are more complex or more distinctive. In support of this notion, picture memory is substantially depressed when stimulus sets are homogeneous (Goldstein & Chance, 1970), and the superiority of pictures as stimulus terms is paired-associate learning is eliminated when the pictures used are highly similar to one another (Nelson, Reed, & Walling, 1976). However, at least some informational differences have been shown unlikely to account for the superiority of picture stimuli over words in memory tasks. Nelson, Metzler, and Reed (1974), for example, found no effect of the amount of pictorial detail on recognition, indicating that it is not the amount of detail that a picture provides which leads to its being better remembered. A similar result was found by Paivio et al. (1968).

The explanation of the picture-superiority effect is likely to remain controversial. Those who wish to attribute it to superficial stimulus factors feel that the concept of visual memory is not necessary to explain the phenomenon. They argue that in order to attribute the effect to visual memory, it is necessary to show that it remains even when such factors as stimulus discriminability and informativeness are equated for pictures and words. On the other hand, if it is argued that visual memory is specialized to retain the more specific content that pictures provide, relative to words, then the greater informativeness and discriminability of pictures are not mere uncontrolled "stimulus factors," but rather constitute the essential difference between pictures and words that visual memory functions to preserve. According to this view, the picture-superiority effect is not inevitable, and elimination or reversal of the effect does not disprove the existence of visual memory. Rather, picture superiority is assumed to arise when distinctive information from a picture is retained in memory, and it is precisely the function of visual memory to retain this information.

Definition by Form: The Analogue Criterion

The Nature of the Definition

The next definition of visual memory focuses on its form rather than its content. This definition stipulates, as a criterion for visual representations, that they be "analogue" in form. The alternative to analogue is generally called "propositional." A proposition is sometimes defined as the internal counterpart of a sentence (Anderson, 1978). Thus, in this definition, propositional representations play the part that verbal representations played in the previous definition. The requirement that visual representations be analogue has used several meanings of the term; we shall consider three.

Analogue as Continuous.   Previously it was proposed that a function of visual memory was to represent information that could not be articulated. The problem was raised that many visual attributes that might seem inarticulable could in fact be described in words, at least well enough to allow a verbally remembered stimulus to be discriminated from a distractor on a recognition test. But suppose we could show that for *any* verbal description that might be assumed to be applied to a stimulus X, there is still a stimulus Y, matching on all the verbally described attributes but still visually distinct from X, which subjects can discriminate from X on a memory test. In other words, no verbal description, however precise, would suffice to allow the observed powers of discrimination. The basis for discrimination in this case would have to be a nonverbal memory representation.

It is essentially this approach that is attempted by experiments which purport to show that spatial information is retained in memory in a form which preserves continuity, in the mathematical sense. If memory represents continuous information, subjects could memorially discriminate a visual item X from another item that lies *arbitrarily* close to X along the continuous dimension. (For example, X might be a line with a marked point; the alternative stimulus, the same line with the marked point near X.) But a verbal description would necessarily describe X in terms of discrete values, which would not permit infinitely fine discrimination. Retention of continuous spatial information would therefore require that a representation exists in memory which is not equivalent to the representation of words. This representation, which is capable of conveying continuous dimensions continuously, has been called "analogue."

A drawback to this definition of analogue is that memory can at best only approximate a continuous dimension. The very fact that two points cannot be perceptually discriminated within a certain range of separation means that their representation cannot be infinitely fine-grained. But if perception—and thus memory—is not continuous, a discrete representation can be found that will account for the ability to discriminate between any two discriminable items. Such a discrete representation need not be analogue; it could be "propositional."

Analogue as Quasi-pictorial. Given that images cannot be strictly continuous, a modified version of the analogue criterion has been considered. Analogue representations are now said to be *picturelike,* rather than pictorial. In this version, the strict continuity requirement has been relaxed in favor of the requirement that analogue representations convey interval rather than merely ordinal dimensions; that they convey "metric" measures of space (Kosslyn, Ball, & Reiser, 1978). Also, the strict pictorial view has been modified, so that it assumes that analogue depictions of visual stimuli portray them as perceived, as output from perceptual processes, rather than as they are received by the sense organs. Such depictions, for example, would have sharpened edges around objects, variation in degree of resolution over the represented field, and might even change dynamically (Anderson, 1978; Kosslyn & Schwartz, 1977).

Can visual-memory representations, as defined by this version of the analogue criterion, be distinguished from propositional representations? Kosslyn (1980, 1981) has argued that they can. He has a particularly well developed model of visual memory that has been embodied in a computer simulation. The model incorporates several components. One is a visual buffer, which provides a "surface" representation of a visual stimulus that functions much like a picture of the stimulus with limited resolution. In the simulation, the visual buffer is a matrix of spatial coordinates (currently in two dimensions). To represent a stimulus, cells in the matrix are activated in correspondence with points on the stimulus. Thus, the surface representation is like an internal, digitized picture.

The surface depiction of a stimulus in the visual buffer is short-term and must be actively maintained. To provide for long-term representation of a visual stimulus, there is another component in Kosslyn's model, consisting of long-term counterparts of surface images. The long-term stimulus representation is a list of cells which are to be activated in the visual buffer when the stimulus is realized as a surface image. This is called a "literal" representation of the stimulus. There is yet another, nonliteral, version of the stimulus in long-term memory. It stores (in propositional form) a list of facts about the stimulus, including names of its parts and their locations on the object and names of associated categories.

From this brief description, it can be seen that visual memory in Kosslyn's model is, in toto, quite complex. It incorporates short-term and long-term representations; it has not only quasi-pictorial elements (the surface representation) but also clearly propositional ones. Kosslyn has argued that the surface image of a stimulus is, in particular, distinct from other forms of representation. It is said to *depict* the stimulus, whereas propositional representations are said to *describe* it. Several distinctions between the depictive representation (or "image") and propositions have been offered, including (Kosslyn, 1980, p. 32): Images do not contain discrete component elements or interelement relations; images do not have clear rules of formation; images are not abstract, categorical concepts; images cannot be proclaimed true or false. In contrast, all these characteristics *do* apply to propositions: Propositions have distinct component concepts and relations among them; they are formed according to an internal grammar, much as a sentence is; their component concepts are often abstract categories rather than specific items; and (again like a sentence) they can be declared true or false. The surface image is therefore said to function quite differently from propositions, even though it might ultimately be reducible to propositional elements (like the list of points in the literal representation in long-term memory, which can be written propositionally).

Analogue as Cognitively Unmodifiable.   Yet another definition of analogue representations has been offered by Pylyshyn (e.g., 1980, 1981). He argues that the functioning of a representation obeys two different kinds of constraints. At one level, there are built-in, fixed, species-universal constraints, due to the medium in which the representation is based—Pylyshyn calls this the "functional architecture" of the representation. At a second level, there are the constraints imposed by processes that work within that functional architecture—the algorithms, as Pylyshyn terms them. For an analogy, the language with which a computer programmer works is functional architecture; the program written is an algorithm. Both constrain the computer's performance.

When a psychological representation is processed, and some pattern of behavioral measures is found, the question arises, what kinds of constraints caused that pattern—constraints imposed by the functional architecture that was used or by the processing algorithm? According to Pylyshyn, the definition of "analogue" demands that the constraints be based on the functional architecture. That is, if behavioral measures reflect built-in constraints, the representation that was processed to produce those measures was used in an analogue manner.

Consider, for example, that under some conditions, when a subject is told to mentally scan between two locations on an imagined map, the scan time is linearly related to the interlocation distance on the actual map (Kosslyn et al., 1978). If the representation were a physical map and scanning were done by moving the eye, greater distance should produce longer scanning time. An internal equivalent of the map like Kosslyn's surface representation could produce the same result: Longer scan time for greater distance would occur if more distant points were separated by more cells in the visual buffer and the internal scanning process proceeded in a cell-by-cell fashion. This sort of surface image would therefore constitute an analogue representation of the map by Pylyshyn's criterion as well as Kosslyn's.

However, the linear relation between mental scan time and distance scanned does not guarantee that an analogue representation was processed; it might result from the algorithm that was used rather than from functional architecture. Suppose, for example, that a subject performed the task as follows: First, he or she accessed the two locations from an internal list of coordinates; then the interpoint distance was computed; then knowledge about the usual relationship between travel time and traveled distance was used to produce an estimated scanning time; then that time was waited before responding (note that this processing need not be conscious). In this case, the representation would not be analogue, by either Pylyshyn's criterion (because the behavioral measure came from the algorithm and not the architecture) or Kosslyn's (because a quasi-pictorial representation was not processed).

It should be clear from this example that it will not be easy to determine just when an analogue representation is being used, by Pylyshyn's criterion. Indeed, there is substantial controversy on the matter. According to Pylyshyn, there is a good test for determining whether observed data are due to analogue processing. If the data result from processing a fixed, built-in, immutable architecture, they should not change with manipulations of subjects' strategies, knowledge of the expected result, practice, or the like. The processing should not be, in Pylyshyn's words, "cognitively penetrable." But if the subject's beliefs, knowledge, or goals affect the results, then the process is not operating on an analogue representation. By showing that many imagery processes are cognitively penetrated, Pylyshyn (1981) attempts to show that images are not analogue. (For example, subjects cannot form an image of two colored transparent filters superimposing, unless they know what color should result.) Kosslyn counterargues (1981) that because behavioral data result from *processes* that act on representations, the origin of cognitive penetration is unclear. In particular, subjects' beliefs and knowledge might influence their processing (producing evidence for cognitive penetration), despite the fact that the processed representation was analogue (and therefore cognitively unmodifiable).

To further complicate matters, Anderson (1978) has suggested that because both processes and representations together determine behavior, the form of any representation is indeterminate. For any explanation of behavior in terms of one representation, there can be another explanation that uses a different representation and modifies the processes so as to accommodate the difference. In rebuttal, it has been argued that some representation-process pairs are more believable than others that make the same predictions. By believable is meant less ad hoc, more general, more constrained, and so on. If the notion of quasi-pictorial representations makes predictions (such as that mental scan time will increase with distance scanned) that other, seemingly equivalent, models do not, it should be chosen in preference to alternative notions. (For relevant discussion, see Anderson, 1979; Hayes-Roth, 1979; Keenan & Moore, 1979; Pylyshyn, 1979.)

The critical data that are predicted by analogue models concern parallels between operations performed in the external world, on physically present objects, and those performed mentally. If analogue representations, by virtue of their functional architecture or inherent properties, constrain performance in a manner comparable to constraints imposed by physical properties of objects, then one can predict behavioral patterns for mental performance, based on expectations for physical performance. The monotonic relationship between mental scanning time and scanned distance is one such prediction.

The Function of Analogue Representations

Suppose we assume for the moment that we have a visual memory with the "functional architecture" to provide "quasi-pictorial" depictions of visual stimuli. What function would such depictions serve? In general, the advantage of analogue representations would be that they could be processed in a manner that is in some sense analogous to viewing a physically present scene. Most of the literature to be reviewed here examines just this possibility, by investigating how visual representations are scanned, transformed, integrated, and so on. A number of such processes can be combined under the general label, "visual problem solving."

Visual Problem Solving.   What is a "visual problem"? Factor-analytic studies of performance on tests of visual-spatial intelligence (reviewed in McGee, 1979) suggest the following definition: A problem is visual if (a) information about a visually presented stimulus is interrogated, and (b) the response requires knowledge either about the spatial arrangement of the stimulus's components or about a transformation of the entire stimulus over space (e.g., by rotation). Since the requirements stated in part b of this definition represent factors that have been isolated in visual intelligence tests (McGee, 1979), the problems that compose such tests obviously fit the definition. Typical examples would be determining whether Picture A is a component of Picture B, or determining whether A could be transformed into B by a given operation such as folding.

What may be more important is what is excluded from this definition, namely, tasks in which the response to a visual stimulus is made on some basis other than transforming it over space or interrelating its visual components. This would include object naming, for example, although visual attributes of the object are obviously relevant, because the response is based on categorical assignment of those attributes. Tasks in which a visual stimulus is used to symbolize a concept rather than to provide specifically visual information would also generally be excluded from the definition of visual problems. When mental arithmetic is performed following a visual display, for example, it would not be considered visual problem solving, despite the common subjective impression that a visual image is used to keep track of intermediate states in the problem's solution and despite the relevance of the spatial position of digits, because that solution is based on symbolic interpretation of the stimulus. Map reading could be termed a visual problem, however, to the extent that it interrogates knowledge of the arrangement of spatial locations (and indeed, it shows a relation to measures from visual aptitude tests—Thorndyke & Stasz, 1980).

There is a variety of evidence for the use of a uniquely visual memory in visual problem solving. One source is the tests-and-measurements literature. The very fact that factors can be isolated on which individuals vary when performing visual problems, but not other types, suggests that these problems tap a distinct mode of cognitive processing. Another source of evidence comprises studies indicating that visual problem solving shares capacity with visual perception. What is generally demonstrated is that when a visual problem must be solved concurrently with perception of visual stimulation (such as tracking a pursuit rotor), performance on one or both tasks decreases, relative to a control condition where one of the tasks is replaced with a nonvisual counterpart (e.g., Baddeley, Grant, Wight, & Thompson, 1975; Brooks, 1968). Interestingly, Baddeley et al. found evidence for capacity sharing between perception and tasks requiring interrogation of positions is space, but not in tasks where the stimulus merely symbolized a concept rich in visual content (such as during learning of a list of concrete nouns).

The link between visual problem-solving tasks and analogue representations lies, as indicated above, in data suggesting that the problem-solving transformations, performed mentally, are constrained in manners analogous to constraints on physical transformations. An outstanding task from the cognitive-psychology literature that makes this point is one developed by Shepard (reviewed in 1978b). Subjects are asked to indicate whether two visual stimuli are identical, within an angular rotation. The time to respond in this task is found to increase regularly (often linearly) with the angular separation of the two stimuli. Since a physical rotation would take longer, the greater the degrees to be rotated, this result has been taken as evidence for a process of mental rotation, operating on an analogue image.

Cognitive Mapping.   A number of studies have used tasks in which subjects were interrogated about their knowledge of previously memorized maps, and the results similarly suggest analogue processing. In a study described previously, Kosslyn et al. (1978) asked subjects to scan between locations on a memorized map and press a button when they had reached the target location. The scanning time (i.e., the time between the signal to start scanning and the button-press response) increased linearly with the scanned distance, a result which the authors attributed to analogue processing. (However, others have shown that subjects know what results are expected and could, as Pylyshyn suggests, have produced them by nonanalogue processing—see Mitchell & Richman, 1980.)

Other tasks, in which subjects are not explicitly told to form an image of a map and scan over it, also give increasing distance-time functions. Putnam and Klatzky (1981) asked subjects to indicate which direction between two points on a circular map was the shorter (or longer) distance. For example, subjects indicated whether Moscow was closer to San Francisco in an Eastward or Westward direction. For subjects' naturally learned maps, experimentally learned maps, and perceptually displayed maps, the response time increased as the shorter distance between the two locations increased. This suggested that the task was performed by "scanning" from the first location to the second in both possible directions and outputting a response when the shorter scan hit the target. In this case, the results indicate that the scan time increased with the distance scanned, as would be predicted by an analogue model.

Definition by Mapping Process: The Perceptual/Conceptual Criterion

The Nature of the Definition

Consider Kosslyn's simulation model for mental imagery and its two forms of visual representation, the surface image and the underlying list of points in long-term memory. Because only the surface image is said to be analogue (in the sense of picturelike), if we applied a strict analogue criterion for visual memory, we would say that the surface image was in visual memory and the underlying representation was not. Yet, the two are informationally equivalent. Both provide a point-by-point (or cell-by-cell) description of the stimulus, in contrast to a description of its meaningful properties. On this basis, it might be argued that both should be incorporated into visual memory, despite their formal differences. But if so, we then must define visual memory on some basis other than its form of representation. The next definition of visual memory to be considered does just that. Under this definition, any point-by-point description (whether an active image or its long-term counterpart) would be put in the class of "perceptual representations." This class is contrasted with "conceptual representations," or meaningful descriptions.

To understand the perceptual/conceptual criterion, recall that a representation in general is the result of a mapping from some represented world into a representing one. The previous criteria for defining visual memory proposed that the visual representation has a unique content (i.e., maps unique information from the represented world) and that it has a unique form (i.e., the objects and relations in the represented world are specific to the visual modality). Here, in contrast, we focus on the mapping process itself, the information-processing activities that result in a mapping from visual stimuli into memory.

According to the present criterion, two types of mapping processes should be considered. One is perceptual, directly associated with the sensory apparatus. The other is conceptual, the result of meaningful thinking about what is perceived. Visual memory is associated with the perceptual process. That is, visual memory is said to hold the sort of information that is extracted during perception, without recourse to meaning (except insofar as meaning directs the perceptual process, for example, by determining where the eyes fixate). Perceptual information is, in principle, as extractable from a nonsensical display as from a meaningful one (unless meaningfulness is correlated with the perceptual "goodness" of the display). Conceptual information, in contrast, directly depends on the meaning of a display. It describes visual stimuli in terms of the semantic concepts they portray. Some semantic concepts might pertain to visual attributes, but many would not.

Note that perceptual information in memory need not be restricted to information derived from an actual stimulus. There might be a "perceptual" memory representation for an event that had no direct physical counterpart, such as a bizarre mental image. To accommodate this situation, we will state that information in memory is "perceptual" if it *could be* extracted from a stimulus by perceptual processes, given that such a stimulus existed. The information is represented *as if* it resulted from a perceptual mapping process, whether or not it actually did. In short, it is the perceptual "mappability" of information in memory that determines it to be a visual-memory representation.

Although the perceptual/conceptual criterion is based on the mapping process, the ultimate interest must be in the nature of the resulting representation. This criterion might seem merely to beg the question of what constitutes visual memory, if it offered no insights into the products of perceptual mapping. We must therefore ask what the nature of perceptual information in memory might be.

One way to determine what information about a visual event might be perceptual is to ask what a computer is capable of extracting from a visual input, without the influence of its conceptual meaning. In essence, this approach equates perceptual information with what can be extracted in perception prior to the "Höffding step," the point where information extracted by sensors makes contact with previously acquired knowledge about categories, and beyond which, conceptual information can be extracted.

Suppose, for example, that we expose a visual stimulus to an optical sensor and compute a digitized version of the stimulus. Now suppose that we stop at the point of digitization, and we assume that this is the final product of perceptual mapping. We would be stating that visual-memory representations, as defined by the perceptual/conceptual criterion, are like digitized pictures (a view similar to that of Kosslyn). However, to stop at this point would be premature. Given an appropriate algorithm, a computer can do much more than digitize a stimulus, without recourse to its meaning (e.g., Duda & Hart, 1973; Marr, 1979; Raphael, 1976). It can divide the digitized matrix into regions based on brightness levels and determine where edges exist. It can infer the depth in the third dimension of points on two-dimensional images and determine the orientation of the surface at those points, relative to the viewing perspective; it may even describe the image as composed of a set of regular geometric shapes. Is this information perceptual? Insofar as it can be extracted without stimulus categorization, it can be attributed to the visual representation, as defined by the perceptual/conceptual criterion.

Now let us push the hypothetical program beyond the Höffding Step. Suppose it has, stored in memory, a set of categories, into which the visual input can be mapped on the basis of the information derived from initial analysis—such as division into regions, projection into three dimensions, and shape analysis. The computer might now substitute, for sections of the input that were previously labeled Region 1, Region 2, and so forth, new labels: person, arm, house, and the like. Now suppose that the computer has a memory store used for natural-language processing, wherein concepts are interassociated to form factual knowledge (cf. Anderson & Bower, 1973; Quillian, 1969). Now it may be able to output, ''The scene contains a boy, which is a male human, nonadult, in Region 1.'' We seem to have entered the realm of conceptual representation, once we passed the Höffding step of categorization. Thus we can draw the line between perceptual and conceptual information at the point of assignment of the stimulus to a meaningful category. All information acquired before that point is ''perceptual,'' and all information acquired afterward is ''conceptual.''

This attempt to determine the nature of perceptual information is idealized, of course. Although we might find the Höffding step relatively unambiguously in a computer, it is well known that in human pattern recognition, conceptual knowledge can affect perceptual processing that operates near the sensory periphery. This means it may be difficult to isolate any body of information that is ''purely perceptual.'' Nonetheless, this characterization of perceptual information offers at least some insights into what the nature of that information might be. And by the perceptual/conceptual criterion, visual representations convey such perceptual information.

Although the perceptual/conceptual criterion does not explicitly address the form and specificity of content of visual memory, it has implications for both. Consider first the formal differences between perceptual and conceptual information. To the extent that semantic concepts generally have lexical counterparts, that is, are nameable, the representation of a visual event in terms of concepts would be closely connected to the lexicon (the portion of long-term memory that describes graphemic, acoustic, and articulatory properties of words). In short, conceptual information would be closely associated with verbal descriptions. But perceptual representations might use different memory structures, which need not be tied to verbalization. To this extent the two representations would have different structures for mapping visual information—different forms. It might be argued, too, that perceptual descriptions would be more specific than concepts, which represent categories of information (a similar argument was made earlier for words).

The Function of Perceptual Representations

According to the perceptual/conceptual criterion, visual memory contains information of the sort extracted during perceptual processing. This close tie to perception links this particular definition to an important function that visual memory has been proposed to serve, namely, to replace perceptual processing. It has been suggested in several contexts (see below) that a visual representation activated in memory can function like perceptual information extracted from a physical stimulus. The perceptual/conceptual definition of visual memory suggests how this could occur. If visual memory information is essentially identical to perceptually evoked information, as the definition proposes, processing of the former might effectively substitute for the latter. I consider here two situations in which memory has been proposed to substitute for perception: priming tasks and visual aftereffects.

Priming Tasks. In a priming task, in general, one stimulus facilitates the processing of another, subsequent stimulus. That is, the first increases the accuracy and/or reduces the speed of responses to the second. In a task that directly addresses this phenomenon, the subject is presented first with a "prime" stimulus, then with "target" stimuli, about which a decision is to be made. The prime stimulus predicts what the target stimuli are likely to be. When the prediction is correct, the subject's response to the target stimulus is speeded (e.g., Posner & Snyder, 1975; Rosch, 1975). This has been explained by assuming that the processing of the prime and target stimuli share common elements. For example, in terms of memory models that treat processing as the activation of memory locations, the prime may activate memory locations in common with the target stimulus. Note that a prime can speed processing even when it bears no direct physical resemblance to the target stimulus, indicating that the effect does not rely on memory for the prime at a sensory level. Instead, it has been assumed that some residual effect of the prime replaces perceptual analysis that would otherwise occur when the predicted stimulus was first exposed (Beller, 1971).

In priming experiments, the preliminary stimulus that anticipates a subsequent item plays no direct role in the response decision about that item. In another type of task where a similar phenomenon has been inferred to occur, the preliminary stimulus provides part of the information needed to make the response. Tasks of this type require speeded responses to pairs of stimuli, one of which plays the role of a prime.

This situation arises, for example, in same/different judgments of successive stimuli (reviewed in Posner, 1978, Ch. 2). When two stimuli are presented in visual form, there is evidence that the judgment as to whether the two are identical can be made by comparing the second stimulus to a perceptually derived "physical code" (i.e., representation of physical attributes) of the first. Such evidence consists, for example, of the finding that response time is sensitive to the physical similarity of the items but not their nominal similarity. More important for the present discussion is the case where the first item is not explicitly presented, but instead its identity is cued more abstractly, for example, by an auditory label. Generally, as subjects are given more time (e.g., up to a second or so) after the first stimulus and before the second in this situation, their response times converge on the times for the corresponding task with both stimuli physically presented. This is said to occur because over the interstimulus interval, a physical (perceptual) code can be generated or activated in visual memory, which functions like the encoding of the first stimulus when it is visually presented and perceptually processed. In support of this inference, variables manipulating physical parameters of the stimuli have similar effects in the perceptual and memorial situations (Posner, 1978; see also Podgorny & Shepard, 1978).

Visual Aftereffects. A second instance where processing in visual memory has been proposed to replace processing evoked by a physical stimulus is provided by studies of Finke and associates (Finke, 1979; Finke & Schmidt, 1977, 1978). They have reported that long-term visual aftereffects like those that occur subsequent to visual stimulation can be produced by *imagined* stimulation. In this case, the imagining of the stimulus, which uses visual memory, replaces the viewing of the actual stimulus. Finke and Schmidt investigated the role of imagery in the McCollough effect, which occurs after subjects view patterns of bars on colored fields, alternating between horizontal and vertical bars on complementary colors. When they are subsequently exposed to horizontal or vertical bars on a white background, they report seeing the complement of the color that was initially viewed with bars of the given orientation. Finke and Schmidt found that subjects who *imagined* the initial bar patterns showed significant complementary-color aftereffects, the magnitude of which was greater for subjects who reported having vivid imagery than those who did not. Moreover, the result occurred even when subjects' intuitions predicted quite a different result—namely, that they were supposed to see, when given the black-and-white test pattern, the same (not complementary) color as had initially been imagined with bars of the given orientation.

There are limits to the commonality of perception and visual memory in the McCollough phenomenon. Finke and Schmidt reported that the effects were weaker under imagery than under perception, which suggests, reasonably enough, that visual memory could be used to replace only some of the mechanisms potentially underlying the effect. Kunen and May (1980) suggested that the imagery phenomenon is dependent on subjects' awareness of the critical properties of their imagined stimuli. They used adapting patterns containing two kinds of spatial frequency components. Imagining such patterns was found to produce the McCollough effect specifically for those spatial frequency components that were perceptually salient and likely to be consciously detected, whereas perception produced effects even for nonsalient components. This evidence that the imagery phenomenon is under cognitive influence might be used by Pylyshyn to deny that analogue representations produce the effect. Under the current perceptual/conceptual criterion, however, the Kunen-May results indicate only that conceptual processing may determine what is perceptually activated. These results therefore do not refute the possibility that functional equivalence of imagery and perception derives from a uniquely visual memory. (Note that the cognitive effect in this study is the influence of subjects' awareness of properties of the stimuli they imagine. This might be compared, for example, to awareness of seeing the ''wife'' or ''mother-in-law'' in the well-known reversible figure. It is quite different from another potential source of influence— subjects' intuitions about the *effects* their imagery will have—which Finke and Schmidt found could not account for their results. For further discussion of this study, see Broerse & Crassini, 1980, 1981; Finke, 1981; Kunen & May, 1981.)

In a related study, Finke (1979) had subjects imagine themselves making errors in a task of pointing at an exposed target while their hand and arm were obscured. Like subjects given error-inducing prismed lenses who actually saw their errors, those who imagined them showed improvement with practice and an aftereffect when the error induction was removed—errors in the reverse direction of those induced. Again, the effect was greater for images rated as vivid than for those rated as nonvivid. Moreover, the imagined errors apparently affected fairly peripheral levels of the haptic system. This was indicated by several facts: The response to an imagined movement error was sensitive to small variations in the location of the erroneous motion, suggesting that the imaginal representation was quite precise in its depiction of spatial extent. And intermanual transfer of the error effects (which requires central mediation) was only partial. Finally, effects were observed even when subjects knew that the imagined errors were not real errors, which would presumably eliminate solely cognitive sources of adaptation, that is, conceptual understanding and conscious reasoning about the task. These results suggest that this situation produces a memorial replacement for *perceptual* processing.

The Definitions Reconsidered

What have we learned thus far? We have examined three ways of defining visual memory, each focusing on a different aspect of the visual representation, each linking visual memory with different functions.

The most important common element in all three definitions is that visual memory is contrasted with another form of memory, which is closely tied to the verbal system. Whether we call this alternative form conceptual, propositional, or simply verbal, it is presumably the component of memory that underlies our linguistic ability. Combining the three definitions, we arrive at a formulation of visual memory as relying on representations with a modality-specific *form*, which resembles the output from perceptual *processes* and has a highly specific *content*. I call such a representation "pictoliteral," a term which is not tied to any one definition more than the others. The contrasting representation has been described as non–modality-specific, a product of post-perceptual processing beyond the "Höffding step," and having an abstract content. I call such a representation "conceptual," a term which seems to capture *non*visual memory as characterized by all three definitions of visual memory.

The distinction between pictoliteral and conceptual memory is hardly a new one. Psychologists have often tried to differentiate between thought processes associated with language, often characterized as logical and analytical, and those which are associated with visualization, often characterized as wholistic and non–rule-governed. Although the distinction is not new, its pervasiveness in the information-processing theories of visual memory that were reviewed here is worth noting. The contrast with language appears to be critical to defining visual memory.

None of the definitions we have considered is without problems. In the case of the visual/verbal definition, there is the problem of determining what level of specificity can be achieved with verbal representations. Without constraining verbal specificity, it is difficult to determine what visual representations can accomplish. The analogue criterion is problematic because of the interdependence of the form of a representation and the processes that act on it. This interdependence means that representations with different formal properties may make equivalent behavioral predictions. It also means that the phenomenon of cognitive influence on visual processing cannot readily be attributed to influence either on the form of representation used or on its manner of processing. The perceptual/conceptual criterion is problematic because, by focusing on the mapping process, it makes minimal assumptions about the nature of the resulting representation—which is, after all, the matter of principal interest. Moreover, because we can visualize things we have never perceived, the equating of visual memory with things perceptual must be opened up to things that *can be* perceived, not just things that *are* perceived. The looseness of this definition is an important flaw.

These problems notwithstanding, the three definitions of visual memory seem to converge on a "pictoliteral" representation that is distinct from the underpinnings of language. The next section of this chapter goes on to consider how these two representations might function together.

PART II: ACROSS THE VISUAL/NONVISUAL BOUNDARY

The present section of this chapter considers the interactions between pictoliteral and conceptual representations. That is, where previously the functions of visual memory were considered with minimal reference to nonvisual contributions, these same functions are now extended to encompass the joint involvement of pictoliteral and conceptual representations.

Three kinds of visual/nonvisual interaction are considered here. As noted above, each is an extension of a function of visual memory that was associated with a definition in Part I. First, there is the function that was attributed to visual memory when it was defined by the visual/verbal criterion. That function was to store highly specific information about visual stimuli. In the first section of Part II, we extend this function to consider how such information might be combined with less specific information, of the sort provided by conceptual representations, to produce a composite memory code for visual events.

Next there is the function associated with visual memory as it was defined by the analogue criterion. This function was to provide a representation that could be processed like viewing a picture. In the second section of Part II, we consider how such an analogue representation could be internally "viewed" to produce conceptual information, a process which will be called "pictoliterally driven."

Finally, there is the function associated with the perceptual/conceptual criterion for defining visual memory. This function was to replace perceptual processing with activation in visual memory. In discussing this function, little attention was paid to how the activation originated. The fact is that paradigms like the priming procedure, which are used to demonstrate the perceptual activation function, generally initiate the activation by providing a verbal cue. Thus the process begins with the designation of a concept and proceeds to the activation of pictoliteral information. This type of interaction between conceptual and pictoliteral representations is called "conceptually driven," and it is considered in the third section of Part II.

Role of Visual and Nonvisual Memory in Representing Visual Stimuli

This section considers how visual stimuli or events might be represented in memory by a combination of pictoliteral and conceptual information. The memorial representation of some visual input will be called the memory "episode" for that input, following Tulving's (1972) distinction between *semantic* and *episodic* memory. (The former represents general knowledge about the world, independent of a particular encoding context; the latter represents events in one's life, encoded under a particular temporal and physical context.) An episode has been characterized (e.g., Flexser & Tulving, 1978) as a bundle of information of different types, such as data about the context in which a stimulus occurred, semantic and physical properties of the stimulus, the encoder's state, and the like. In the same vein, an episode for a visual stimulus might combine several types of information. For our purposes, the interest lies in its potential for combining pictoliteral and conceptual information.

In the following discussion, I first develop the idea that the episode for a visual stimulus includes both of these types of information. Then I discuss their interdependence. Specifically, I consider how the conceptual information associated with a visual stimulus might influence what pictoliteral information is encoded from it, the fate of that pictoliteral information while the stimulus is stored as a memory episode, and the retrieval of pictoliteral information from that episode.

Two Types of Information in Visual Episodes

The idea that visual stimuli, such as pictures, are represented by two distinct types of information is frequently expressed. (Indeed, it is the fundamental assumption of the visual/verbal criterion for defining visual memory.) One use of this notion is in the pictorial encoding model of Nelson and associates (Nelson & Reed, 1976; Nelson, Reed, & McEvoy, 1977), which assumes that a "sensory code" for a picture, representing its visual features, becomes available early in encoding, and that a distinct "semantic code" becomes available somewhat later. This sensory/semantic distinction has been found useful in predicting when memory performance with verbal stimuli will equal or better that with pictures.

The notion that picture-memory performance reflects both visual and verbal-conceptual types of storage is consistent with studies of the effect of verbalization at exposure on memory for pictures. One would assume that verbalization would augment the verbal code and improve performance. Consistently with this idea, verbalization has been found to improve picture recognition, and the suppression of verbalization, to impair it (Freund, 1971); and verbalizing a detail has been shown to increase the probability that the picture containing it will subsequently be recognized (Loftus & Kallman, 1979).

Given the idea that a picture's memory episode includes two distinct types of information, the question arises as to how structurally independent they are. Without making detailed structural assumptions about the nature of memory, we can consider two possibilities. For one, pictoliteral and conceptual information might be in two distinct codes, which are associated only by virtue of their representing the same stimulus. Alternatively, conceptual and pictoliteral components might be structurally related in a common code.

An interesting indication that this second possibility might hold, at least for some pictorial stimuli, comes from work on memory for maps. Stevens and Coupe (1978) showed that people often have misconceptions about geographical locations. For example, they think that Reno is east of San Diego (it is not). These misconceptions are quite predictable on the basis of the locations' superordinates: Most of Nevada, in which Reno is located, is east of California, in which San Diego is located. Results like these, and similar errors that have been experimentally induced by Stevens and Coupe, suggest that the memorial representation has a hierarchical character, in which information about large regions is stored superordinate to more specific locational information. When a decision about locations cannot be determined from the more specific level, it may be inferred from the more abstract level. If we go a step further and equate the specific information with a pictoliteral representation, this suggests a hierarchy in which pictoliteral and conceptual data are structurally interrelated.

In summary, the preceding suggests that the memorial episode for a visual stimulus includes both pictoliteral and conceptual information. I now turn to the question of how conceptual information derived from, or associated with, a visual stimulus influences the processing of the pictoliteral component of its episode. More specifically, the following sections are concerned with how conceptual interpretation might influence what pictoliteral information is encoded from a visual stimulus, the fate of that information in storage, and what can be retrieved.

Before beginning the discussion, we must consider the problem of how to identify when performance in some experiment relies on pictoliteral information. In general, as the first part of this chapter points out, it is quite difficult to determine when a specifically visual type of memory representation is being used. How, then, can we unambiguously interpret an experiment as demonstrating conceptual influence on *pictoliteral* information processing? Following the guidelines set out in Part I, the present discussion will infer that pictoliteral processing is being measured in some experiment if the measure taps memory for idiosyncratic visual details of a stimulus, or if the measure directly taps perceptual processes, or if the experiment uses a task thought to produce ''analogue'' processing (i.e., in which the stimulus information appears to be treated quasi-continuously). Although it still cannot be proved that we are observing conceptual influence on pictoliteral (as opposed to conceptual) representations and their processing, the use of these operational definitions for pictoliteral representations will at least allow for hypotheses about the nature of conceptual/pictoliteral interactions.

Conceptual Influence on Encoding Visual Stimuli

The first interaction to be considered is how concepts derived from or presented with a picture influence what visual detail (and presumably, that means pictoliteral information) from the picture is encoded into memory. A very relevant study is that of Friedman (1979), who examined subjects' eye fixations on objects in scenes and their subsequent ability to recognize those objects from among visually similar, categorically identical, distractors. (This provides a test of memory for visual appearance, rather than category.) Friedman found that expected objects (like a stove in a kitchen) were fixated less than unexpected ones, indicating that conceptual expectations about objects in scenes directed the intake of visual information. And even when viewing time was controlled, memory for the visual appearance of low-probability objects was better than for high-probability ones. This suggests that the low-probables were encoded more extensively, as well as looked at longer.

Friedman's work can be interpreted as illustrating the influence of a conceptual "schema" on visual encoding. In general, a schema is defined as a memorial structure that conveys generic information about some concept, characteristics that its exemplars tend to have in common. In these terms, Friedman's results indicate that objects which are not part of the schema for a certain type of scene (like a kitchen) are subjected to greater amounts of visual encoding.

A more general type of schema for visual stimuli—one for scenes in general—has been studied by Mandler and associates (Mandler & Parker, 1976; Mandler & Ritchey, 1977). They proposed that a visual stimulus that can be related to a "scene schema" should be remembered better than one that cannot. In particular, if the stimulus is an array of pictures of common objects, it should be remembered better when the objects form a scene (in which case the scene schema could be applied) than when they are randomly arranged. Mandler's studies used memory tests that varied the relation between originally seen objects and distractors, in order to determine just what aspects of the stimulus were better encoded in a scene than a nonscene. In general, there was superior retention not only of objects' identities but also of their relative locations when the objects were in scenes. The latter finding suggests that the scene schema might provide a framework for encoding at least some visual details of the scene.

A rather specific type of scene schema that has been related to visual encoding is a schema for scenes portraying actions, such as the act of reading. Goodman (1980) studied memory for objects in scenes which exemplified some common action, and she varied the relevance of objects to the action (e.g., a book is highly relevant to reading; a plant is not). Retention of the objects' visual appearance was assessed by using a recognition test in which the distractors were in the same basic category as the original items, and the two had to be discriminated on the basis of appearance. Like Friedman, Goodman found that the appearance of highly relevant objects was not remembered as well as that of irrelevant objects. This suggests that an action schema determined objects' relevance, and more extensive visual encoding processes were applied to the low-relevant items.

In summary, the preceding suggests that schematic concepts that are evoked when scenelike displays are presented can play an important role in encoding of specifically visual information. If the display cannot be interpreted as a scene (no schema is applied), encoding suffers. If a schema is activated, the relevance of objects in the scene to that schema affects encoding. Objects that are unexpected in a scene appear to receive greater perceptual processing, and their visual appearance is better remembered. It is interesting to note that these results for encoding of visual details about scenes appear to have direct counterparts in the memory-for-text literature, where the ability to evoke a schema has been found to facilitate memory for a text (e.g., Dooling & Lachman, 1971), and where sentences which are atypical of a schematic topic are remembered better than typical sentences (Graesser, Gordon, & Sawyer, 1979).

Work of Klatzky, Martin, and Kane (1982 a,b) on the influence of socially relevant schemata—categories for human faces—presents somewhat of a contrast to the scene research, however. The categories they studied were occupations—''salesman,'' ''athlete,'' and the like. The existence of such categorical representations for faces was demonstrated by subjects' agreement on which faces matched which occupations. Moreover, the presentation of a category name was found to influence speeded decisions about faces' visual properties (i.e., whether two half-faces came from the same person) when the face followed the label by well under a half second. In investigations of the role of such categories in memory for faces, Klatzky et al. presented faces along with matching occupational labels or, in control conditions, with mismatching labels or arbitrary names. The effects of a matching label on subsequent face recognition were small, but consistent. However, they were not uniformly positive: Viewing a face along with a matching occupational title improved recognition of that face, but also led to more false recognitions of similar faces. Thus, in this case the category's activation appears to have led to the encoding of general category-relevant information—which may have pertained to visual appearance—but not to have enhanced the encoding of particular features of the presented face.

Work by Newtson and associates (e.g., Massad, Hubbard, & Newtson, 1979; Newtson, 1976) suggests that the notion of conceptual influence on encoding pictoliteral information might be expanded from static scenes to behaviors that extend over time. In a series of studies, Newtson has examined how observers break a sequence of behaviors into units, each corresponding to a meaningful action. It is theorized that the act of perceiving behavior over time consists of just such a segmenting process. Two additional assumptions are important for present purposes. One is that the transitions between meaningful-action units are particularly informative, so that the visual encoding process emphasizes these points. The second is that the observer's conceptual set for interpreting the behavior affects how it is segmented. These assumptions imply that observers take in, during the course of perception, different features of the behavior according to their acts, which implies in turn (assuming that pictoliteral encoding directly reflects perception) that different features will be pictoliterally represented in memory. Massad, Hubbard, and Newtson (1979) investigated these ideas by giving observers one of two possible interpretations for an ambiguous sequence of events. How the subjects segmented the sequence was found to differ, depending on which of the two potential interpretations they were given.

There are some criticisms of the Newtson approach. For one, as will be discussed below, and as Massad et al. note, a locus at initial perception is not the only possible site of interpretation effects. Ebbesen (1980) has raised the possibility that the action-segmentation task used by Newtson may not tap directly into perceptual processing, but may instead require a secondary process (e.g., a decision about action boundaries) in its own right. This does not necessarily mean that the idea that conceptualization influences perception of behavior is wrong, but it does mean that the segmentation task may not be a direct indicant of what happens during early visual processing. These problems notwithstanding, the idea that conceptual interpretation may influence what pictoliteral information is encoded into memory from an extended behavior remains a viable and intriguing one.

Conceptual Influence After Encoding

Once a visual input has been presented, and pictoliteral information has been encoded, how amenable is that information to influence from conceptual interpretation? One answer to this question was proposed by the early Gestalt psychologists. They suggested that while a visual form was stored in memory, it was subject to mental forces which transformed it in the direction of greater regularity and conformity with familiar figures. In a much cited study, Carmichael, Hogan, and Walter (1932) showed subjects ambiguous forms, along with disambiguating labels (e.g., "eye glasses" vs. "dumbbells"), and found that subsequent reproductions were distorted toward conformity with the labels.

A more contemporary demonstration of this sort of phenomenon was provided by Daniel (1972) who devised a set of stimuli that varied along a shape continuum, one end of which was a familiar form and the other a gross distortion of that form. Subjects were presented with the midpoint of the continuum, accompanied by a label that named the familiar form. They were then tested for recognition either immediately or at a delay of up to 2 days. With the delay, false recognitions shifted toward the familiar-form end of the continuum, suggesting that the label biased subjects' memory for the form's appearance.

There are a number of potential explanations for memory distortions produced by labeling. One is the original Gestalt hypothesis, that the form's representation was gradually modified by autonomous cortical forces. Riley (1962), in an excellent review of the literature on such experiments, concludes that this hypothesis is essentially untestable, due to the inability to manipulate "autonomous" forces.

Another explanation of the form distortion phenomenon is that it arises at the time of the response. The idea is that subjects remember the conceptual category of the original form as they forget its details. When they are tested, they are more willing to accept as a distractor on a recognition test, or draw, an item that is consistent with the remembered category. Yet another explanation attributes the phenomenon to selective encoding, rather than from post-encoding sources. In this view, subjects best encode those aspects of the figure that are consistent with its conceptual category. As a result, these consistent aspects are retained when others are forgotten. Over time, this moves the form's representation toward consistency with the concept.

Another type of memory inaccuracy induced by conceptualization can be more unambiguously attributed to post-encoding effects. This is the finding that a concept introduced after a visual stimulus has been encoded, which conflicts with that stimulus, can impair memory for its visual properties. To show this, Loftus (1977; Loftus, Miller, & Burns, 1978) has used a technique which first presents a visual event, such as slides or a film, and then introduces false conceptual information—under the guise of post-event questions. For example, subjects who viewed a car accident, in which a green car passed by incidentally, may be asked a question which presupposes that the car was blue (Did the blue car that drove by . . .). Later, the subjects are given visual recognition tests, probing for the influence of the false conceptual information on memory for the initial visual input. And there is such influence—for example, presupposing that a car was blue, when it was actually green, shifts subjects' color reports toward blue. Such effects occur even when subjects are warned, at the time of test, that false information might have been introduced earlier, although they do not occur when subjects have an a priori expectation that misleading information will be introduced (Dodd & Bradshaw, 1980).

The mechanism whereby post-event concepts influence memory in these studies is not clear. One possibility is that the concept initiates activation of related pictoliteral information, which is (erroneously) added to or even replaces the original episode. One of Loftus's findings—that subjects tend to select, on a memory test, a color that lies between the one originally viewed and the one mentioned in a post-event question—suggests that the two colors were effectively integrated (see Loftus, 1979). As an alternative mechanism for post-encoding effects, conceptual information might remain in conceptual form and simply dominate the original pictoliteral data. Results from pilot experiments performed by Laura Miceli and myself suggest that this latter may be true in at least some cases. We had subjects view scenes intermixed with related sentences. Some sentences provided an abstract label for an object in a previous scene (e.g., for mittens, "handwear"). Later, subjects were asked to pick out the original from two versions of the scene, both of which fit the abstract label (e.g., one with mittens and one with gloves). In some cases their ability to do so was impaired, relative to a condition using irrelevant sentences. Since the abstract label was consistent with the original object and should not have led to the generation of new pictoliteral detail (if anything, the old object should have been retrieved and rehearsed when the label was given), this suggests that the label may have conceptually interfered with the original pictoliteral data. Still other evidence that post-event information does not replace pictoliteral data comes from Bekerian and Bowers (1983), who found that the influences of post-event questions were eliminated when the test-item sequence was yoked to the sequence of initial events. Presumably this type of test provided a highly effective retrieval cue, facilitating access to the initially encoded representation.

Conceptual Influence on Retrieving Visual Episodes. I next consider whether conceptual interpretation of a visual input can influence the retrieval from memory of pictoliteral information about that input. Finding the proper test for this is somewhat of a problem. In general, it is assumed that a recognition test which uses distractor items that are visually similar to (and in the same verbal category as) original items provides a test for retention of visual detail. But recognition also minimizes the demands for retrieval. For this reason, drawing responses and verbal reports about visual details might be better used to assess retrieval of pictoliteral information (although the verbal report is problematic, insofar as pictoliteral data are supposed to be minimally verbalizeable).

On this basis, a study of Brewer and Treyens (1981) dealing with schema effects on memory for visual displays offers some evidence that conceptual assignment can influence retrieval of pictoliteral detail. They studied memory for objects in a well-known type of place, a student's office, and their retention tests asked for verbal descriptions of the objects and drawing recall. Objects which would be expected in a student's office were described and drawn better than unexpected objects. Given the evidence (previously cited) that *un*expected objects will be viewed more and encoded better, it would appear that this advantage for expected objects is not an encoding effect. Moreover, other data indicated that it arose at retrieval: Even when only those objects for which strong recognition responses had been given were considered, recall of schema-expected objects was greater. This indicates that of the objects represented in memory (those strongly recognized), the expected ones were more retrievable in recall.

Summary of Visual Episodes

To summarize the foregoing, this section of Part II considered how visual and nonvisual memory components might interact to represent visual stimuli as memory "episodes." First, it was suggested that both types of memory representations, pictoliteral and conceptual, contribute to the episode for some visual display. Next, the interdependence of these contributions was assessed. There is strong evidence that the conceptual interpretation of a stimulus (as induced, e.g., by its categorization with respect to some schema, or by an ad hoc label that an experimenter supplies) influences the encoding of its visual details. There is also evidence that concepts can facilitate the retrieval of visual-appearance information about a stimulus. The question of whether conceptual interpretation can affect the pictoliteral representation of a visual stimulus after encoding is more problematic. Although it has been dififcult to show changes due to autonomous mental forces, it nevertheless is clear that introducing a conflicting concept can impair memory for the visual content of a previously seen stimulus.

Pictoliterally Driven Processing

I now turn to a form of conceptual/pictoliteral interaction that is suggested by the analogue criterion for defining visual memory. According to that definition, visual-memory representations can be processed analogously to pictures, as if by an internal viewing process. To extend this function to incorporate conceptual representations, I consider the possibility that concepts might be derived from a "quasi-pictorial" representation. This type of process will be called pictoliterally driven.

As was mentioned previously, a distinction is made here between pictoliterally driven processes, which proceed from a visual-memory representation to conceptual information, and processing that proceeds in the reverse direction, which is called "conceptually driven." This pair of labels is parallel to one used in theories of perception and cognitive processing—"data driven" and "conceptually driven" (e.g., Norman & Rumelhart, 1975). "Data driven" refers to processing that uses information, or data, from a physically present stimulus. Since I am referring here to information from the internal counterpart of a stimulus, I substitute "pictoliterally driven." "Conceptually driven," in the perceptual domain, refers to processing that originates with expectations about what stimulus might be occurring, then derives expectations for its perceptual content. The current meaning of the term is similar; again it refers to processing that originates with relatively abstract concepts rather than with information about specific visual events.

Shepard (1978a), in a review of famous examples of the creative use of imagery, describes several instances that may make this distinction clearer. Consider the case of the chemist Kekulé, who reported that he mentally observed moving particles, thought of them as atoms, and then from their configuration, deduced how they might combine to form molecules. This can be hypothesized to be an example of pictoliterally driven processing, because it began with representation of visual forms, which was then translated into the concepts of atom and molecule. In contrast, Watt's invention of the steam engine began with abstract concepts that were not particularly visual, namely, the knowledge that steam could be induced to rush from one vessel into another, where it could then be cooled. This knowledge led to an arrangement that specified the physical characteristics of the mechanism that could be used. According to Watt, "The whole thing was arranged in my mind." This phrase suggests that from the ideas about the function of the steam engine was derived a pictoliteral representation—this would be conceptually driven processing.

Of course, I cannot "prove" that processing originated with pictoliteral or conceptual information. One has only to look at the imagery literature to see that this is a major point of contention. For example, consider a task as straightforward as defining the word "goatee." Many persons, when asked to do this, report seeing a mental image of a goatee and even stroke the chin, as if the image were transferred to their own face. This suggests that the definition might be achieved by first accessing pictoliteral information from the word goatee, then deriving the verbal description from it. But an anti-image theorist would argue that the image is merely an ancillary phenomenon, and that the definer has translated a stored conceptual description into words.

My purpose here is not to prove one of these views correct but to explore how the concepts of pictoliterally and conceptually driven processing might be applied. Accordingly, I begin with a look at processing that might initiate at the pictoliteral end and culminate in concepts.

To start with, note that the act of perceiving a visual stimulus can be characterized as a pictoliterally driven process, according to the sort of model outlined under the perceptual/conceptual criterion—in which a stimulus is first processed in visual memory, then (beyond the Höffding step) on a conceptual basis. (This model ignores expectancy effects in perception.) But of more interest here is the case where there is no stimulus physically present to provide the initial pictoliteral information, but instead the information is in memory. Here, pictoliterally driven processing might be likened to an *internal* process of perception.

Such a process has been called by Kerst and Howard (1978) "re-perception," by which is meant memorial processing of information that was once perceived from a visual stimulus, in such a way as to essentially duplicate the initial act of perception. Kerst and Howard suggested this process to account for data from psychophysical judgments of visual stimuli; from memory. Their subjects were asked to assign magnitude estimates for the area of, and distance between, geographical regions (e.g., states) which were either perceived from a map or remembered from general knowledge. Both perception and memory gave rise to typical power functions relating judged magnitude to actual stimulus magnitude. Moreover, the exponent of the memory function was approximately the square of that of the perception function. This is predictable from the idea that subjects in the memory condition re-perceived the stimulus. A remembered stimulus would undergo two transformations—once in original perception, then again in re-perception from memory—which would square the transformational effect.

Another task where reperception has been theorized to occur is in comparing stimulus magnitudes. In a magnitude-comparison task, subjects are given two stimuli and asked which has the greater (or sometimes lesser) magnitude along some dimension. Typically, the time to make this judgment increases as the difference in the two magnitudes decreases. For example, it takes longer to determine that a bear is larger than a dog than to determine that a bear is larger than a mouse. Paivio (1975, 1978) suggests that performance in such a task is achieved by retrieving visual images of the two objects (in some canonical size), re-perceiving them to determine their magnitudes, and comparing the magnitudes. Paivio (1975) showed that performance in the task is faster when the items are represented by pictures than when they are words, and that size anomalies (e.g., showing a mouse larger than a bear) slow responses when the items are pictures but not when they are words. These data are taken in support of the re-perception model, because assuming that pictures have faster and more direct access to the image store than words, we would expect responses to pictures to be faster and impaired by visual distortion.

Not only are visual properties derived from pictoliteral information, but quite abstract properties can be as well, according to Paivio (1978). Magnitude comparisons of pleasantness, like those of size, for example, are faster for pictorial than verbal stimuli. Paivio suggests that this might reflect the acquisition of affective information from images of the compared objects. This would constitute pictoliterally driven processing that culminated in access to information about the stimulus that is not directly visual.

By "re-perception" is not meant some unreeling of a perfect, photographic representation of past events, from which any concept may be derived. The extent to which conceptual information can be derived from pictoliteral depends on the latter's quantitative characteristics, of course; we cannot re-perceive what is not encoded in memory. It may also be limited by the qualitative nature of the pictoliteral data. If the memory structure ties pictoliteral information to some set of concepts (cf. the discussion about map memory), it might be impossible to generate a different set of concepts from the same information.

An indication of this sort of limit on pictoliterally driven processing comes from a previously cited study by Massad et al. (1979). They presented subjects with a brief film having geometric forms as its "characters," which could be interpreted either as a theft or an attack. Subjects' evaluation of the characters (e.g., as good or bad) varied according to the interpretation they had been given before the viewing. The finding of interest concerns subjects who were given one interpretation before seeing the film, then a second interpretation afterwards. Their evaluation of the characters remained unchanged when given the new interpretations, *unless* they were allowed to see the film anew. This suggests that subjects were unable to retrieve a pictoliteral representation of the film and reinterpret it. (For another "Gedanken" example, this might be likened to perceiving the famous wife/mother-in-law ambiguous figure as a mother-in-law at first viewing, then "seeing" the wife by reexamining the figure in memory. It might be possible to conceptualize the wife as present, but would this conceptualization result from the same sort of perceptual apprehension as in the initial viewing?)

Conceptually Driven Processing

The third type of conceptual/pictoliteral interaction is suggested by the perceptual/conceptual definition of visual memory. This interaction, called conceptually driven processing, is pictoliterally driven processing in reverse. It begins with conceptual information and results in activation of pictoliteral information.

An example that has previously been discussed comes from the priming task. Recall that in theory, subjects in this task use a verbal prime to access information which is sufficiently veridical that it can replace a component of perceptual processing. By the perceptual/conceptual criterion, the information so accessed is pictoliteral, and it has been activated from a verbally denoted concept.

Although the priming literature generally suggests that activating a pictoliteral representation for some concept will facilitate perception of the concept's exemplars, there are some situations where the reverse seems to hold. A classic experiment by Perky (1910—others are reviewed in Segal, 1971) found that subjects' ability to detect a brief target was reduced, rather than facilitated, if they were instructed to maintain an image of the target during its presentation. Reeves (1981) found that the impairment effect only occurred if the target was in color, which suggests that the activation of pictoliteral information about color may have interfered with operation of specifically color-processing mechanisms. It appears that further research is needed to clarify when conceptually driven processing will be beneficial versus detrimental to perception. (See Farah & Smith, 1983, for a relevant study with auditory imagery.)

The priming literature emphasizes the effect of conceptually driven processing on perceiving, but it may affect remembering as well. A literature that is relevant concerns imagery effects in verbal learning. In a variety of experiments, it has been shown that when words are presented under instructions to form a mental image of their referents, or simply when concrete nouns (assumed to evoke spontaneous images) are presented, memory is enhanced. Paivio (1971) has interpreted this effect by assuming that under imagery instructions, a visual-memory representation corresponding to the word is formed, and that when this is added to its nonvisual representation, memory for the word is boosted. A similar finding is that it is highly effective to encode word pairs by integrating the underlying concept in a mental image. The imagined representation has therefore been proposed to be highly integrative, presumably because it conveys the spatial interaction of the represented concepts.

Paivio's interpretation of these effects essentially attributes them to conceptually driven processing. That is, it is assumed that words evoke concepts, which in turn activate pictoliteral information, which is both integrative and memory-facilitative. Not everyone accepts this explanation, however. Anderson and Bower (1973) have argued, for example, that imagery instructions merely motivate subjects to increase tbe amount of information encoded. Item concreteness effects have been attributed—not necessarily convincingly—to nonvisual correlates of concreteness such as meaningfulness (see Kieras, 1978). Such correlates might explain some effects at least, such as why even blind subjects show an advantage in recall for highly imaginable words (Craig, 1973). But it is also possible that imagery effects on verbal memory reflect conceptually driven processing.

Some newer studies have extended imagery effects on memory. Peterson and associates (e.g., Peterson, 1975; Peterson, Peterson, & Ward-Hull, 1977) have compared memory for a set of numbers over several conditions—where the numbers are merely memorized by rote, where they are seen in a matrix, and where they are imagined in matrix form. The imagined matrix appears to be an effective device for aiding memory for numbers.

Ritchey and Beal (1980) varied the size and complexity of the images that subjects formed for nouns in a list. To manipulate size, they simply told subjects how large an image should be formed. To manipulate complexity, they followed a finding of Kosslyn (1975), which was that the details of objects imagined next to something complex appear to be less accessible than the details of objects imagined next to something simple. Presumably, due to limitations on imagery capacity, an object imagined next to something complex must itself be simple. Ritchey and Beal found that objects that were presumably imagined in more detail (i.e., in a larger size, or next to a simple matrix) were recalled better. This suggests that the boost in memory from conceptually driven processing may vary with the amount of pictoliteral information that is activated.

Conceptually driven processing, like pictoliterally driven, appears to have its limits. Finke (1980; Finke & Kurtzman, 1981) has pointed out that there are circumstances where imagery cannot replace perception. One instance is in color afterimages, which are formed when an object is fixated by the eyes but not when it is merely imagined. Thus, even when one has a strong subjective impression of having activated pictoliteral information—formed an image, in more common parlance—this information may not be suficient to produce certain kinds of visual effects. Finke proposes that these cases are more likely to arise when the perceptual effects being replaced are quite peripheral. Concepts cannot ''drive'' to the outer regions of the perceptual system, it would seem.

SUMMARY

This chapter attempted to describe definitions for, and functions of, visual memory, both in isolation from and in interaction with nonvisual memory. Part I considered three means of defining a memory representation that could be called visual—by its specificity, relative to that of words; by its structural form; and by its close relation to perceptual stages of information processing. These three definitions were combined in ''pictoliteral,'' a term which assumes that there does exist a visual-modality specific representation, but is not tied to any one definition of it.

In Part II, the interaction between pictoliteral and nonpictoliteral, or ''conceptual,'' representations were considered. In correspondence with the three definitions, three types of interaction were considered. Pictoliteral and conceptual information might combine to form memory episodes for visual stimuli; concepts might be derived anew from stored pictoliteral information; and concepts might drive the activation of pictoliteral representations.

The separation of criteria for defining visual representations and the corresponding separation of their functions are particularly important aspects of this review. It appears that saying what visual memory *is* carries strong implications for what it *does*. Thus, although convergence on a single definition may be desirable, the separation of definitions also has its benefits in organizing visual-memory functions. The present exploration of those benefits was primarily confined to tasks familiar to researchers in cognition and perception. It would be interesting to extend it to the social domain. For example, one could ask how the interpretation of a social event determines what visual information is encoded; whether re-perception of an event re-evokes affective responses; or whether expectations about a socially relevant visual stimulus, such as a face, affect responses to the stimulus that actually occurs. According to the present analysis, these are the sorts of phenomena that we should find resulting from the functioning of visual memory in social cognition.

REFERENCES

Anderson, J. R. Arguments concerning representations for mental imagery. *Psychological Review,* 1978, *85,* 249–277.

Anderson, J. R. Further arguments concerning representations for mental imagery: A response to Hayes-Roth and Pylyshyn. *Psychological Review,* 1979, *86,* 395–406.

Anderson, J. R., & Bower, G. H. *Human associative memory.* Washington, D.C.: V. H. Winston & Sons, 1973.

Atkinson, R. C., & Shiffrin, R. M. Human memory: A proposed system and its control processes. In K. W. Spence & J. T. Spence (Eds.), *The psychology of learning and motivation: Advances in research and theory* (Vol. 2). New York: Academic Press, 1968.

Baddeley, A. Applied cognitive and cognitive applied psychology: The case of face recognition. In L-G. Nilsson (Eds.), *Perspectives on memory research.* Hillsdale, N.J.: Lawrence Erlbaum Associates, 1979.

Baddeley, A. D., Grant, S., Wight, E., & Thompson, N. Imagery and visual working memory. In P. M. Rabbitt & S. Dornic (Eds.),. *Attention and performance* (Vol. 5). New York: Academic Press, 1975.

Bahrick, H. P., Clark, S., & Bahrick, P. Generalization gradients as indicants of learning and retention of a recognition task. *Journal of Experimental Psychology,* 1967, *75,* 464–471.

Bartram, D. J. The role of visual and semantic codes in object naming. *Cognitive Psychology,* 1974, *6,* 325–356.

Beller, H. K. Priming: Effects of advance information on matching. *Journal of Experimental Psychology,* 1971, *87,* 176–182.

Bencomo, A. A., & Daniel, T. C. Recognition latency for pictures and words as a function of encoded-feature similarity. *Journal of Experimental Psychology: Human Learning and Memory,* 1975, *1,* 119–125.

Bekerian, D. A., & Bowers, J. M. Eyewitness testimony: Were we misled? *Journal of Experimental Psychology: Learning, Memory, and Cognition,* 1983, *9,* 139–145.

Brewer, W. F., & Treyens, J. C. Role of schemata in memory for places. *Cognitive Psychology*, 1981, *13*, 207–230.

Broerse, J., & Crassini, B. The influence of imagery ability on color aftereffects produced by physically present and imagined induction stimuli. *Perception & Psychophysics*, 1980, *28*, 560–568.

Broerse, J., & Crassini, B. Misinterpretations of imagery-induced McCollough effects: A reply to Finke. *Perception & Psychophysics*, 1981, *30*, 96–98.

Brooks, L. R. Spatial and verbal components of the act of recall. *Canadian Journal of Psychology*, 1968, *22*, 349–368.

Carmichael, L., Hogan, H. P., & Walter, A. A. An experimental study of the effect of language on the reproduction of visually perceived form. *Journal of Experimental Psychology*, 1932, *15*, 73–86.

Craig, E. M. Role of mental imagery in free recall of deaf, blind, and normal subjects. *Journal of Experimental Psychology*, 1973, *97*, 249–253.

Daniel, T. C. Nature of the effect of verbal labels on recognition memory for form. *Journal of Experimental Psychology*, 1972, *96*, 152–157.

DeSoto, C. B., London, M., & Handel, S. Social reasoning and spatial paralogic. *Journal of Personality and Social Psychology*, 1965, *2*, 513–521.

Dodd, D. H., & Bradshaw, J. M. Leading questions and memory: Pragmatic constraints. *Journal of Verbal Learning and Verbal Behavior*, 1980, *19*, 695–704.

Dooling, D. J., & Lachman, R. Effects of comprehension on retention of prose. *Journal of Experimental Psychology*, 1971, *88*, 216–222.

Duda, R. O., & Hart, P. E. *Pattern classification and scene analysis*. New York: Wiley, 1973.

Ebbesen, E. B. Cognitive processes in understanding ongoing behavior. In R. Hastie, T. M. Ostrom, E. B. Ebbesen, R. S. Wyer, Jr., D. L. Hamilton, & D. E. Carlston (Eds.), *Person memory: The cognitive basis of social perception*. Hillsdale, N.J.: Lawrence Erlbaum Associates, 1980.

Farah, M. J., & Smith, A. F. Perceptual interference and facilitation with auditory imagery. *Perception & Psychophysics*, 1983, *33*, 475–478.

Finke, R. A. The functional equivalence of mental images and errors of movement. *Cognitive Psychology*, 1979, *11*, 235–264.

Finke, R. A. Levels of equivalence in imagery and perception. *Psychological Review*, 1980, *87*, 113–132.

Finke, R. A. Interpretations of imagery-induced McCollough effects. *Perception & Psychophysics*, 1981, *30*, 94–95.

Finke, R. A., & Kurtzman, H. S. Area and contrast effects upon perceptual and imagery acuity. *Journal of Experimental Psychology: Human Perception and Performance*, 1981, *7*, 825–832.

Finke, R. A., & Schmidt, M. J. Orientation-specific color aftereffects following imagination. *Journal of Experimental Psychology: Human Perception and Performance*, 1977, *3*, 599–606.

Finke, R. A., & Schmidt, M. J. The quantitative measure of pattern representation in images using orientation-specific color afteraffects. *Perception & Psychophysics*, 1978, *23*, 515–520.

Flexser, A. J., & Tulving, E. Retrieval independence in recognition and recall. *Psychological Review*, 1978, *85*, 153–171.

Freund, R. D. *Verbal and nonverbal processes in picture recognition*. Unpublished doctoral dissertation, Stanford University, 1971.

Freidman, A. Framing pictures: The role of knowledge in automatized encoding and memory for gist. *Journal of Experimental Psychology: General*, 1979, *108*, 316–355.

Glanzer, M., & Clark, W. Accuracy of perceptual recall: An analysis of organization. *Journal of Verbal Learning and Verbal Behavior*, 1962, *1*, 289–299.

Goldstein, A. G. The fallibility of the eyewitness: Psychological evidence. In B. D. Sales (Ed.), *Psychology in the legal process*. New York: Spectrum, 1977.

Goldstein, A. G., & Chance, J. Visual recognition memory for complex configurations. *Perception & Psychophysics*, 1970, *9*, 237–241.

Goodman, G. S. Picture memory: How the action schema affects retention. *Cognitive Psychology*, 1980, *12*, 473–495.

Graesser, A. C., Gordon, S. E., & Sawyer, J. D. Recognition memory for typical and atypical actions in scripted activities: Tests of a script pointer + tag hypothesis. *Journal of Verbal Learning and Verbal Behavior*, 1979, *18*, 319–332.

Hayes-Roth, F. Distinguishing theories of representation: A critique of Anderson's "Arguments concerning mental imagery." *Psychological Review*, 1979, *86*, 376–392.

Keenan, J. M., & Moore, R. E. Memory for images of concealed objects: A reexamination of Neisser and Kerr. *Journal of Experimental Psychology*, 1979, *5*, 374–385.

Kerst, S. M., & Howard, J. H., Jr. Memory psychophysics for visual area and length. *Memory & Cognition*, 1978, *6*, 327–335.

Kieras, D. Beyond pictures and words: Alternative information-processing models for imagery effects in verbal memory. *Psychological Bulletin*, 1978, *85*, 532–554.

Klatzky, R. L., Martin, G. L., & Kane, R. A. Influence of social-category activation on processing of visual information. *Social Cognition*, 1982, *1*, 95–109. (a)

Klatzky, R. L., Martin, G. L., & Kane, R. A. Semantic interpretation effects on memory for faces. *Memory & Cognition*, 1982, *10*, 195–206. (b)

Klatzky, R. L., & Stoy, A. M. Using visual codes for comparisons of pictures. *Memory & Cognition*, 1974, *2*, 727–746.

Kolers, P. A., & Ostry, D. J. Time course of loss of information regarding pattern analyzing operations. *Journal of Verbal Learning and Verbal Behavior*, 1974, *13*, 599–612.

Kosslyn, S. M. *Image and mind.* Cambridge, Mass: Harvard University Press, 1980.

Kosslyn, S. M. Information representation in visual images. *Cognitive Psychology*, 1975, *7*, 341–370.

Kosslyn, S. M. The medium and the message in mental imagery: A theory. *Psychological Review*, 1981, *88*, 46–66.

Kosslyn, S. M., Ball, T. M., & Reiser, B. J. Visual images preserve metric spatial information: Evidence from studies of image scanning. *Journal of Experimental Psychology: Human Perception and Performance*, 1978, *4*, 47–60.

Kosslyn, S. M., &Schwartz, S. P. A simulation of visual imagery. *Cognitive Science*, 1977, *1*, 265–296.

Kunen, S., & May, J. G. Spatial frequency content of visual imagery. *Perception & Psychophysics*, 1980, *28*, 555–559.

Kunen, S., & May, J. G. Imagery-induced McCollough effects: Real or imagined? *Perception & Psychophysics*, 1981, *30*, 99–110.

Loftus, E. F. Shifting human color memory. *Memory & Cognition*, 1977, *5*, 696–699.

Loftus, E. F. *Eyewitness testimony.* Cambridge, Mass.: Harvard Press, 1979.

Loftus, E. F., Miller, D. G., & Burns, H. J. Semantic integration of verbal information into a visual memory. *Journal of Experimental Psychology: Human Learning and Memory*, 1978, *4*, 19–31.

Loftus, G. R., & Kallman, H. J. Encoding and use of detail information in picture recognition. *Journal of Experimental Psychology: Human Learning and Memory*, 1979, *5*, 197–211.

Mandler, J. M., & Parker, R. E. Memory for descriptive and spatial information in complex pictures. *Journal of Experimental Psychology: Human Learning and Memory*, 1976, *2*, 38–48.

Mandler, J. M., & Ritchey, G. H. Long-term memory for pictures. *Journal of Experimental Psychology: Human Learning and Memory*, 1977, *3*, 386–396.

Marr, D. Representing and computing visual information. In P. H. Winston & R. H. Brown (Eds.), *Artificial intelligence: An MIT perspective* (Vol. 2). Boston: MIT Press, 1979.

Massad, C. M., Hubbard, M., & Newtson, D. Selective perception of events. *Journal of Experimental Social Psychology*, 1979, *15*, 513–532.

McGee, M. G. Human spatial abilities: Psychometric studies and environmental, genetic, hormonal, and neurological influences. *Psychological Bulletin*, 1979, *86*, 889–918.

Mitchell, D. B., & Richman, C. L. Confirmed reservations: Mental travel. *Journal of Experimental Psychology: Human Perception and Performance*, 1980, *6*, 58–66.

Nelson, D. L., & Brooks, D. H. Independence of phonetic and imaginal features. *Journal of Experimental Psychology*, 1973, *97*, 1–7.

Nelson, D. L., & Reed, V. S. On the nature of pictorial encoding: A levels-of-processing analysis. *Journal of Experimental Psychology: Human Learning and Memory*, 1976, *2*, 49–57.

Nelson, D. L., Reed, V. S., & McEvoy, C. L. Learning to order pictures and words: A model of sensory and semantic encoding. *Journal of Experimental Psychology: Human Learning and Memory*, 1977, *3*, 485–497.

Nelson, D. L., Reed, V. S., & Walling, J. R. Pictorial superiority effect. *Journal of Experimental Psychology: Human Learning and Memory*, 1976, *2*, 523–538.

Nelson, T. O., Metzler, J., & Reed, D. A. Role of details in the long-term recognition of pictures and verbal descriptions. *Journal of Experimental Psychology*, 1974, *102*, 184–186.

Newtson, D. Foundations of attribution: The perception of ongoing behavior. In J. Harvey, W. Ickes, & R. Kidd (Eds.), *New directions in attribution research* (Vol. 1). Hillsdale, N.J.: Lawrence Erlbaum Associates, 1976.

Norman, D. A., & Rumelhart, D. E. *Explorations in cognition*. San Francisco: W. H. Freeman & Co., 1975.

Paivio, A. *Imagery and verbal processes*. New York: Holt, Rinehart, and Winston, 1971.

Paivio, A. Perceptual comparisons through the mind's eye. *Memory & Cognition*, 1975, *3*, 635–647.

Paivio, A. Mental comparisons involving abstract attributes. *Memory & Cognition*, 1978, *6*, 199–208.

Paivio, A., Rogers, T. B., & Smythe, P. C. Why are pictures easier to recall than words? *Psychonomic Science*, 1968, *11*, 137–138.

Palmer, S. E. Fundamental aspects of cognitive representation. In E. Rosch & B. B. Lloyd (Eds.), *Cognition and Categorization*. Hillsdale, N.J.: Lawrence Erlbaum Associates, 1978.

Perky, C. W. An experimental study of imagination. *American Journal of Psychology*, 1910, *21*, 422–452.

Peterson, M. J. The retention of imagined and seen spatial matrices. *Cognitive Psychology*, 1975, *7*, 181–193.

Peterson, M. J., Peterson, L. A., & Ward-Hull, C. Rehearsing and maintaining mental matrices. *Journal of Verbal Learning and Verbal Behavior*, 1977, *16*, 371–381.

Pick, H. I., Jr., & Saltzman, E. *Modes of Perceiving and processing information*, Hillsdale, N.J.: Lawrence Erlbaum Associates, 1978.

Podgorny, P., & Shepard, R. N. Functional representations common to visual perception and imagination. *Journal of Experimental Psychology: Human Perception and Performance*, 1978, *4*, 21–35.

Posner, M. I. *Chronometric explorations of mind*. Hillsdale, N.J.: Lawrence Erlbaum Associates, 1978.

Posner, M. I., & Snyder, C. R. R. Facilitation and inhibition in the processing of signals. In P. M. A. Rabbitt & S. Dornic (Eds.), *Attention and Performance* (Vol. 5). New York: Academic Press, 1975.

Putnam, W., & Klatzky, R. L. Processing locational information from memorial and perceptual maps. *American Journal of Psychology*, 1981, *94*, 223–345.

Pylyshyn, Z. W. Validating computational models: A critique of Anderson's indeterminancy of representation claim. *Psychological Review*, 1979, *86*, 383–394.

Pylyshyn, Z. W. Computation and cognition: Issues in the foundations of cognitive science. *The Behavioral and Brain Sciences*, 1980, *3*, 111–169.

Pylyshyn, Z. W. The imagery debate: Analogue media versus tacit knowledge. *Psychological Review*, 1981, *88*, 16–45.

Quillian, M. R. The teachable language comprehender: A simulation program and theory of language. *Communications of the Association for Computing Machinery*, 1969, *12*, 459–476.

Raphael, B. *The thinking computer: Mind inside matter*. San Francisco: Freeman, 1976.

Reeves, A. Visual imagery lowers sensitivity to hue varying, but not to luminance varying, visual stimuli. *Perception & Psychophysics*, 1981, *29*, 247–250.

Riley, D. A. Memory for form. In L. Postman (Eds.), *Psychology in the making*. New York: Knopf, 1962.

Ritchey, G. H., & Beal, C. R. Image detail and recall: Evidence for within-item elaboration. *Journal of Experimental Psychology: Human Learning and Memory*, 1980, *6*, 66–76.

Rosch, E. Cognitive representations of semantic categories. *Journal of Experimental Psychology: General*, 1975, *104*, 192–233.

Rosch, E., Mervis, C. B., Gray, W., Johnson, D., & Boyes-Braem, P. Basic objects in natural categories. *Cognitive Psychology*, 1976, *8*, 382–439.

Segal, S. J. *Imagery: Current cognitive approaches*. New York: Academic Press, 1971.

Shepard, R. N. Recognition memory for words, sentences, and pictures. *Journal of Verbal Learning and Verbal Behavior*, 1967, *6*, 156–163.

Shepard, R. N. Externalization of mental images and the act of creation. In B. S. Randhawa & W. E. Coffman (Eds.), *Visual learning, thinking, and communication*. New York: Academic Press, 1978. (a)

Shepard, R. N. The mental image. *American Psychologist*, 1978, *33*, 125–137. (b)

Snodgrass, J. G., Wasser, B., Finkelstein, M., & Goldberg, L. B. On the fate of visual and verbal memory codes for pictures and words: Evidence for a dual coding mechanism in recognition memory. *Journal of Verbal Learning and Verbal Behavior*, 1974, *13*, 27–37.

Stevens, A., & Coupe, P. Distortions in judged spatial relations. *Cognitive Psychology*, 1978, *10*, 433–437.

Thorndyke, P. W., & Stasz, C. Individual differences in procedures for knowledge acquisition from maps. *Cognitive Psychology*, 1980, *12*, 137–175.

Tulving, E. Episodic and semantic memory. In E. Tulving & W. Donaldson (Eds.), *Organization and memory*. New York: Academic Press, 1972.

Author Index

Numbers in *italics* indicate pages with complete biliographic information.

A

Abelson, R. P., 77, 80, 82, 85, 87, 89, 94, 95, 96, 98, 103, 137, 142, 143, *144, 149,* 172, 179, 183, *202, 210*
Adams, M. J., 35, *66*
Adams, N., 48, *69,* 186, *210,* 218, 229, *231*
Adler, A., 152, *202*
Allen, R. B., 33, 54, 55, 56, *58, 61,* 109, *144,* 158, *204,* 214, 229, *229, 230*
Allport, G., 152, *202*
Anastasio, E. J., 49, *61*
Anderson, B. J., 77, *144*
Anderson, D. C., 27, *58*
Anderson, J. R., 6, 14, 23, 29, 40, 41, 48, 53, *58, 67,* 115, 118, 119, *144,* 160, 171, 176, 177, 178, 180, 185, 186, 195, 197, 200, 202, *202, 203, 207, 210,* 216, 218, 220, 222, 223, 225, 227, 229, *229, 230,* 240, 241, 243, 244, 248, 264, *266*
Anderson, N. H., 22, *58,* 76, 94, 112, 116, 121, 129, *144, 145,* 190, *202*
Anderson, R. C., 23, *58, 62,* 159, *202*
Anderson, R. E., 32, 33, 40, *65*
Anisfeld, M., 26, *58,* 221, 227, *230*
Apple, W., 153, *207*

B

Arbuckle, T. Y., 24, *64*
Asch, S. E., 22, *58,* 111, 116, *145,* 190, 200, *202*
Atkinson, R. C., 13, 33, 40, 50, 51, 52, 54, 56, *58, 59, 60, 62, 64,* 216, *230,* 236, *266*

Baddeley, A. D., 24, *59,* 199, *202,* 239, 245, *266*
Bahrick, H. P., 13, 24, 40, *59,* 165, 166, *202,* 238, *266*
Bahrick, P., 238, *266*
Baillet, S. D., 161, *206*
Ball, T. M., 241, 243, 245, *268*
Bandura, A., 152, *202*
Banks, W. P., 27, 31, 32, *59,* 106, *145*
Barclay, J. R., 84, *145,* 187, *203*
Bargh, J. A., 166, 177, *202, 203, 212*
Barkowitz, P., 199, *203*
Baron, R. M., 154, *203, 208*
Bartlett, F. C., 187, 201, *203*
Bartram, D. J., 238, *266*
Battig, W. F., 13, *59*
Baumgardner, M. H., 194, *207*

271

Subject Index

Note: This is a composite index for all three volumes of the *Handbook.* Volume numbers are indicated by Roman numerals preceding the page numbers.

memory, relation to, II: 190–195
and motivation, I: 267
persistence of, I: 270–275
and personality, I: 205
and self, III: 155–156
primitive or advanced, I: 246–254
types of,
    availability, I: 193, 204, 209–218, 234–235, 248–251. II: 190–193
    representativeness, I: 193, 197–209, 226–228, 234–245, 249–251
    simulation, I: 193, 218–224, 229–230, 249–251
Hierarchies, I: 98–102
Hypothesis testing, I: 213

I

Illusion of control, I: 226–227. III: 139
Illusory correlation, I: 217–218, 267
Imagery, I: 45, 58, 122 124. II: 242, 246, 249–251, 264
vs. word concreteness, II: 264
in Kosslyn model, II: 242, 246
substitute for perception, II: 249–251
Implicational molecules, II: 85–94
definition, II: 85–87
implications for cognitive balance, II: 87–91
role of,
    in attribution, II: 91–92
    in cognitive balance, II: 87–91
    in syllogistic belief organization, II: 92–94
Inconsistency of information,
    effect on recall, II: 98–101, 124–129, 169–172
    evaluative vs. descriptive, II: 128–129
Individuating information, I: 230–234
Inferences (*see also* Social inference), I: 74, 80, 84, 86–87, 108–109
    from schemas, I: 148
    from event sequences, II: 109–110
Information, ease of generating, I: 215
Information integration theory, I: 191
Information processing,
    levels of, I: 43
    limitations on, I: 194–195. III: 1–2, 6–7, 11–12, 29, 33, 35
    parallel vs. serial, I: 43
    psychology of, I: 129, 135
Innate perceptual biases, III: 17–18

Introspection, III: 142
Involvement, as determinant of conscious processing, III: 32–33, 35–37

J

Judgment (*see also* Inference)
    components of,
        discrimination, III: 241–242
        identification, III: 238–246
        recognition, III: 238–246
        recognition, III: 237, 243–247
        scaling, III: 238, 242–248
        stimulus detection, III: 238–246
    context effects in, III: 245–248
    contrast effects in, III: 248, 252
    input processes in, III: 239–242
    meaning of, III: 237
    mediating function of, III: 238, 251–252
    output processes in, III: 238–239, 242, 247, 253
    theories of,
        range-frequency, III: 248
        signal detectability, III: 239–251

K

Knowledge, representation of (*see also* Schemas)
    acquisition of, I: 51–58
    analogues, II: 240–242
    as a mapping, II: 235, 247
    perceptual vs. conceptual, II: 246
    propositional, II: 240–242
    specificity of, II: 236
Korsakoff syndrome, III: 134, 168

L

Labeling
    context effects on, III: 106–107
    role in memory, III: 104–106
Law of small numbers, I: 199
Learning,
    as affected by prior knowledge, II: 185–186
    implicit, I: 56–57
    social, I: 51
Linear orderings,
    of event sequences, II: 106–108
    processing of, I: 58–60
Linear separability, I: 93–94